The New Elite

in Post-Communist

Eastern Europe

Vladimir Shlapentokh,
Christopher Vanderpool,
and Boris Doktorov
Editors

The New Elite in Post-Communist Eastern Europe

Texas A&M University Press

College Station

First edition
The paper used in this book
meets the minimum requirements
of the American National Standard
for Permanence of Paper
for Printed Library Materials,
z39.48-1984.
Binding materials have been chosen
for durability.
∞

For a complete list of books in print
in this series, see the back of the book.

Library of Congress Cataloging-in-Publication Data

The new elite in post-communist Eastern Europe / edited by Vladimir
    Shlapentokh, Christopher Vanderpool, and Boris Doktorov.
        p.   cm. — (Eastern European studies ; no. 10)
    "This book grew out of an international conference "The New Elite
in the Post-Communist World," held at Michigan State University on
November 2–4, 1994"—Pref.
    Includes bibliographical references and index.
    ISBN 0-89096-895-0
    1. Former Soviet republics—Politics and government Congresses.
I. Shlapentokh, Vladimir.   II. Vanderpool, Christopher K.   III. Doktorov,
Boris Zusmanovich.   IV. International Conference "The New Elite in the
Post-Communist World" (1994 : Michigan State University)   V. Series:
Eastern European studies (College Station, Tex.) ; no. 10.
DK293.N48   1999
306'.0947—DC21   99-21472
                                                                      CIP

To Galina Starovoitova,

a prominent Russian democrat

murdered in 1998

Contents

Tables

Series Editor's Statement

The editors of this collection break new conceptual ground in political science by using the neglected theories of Pareto and Mosca to explain what is readily known—but rarely acknowledged—about post-Communist Russia: the former Communist elites have circulated into the new, so-called Democratic elites, so that the Russian people are still being ruled by an aristocracy. In many cases, they are being ruled by the exact same former Communists who ruled them in the despised years of Communist rule. From Boris Yeltsin on down, most Russian leaders, cabinet members, and members of parliament are ex-Communists. The true dissidents, democrats, and anti-Communists did not and still do not have much of a chance to gain power or social influence. This is the theory of the "circulation of elites" applied to a new situation, the development of post-Communist Russia. Shlapentokh, Vanderpool, and Doktorov lay the groundwork for appreciating the contributions in the other essays with this provocative, and I think accurate, conceptual template.

Thus, this book is a refreshing departure from the unrealistic fantasies of Francis Fukuyama's *The End of History and the Last Man* (New York: Free Press, 1992), which promised us that post-Communist Russia would become democractic, along with the rest of the world, and the world's only remaining problem would be boredom with so much democracy. It is difficult to imagine now, nearly a decade after the fall of Communism in the Soviet Union and Eastern Europe, that such musings could have captured the imaginations of *most* journalists, authors, professors, and analysts concerned with postcommunist development in the early 1990s. But this is precisely what happened. In stark contrast to these hyperoptimistic fantasies, the present book is exactly on target concerning the reality of post-Communist Russia: Instead of Russia becoming more democratic, adopting free markets and otherwise becoming like the United States, contemporary Russia is run by mafias; it is most undemocratic; and it is basically repeating many authoritarian features of the former Communist regime under new names. It is an open question whether a sobering assessment of Russia's future by Western analysts in the early 1990s might have prevented this dismal outcome. The starry-eyed optimists who followed in Fukuyama's wake simply did not diagnose Russia's problems correctly, and prescribed the wrong "medication," namely, "shock economic therapy." The cruel suffering inflicted on the Russian people by this shock therapy turned even moderates in Russia against the United States and the West. Another open question is whether Russia's contemporary problems can be resolved eventually. Will Russia ever join the orbit of democratic nations, or is it fated to relive the nightmare of autocracy over and over again?

It is certainly the case that political scientists in general and students of Russia and the former Soviet Union in particular, *could have* made the correct diagnosis. As early as 1953, Dinko Tomasic published a book entitled *The Impact of Russian Culture on Soviet Communism* (Glencoe, Ill.: Free Press), in which he isolated autocratic "habits of the heart" among the Russian people that were overruling the other, more democratic and peaceable cultural traits. Tomasic noted that Russia was autocratic before and during Communism, and predicted that without insight, it would be autocratic following Communism. Alas, this is exactly what happened. Had the think tanks and analysts who staff them only pursued Tomasic's line of reasoning and inquired into how the peaceable, democratic habits of the heart could have been nurtured in Russia, how the elitists and autocrats could have been tamed—how different things might be today! Instead, most Western analysts eschewed the cultural argument, reasoning, incorrectly, that all of the world's cultures are basically the same, and what works in the United States and Western Europe can be transplanted easily into Russia and other nations. If only all those experts on Russia and the former Soviet Union of a decade ago had taken seriously the field of cultural studies!

But the editors and authors of the present book do not look back with regret nor acrimony. Instead, they give us a sobering, scholarly, and realistic assessment of where Russia stands today. And most importantly, they document their claims with empirical data from opinion polls and other data sources. The result is a book that is neither pessimistic nor optimistic, neither cynical nor divorced from reality. It is a book that assesses the serious problems in contemporary Russia yet finds places in the data where the careful reader can find reasons for hope and real democratic progress.

—Stjepan G. Meštrović
Series Editor

Preface

This book grew out of an international conference, "The New Elite in the Post-Communist World," held at Michigan State University on November 2-4, 1994. The conference was organized by sociologists Vladimir Shlapentokh and Christopher Vanderpool with the assistance of political scientist Christopher Sprecher. Participants were major scholars, public opinion leaders, and representatives of the new elite groups in Russia, Eastern Europe, and the new states of the post-communist world. Representatives from major international and national governmental and nongovernmental organizations as well as United States and Western European scholars presented papers at the conference.

The conference addressed the following central question: Given that most of the power in the communist systems were controlled by institutions dominated by the state, how is power being organized when the state is no longer dominant? With new power systems come new dominant elites. The conference identified new elites controlling the political, economic, cultural, and scientific institutions of the new state systems.

Following the conference, several of the discussants (scholars from around the globe) prepared chapters for this book. The collection explicates the nature of power in the postcommunist world in the historical context of the period immediately after the fall of the Soviet Union by 1) identifying the new elites who controlled the political, economic, cultural, and scientific institutions of the new state systems; 2) pinpointing the characteristics of the new elite and the ways they gained power; 3) elucidating the relationships between the old and new elite; 4) defining the new patterns of relationships of elite women in society;

and 5) surmising the intricacies of the criminal and oligarchic elite, their relationship to each other, as well as their effect on postcommunist society as a whole.

This volume is divided into four sections: 1) theoretical issues of the new elite; 2) discourses on the former Soviet republics; 3) the elites in the regions of the Russian Federation; and 4) a comprehensive evaluation of elites in different sectors of postcommunist society.

In many respects, this book is unique in its attempt to develop a comprehensive analysis of the new elite in most post-Soviet republics. The editors permitted the authors to use different definitions of the elite in order not to stifle the debates on this subject. The work closest to our own project (a manuscript edited by Ivan Szelenyi) was not, to our knowledge, published as a book, at least not in English. Another book, *Elites in Transition,* by Heinrich Best and Ulrike Becker is similar to our project but much narrower in its scope.

Our collection has an exceedingly strong empirical basis. The majority of contributors conducted direct sociological studies on the issues pertaining to their respective chapters. The comparative approach of this book is another very important virtue. Our project has the advantage of delineating a diversity of views on the political and social processes of postcommunist societies.

In the introduction, we discuss the theory perspectives involved with both communist and postcommunist sociological studies, especially the way in which theoretical concepts in the literature changed in the wake of the collapse of the Soviet empire. A major objective of the book is to introduce the reader to some of the more important issues that were inspired by the birth of a new social species—postcommunist societies.

The support of Dr. Blair Rubble and the staff of the Kennan Institute for Advanced Russian Studies of the Woodrow Wilson Center in Washington was essential for the development and success of the conference. Dr. Rubble's creative insights, critiques, and encouragement were particularly important for the evolution and implementation of the conference. The Kennan Institute also enabled us to bring to Washington for a set of briefings key conference participants who outlined the significance of the birth of a new elite for international relations.

We would like to thank Michigan State University's provost Lou Anna K. Simon and the Office of the Vice President for Research and Graduate Studies; the deans of the Colleges of Social Science, Arts and Letters, Agricultural and Natural Resources, Communication Arts and Sciences, Natural Science, Engineering, International Studies and Programs, and James Madison College; the directors and chairs of the Institute for International Agriculture, International Business Center, Institute for Public Policy and Social Research, Center for Advanced Studies in International Development, Center for European and Russian Studies, School of Criminal Justice, and Department of Political Science.

A special thanks to the staff of the Sociology Department for their assistance with the conference and follow-up activities.

Our deepest gratitude goes to Joshua Woods for his outstanding editing of this manuscript. He meticulously executed the difficult task of refining and polishing the translations of these international works. His bright determination and organizational excellence also served, in many ways, as a driving force for the finalization of this book.

The New Elite

in Post-Communist

Eastern Europe

Introduction

Vladimir Shlapentokh and Christopher Vanderpool

History is the empirical rack upon which ideologies, utopian visions, and theories are stretched and torn apart. People and their leaders create events that shatter the characterizations, myths, and paradigms held by others and even themselves. Beliefs and theories that supposedly aided us in understanding how a nation or society acted and how its future was to unfold blind us from considering vast undercurrents of structural discontinuities and strain that are building up to a flood of new forms of social patterns and change. Such has been the case in the devolution of communist systems and the evolution of a post-communist world.

Leaders and peoples in nation-states throughout the world believed that the East-West conflict was as permanent as the structured inequality between the North and South in the world system. Cold war ideologies defined the political, economic, and social chasms that divided the communist and noncommunist worlds. Bourgeois-dominated political economies clashed with communist-dominated socialized production systems. Most important, social and historical change within each system was seen as an outcome of internal forces generated by democratic capitalist class systems or by authoritarian centralized party bureaucracies.

Within the last decade, history has challenged the worldviews scholars, political leaders, and others had of the nature, potential, and future of communist and noncommunist states. Within the social sciences, theories of class analysis based on Marx's original conceptualizations were used to explain processes of inequality and social change within and between societies in the global system. Most scholars in the West found it difficult to apply class theory to the socialized production systems in the Soviet Union, Eastern European nations, China, and Cuba. So class analysis was and continues to be the way social scientists understand history and change in noncommunist societies.

This was a very comfortable way of envisioning the world. These fixed paradigms gave us certainty about how to explain our past, understand the present, and predict the future. History shattered this illusion so much so that Francis Fukuyama could announce that this was the "end of history" as we have known it. Why? Because our ideologies, utopia, and theories could no longer define and shape our understanding of history. It was not the end of history but an end to our illusions.

A part of history did end. The cold war, which had structured the world system since World War II, went into the dustbin of history. The communist systems of the Soviet Union and Eastern Europe were shattered. The hegemonic stranglehold of the Soviet Union on Eastern Europe was permanently broken. Poland, Romania, Hungary, Slovenia, and the Czech Republic have tasted the springtime of freedom and have quickly moved to create new social institutions to reshape their political economies. So too have the Baltic States of Estonia, Latvia, and Lithuania. Slovakia and Bulgaria are still struggling through the transformation process. But the turmoil and chaos of Albania, Yugoslavia, Bosnia, and Macedonia hang as a specter of what might happen if the new institutionalization processes break down or are misdirected.

History has ended for the Soviet Union and the imperial system it inherited from the czarist past. In its place, Russia and the Commonwealth of Independent States (CIS) are creating a new history that is still unfolding with uncertain forms. Without a democratic and independent past to look to as a guidepost toward the future, there are frequent and deep political conflicts and a hesitancy to embrace fully the notion of an independent citizenry controlling its political destiny. Their economies have not been able to lead to a sustained system of privatized production. Russia and the CIS are cursed with an economic infrastructure more characteristic of the 1930s than of an economy in the postindustrialized world of the information age. Moreover, the ranges of social institutions that are taken for granted in many societies—political, legal, welfare, economic, and religious institutions that form the basis of civil society in democratic political economies—are absent, not functioning, or just being formed. There is a massive social institutional vacuum that has yet to be filled.

Without such institutions, it is difficult to develop a notion of what is the public good and how to create and sustain it. At the same time, there is no way to act authoritatively with a sense of legitimacy granted by the citizenry. In this vacuum, power is used in its most naked and abrasive forms by elites, both new and old, seeking to maximize their own private interests while the masses are bewildered by the collapse of the securities they had in the old system and the vast uncertainties and risks of the newly formed present. Yet the dynamic and complex relationships between elites and the masses will be the basis upon which the new societies and states of the postcommunist world will be formed. They are learning one of the fundamental truths of history: "In history there may be total defeats, but there are no final solutions. So long as human beings exist, there is no exit from the traumas of history."[1]

From Class Theory to Elite Conflict

For almost three decades, social scientists largely looked to class theory for an explanation of major social changes transforming political economies. Classes shaped and determined distributions of power. Class struggles and structural contradictions led to the emergence of new modes of production. These images of the forces shaping history were shared by Marxist theoreticians in communist societies.

The events in the collapse of the communist world in Europe have led to a resurgence of an earlier conceptualization of how power is distributed in societies. Class struggle has been replaced by elite conflicts. Oscillations in political economies are seen more as the result of actions taken by governing and nongoverning elites and less as the result of class structuration processes, yet class theory continues to inform elite theory. The concepts of ruling class and power elite are closely interwoven. Gradually, a reconsideration of elite theory is informing an understanding of history and the processes structuring its outcomes.

The Formation of Elite Theory

The earliest formulations of elite theory were developed by Vilfredo Pareto and Gaetano Mosca.[2] Two conceptualizations of those at the top of a power hierarchy were developed: the elite and the ruling class. The elite is composed of all those who occupy the most important, powerful, and privileged positions in a society and who make strategic decisions in the field under their control—in public and private organizations, including governments, parties, business, unions, media, and various other institutions in society.[3]

There are two types of elites according to Pareto: governing and nongoverning.[4] Those elites who actually exercise the political functions of a government or who control the outcomes and policies of government are the governing elite. Sometimes the nongoverning elites are referred to as the political class. Pareto's nongoverning elites are Mosca's ruling classes. A ruling class is composed of those powerful and privileged elites who influence and sometimes control those who govern and those who obey.[5] They do not hold political office or perform a political function, but they often determine the policies, processes, and outcomes of politics.

The ruling class holds dominant positions in the major institutions of a society. They control decision making and centrally control the flow of resources, information, and values in institutions and the social organizations that comprise them. They also help create, change, and, at times, limit the types of interdependent linkages that emerge among institutions. In this sense, they are strategic elites who exercise considerable power in their institutional spheres of influence.[6]

These are very key concepts for understanding what is happening to power structures in the postcommunist world. New strategic elites are beginning to control the flow of resources and information in Russia, the CIS, and Eastern Europe as new social institutions emerge out of the collapse of the totalitarian state system. The old strategic elites of the *nomenklatura* (the highest level of Soviet officials selected and endorsed by party committees) are being challenged by new institutional power brokers. Yet, at the same time, many of the old communist elites are now members of the new capitalist elite. Abrupt shifts of power are occurring as these strategic elites form competing ruling-class formations. The old governing elites of the communist party desperately try to hold on to the last vestiges of state power as a new governing elite is rising to the control of politics in the new state system. The emergence of a market economy does not mean an increase in political and economic equality. Rather, new forms and heightened inequality mark the new regimes.

As if following the script provided by Pareto, there is a circulation of elites under way in the postcommunist world. The spirals of uncertain forms that the power structures are taking, particularly in Russia and the CIS, are largely the result of the ebb and flow of power shifts between a governing elite and a nongoverning elite, of challenges to an elite by a counterelite. This is why the political systems of the postcommunist world are so unstable. Stability will occur only when a new governing elite is ascendant.[7]

The Iron Law

The transitions in power and the transformations of the social structures are marked by high degrees of upheaval in the political system.
From the outside looking in, it appears that the political situation is so
fluid that chaos rules society. But this is an illusion. There is at work
an "iron law of oligarchy."

There is a springtime of freedom as the old governing elite loses its
grip on power and the totalitarian state system collapses. There is a
hope that true democracy will emerge and that a parliamentary and
multiple-party system will provide adequate checks and balances to
control the power of the elite and to advance and protect the interests
of the masses. But underneath, the iron law is at work. All political
systems and large-scale organizations are ruled by a few who seek to
maximize their interests and have only limited concern with those
who are below them in a power hierarchy. The reality of this iron law
of oligarchy, as first formulated by Michels in 1915, is a true shock for
the newly formed public citizenry.[8]

The iron law of oligarchy and the law of the circulation of elites "destroys the thesis of the possibility of a society without social levels."[9]
For a citizenry raised in the belief of a Marxian utopian vision of a
classless society and rudely suffering under the yoke of the selfish
greed of the communist party elite and its dominant bureaucracy, the
hope of a humane society that cares for its people is shattered.

So too is the hope of the establishment of a stable transition to a
democratic form of government. The citizenry longs for a system in
which there are predictable outcomes in the political institutions, a
possibility of voting into office those who will create constitutionally
based laws, and the constraints that a democratic checks-and-balances
system between the legislature, executive, and judicial branches of
government provide. The working out of the iron law of oligarchy un-
masks parliamentary democracy. As Mosca warned, "Parliamentarianism [is] a reality of intrigue, of imbroglios, of manifold interests dis-
honest by their own nature and demanding a constant stream of lies.
Beneath the fiction of the sovereign people, parliamentarianism leads
to a minority of ambitious and unscrupulous manipulators concerned
principally with their own ends."[10]

The shocks of the iron law and the continuous chaos in society resulting from the struggles in the circulation of the elite and the vast social change under way propel the citizenry to consider some way out
of this political, economic, and social turmoil. They begin to think that

a benign Machiavellian prince may be able to restore order, provide security, and establish a course toward a predictable future. They may try to "escape from freedom," lunging backwards toward the stability that authoritarian rule offers.[11]

Elites and Transitions to Democracy

This foreboding possibility may only be the reaction to the strains, contradictions, risks, and uncertainties of a state undergoing a massive structural revolution in its political, economic, and social systems. Some of the newest formulations of elite theory attempt to portray what types of elite formations are most likely to assist in the process of transition to democracy.

One of the most important conditions facilitating the development of stable democratic systems is the emergence of a consensually unified elite. Higley and Burton argue that a disunified elite is the source of political instability that marks democratic transitions and breakdowns along the path toward democracy. Prior to the transition to democracy, an ideologically unified elite control the political regime and provide a basis of stability. This stability is a result of an elite formation that appears to perpetuate itself indefinitely by penalizing dissent and by a consistent application of ideology to political issues and policy questions. Changes in the political system and struggles among elites, especially when there is a disintegration of a totalitarian state run by an ideologically unified elite, produces a period of intense political conflict.[12]

Successful transitions to democracy require the emergence of a consensus among elites on 1) the rules and codes of political conduct that define appropriate and inappropriate political action; and 2) the development of a set of structured links and networks to each other that allow for reliable and effective interaction and access to each other and other strategic elites.[13] This consensus allows for elites to develop political outcomes that are positive-sum. Politics are seen as contexts for bargaining and not requiring zero-sum conditions where one elite gains and another loses. Politics are not seen as war but as a decision-making process. Such conditions supportive of democracy require non-zero-sum conditions to exist in the political economy, that is, the supply of societal resources is greater than the demand for those resources.

Elite disunity originates in the process of state-formation and results in unstable political regimes. Such instability is marked by irregular and attempted seizures of power from the executive branch and the orchestration of seizures of power, possibly by force, by competing elites.[14] Instability increases as zero-sum power conditions emerge, that is, the demand for societal resources far exceeds the supply of such resources.

A transition to a stable democracy requires an elite settlement in which elites and counterelites agree to reorganize their relations and negotiate compromises on the key points of their conflict with each other. Two types of conditions stimulate the emergence of an elite settlement: 1) The elite conflict may be so intense and costly that all parties are exhausted and find no clear victor to their political war; and 2) a major societal crisis propels the elite to develop some unity and consensus in order to avoid system collapse and disintegration. Usually the latter are the result of failures, abuses, and weaknesses of the incumbent heads of state and their policies and actions.[15]

The move toward democracy may lead to compromises that sustain nondemocratic or quasi-democratic systems and their elites in power for protracted periods—for example, Portugal's transition to democracy by developing a "Kerensky" form of government with long periods of inattention to the state followed by intense but short periods of panic. The end only came when moderate military officers demilitarized Portuguese politics. Similarly, Brazil's long march to democracy has been marked by a gradual process of state intervention and nationalist protection governed by a military elite assisted by bureaucratic elites controlling major state bureaucracies. Few elites were willing to incur the costs of transforming the state bureaucracy. So they adopted a system of representation in which appointment processes bolstered and supported economic and political elites. At the same time, they instituted a system of succession of military presidents that gradually fostered a return to civilian rule.[16]

Analysts of developments in Russia, the CIS, and Eastern Europe have begun to assess the implications of elite formations and the transition to democracy. Genov provides a sober assessment of the action of political elites in support of the collective good. He argues that the "chronic illnesses of democracy" become acute during the period of political instability following the collapse of the communist system. Parliamentary democracy involves gross emphasis on attainment of individual preferences and interest rather than being an arena in which rational processes are used to evolve policies and decisions to support the collective good. He points to a need for a process of rationalization in the transition to democracy that will end the control of culture by ideology so characteristic of communist systems and will provide a way for the emergence of new bases for the development of ultimate values. These bases or foundations are embedded in the new rights to private property, free speech, and freedom of religion.[17]

Critical too is the compression of time. Social events are moving so rapidly and with such a massive impact that social time is dramatically accelerated.[18] People want radical transformations to occur peacefully in the shortest period of time without massive social costs and instability. Since this is not possible given the depth of social, political, and economic transformation that is necessary to support a democratic civil society, people are growing impatient and believe that change is being blocked or delayed. The result is a high degree of alienation and anomie among the people. The lack of ultimate values and ends reduces all social action to an instrumental level, especially action in the political system by elites. It is not surprising that crime, corruption, suicide rates, and lack of adherence to governmental regulation are the accompaniments of the collapse of communist regimes.

Sztompka sees such impacts evident in the emergent democracy of Poland. A "culture of distrust" is pervading all levels of Polish society. There is very little trust in social institutions, especially in the political and economic system. Trust enables a citizenry to construct a political, economic, and social reality that is known to them as an arena for activism and freedom. Moreover, the greater the degree of trust the more a people can "take for granted" these realities. But in the rapid transition to democracy in Poland and elsewhere in the postcommunist world, there are frequent breaches of trust, a lack of social institutions that can establish and guarantee trust, and a steady flow of elite actions that involve coercion and the use of naked power. Sztompka notes that people "feel cheated, disenchanted, disappointed; they either develop strong hostility towards earlier objects of trust, or fall into apathy, resignation and withdrawal. Creative mobilization is terminated, demobilization proceeds, and passivism spreads out. Activity towards formerly trusted objects is now motivated by blind hatred and takes destructive forms."[19]

Part of the source of this distrust is the rise of an "environment of risk" and uncertainty among the citizenry.[20] Rising unemployment and its threat generate anxiety and frustration. Free competition and market transitions lead to increasing inflation, a devaluation of home-country products and production systems, and massive capital accumulation by the new elite. The political economic system resembles the Wild West, in which cowboy entrepreneurs have frequent economic shootouts with their opponents. Moreover, the society is going through a period of economic shakeups that resemble the nineteenth-century

period of robber barons in many Western democratic political economies, yet it is equally true that conditions in present-day Poland also
are characteristic of contemporary U.S. society.

Adding to the uncertainty is the fragmented mosaic of laws and regulations combining old and new rules of conduct.[21] There is so much inconsistency in the application and interpretation of law and conduct
that there is very little continuity in society. Compounding this con-
fusion is the emergence of a new set of political voices, each claiming
to represent and speak for the people. The cacophony of political parties, clubs, and factions numbs the public and increasingly delegiti-
mates anyone claiming to have the authority to make legitimatized decisions for the collective good. All those who could act as guardians of
the public, from judges, lawmakers, and police, to heads of public bureaucracies, are viewed as biased or corrupt. Under such conditions,
the general collapse of society and the disintegration of the political
order is a real possibility.

Such threats may give insight into why China has attempted to
delink the process of transition to a market economy from the transition to democracy. The crushing of the nascent democratic movement
in Tiananmen Square was a clear message that the Chinese Communist
Party would foster economic growth without encouragement of the
formation of democratic politics. Nee's analysis of social inequalities in
the reform of state socialism and his more recent analysis of the linkage between market transitions and societal transformation provide a
considerable contrast to the preceding analysis and that provided in
the chapters that follow.[22]

In the transition to a market economy, an elite group of entrepreneurs has emerged.[23] Many of these are cadres of the party bureaucracy and are equivalent to the nomenklatura in the former Soviet
Union. While they did gain an advantage in the marketplace, overall
increases in inequality were modest in the early stages of market transition. There is some evidence that the increasing economic development provided boosts in household income to even the lowest levels of
Chinese societies.

Nee also notes that there is some control over the power and privileges enjoyed by an administrative elite and they may even experience
a decline in them.[24] If local production markets grow, entrepreneurs,
managers, and workers in private firms gain income and become mobile. In many cases, their mobility exceeds that of the administrative
elite.

The market transition in China has also been controlled by the absence of a full-scale program of privatization.[25] Rather the dominant form of property is publicly owned. Such property provides a basis for continuing economic activity for the administrative elite. This is quite a contrast with Russia and Eastern Europe, where a more rapid move to private property rights has occurred. The slow pace of fiscal reform in China provided a pathway for the rise of local and regional corporatism.

At the same time, there has been an equally slow pace for the emergence of a civil society.[26] The extension of citizen rights has been limited and constrained by a strong, centralized state power structure. The central state does not resist intervening with force when necessary to protect its control over power in the political economy of China. Yet, it is clear that there are new relationships and interdependencies emerging between the power elite of the Chinese Communist Party and the entrepreneurial elite of the newly emergent marketplace. Moreover, the central state system must develop new ways of relating to local and regional elites who are strengthening the pace of economic development in China. As long as rapid economic growth continues without major crises or political uncertainties, the collapse of the communist elite is not likely. But should there be a breakdown in economic development, political turmoil might occur and the nongoverning elite may challenge the governing elite of the Communist Party.

The New Social Reality and New Issues

While traditional theories on elites help us understand the emergence of elite groups of the past, the elite that emerged on the ruins of communist regimes attracted the attentions of scholars and required from them new concepts and even new methodology. Moreover, these new developments, as often happens in social science, encouraged researchers to look at old issues from a new angle as new societies feature phenomena never before studied. This book provides readers with many ideas and data about these new developments.

The Origin of Elites: Are the Nomenklatura the Same as the New Elite?

The origin of the new elite and the impact of the old party nomenklatura on its composition has been a subject of many debates—some of which are reflected in this book.[27] Two schools of thought emerged in the 1990s: one insists that the old-party nomenklatura managed to transfer themselves from the old to the new elite in postcommunist countries. This school can be called Stalinist in the sense that its proponents believed as the bolsheviks did, particularly Stalin, that the social origin of an individual shapes his or her mind and style of life.[28] Stalinists would argue that the old nomenklatura elite determines much of the mentality and style of behavior of the new ruling class. What is more, some authors like Egor Gaidar speak of "the nomenklatura revenge" and insist that "the old nomenklatura" even "assimilated" new cadres and managed to restore the previous spirit of the party apparatus.[29]

Another school supposes that although social background is important, the nomenklatura will think and behave much like those members of the elite without a nomenklatura past. This school is closer to Marx, who insisted on the great malleability of human beings in their adjustment to a new social milieu.[30] The authors of this book hotly debate this subject, joining more or less categorically to one or another school (for instance, see chapters by Keller, Krishtanovskaia and White, Loiberg, Gaidys, and Marchenko). In our opinion, the available data more clearly supports the second school and the claims that the elite with a nomenklatura past behave much like the rest of the elite when faced with the same conditions.[31] Indeed, the new post-communist regimes offer former apparatchiks who joined the new elite what they were denied in the past: independence from superiors, no fear of being dismissed at short notice, a much higher standard of living, the right to conspicuous consumption, the freedom to travel abroad, to go to church, to have friends and lovers as they wish, and many other bonuses that the rigid communist system did not permit them.[32]

It is also interesting to note that the first school of thought may be wrong simply because the number of new elites with a nomenklatura past is not very high, particularly at the top of the political and business elite. In Krishtanovskaia and White's chapter the reader will find data on the various social backgrounds of new elites that support this thesis. Their list of the one hundred most influential political figures in Russia includes no more than 10 percent of the old Soviet nomenklatura, while the rest are new.[33] In the provinces, the number of old apparatchiks is higher than in Moscow, as can be seen from Stykow's chapter on the Saratov region, Farukshin's chapter about Tatarstan, and Shubkin's chapter about the Altay region. However, the most prominent and known local leaders—like Valentin Fedorov in Sakhalin, Boris Nemtsov in Nizhnii Novgorod, Eduard Rossel in Ekaterinburg, and Anatolii Sobchak in Petersburg—have no party apparatus background.

Even those who were apparatchiks and now work for the new regime no longer belong to the nomenklatura, a stratum that ceased to exist along with the control of the Communist Party. In addition, they are not united by any central body like members of some secret order. In fact, a new dominant elite emerged that partially incorporated many former apparatchiks.

While much of what was explained above is more relevant to Russia, the specific features of the formation of new elites in other post-Soviet republics should not be ignored. The degree of continuity in personal composition between old and new elites was much lower in some non-Russian republics simply because Russians as the dominant nation as well as their collaborators from the local population lost their control over them and new national cadres were able to attain the top level of power. This was supported by the authors of this book, including Gaidys in the case of Lithuania, Solonar in Moldova, and, to some degree, Churilov in Ukraine and Snapkovskii in Byelorussia. At the same time, in Kazakhstan, as can be seen from the chapter written by Kadyrzhanov (as well as from Kandinov's chapter on Uzbekistan), the role of the old nomenklatura in the new elite is perhaps even greater than in Russia. However, in all republics, the "old elite" adjusted quite rapidly, even ideologically, and not only in relation to the new realities, in particular the acceptance of the nationalist issue as the core of the official ideology.

New Elites in the Climate of Permanent Instability

The formation of the new elite took place during a period when law and order was widely ignored by all social actors. The state was extremely weak and corruption was rampant within law enforcement agencies. By all accounts, even in the wildest years of development of capitalist societies in America or Europe the contempt for law was never so apparent as it was in Russia, Ukraine, Lithuania, and Kazakhstan. Even in the Czech Republic, one of the more "civilized" postcommunist countries, disregard for law, as President Vaclav Havel complained, is the most telling feature of life. Postcommunist societies, especially those of the former Soviet Union, are divided into different clans with their own political and economic bases that regularly violate law—often seemingly like a "war of all against all." The borders between property, power, and crimes in such societies are extremely blurred, and almost all active people in politics, business, and even culture are in one or another way engaged in illegal activity.[34]

In the climate of lawlessness, members of the elite, particularly in the former Soviet republics and much less so in the former Soviet satellites in Eastern Europe, feel quite insecure. They consider their current positions temporary and are not sure whether the current new political regime will persist. There is a real threat that the rules of the game will be revised and the structure of the political and cultural landscape will change.[35] Some elites even worry that the results of privatization will be overhauled.

This deeply rooted feeling of insecurity has a dramatic influence on the mentality and behavior of the elite of the postcommunist world. First of all, long-term goals lose out to an ever-present ambition for short-term gains. This means that laws are often ignored as the elite use their positions for their immediate benefit. Second, in preparation for emergencies, most members of the elite regularly and illegally amass fantastic amounts of money in foreign banks while purchasing real estate abroad. They also send their children to foreign schools, directing them to establish themselves while arranging a safe haven for the rest of the family. In this respect, postcommunist moguls are very different when compared to the robber barons of European and American industrialization who invested their money in the economy of their own country. Third, the new elites, with their fixation on satisfying their immediate interests, do not cultivate professionalism. It is clear that many of those recruited for the top positions in politics and business were hired not for their professional ability but for their loyalty. Grushin discusses this issue and the incompetence of the new Russian elite at great length in the second chapter of this book. Fourth, and most important, national interests play a weak role in the decision-making process of the members of the elite. Absorbed by their own private interests and struggles, they demonstrate much more egotistical behavior than elites in democratic societies who, while also quite egotistical, understand that the prosperity of their countries is also in their ultimate interests.

The study of the elites in postcommunist society accentuates the importance of the stability of the elites in any society as a powerful factor for social and economic progress. Of course, there are a number of nations where the stability of the political elite is not very high. Italy can be cited with some reservations as an example. However, this instability is not extended to the business elite, whose stability is guaranteed by the invulnerability of private property. This is not the case in Russia, Ukraine, or Moldova, where the owners of large fortunes never feel confident in the stability of property rights.

The Collusion Between Elites:
Rent Givers and Rent Seekers

The collaboration between various types of elites, and, in the first place, between political and business elites (oligarchs), is typical for any society, including the most democratic societies. However, in the postcommunist world, as well as in almost all countries moving toward liberal capitalism, because of lawlessness and overwhelming corruption, the complicity of elites has reached the highest level.[36] Luneev and Gaidys examine this development in their chapters. What is more, the criminal elite are added to the collusion and work along with the other elites in the illegal distribution and redistribution of limited resources. In 1997, after almost blindly accepting privatization and the free market as the irrefutable keys to making any society "normal" and healthy, international organizations like the World Bank began to pay close attention to corruption and "robber capitalism" or "crony capitalism" as formidable obstacles to social and economic progress, obstacles that cannot be autonomically overcome by market forces.[37]

While business elites come up as rent seekers, politicians and, to some degree, criminals play the role of rent givers. "Rent seeking" can be defined as a firm's attempt at receiving extra profits by becoming an exclusive, politically backed monopoly. Rent seeking and rent giving stand in dramatic opposition to the conditions of fair economic and political competition.[38] Legally run institutions (private and public firms and companies) strive for (or seek) privileges from the state as well as from criminal structures that will help them generate the power and control of a monopoly. The actual methods and instruments of rent seeking and giving are designed to be concealed. They range from outright bribery to the sales of subsidies, tax privileges, price supports, tariffs, farm or import quotas, and licenses.[39] Of no less importance is the immunity against criminal investigations, which the elites along with criminals have taken advantage of.

While rent seekers are greatly benefited by their privileges, the rent givers also profit. The payoffs from rent seekers allow them to maintain and expand their own political power. It takes "big" money to be elected and reelected for key positions at the national and regional level. Even a growing number of criminals are using the money from business oligarchs to enter the official political system.[40]

The exchange of wealth for political power is well known in the behavior of oligarchic societies.[41] However, the basic idea of exchange does not adequately explain the relationship between political power and big money. The term "exchange" implies that the participants are both losing and receiving something simultaneously. In the case of "rent seeking," however, the partners only gain: bureaucrats receive monetary support that perpetuates their political power, while oligarchs procure special privileges that generate wealth and power far greater than the oligarch's initial payoff to the bureaucrat.

Rent seeking and rent giving, and the corruption that stems from them, are universal phenomena. Many American economists have studied the effects of rent seeking in the United States. However, most experts consider the current level of rent seeking activity in postcommunist countries comparable only with Colombian corruption. Among the most successful rent seekers are the companies vying for special state privileges in foreign trade, the extracting industry, and the financial sector. Every major corporation has its "own people" in the government and the Duma as well as in local governments.[42]

One of the most important features of an oligarchy (noted by Aristotle)[43] is the purchasing of political positions, which, in turn, bolsters the oligarch's economic and political power. This practice not only allows for additional pecuniary revenue but enhances the social prestige of the buyer. The practice ranges from buying nobility titles, as was common in the Middle Ages, to buying ambassadorial offices in the United States with lavish donations to a successful contender in the presidential elections. This phenomenon, the buying and selling of political offices, escalated in post-Communist Russia.

The Criminality of the New Elite

The interaction between criminal leaders and the members of the political and business elite is typical for any society. It is much more intensive, however, in the postcommunist world than in any democratic society. Here, Russia is again a revealing case.

Criminals in Russia, Ukraine, and several other countries replace the state as a guarantor of order as well as a mediator in commercial disputes. Practically every small to midsized business as well as several big companies and state enterprises are forced to go into collusion with leaders of gangs in order to have their own *krysha* (or roof). A krysha is a criminal organization that receives 10 to 20 percent of the profit from each business in exchange for supplying protection, or a "roof," from other mafias. What is more, a krysha offers the only real option to resolving disputes with clients who refuse to pay for delivered goods, or with companies that do not pay off their debts.[44] The criminal organization is used also by businesspeople to destroy their competitors and thereby maintain their monopoly.

Members of the political elite also actively corroborate with criminal chieftains, as Luneev shows in his chapter, as well as in his other works.[45] Politicians need criminals for help in their election campaigns and in laundering money they receive as bribes.

In the last few years, the power of criminal organizations has gone far beyond economic matters. Criminal organizations have started taking control of political institutions, particularly the police, courts, procurators, as well as certain mayors and local dumas. These organizations use threats, bribes, and even murder to achieve their goals.[46]

A number of authors (Stanislav Govorukhin, for example) have attempted to emphasize that Russia has been "a criminal society" since 1992–93. Govorukhin's book *The Great Criminal Revolution* and other articles about the effects of the criminal layer on Russia have all been rejected by the Kremlin as exaggerations. However, in a radio conversation at the end of 1997, Yeltsin himself talked about "the intentions of criminal structures to take control of the country."[47]

Criminals are active participants in the election process. In 1997 and 1998, several individuals with serious criminal records were elected to various positions, from mayors to deputies of local parliaments. Certain state and regional members of parliament are well known for their direct connection to criminal organizations. Criminal organizations control local administrations; they dictate the selection of "cadres"; they control business policies; and they protect themselves from legal persecution.[48]

A Russian scholar described the criminal layer in Russia as a "parallel, shadow state with its own government, army, police, court, population and economy." He contends that all agencies of this state work extremely effectively in comparison with similar bodies in the legal Russian state.[49]

The Special Status of Oligarchs in Post-Communist Society

The weakness of the state and law enforcement agencies led to several developments similar to those that existed during early feudalism. The members of elites—both business and political—as well as ordinary people do not receive enough protection from state agencies.[50]

With the growing awareness of the state's unwillingness or inability to protect society, large and small businesses have resorted to three methods of protection, which date back to the Middle Ages: 1) develop a link with the criminal layer by hiring criminals to provide a "roof"; 2) garner the support of people from legitimate law enforcement offices by paying them salaries that greatly surpass their official incomes; or 3) create a professional (private) guard or small army. Similar developments are also occurring in several other countries, such as Ukraine and Kazakhstan, but to a lesser degree. Large corporations usually rely more on their own resources of defense, though even some of the biggest banks do not completely dismiss their contact with criminals who provide protection. The members of these private armies are recruited from the former police force and KGB, as well as from professional athletics (mostly sports related to unarmed combat). Most security forces are headed by experienced military leaders, usually former officers or generals. Regardless of how well equipped these private armed services are, they must maintain good relations with criminal structures and observe the rules of the game.[51]

In postcommunist republics, "hired gun" is now considered a normal occupation. In Soviet times, only members of the Politburo had personal wardens.[52]

Anti-Democratic Attitudes of the Dominant Elite

One of the most important characteristics of the elite who came to power in the postcommunist world is their deep antidemocratic sentiments, which they try to hide but which are revealed in many ways. The ruling political elite often humiliate liberal institutions. There were numerous examples of this during 1993–98. Avraamova, who studies the political attitudes of the Russian elite, puts forth a great deal of data in his chapter in support of this thesis.[53]

Oligarchs in their own turn have downgraded the fledgling Russian democracy, a tendency also true for other countries (including Western countries). Oligarchs cynically exert direct control over leading television channels and newspapers.[54] Media objectivity was considered poor following the summer of 1996, but it only worsened during the "bank war" in 1997. Consequently, many Russians consider the present media just as restricted as the Communist media of the past.

Oligarchs make it very difficult to carry out a fair election campaign. It is commonly believed that just about anyone could win an election with the right financial backing. The impact of wealthy individuals on the outcomes of elections is particularly strong at the local level. There are two major motivations for entering politics (that is, local parliaments): 1) to increase political leverage for rent seeking and 2) to gain immunity from potential criminal persecution. Local parliaments became especially attractive to businesspeople when, under their influence, the parliament began permitting deputies to combine their businesses and their duties as deputies. Following the election of local legislatures in 1997, a Moscow political scientist noted, "the actual regional parliaments in Russia come up as nothing more than an oligarchic organization, free from professional legislative responsibilities."[55]

As previously mentioned, like the oligarchic layer, criminal structures also denigrate democratic institutions. Criminals have penetrated all levels of the liberal layer, taking leading positions as deputies of parliament (national and local) as well as administrative positions. The criminal layer also has a negative effect on the market in post-Soviet republics. Natural competition is hindered by various criminal activities. Free competition between small and midsized businesses is practically impossible. Organized crime has a hand in the redistribution of state property.

Quite possibly the most dangerous threat to the liberal sector, ironically, comes from the democratic institutions. The majority of the Russian parliament between 1992 and 1998 was inclined toward authoritarianism, as the deputies are more worried about keeping their seats than supporting democratic institutions. As a result, they often abuse the power of their positions and lose the respect of the masses.[56]

Moreover, many members of the Russian intellectual elite who in the recent past favored democratic principals lost their faith in the ability of their nation to forge a democratic society. Intellectuals see the population as incompetent and full of bias and therefore unable to make correct decisions during the election process. In effect, intellectuals directly or indirectly support the oligarchic ideology. Some intellectuals backed the idea of postponing the presidential election in the summer of 1996, when threatened with the possible victory of the Communists.

Disappearance of the Individual Inferiority Complex

Elites in communist societies had an exceedingly complex and often contradictory attitude toward the West. Despite public harangues about their exceptionalism and superiority over the West, the elites from communist societies always fostered an inferiority complex with regard to Western countries. While elites perceived the West as deeply hostile toward their countries, they also considered their nations a part of Western civilization. The conflict between Westernizers and nationalists in the nineteenth and twentieth centuries could not eclipse the deep attachment of communist elites to the West, despite how Slavophiles eagerly criticized it.[57]

Communist elites have always dreamed of reaching a level of equality with the ruling classes in France, England, and America, countries that served, at different times, as models for their countries. Interest in the West (which was imbued in communist society) heightened again in postcommunist society. The new rulers vowed to turn their countries into "normal" Western-type societies in a short period of time. Paradoxically, the "new" attitude toward the West, in contrast to the communist past, does not incorporate an individual inferiority complex. Only ten years ago, an official or intellectual from a communist country looked at his or her colleagues in the West with a great deal of envy (mostly for material reasons), but this is no longer the case. A postcommunist bureaucrat, or a leading newspaper/television journalist, often earns (legally or illegally) more than his or her American counterpart. Their homes and the quality of their vacations could probably arouse jealousy among many Westerners, even those who consider themselves wealthy.

While politicians, businesspeople, and journalists from several post-Soviet republics rejoice in their newfound wealth, however, they have lost the self-esteem and pride of representing a superpower, a great country. Some of them still remember how they were treated abroad as the emissaries of the USSR, a country that could compete on almost any level (military, scientific, cultural) with any country in the world. Today, post-Communist elites feel not dignity but national humiliation. With their material needs fully satisfied, the members of the Communist elite are particularly sensitive to the views that their country lost, and probably forever, its special standing in the world. At best, elites can now only claim to be part of a second-rank country. In 1997, many "new Russians" wanted to combine both a high material standing and the status of superpower, whatever the price for the Russian masses. In light of this analysis, it is quite understandable that often the more successful one is, the more one fumes about Russian greatness.[58]

"New liberals," in order to justify their latest ideological stance toward the West and their feelings of equality or even superiority over the Western elite, are now looking for defects in the Western way of life, defects that must have eluded their attention only a few years ago when they praised the Western lifestyle. They have concluded that all the flaws of contemporary Russia, particularly the high level of corruption and criminality, the blatant violations of democratic principles, and the venality of the media are at the same if not higher levels in America and other Western countries. It has now become fashionable to speak contemptuously about American culture. The denunciations of the American style of life are similar to the articles prepared by hack

Soviet propagandists before 1985. Once again, Russians read in the most liberal publications such stereotypical rebukes as "the Western style of life recognizes only one idol—money" and "all humanitarian slogans are only for show." [59]

The People's Attitudes Toward the Elite

The formation of the new elite in the postcommunist world aroused a largely ignored issue: the public's attitudes toward the elite. The gap between the elites and the masses is significant in any society. However, the size of this gap varies from society to society, and from nation to nation. All empirical data suggests that this gap in postcommunist societies is enormous, and definitely much more vast than under the communist regimes. This alienation is especially evident when considering the political elite.

Most people are sure that the majority of politicians are corrupt and that the majority of businessmen are crooks. This is definitely true of post-Communist Russia where no politician was able to garner more than 10–12 percent of popular support between 1993 and 1998. Only 3 percent of Russians believed that Russian politicians "are in essence honest people." Russians rejected in 1992–94 the idea that the Russian leaders, including those elected by them, are concerned about the interests of the country. Instead, they are confident that they are absorbed only with the enrichment and preservation of their power. [60]

Ordinary people resent the almost criminal origin of the wealth of new elites as well as their obvious disregard for the plight of a significant part of the population who had a difficult time adjusting to the new conditions of life. Today, ordinary Russians are indifferent if not completely unsympathetic toward the violent tribulations of oligarchs. [61]

The great hostility of the masses toward the elites is extremely important because it threatens the existence of democracy. If the elites lose touch with the rest of the population, the fate of democracy will be in jeopardy, and with such discontent the chances for the emergence of populist demagogues will increase, not only in Russia or Ukraine but in almost all postcommunist countries.

Conclusion

One cannot yet forecast the end of political, economic, and social transition in Russia, the CIS, and Eastern Europe. The fate of these nations is highly dependent on the quality of the elites. The authors of this book are very critical of the elites in their respective countries, yet most of them are still optimistic that in time the elites will become more responsible to their people, that, in the not-so-distant future, they will be less corrupt and much more devoted to democratic principles.

Of course, nobody is so overly romantic that they believe the elites will soon be ideal rulers of society. The authors are well aware that most elements typical for the elites in democratic societies were criticized by radical and liberal thinkers in the past. It is evident, as C. Wright Mills noted, that the power elite are not solitary rulers but well linked to each other and pressure groups. The power elite links old and new elites across local, regional, and national levels to support one another's power base. Acting in concert, they form a consensus elite who use lawyers, scholars, religious leaders, doctors, and bureaucrats as their servants of power to manage the political economy. This is how policy is made and implemented in democratic state systems. Dense social networks are arenas where decisions are made that determine "who decides, who sits, and who benefits." [62]

Having control over the decision-making process, the elites in democratic societies tend to pursue their egotistical interests, act as rent givers and rent seekers, expose themselves to corruption and, in some cases, entertain some dubious connections to the criminal world. However, democratic institutions, free elections, and a free media do not permit elites to go too far into semilegal or illegal domains. In order to survive and reproduce, elites are forced to observe the democratic rules of the game and serve, even if reluctantly, the interests of the majority of the population.

It is the hope of all who participated in this book that postcommunist nations will reach a level of maturity where the elites of those countries will be at least comparable in positive and negative features to the elites in Western democracies.

Part 1

Post-Communist Elites
An Overview

1

From *Nomenklatura* to New Elite

Olga Krishtanovskaia and Stephen White

Revolutions, according to Vilfredo Pareto, are above all a matter of elite transformation. The revolution in Eastern Europe at the end of the 1980s brought on changes in government and a shift toward pluralist and democratic politics throughout the region. Today, many of these changes look less decisive. Former communist parties have returned to power in Hungary, Poland, Lithuania, and Bulgaria. In Romania, there has been a shift in leadership but less clearly a change of political regime. Former communists maintained their positions in Serbia and in Slovakia, and there has been a transformation of the nomenklatura in much of former Soviet Central Asia. In Russia, the Communist Party left office but was revived in the beginning of 1993. It fared well at the polls in the December election of that year and was by far the largest party in the Duma elections that took place in December, 1995. The Russian public, for their part, remained committed to the concept of a USSR. They rated their new political system lower than the one they had experienced in the Soviet years. Furthermore, they believed the Communists were still in power.[1]

Views differed as to the extent to which communists or former communists were, in fact, still in power throughout the Central and Eastern European countries. There was relatively little direct continuity in the Czech Republic, where the Communist Party quickly became a marginal force, and only a limited degree of continuity of leading personnel in Poland. In Russia, some argued that there was "relatively little overlap between the Gorbachev and Yeltsin political elites." Others pointed to the very high degree of continuity at local levels in the early post-Soviet period, and went on to emphasize the continuities in post-Communist government more generally. As a commentator for

Nezavisimaia Gazeta put it, if an observer had gone to sleep in Russia at the start of 1990, then awoke at the end of 1992, he would conclude that the reformist wing of the Communist Party headed by Boris Yeltsin had finally come to power.[2]

Clearly, as the changes at the leadership level increase, the Russian and Eastern European transition can be more readily considered a revolution. At the same time, we need to differentiate between changes in central government and in the regions; between changes in different sections of the central government; and between rates of change in different subperiods. We need to know if the elite has been changing in terms of age and gender, social and geographical origin, national composition, and levels of education. Above all, we need to know the extent to which the Russian elite has recruited its membership from the Soviet nomenklatura of the past, and from which of its constituent groups. In the discussion that follows, we consider some of the operating principles of the former nomenklatura and examine the ways in which they attempted to protect their position, mostly through privileged access to the market, in the late 1980s. The final section of this chapter provides a sociological portrait of the Russian elite of the mid-1990s and discusses the extent of its origins in the Soviet system.[3]

Defining and Measuring the Elite

Generally, an "elite" is a ruling group in society. We define the elite in largely positional terms: on the basis of their occupancy of posts that involve the making of decisions of national importance. Included are the deputies of the Russian Federal Assembly who were elected in December, 1993, government officials, the Russian president, and his closest associates. We have not separately distinguished the leaders of the major political parties or the heads of regional administrations as these two categories account for the bulk of the membership of the Russian Parliament.

A separate business elite is a constituent part of the ruling elite, whose influence on public policy is defined by their position in the most important sectors of the economy and by the assets they control.[4]

Our analysis is based upon a series of investigations conducted between 1989 and 1994 by the Sector on Elite Studies of the Institute of Sociology of the Russian Academy of Sciences.[5] The main methods of study included informal in-depth interviews with members of the elite; formal interviews; surveys of expert opinion; observation; the study of official biographies; press analysis; and the study of official documents and statistics. The core of the study was based upon an examination of official biographical directories,[6] as well as a series of interviews with elite members themselves, conducted by the Sector of Elite Studies in association with the University of Glasgow. Altogether, 3,610 biographies were analyzed, consisting of members from the Brezhnev elite (57 members of the government, 1,500 deputies of the USSR Supreme Soviet, 282 members of the Communist Party of the Soviet Union (CPSU) Central Committee, 26 Politburo and Secretariat members, and 131 *obkom* first secretaries); the Gorbachev elite from 1985 to August, 1991 (consisting of 251 Russian Supreme Soviet deputies, 371 members of the CPSU Central Committee that were elected in 1990, 35 members of the Politburo and Secretariat, and 132 obkom first secretaries); and the Yeltsin elite from September, 1991 (consisting of 35 members of the Russian government, 44 members of the higher ranks of the presidential administration, 68 heads of regional administrations, 35 party leaders, 100 members of the business elite, and 543 members of the Federal Assembly).

Our elite groups consist of six main sections: 1) the government (before 1985, during the Gorbachev years, and in 1993); 2) Parliament (for the Brezhnev period, the 11th Supreme Soviet of the USSR that was elected in 1984; for the Gorbachev period, the Supreme Soviet of the Russian Socialist Federation of Soviet Republics (RSFSR) that was elected in 1990; and for the Yeltsin period, the Federal Assembly of the Russian Federation that was elected in December, 1993); 3) the party elite (for the Brezhnev period, the CPSU Central Committee that was elected at the Twenty-seventh Party Congress in 1986; for the Gorbachev period, the Central Committee that was elected at the Twenty-eighth Party Congress in 1990; and for the Yeltsin period, the leaders of the major Russian parties as they stood in 1993, the section that, despite the change from a single to a multiparty system, manifested the greatest degree of direct continuity); 4) the top leadership (for the Brezhnev period, the members and candidate members of the Politburo and the secretaries of the Central Committee as of January, 1985; for the Gorbachev period, the members and candidate members of the Politburo and the secretaries of the Central Committee as of January, 1991; and for the Yeltsin period, the president's immediate associates, the leading members of his administration, his advisors, and members of the presidential council); 5) the regional elite (for the Brezhnev period, the obkom first secretaries that were in office at the start of 1985; for the Gorbachev period, the obkom first secretaries that were in office in 1990; and for the Yeltsin period, the heads of regional administrations as of 1993); and finally 6) the business elite (for the Yeltsin period alone, consisting of the heads of the largest banks, exchanges, and industrial-financial groups).

The Soviet Nomenklatura

In order to understand how the elite changed in the post-Soviet period, we must understand how it formed over many decades of single-party, Communist rule. As this is a subject that has already been discussed in the scholarly literature, we will simply identify a number of the elite's most distinctive features.[7]

The elite had a precise form as a result of its institutionalized character. Lists of leading positions were maintained in the Central Committee apparatus. Appointment to these leading positions was impossible without the agreement of the party hierarchy. The highest ranked members of the nomenklatura, that is, the holders of positions to which appointments required the approval of the Politburo, or Secretariat of the CPSU Central Committee, were in effect the national elite. Equally, in spite of the varied character of the positions that were included in the upper nomenklatura, the Soviet elite was monolithic in nature, extending across all spheres of party, state, and social life. Its monolithic character was assured by the fact that all its members were Communists and by the manner in which all leading appointments had to be made or at least approved by higher-level party bodies. Elite members were obligated to espouse Marxism-Leninism and other conventions of Soviet public life.

The structure of the Soviet elite can be derived from the composition of the membership of the CPSU Central Committee. The following groups were always represented: the national leadership (the Politburo and Secretariat of the CPSU Central Committee, which were, in effect, political executives); the leading officials of the Central Committee apparatus (the national administration); the most important regional party first secretaries; the prime minister and other leading members of the government; the most important members of the armed and security services; leading diplomats; and the leaders of youth, trade union, and cultural organizations. Formally, the Central Committee and Supreme Soviet also included workers, collective farmers, engineers, and scholars. This group of "ordinary Soviet people" had a purely decorative character: its function was to demonstrate that the USSR was a state run by cooks rather than professional politicians (as Lenin put it).[8]

The Soviet nomenklatura elite was strictly hierarchical. As early as the Stalin era, all nomenklatura positions were divided into fourteen ranks.[9] The General Secretary of the CPSU Central Committee was at the highest level, followed by members of the Politburo, candidate Politburo members, and the Central Committee secretaries. The next rank in the hierarchy consisted of the nomenklatura of the Politburo (those with positions that were appointed and approved at Politburo level). This group included the first and (sometimes) second secretaries of Republican Party organizations, the first secretaries of regional party committees, all-union ministers, the military hierarchy, ambassadors to all the socialist countries (as well as the ambassadors to the largest capitalist countries), directors of the largest military-industrial enterprises, the leading officials of the creative unions, and the editors of central newspapers and journals. The level below this group was the nomenklatura of the Central Committee Secretariat, which included deputy ministers, the second secretaries of regional party committees, the heads of regional Soviet executives, and so forth. Then came positions that required the approval of the relevant Central Committee department, followed by positions that needed approval from regional, urban, and district party committees. The lowest level positions were those approved by local party branches.[10] The hierarchical principle required a steady progression through these stages, from level to level: it was similar in many ways to an army hierarchy, and (as in the armed forces) exceptions were rare.

The nomenklatura system had mechanisms that limited self-recruitment, or *semeistvennost'*. According to an informal convention, the children of higher-level officials never inherited positions with the same level of seniority as their fathers. Rather, "elite children" had a series of special professional niches, often connected with work abroad and supported by a nomenklatura system of education at elite institutions, particularly those that trained economists, diplomats, and journalists specializing in international affairs. As a result of the restrictions on internal recruitment, the nomenklatura was replenished to a large extent by new members from other sections of society, including the intelligentsia, working class, and collective-farm peasantry. The biographies of Central Committee members for the whole period of Soviet rule demonstrate how few of the members had a Moscow or big-city background. Furthermore, there were almost no members who had themselves been brought up in nomenklatura households (this principle began to be violated in 1986 when Brezhnev's son Yurii and son-in-law Churbanov joined the Central Committee; both had been expelled by the following party congress, in 1990).

The nomenklatura, in addition, required its members, particularly those who were likely to obtain advancement, to serve in different parts of the country. The traditional nomenklatura career trajectory began with study in Moscow, followed by work in the Soviet, Komsomol, economic, or party apparatus at the district level. The member would then be recalled to Moscow for a one- or two-year stint in the Central Committee headquarters, and then a return to the provinces to a higher-level post (often an obkom first secretaryship).

Apart from geographical mobility, another characteristic was a change in career specialization. During the Brezhnev period a number of typical nomenklatura career patterns developed, all of them under Central Committee auspices: party-economic, Komsomol-party, Soviet-party, and party-diplomatic. The most typical was a career that moved upwards from Komsomol to party work, or from party to Soviet work and back, or from economic to party work and back. There were also "pure" career progressions, most often on the part of economic administrators. In such cases, the people involved moved upwards at the same factory to the level of director, then into the relevant ministry and eventually to the rank of minister. The party-diplomatic career type, by contrast, was a feature of the decline of the nomenklatura, with ambassadorial posts in less important countries being filled by disgraced politicians as a form of honorary retirement.

The nomenklatura was served by a comprehensive and finely differentiated system of privileges. In Voslensky's words, "the nomenklatura lived in another, entirely different, and special country" from which ordinary citizens were "carefully isolated."[11] The existence of a system of this kind was related to the chronic deficits that existed throughout the Soviet period. Members of the nomenklatura were not rich in the conventional sense but were removed from hardships by their positions and allowed to enjoy a better quality of life. Their money incomes were generally high, but their living standards were sustained by a whole system of indirect payments and benefits. Prices in official restaurants were significantly below the real costs, certain forms of recreation were heavily subsidized, and so forth. Nomenklatura members were also given flats and dachas in the most fashionable areas; the rentals were symbolic.[12]

Apart from this, a well-developed distribution system supported the special needs of nomenklatura members. At food processing plants, for instance, there was always a section producing higher-quality foodstuffs for the elite. Special construction companies looked after their housing requirements at a level far above those of ordinary citizens. There were special ateliers, special shops, special polyclinics, and even (a labor veteran complained) special graveyards.[13] Privileges were provided strictly according to rank, and each rank in the nomenklatura ladder had its own list of benefits. In addition, there was a system of special nomenklatura education. It included the Higher Komsomol and Party Schools, the Academy of Social Sciences attached to the CPSU Central Committee, and the Academy of the National Economy. The Higher Schools were generally concerned with the training of the local and regional nomenklatura members and sometimes provided a local official with the educational qualifications that were felt to be appropriate. The Moscow Party School, the Academy of Social Sciences, and the Academy of the National Economy were, by contrast, institutions for raising the qualifications of nomenklatura members. A placement at any of these institutions meant, in practice, that the official concerned was being prepared for advancement to a still higher position.

From Power to Property

As the Soviet system began to change under the impact of the Gorbachev reforms, so too did the patterns of elite advantage that had become established over decades of Soviet rule. And as political position became a less secure guarantee of those advantages, the emphasis shifted to private property, as Trotsky had predicted many years earlier.[14] One of the most significant ways this transition took place was through the alternative or "Komsomol" economy that began to develop in the late 1980s under the supervision of Yegor Ligachev.[15] Its focus was the Coordinating Council of Centers of Scientific and Technical Creativity of Youth (TsNTTM), established in 1987 and staffed by Komsomol officials, with a network of centers attached to every district party committee in Moscow. These were, in effect, the first commercial structures of any kind in the former USSR, and it was through these centers that many in the first wave of new Russian entrepreneurs became established, including Konstantin Borovoi, a computer scientist who moved into Komsomol business and thereafter established the country's leading raw materials exchange and his own political party; Igor Safaryan, who progressed from a Komsomol center to a cooperative and then his own firm of brokers; Konstantin Zatulin, a Moscow history graduate who gave up his dissertation to work for the economics secretary of the Komsomol Central Committee and then became chairman of "Entrepreneurs for a New Russia"; and Mikhail Khodorkovskii, who graduated from a deputy Komsomol secretaryship at the Mendeleev chemistry institute to the chairmanship of Menatep Bank.[16]

The "Komsomol economy" took its origin from a resolution adopted by the CPSU Central Committee on July 25, 1986, in which it approved a proposal from the Komsomol that it establish a network of scientific and technical centers for the benefit of its members. The new centers were supposed to operate on a commercial basis, based on agreements with enterprises and providing services that were not otherwise available. A series of more formal agreements followed in the course of 1987, including one in March that established a Coordinating Council for the Scientific-Technical Creativity of Youth under the chairmanship of Deputy Premier Boris Tolstykh. By the end of the year, the term "Komsomol economy" had come into regular use among Komsomol officials, and it was repeatedly employed by First Secretary Victor Mironenko in his address to a Komsomol plenum in December, 1987. He was able to report that coordinating councils had been established in most republics and regions and that more than sixty centers were already operating in towns throughout the country.[17]

The scope of the new centers was extended considerably during 1988, allowing them to engage in the manufacture of consumer goods and to establish economic relations with foreign firms and organizations. They could set their own prices for the goods they imported from abroad and were relieved of all customs duties. The Law on Cooperatives, adopted in May, 1988, was modified as a result of pressure from the Komsomol to cover "other public organizations," allowing the new youth centers to broaden the base of their activity. Complaints soon reached the government that youth organizations had been buying and reselling video recorders, computers, and other technological items at inflated prices and with "crude violations of the law"; Gorbachev, addressing the Twenty-first Komsomol Congress in April, 1990, warned that it was not appropriate for the party's youth movement to become involved in this sort of "middleman activity." Nevertheless, the system was developing its own momentum; there was already a youth commercial bank, an import-export center, and a network of fashion shops, and by 1990 more than seventeen thousand youth cooperatives were in operation, employing about a million staff members.[18]

The Komsomol and its youth centers performed a number of important functions in the establishment of early Russian capitalism, including converting paper assets into liquid cash. Not a single state enterprise in the late 1980s had the right to conduct a relatively simple operation of this kind. Armed with this concession, the new centers of scientific and technical creativity were able to charge a rate of up to 30 percent on the profits that arose from such transactions; of these profits, 5 percent were remitted to the CPSU Central Committee.[19] Formerly, the privileges of the nomenklatura had been given largely in kind, reflected in the granting of state property for private use or in special services. Now the privileges began to acquire an increasingly "monetary" character. The members were allowed to engage in activities that were prohibited for others and to make profits from such activities. During the perestroika period, the main privileges of this type were 1) joint enterprises, 2) cash assets, 3) credits, 4) property, 5) import privileges, and 6) privatization benefits.

The Establishment of Joint Enterprises

The nomenklatura had always been distinguished by its special relationship with the outside world—and for many reasons not necessarily connected with high politics. The difference between the official and unofficial exchange rates for the ruble, for instance, made any foreign economic activity profitable and gave opportunities for a speculative gain to anyone who was able to travel abroad. Contacts with the West were not simply agreeable and prestigious, they were also lucrative. In the broadest terms, the Soviet government itself was involved in commerce during Brezhnev's years of "developed socialism." Staff members of the Ministry of Foreign Trade, for instance, bought and sold commodities on the American stock exchange; and several grain deals in the 1960s and 1970s are still remembered in ministerial circles as enormously profitable.[20]

From the very first stages of economic reform, the question of foreign dealings came to the leadership's close attention. An association of joint enterprises was established in 1988, headed by Lev Vainberg, who joined a consultative council on entrepreneurship under the Gorbachev presidency in 1991 and was himself the director of a French-Italian-Soviet joint enterprise and vice president of the Scientific-Industrial Union (later the Russian Union of Industrialists and Entrepreneurs). The first joint enterprises to be registered by the USSR Ministry of Justice were directly linked with the CPSU; the very first Soviet-American joint enterprise, Dialog, was established in 1987 under the party's direct patronage. Through its "authorized organizations" (the Main Computing Center of the All Union Exhibition of Economic Achievement (VDNKh), the Computing Center of the State Committee of Science and Technology of the USSR (VO Vneshtekhnika pri GKNT SSSR), and the automobile factory (KamAZ) the party invested twelve million rubles in the founding capital of the joint venture. After six months, Dialog in turn became the founder of another joint enterprise, Perestroika, whose president was Andrei Stroev, a relative of Yegor Stroev, who was at that time a Central Committee secretary.[21]

One of the first joint enterprises, Vneshkonsul't, founded in 1988, was established with the participation of a similar range of "authorized representatives" of the CPSU (once again, Vneshtekhnika and the Main Computing Center of VDNKh). The foreign participant was the Finnish concern, Sarka-Sov Consulting (in practice, a foreign-based Soviet firm). Soon Vneshkonsul't became the partner of one of the world's most important business consultant firms, Ernst and Young, forming the joint enterprise, Ernst, Young and Vneshkonsul't. The "authorized organizations" that used the financial resources of the CPSU Central Committee to establish joint concerns included, in the agricultural sphere, RSFSR Gosagroprom and its affiliates; in the cultural sphere, the Bolshoi Theatre and the Kremlin Palace of Congresses; in computers, the Main Computing Center of VDNKh and Vneshtekhnika; and in the various business spheres, the Znanie Society, the All-Union Trade Union Council, the Moscow and regional sections of Zhilsotsbank, the Komsomol Central Committee, and others.

There were other, less recognized organizations that also became agencies and through which the party began to adapt to a market environment. In a single day (January 11, 1989), for instance, a specialized medical cooperative in Donetsk established three joint enterprises with a total capitalization of $50 million: Rida (with the Brazilian firm Brital), Koyana (with the same Brazilian firm), and Valeo (a joint venture with the Italian firm Imar). None of these enterprises had foreign shares exceeding 25 percent of the total investment. According to an analysis of the founding documents that were registered in the USSR Ministry of Justice, their role was rather to facilitate a process by which party-controlled assets could be converted into the more defensible form of an enterprise with foreign as well as Russian ownership and management.

The Conversion of Assets into Cash

During the perestroika years, only the National State Bank had the privilege of converting its nominal assets into cash. Money, at this time, was of two kinds: cash *(nalichnye)* and nominal *(beznalichnye)*. Only cash was money in the real sense; bank credits were necessary for purely paper transactions between state organizations. An enterprise deducted what it needed for the pay of its employees, whose rates of remuneration were strictly regulated by the state, and no other source of income was possible than the one that arose from a regular salary or bonus payment. "Ready cash" had to be limited; otherwise there would be serious social tensions in the circumstances of general shortage. The creation of the new centers, as a means of converting paper credits into cash, was not only a contribution to the emergence of a Soviet market, it was also one of the causes of the deepening problem of inflation. In Komsomol circles, the scientific and technical centers began to be called the "locomotive of inflation." The means by which money was processed in this way was itself a profitable and privileged one.

Advantageous Credits

In order to obtain credit at low levels of interest (sometimes without payment at all), it was necessary to belong to the nomenklatura or to have close links with highly placed officials. In the perestroika years, it was particularly profitable to obtain a credit in foreign currency. At this time, there were three rates of exchange to the dollar: the state rate, the commercial rate, and a special tourist rate. While the commercial and tourist rates gradually increased, moving closer to the level at which currencies changed hands on the black market, the state exchange rate remained the same: 65 kopeks for a U.S. dollar. This is what made foreign currency credits so profitable. Typically, a firm might obtain a credit of one million U.S. dollars for a month, sell the dollars on the black market for, say, 10 rubles each, then return the credit to the state at the official rate of exchange, leaving a profit of more than 9 million rubles. The first commercial banks, operating with the support of the state itself, were able to make profits in the same way.

Property Transactions

In the early years of economic reform, only firms that were connected with the nomenklatura had the right to engage in property transactions. There were several reasons for this. In the first place, no one else owned any property. The mass population lived in state apartments, and enterprises were also based on state ownership. Consequently, the officials that disposed of state property had enormous scope for their activities. While the first commercial firms were being established, some of the best state property was sold at advantageous prices to firms that had been established with the participation of the nomenklatura. The nomenklatura, in this way, sold itself its own property at nominal prices. The Most Group, for instance, which is now one of the most powerful financial and industrial associations in Russia, bought several buildings in the center of Moscow for several tens of thousands of rubles, which was less than half the market value at the time.

In the Soviet period, the CPSU had been the owner of a large number of buildings in which its full-time officials, publishing houses, educational institutions, rest homes, living quarters, and hotels were accommodated. These party buildings were the country's "gold fund"; they were the best buildings, located in the most convenient and prestigious locations, and had been well maintained. During the perestroika period, the nomenklatura began to receive a profit from the rental of these establishments. The best rest homes, clinics, tourist bases, and hotels were typically made available to foreign firms, and joint enterprises were actively established. A full-scale nomenklatura war developed over the right to make use of the Central Committee hotel, "October 1"; the final victor was the administration of the Russian president himself. Similarly, offices in the best buildings in the center of Moscow were rented out at low rates to firms that had nomenklatura contacts. Indeed, in the mid-1990s, it was still possible to judge how close a firm was to the party elite of the Soviet period by where it was located. The offices of a number of firms directed by Konstantin Zatulin, for instance, are in the complex of buildings on Old Square, where the Central Committee offices had been located. Zatulin, now a well-known politician and businessman, was (as we have noted) a former advisor to the Komsomol with special responsibility for the "youth economy." [22]

Privileges in Import-Export Operations

As in other spheres, the right to engage in foreign commercial operations was restricted during the perestroika years. Special firms were created by the nomenklatura to serve as a form of contact between domestic producers and their foreign clients. For other firms, there was no means of access to the foreign market, and the profits that derived from the export of raw material and other competitive goods went directly into the pockets of these nomenklatura companies. A different procedure was followed in the case of imports. A system of state purchase prices for imported goods was still in operation with a number of bodies that made the necessary arrangements. Commercial bodies were founded in their place whose function was the retail sale of imported goods; the difference between state and retail prices was considerable and prices remained at the discretion of the owners of these new commercial importers.

Privatization of the State by the State

Privatization of the state by the state takes place when public officials, using their formal powers, privatize those sections of the state for which they are themselves responsible. This process began in 1987 and was largely concluded by the time a privatization program for the population at large was ready to be launched. Privatization of this kind included wholesale changes in the system of economic management, banking, and retail sale, and the sale of the most profitable enterprises. Ministries, for instance, were turned into concerns. The minister typically retired or became a consultant to the concern that succeeded the ministry. The president of the concern, as a rule, was a former deputy minister. The concern acquired the status of joint stock company. The shareholders were typically among the most senior members of management. The ministry's property in this way became the private property of its leading officials. These leading officials did not simply privatize the organization for which they were responsible but did so for their own benefit.

The privatization of banking took place in a similar fashion. The reforms, undertaken in 1988 and 1989, led to the collapse of what had been a unitary and closely regulated system, a system that was no longer able to adapt to the new requirements. Promstroibank and Zhilsotsbank, together with their regional affiliates, were dissolved entirely. Each part of the former system became a commercial bank. The buildings, the staff, the equipment, and often the management remained the same. What changed was the name and the means by which profits were distributed. Zhilsotsbank, for instance, became Mosbiznesbank, under the continued presidency of Viktor Bukato. Promostroibank retained its former name, simply adding the word "commercial." Its president, as before, is Yakov Dubenetskii.[23]

A number of new commercial banks were created with the direct participation of officials of the Ministry of Finance. One of the main Russian banks, Imperial, was established under the auspices of the ministry's department for relations with commercial banks, which was headed, at that time, by Sergei Rodionov. Rodionov duly became the new head of Imperial. Several other commercial banks were established on the basis of what was apparently a fresh initiative, but the history of their establishment, and the biographies of their directors, suggests a rather different interpretation. One of the first commercial banks, Menatep, for instance, began life in 1988 as a scientific and technical center for youth creativity under the auspices of the Frunze district committee of the CPSU. Gosbank officials and highly-placed staff in the Ministry of Finance did not receive a majority of shares in the banks of which they became directors. Their contribution to capital assets was generally insignificant. Often their share was sufficient to exercise a dominant influence, which was exercised over what were often very profitable capital assets as well as over the circulation of currency.[24]

Retail trade was privatized in the same way. The Soviet trading system had two main forms: Gossnab, which was responsible for the allocation of the "means of production," and various bureaus responsible for consumer goods. The USSR Ministry of Foreign Trade and its specialized administrations (Eksportkhleb, Eksportles, and so forth) were particularly important parts of this elaborate system. Gossnab duly became the basis upon which the first stock exchanges began to emerge. Major exchanges like the Russian Commodity Exchange (RTSB), the Moscow Commodity Exchange (MTB), and the Moscow Stock Exchange (MFB) were headed by former Komsomol functionaries, and former specialists from Gossnab were invited to take over their management positions. Senior officials of the Ministries of Trade and of Foreign Trade moved quickly to establish commercial structures within the framework of their own organizations, which then monopolized the most profitable sections of the activities for which the former ministries had been responsible.

The most profitable enterprises were also privatized, becoming joint stock companies long before a full-scale program of privatization was instituted. Some of the first commercially established enterprises were Butek, directed by Mikhail Bocharov; Mikrokhirurgiia Glaza, directed by the surgeon and politician Sviatoslav Fedorov; and the KamAZ and AvtoVAZ automobile works, directed respectively by Nikolai Bekh and Vladimir Kadannikov. The manner in which such firms were privatized is unclear, as no legislation had yet been adopted to provide for such changes. Another form of "privatization before privatization" was through the creation of commercial structures based at the factories themselves, typically the creation of a more specialized agency involved in marketing and sales. The factory's production was first classified into competitive and noncompetitive. Noncompetitive output, either because it was of poor quality or because it was simply too expensive, was sold thereafter at state prices, while output for which there was a demand was sold through the factory-based firm. The difference between the state price and the retail price was converted in this way into profits for the factory directors. A factory that had not yet been privatized became a source of material benefit for its management.

The outcome of all these changes was a substantial move toward the conversion of the power of the party-state nomenklatura into private property. The state, in effect, had privatized itself. Formerly, property had been at the disposal of the nomenklatura, but they were denied its private ownership. Now, property moved from public into private hands, typically those of the factory administration. Ministers, by the same token, became the owners of majority shareholdings in privatized companies. Department heads at the Ministry of Finance became presidents of commercial banks, and leading officials at Gossnab became managers of exchanges. During this early, nomenklatura stage of privatization, there were certainly some with no previous involvement in their new sphere of activity. Many of them, indeed, enjoyed a good deal of success. But taken as a whole, it is clear that the process of economic reform took place under the control of the nomenklatura and to its direct material benefit.

The New Russian Elite

As a result of all these changes, what had been a unitary Soviet elite divided into two broad sections: a political and an economic elite. Membership of the first was a consequence of position and of one's standing within the political establishment; the second was made up of people whose influence was based upon their control of capital. The new Russian elite, in other words, became bifurcated.[25]

With the coming to power of Yeltsin, the new elite began to consolidate itself. Yeltsin, as a rule, used officials who had been appointed by Gorbachev or ones he had known himself in the Sverdlovsk party committee. Although the flow of new people into high-ranking positions continued, it was nonetheless clear that the revolutionary period of the transformation of the elite had ended. Structures of executive power had come into being: the administration of the president; the government of the Russian Federation; and the freely elected parliament, the State Duma. The courts alone had not developed into an independent branch of government. The locus of authority was increasingly in the hands of executive bodies. The movement of officials from party to state that had begun under Gorbachev now showed its results. Throughout Russia administrations were being formed from the same sources—the old nomenklatura. And a new pyramid of power arose above the former one.

The Yeltsin leadership took steps to "close" the elite at this stage. The first stage in this process was the dissolution of the Congress of People's Deputies and Supreme Soviet, which had up to this point resisted presidential control. The next step was the adoption of a new constitution, which made it clear that the Parliament of the future would consist, in part, of the heads of regional administrations that the president had himself appointed (they were represented in the upper house, the Council of the Federation) and of political leaders who also came from the former nomenklatura and who were represented in the lower house, the State Duma. Ministers were allowed to combine their positions with seats in the Duma that was elected in 1993, strengthening the influence of the executive within the system of representative institutions.

While formally retaining the two branches of government, the Yeltsin leadership made great efforts to control the work of legislative bodies by methods that included increasing the presence within them of state officials, regulating the election of new deputies as closely as possible, and gradually absorbing the whole system of government within a nomenklatura framework. The Soviet tradition of "selection and allocation of cadres" was in effect revived, and with it the "table of ranks," that is, the hierarchy of positions and corresponding rates of pay that had given rise to the nomenklatura itself when it was established in the early 1920s.

The new system of appointment was as follows: at the apex of the pyramid were the supreme leaders, who occasionally lost their places as a result of high-level political intrigue. In their place, a second and then a third stratum of the old nomenklatura rose to positions of power. Unlike in the Soviet period, loss of position at the apex of the system was no longer equivalent to political death: a former leader, under these new conventions, soon found a position in a new power structure at a slightly lower point in the hierarchy. A process of replacement of this kind took place at different rates in the center and in the localities. In Moscow, the political process was more intensive and the top leadership was replaced more often, giving greater opportunities for lower levels of the former nomenklatura to advance their position. In many of the regions, on the other hand, there were only one or two cycles in the process of elite renewal. In Krasnodar *krai,* for instance, the former chairman of the territorial council, Nikolai Kondratenko, was dismissed for his support of the attempted 1991 coup and replaced by the democrat, D'iakonov. D'iakonov resigned in turn and was replaced by his deputy, Nikolai Egorov, a representative of the "third layer" of the nomenklatura who had not been discredited by his previous activity and now declared himself an "independent politician of centrist views." Unlike in the Soviet period, when resignation meant the end of a political career, both Kondratenko and D'iakonov remained active and influential members of the regional elite. Kondratenko, who became the leader of the local opposition, won a large majority at the polls in December, 1993, and became a member of the Council of the Federation; and D'iakonov went on to head the territorial committee of "Vybor Rossii."[26]

There was a concentration not only of political power but of economic resources. The period of economic reform from 1987 to 1992 was associated with a process of decentralization and collapse of the formerly powerful "vertical" links in the state system of economic management. Formerly, for instance, the banking system had been represented by Gosbank, Promstroibank, Zhilsotsbank, and their local affiliates, and the whole system had been closely regulated by the Ministry of Finance. In the perestroika period, this monolithic system collapsed and a whole series of commercial banks developed in its place, often by simply renaming themselves. A similar process took place in other sectors of the economy.

In 1992, a process of recentralization began to assert itself, but based on horizontal rather than vertical links. Commercial banks were united no longer by their capital but by a range of interrelated activities of other kinds. A variety of new forms of enterprise developed on this basis, including holding companies, groups of companies, and industrial-financial concerns. All of them, typically, were based upon a "mother" firm, whose activities ranged from the sale of computers to the construction of buildings. This mother firm, having accumulated sufficient resources, would then establish "daughter" firms including its own bank and commodity exchange, its own insurance society, its own chamber of commerce, and so forth. A logical development was the establishment of its own joint enterprises (to improve its contacts with the West and to allow its capital to be exported). Similarly, a philanthropic fund might be established, or an investment or pension fund; and the firm would also acquire its own newspapers, its own lobbyists, sometimes its own political parties, and eventually its own security services. Financial groups of this kind had every means thereafter of exercising influence on public policy and on mass opinion.

The new Russian elite, as it had developed by the mid-1990s, may be conceptualized as a three-layered pie. At the top level, there are politicians and their allies, who compete among themselves for power. The middle layer consists of entrepreneurs, who finance the politicians' electoral campaigns, lobbying, newspapers, and television; and at the bottom level are the security services that not only maintain order but also act as a means of influence and contract enforcement. Private security forces of this kind have been established very widely by the largest corporations, or by their agencies, and have also been established on an "independent" basis. The periodic reforms of the KGB have had a number of effects, one of which has been to oblige many of its staff to leave and find alternative employment; and it is former KGB employees who form the core of the security services of major banks and companies. The significance of a Moscow bank has come to be reflected not in its financial position but in whether its security services are headed by a general or merely a colonel from the KGB. The new security services also employ athletes with a specialization in unarmed combat. One of the forms of philanthropy in which the major financial groups engage is precisely the support of clubs for children and young people where karate and other combat sports are taught.

The heads of private security services of this kind are, as a rule, important and well-known figures in their own right. The president of the Lev Yashin fund, Otari Kvantrishvili, was regularly received at the highest levels of the Kremlin;[27] and the heads of the national associations of kick-boxing, field athletics, and kung fu are, as a rule, of considerable political influence. In 1993, the first political party was formed in order to represent their interests, Sportivnaia Rossiia, with branches in local areas as well as in Moscow. The USSR was a major sporting power, and it still provides a home to a large number of outstanding athletes. These new "sports parties" enjoy a considerable public following, especially among young people, whose ideal in life is often to be able to shoot and fight professionally.

The redistribution of power on this basis appears to have been completed and with it the "second Russian revolution" has come to an end. It was a revolution in which a younger generation of the nomenklatura ousted its older rivals. In effect, it was a bourgeois revolution in that it led to a change in the sociopolitical system in the direction of private property and political pluralism. And it involved a redistribution of political power toward a group of younger, more pragmatic nomenklatura, some of whom became politicians and some businessmen. In the economy, there was a corresponding shift of power into property based upon the privatization of the key sectors of the infrastructure: finance, retail trade, international economic relations, and the most profitable sectors of industry (especially the energy and extracting complexes).

Continuity and Change in the Russian Elite

In this final section, we present an analysis of the characteristics of three generations of the Soviet and Russian elite under Brezhnev, Gorbachev, and Yeltsin in order to confirm some of the generalizations

Table 1.1. The Soviet and Russian Elite by Years of Age

	Top leader-ship	Party elite	Parlia-mentary elite	Govern-ment	Re-gional elite	Business elite	Avg. by cohort
Brezhnev cohort	61.8	59.1	41.9	61.0	59.0	n.d.	56.6
Gorbachev cohort	54.0	54.9	44.0	56.2	52.0	n.d.	52.2
Yeltsin cohort	53.1	n.d.	46.5	52.0	49.0	42.1	48.5

Note: n.d. = no data

offered in earlier sections and to give more particular attention to the extent to which the nomenklatura of the Soviet period maintained its position into the post-Communist 1990s.[28] One of the clearest conclusions is that the elite has become significantly younger over the past ten years (see table 1.1). Overall, it has become about eight years more junior. Under Brezhnev, the oldest groups within the elite were the Politburo and the Soviet government, that is, the most powerful functionaries of all; while the youngest was the group of deputies to the USSR Supreme Soviet. There was, in fact, a direct relationship between age and political influence: the greater the age, the greater the authority. The same tends to be true of professional groups in all societies, but it is less clearly the case elsewhere that youth is an indicator of lowly status. In the Brezhnev elite, the relationship was an almost linear one: the youth of parliamentarians was a direct reflection of their relatively low position in the nomenklatura hierarchy. It was not a secret for anyone that the Supreme Soviet of those years played a largely formal role, with its membership based upon national quotas, which in turn determined the share of young people, of women, and of non-Russians that were to be elected.

Under Gorbachev, the ages of the various sections of the elite became more similar: the traditional party-state elite became more youthful, while the relatively freely elected Parliament became three years older. Then, under Yeltsin, there were further changes: the government and regional leadership became almost ten years younger, while the Parliament aged by a further six as it lost the youthful workers and Komsomol members that had formerly been imposed upon it. As the December, 1993, elections made clear, Russian voters, given a choice, generally prefer candidates that are in their late forties, married, and male, with some experience of other spheres of public activity.[29]

The gender composition of the elite in the Brezhnev period was also subject to a quota. About a third of the seats in the USSR Supreme So-

Table 1.2. Women in the Elite (percentage)

	Top leadership	Party elite	Parliamentary elite	Government	Regional elite	Business elite	Avg. by cohort
Brezhnev cohort	3.9	4.3	32.8	0.0	0.0	n.d.	8.2
Gorbachev cohort	5.7	8.4	8.4	2.9	0.0	n.d.	5.6
Yeltsin cohort	2.3	8.6	11.2	2.9	0.0	0.0	4.2

Note: n.d. = no data

Table 1.3. Elites with Rural Origins (percentage)

	Top leadership	Party elite	Parliamentary elite	Government	Regional elite	Business elite	Avg. by cohort
Brezhnev cohort	57.7	59.2	n.d.	45.6	66.7	n.d.	57.3
Gorbachev cohort	48.6	48.5	55.7	35.0	65.6	n.d.	54.6
Yeltsin cohort	12.5	22.9	n.d.	22.9	33.8	22.0	22.8

Note: n.d. = no data

viet were reserved for women, and this was the reason for their relatively substantial representation in Parliament compared with other sections of the elite (see table 1.2). At levels of the nomenklatura where power was actually and not just formally exercised, however, their representation was much less and sometimes nonexistent. Under Gorbachev, there was some increase in the number of women in positions of real authority, but this was matched by a fall in female representation in parliamentary institutions. Women almost doubled their share of the CPSU Central Committee in 1990, but this came when the influence of the Central Committee was itself declining.

In terms of social origin, the old nomenklatura had been predominantly rural. More than half of the Moscow-based party and government leaders, for instance, had a rural background (see table 1.3). In the regions the proportion was even higher. Under Gorbachev there was very little change in this respect in the regions, although in the central institutions of party and state there was a considerable increase in the proportion of leaders that were of urban origin. However, the real change took place in the years that followed. Yeltsin was able to attract a new group of young and well-educated Moscow economists, lawyers, and other professionals into his administration. Those of rural origin dropped to a small proportion at all levels, particularly in the top lead-

Table 1.4. Non-Russian Members of the Elite (percentage)

	Top leader-ship	Party elite	Parlia-mentary elite	Govern-ment	Re-gional elite	Business elite	Avg. by cohort
Brezhnev cohort	23.1	28.4	55.5	24.6	19.1	n.d.	30.1
Gorbachev cohort	51.4	47.4	33.9	15.7	12.5	n.d.	36.3
Yeltsin cohort	27.3	25.7	19.3	17.1	16.2	n.d.	21.1

Note: n.d. = no data

ership, but also in the regions, where a rural origin might have been expected to survive longer. Overall, the proportion of elite members that had been born in rural areas fell to less than half of its level in the years before Gorbachev's accession, and its social origins had been shaped by a very different set of experiences, although they were still far from representative of a society that had been largely urbanized.

It is more difficult to consider changes in the national composition of the elite over the same period, given the collapse of the USSR and the formation in its place of fifteen independent states (see table 1.4). A direct comparison of the Brezhnev and Gorbachev elites with the elite of the Yeltsin years would accordingly be misleading. It was clear, however, that Gorbachev was making some effort under the pressure of events to increase the representation of non-Russians: in the top party leadership their share more than doubled (this reflected a change in the composition of the Politburo, which in 1990 became a body made up of the heads of Republican Party organizations); and in the Central Committee it increased in proportion. Only at the regional level was there a relative fall in the proportion of non-Russians. Under Yeltsin, by contrast, the clearest tendency is for the national composition of each section of the elite to become more similar: under Gorbachev there had been a fourfold difference in the share of non-Russians in the central leadership as compared with the regions, while under Yeltsin the share of non-Russians within each section of the elite varied much less around an average of just over 20 percent, which was itself just above their share of the total population.

The elite was always one of the most educated groups in society. Even in the Brezhnev years, when the leadership was made up pre-dominantly of those of lower socioeconomic status, a higher education of some kind was all but universal. A significant proportion of the nomenklatura of those years, admittedly, had a party or Komsomol higher education, the quality of which could be doubted. During the

Table 1.5. Higher Education among Elite Members (percentage)

	Top leader- ship	Party elite	Parlia- mentary elite	Govern- ment	Re- gional elite	Busi- ness elite	Avg. by cohort
Brezhnev cohort	100.0	92.6	51.3	100.0	100.0	n.d.	88.8
Gorbachev cohort	88.6	74.4	67.9	100.0	100.0	n.d.	84.1
Yeltsin cohort	100.0	100.0	94.0	100.0	97.1	93.0	97.4

Note: n.d. = no data

1980s, it was in fact the parliamentarians who distinguished them-selves, as a result of the fact that all groups of the society, including the highly educated, had their allocated share of seats in representa-tive bodies. Under Gorbachev the relative advantage of parliamentar-ians declined, while regional party first secretaries moved to the fore. The educational level of Parliament nonetheless increased considerably in the Gorbachev years, following the relatively open elections of 1989 and 1990; and there were still more considerable changes in all elite groups during the Yeltsin years, with graduate membership becoming all but universal. (See table 1.5.)

At the same time that a higher education became virtually univer-sal it became less useful as a means of distinguishing among subelite groups. Moreover, it is important to consider other characteristics of educational level. In terms of higher degrees, for instance, there was a clear change from the Brezhnev and Gorbachev years to the elite of the Yeltsin period. About a quarter of the elite had a candidate (the equivalent of an American Ph.D.) or doctor of science degree (a full professor) in the late Communist period (23 percent under Brezh-nev and 29 percent under Gorbachev, with the increase particularly marked within the party leadership); under Yeltsin, the proportion was 48.4 percent, and as high as 70.5 percent in the presidential ad-ministration. There were corresponding changes in the nature of the education that was characteristic of the elite: under Brezhnev it had been predominantly technological, with engineering, military, or agri-cultural specializations particularly prominent. Under Gorbachev, the proportion with a technological education fell, while those with a party higher education increased. Under Yeltsin there was a further fall to 47.2 percent, compared with 71.7 percent under Brezhnev and 67.3 percent in the Gorbachev years; and there was a substantial in-crease in economists and lawyers.

Table 1.6. Elite Members from Outside the Nomenklatura (percentage)

	Top leader-ship	Party elite	Parlia-mentary elite	Govern-ment	Re-gional elite	Business elite	Avg. by cohort
Brezhnev cohort	0.0	6.0	51.3	0.0	0.0	n.d.	11.4
Gorbachev cohort	8.5	28.8	40.6	n.d.	0.0	n.d.	19.5
Yeltsin cohort	25.0	42.8	39.8	25.7	17.7	59.0	35.0

Note: n.d. = no data

Table 1.7. Elite Members of the Yeltsin Cohort Who Served under the Previous Regime (percentage)

	Government	Top leadership	Regional elite	Avg.
Under Brezhnev	31.3	22.7	57.4	37.1
Under Gorbachev	42.9	36.4	39.7	39.7

What about recruitment and renewal? Under Brezhnev it had been all but impossible to enter the elite without passing through the nomenklatura hierarchy or to bypass any of the normal stages of advancement. There were some non-nomenklatura within the CPSU Central Committee and the USSR Supreme Soviet, but these (as in other cases) were "planned" exceptions. There were some changes in the perestroika years, and even the party leadership became accessible to relative outsiders. The most important means of recruitment to the leadership by other than the nomenklatura route was, however, the elections of 1989 and 1990. During the post-Communist years, a still greater proportion were recruited to the elite from those who had not previously been members of the nomenklatura; nearly half of all party leaders and more than half of all the business elite were new people, and so too were a third of all deputies. More striking was the degree of continuity at leading levels of government: three-quarters of the presidential administration and nearly three-quarters of the Russian government were former members of the nomenklatura, and among the regional leadership over 80 percent had similar origins (see table 1.6).

Most of the Yeltsin leadership had spent considerable time in leading positions in the former regime (see table 1.7). Within the Yeltsin elite as a whole, more than a third had begun their progress through the nomenklatura in the Brezhnev years, and more than a third under

Table 1.8. Recruitment of the Yeltsin Cohort by Sector (percentage)

	Top leader-ship	Party elite	Re-gional elite	Govern-ment	Busi-ness elite	Avg
From the nomenklatura as a whole	75.0	57.1	82.3	74.3	61.0	69.9
From sectoral sub-elites:						
Party	21.2	65.0	17.8	0.0	13.1	23.4
Komsomol	0.0	5.0	1.8	0.0	37.7	8.9
Soviets	63.6	25.0	78.6	26.9	3.3	39.5
Economy	9.1	5.0	0.0	42.3	37.7	10.8
Other	6.1	10.0	0.0	30.8	8.2	11.0

Gorbachev; only one in ten were new to the elite, in that they had begun their professional careers in the post-Soviet period. More than half of the current regional leadership began their nomenklatura careers under Brezhnev, and all had inherited rather than acquired their elite status. Among those in the Yeltsin leadership who were former nomenklatura members the average length of service was 11.5 years, ranging from an average of 10 years among members of the Yeltsin government to 14.5 years among his regional administrators. Just as there were typical career paths in all of these periods, there were typical paths from one period to another (see table 1.8). Regional first secretaries, for instance, became chairmen of local Soviets and then heads of local administrations. The presidential administration and the regional elite tended to emerge from former structures of government; the business elite was more likely to have a background in the Komsomol. The Russian government, for its part, became more professional, with its origins increasingly in economic management, diplomacy, and the former security services.

Elites and Post-Communist Transition

This discussion largely shares the conclusions of those who have argued the famous French proverb ("plus ca change") that so much has changed, yet everything is the same. It would, of course, be surprising if the political managers of the post-Soviet system were very different from those who had been responsible for its operation for many years, particularly in Russia, where Communist rule lasted for more than two generations and where many of its assumptions, as surveys have suggested, retained a great deal of support. So it was appropriate that the post-Communist Russian state should be headed by a president who had been a member of the Politburo and Secretariat and by a prime minister who had been a member of the party's Central Committee. The more "indigenous" the regime and the greater its longevity, the greater the extent to which its post-Communist leadership is likely to have its origins in the nomenklatura of the Soviet period.

A broader continuity coexisted, in the Russian case, with a process of circulation within the elite as a younger and less compromised cohort rose to leading positions. This is what a Gorbachev adviser has called the "revolution of the second secretaries."[30] It was similar, in some ways, to the military coups that took place in Africa under the leadership of junior officers, not complete outsiders. For the Hungarians, a change of this kind was best described as a "power metamorphosis" *(metamorphozisa):* it was not a transition from one system to another, but the resolution of an intrasystem crisis and the recuperation of a system of authoritarian power.[31] For Boris Kagarlitsky, "the basic characteristics of the existing system" still remained.[32] For President Vaclav Havel, it was a "velvet restoration." Or as the former Solidarity activist, Andrzej Gwiazda, put it in Poland, "Communism has not collapsed. Maybe it's reclining in a more comfortable position."[33] A process of leadership renewal that was largely confined to the junior ranks of the Communist elite was a part of this evolutionary picture.

A broad continuity also coexisted with a redistribution by sector, as a monolithic elite reconstituted itself as a bifurcated one. Trotsky had long ago argued that the elite would find its privileged position unsatisfactory, as (under Soviet conditions) it depended upon the temporary control of office. Far better, from their point of view, to guarantee their advantage and make it heritable across the generations in the same way as ruling groups in other societies: by the private ownership of property and wealth.[34] It was access to the market, in the first instance, that allowed the nomenklatura to begin to protect their position as the future of the regime became uncertain; afterwards, for many, it was the market and particularly banking that allowed them to retain their position of advantage.

It is likely, in the future, that a still wider range of mechanisms of elite renewal will come into play: particularly access to privileged educational institutions. Already within the Russian elite a number have emerged as particularly important, among them the Moscow State Institute of International Relations (where diplomats are trained), the

Moscow Financial Institute (a source of supply for bankers and entrepreneurs), the Law Faculty of Moscow University and particularly its
Economics Faculty (alma mater for three ministers in the Russian government in 1994, with two more graduates of other faculties). It is also
likely in the future that an increasingly differentiated system of government will throw up local patterns of recruitment and replacement,
with clans (official associations of powerful people from bureaucracy,
business, and criminal sectors) and other associations of particular importance.[35] If this is the case, the Russian political elite will likely share
many of the characteristics of its counterparts in other countries. In
the early post-Communist years, however, its membership is still
largely rooted in the particular circumstances of Communist single-
party rule.

2

The Emergence of a New Elite
Harbinger of the Future or Vestige of the Past?

Boris Grushin

The political elite consists of people directly engaged in politics, as opposed to other elite groups that may affect the political process (such as the economic elite, the entrepreneurial elite, the artistic elite, and the sports elite). Broadly defined, the political elite, in addition to the officials in legislative/executive branches and the leaders of the various political parties/movements, includes the most prominent figures in mass media, top-ranking military personnel, and so forth.

The federal elite level consists of elites affiliated with the top level of the hierarchy, that is, the central authorities and those with political (ideological) control. This excludes local elite (at the municipal, regional, or republican level). Another group, which we call "Politicians 1994," consists of the latter-day elite who emerged after the October assault on the White House. These are the elite who have been in power since 1994.

Russian Political Olympus, Circa 1994

Using an extensive arsenal of techniques, the Vox Populi Polling Service (VP) has been researching the top echelon of Russia's political elite over the course of many years, accumulating a significant amount of data. In 1991, Vox Populi conducted monthly opinion polls for the *Ogonek* magazine on the nation's leaders. These polls, based on a list of prominent political figures, determined the "Man of the Month" (the most visible political figure for the past month). This index was used over the course of about one year to gauge the popularity of the Soviet Union's leading politicians. In 1992, following the collapse of the Soviet Union, these monthly polls were modified, this time at the request of the newspaper *Nezavisimaia Gazeta*. Using direct and open questions, these monthly surveys focused on the politicians who were determined by the opinion polls to be the most influential in charting the country's course of development. The surveys also provided researchers with an opportunity to study the popularity of the leading politicians of the Commonwealth of Independent States (CIS) countries over time.

Starting in January, 1993, the same "individual approach" was expanded to cover not just the leading politicians but a broad spectrum of people comprising the country's political elite. VP collaborated with *Nezavisimaia Gazeta* to start monthly "expert" surveys. Using a ten-point scale, a staff of 50 experts (leaders of major mass media organizations, prominent political commentators, and political scientists) were to determine the 100 most influential politicians in Russia from a precompiled list of 150 names. This list, published regularly by the *Nezavisimaia Gazeta* reveals "who's who" on Russia's political Olympus. To save space, only the top 50 individuals are listed.

The executive branch commands 32 of the top 50 names on the list (9 individuals are members of the president's cabinet); 14 (a respectable number) work in the legislative branch and are not engaged in any executive functions. Leaders of the various political parties and political movements have managed to garner only 7 spots; senior military officers, 2 slots; and people from other law enforcement agencies, 3 slots. Journalists came up empty-handed.

In terms of one's ideological "mind-set," which is measured as one's assessment of the president (naturally, these results are tainted), the president's supporters outnumber those openly opposed to him by almost ten to one. This is hardly surprising, since the number of people appointed by the president is much higher than the number of "unconnected and independent" political leaders. About 20 percent of the entire group are "centrists," that is, moderate opponents of the president who do not hesitate to attack him but who, nevertheless, recognize his authority as completely legitimate.

The top echelon of Russia's political elite is dominated by people from the Center (Moscow) with only five individuals representing local (regional) government bodies. Furthermore, only five people on the list have passed through the "purgatory" of the pre-perestroika command-style administrative system. The rest belong to the new school of politicians whose political career took off during the perestroika years. In fact, the bulk of this group are newcomers on the political scene, emerging after the events of August, 1991.

The data we have paints the following picture of the changing fortunes of Russia's leading politicians. First of all, fluctuations in the perceived political activity of the 50 leading figures is quite common. As a result, shifts in one's rating are insignificant and situation-specific. Second, the list of the "top 100" is very consistent. The same people make up this select group. "Expulsion" from the list (as opposed to the pendulum-like swings in one's rating), as well as the emergence of new names, is extremely rare. For instance, in June, 1993, one single slot changed when Nikolai Travkin was replaced by Alexander Solzhenitsyn; in July the list stayed the same; and in August a new name, General Alexander Lebed (ranked 13th), appeared on the list. It should be noted that the upper half of the list of 100 is quite different from the bottom half. The latter group is predominantly composed of the leaders of various parties and representatives of the legislative, rather than the executive, branch. In the bottom 50 group, the president's staunch opponents are on par (number-wise) with his supporters, and each group is almost twice as weak as the "centrist" wing. Another notable feature of this group is that it has many more representatives of the regional authorities than the top 50 group has.

As we look at who's who among Russia's political elite it may be worthwhile to consider the expert analysis conducted on a monthly basis by the VP Polling Service. One indicator was based on the following question: "Which politicians from among the ones on the big list are likely to be nominated in the next presidential election? Which candidate is sure to be on the ballot?"

Political Elite: Positive Characteristics

The newcomers to the political arena come from very different backgrounds and exhibit extreme variations in other pertinent characteristics. This makes finding common features shared by the majority of Russia's leading politicians a formidable task. Much of our data come from the surveys conducted by the VP Group, which covers the country's leading politicians, including deputies to the State Duma, leaders of the various political parties, top-ranking military officers, and chief executives in the media. For each month, this database contains about 15–20 questions with 50 respondents in each group. The second source of information is my own personal observations of Russia's leading politicians, with many of whom I have had personal contact. Some of my findings were featured in a series of radio broadcasts (Radio Liberty, 1994) entitled *Terra Incognita or Russia in the X Era.*

There is ample evidence pointing to positive qualities of Russia's present-day political establishment. First of all, today's leading politicians are actively involved in the political process. They are truly immersed in the political life of the country, responding (positively or negatively) to new developments, coming up with new proposals, and so on. Unfortunately, all too often this level of intensity creates too much "commotion" and unproductive talk. On the other hand, this kind of involvement (constant public speeches and new proposals made by the politicians of all persuasions, their faces and names appearing in the press and on television every day) fuels passion in society and prevents the government, as well as the opposition and those who want to stick to the "golden middle," from falling into a deep slumber of complacency.

Second, most politicians have developed a certain tolerance, a willingness to compromise and the ability to recognize each other. The aftershock of September–October, 1993, did not go unnoticed, as evidenced by the unusually congenial, albeit formal, signing of the "Social Accord" by the great majority of Russia's political factions. Finally, the third major achievement of Russia's current political elite is a certain consistency of the agenda pursued by the various political groups. This stands in sharp contrast to the former inconsistency, vacillation, and defections from one party to another. As illegal as these practices are (recall the split in the ranks of the Democrats as Gaidar's party, Democratic Choice for Russia, was being formed), it appears that most politicians have settled down as far as their ideological and political tastes are concerned. This relative stability makes it easier to predict their actions.

These new developments are corroborated by the data. It reveals the names of the leading politicians "nominated" monthly by the various political groups; the "nominees" were deemed capable of leading the country out of its current crisis. Discounting certain minor and easily explained inconsistencies (resulting primarily from the day-to-day statements made by the persons being "judged"), each group of respondents is consistent in its attitude and response.

Major Limitations of Russia's Elite

It is actually much easier to pinpoint the weaknesses of Russia's Politicians 1994. Their inadequacies are more numerous and conspicuous. The following three key areas pose special problems for Russia's political elite and appear to stymie the development of new political institutions in Russia.

The first flaw is the total lack of professionalism in the political sphere. Major qualitative shifts in the political structure of the country call for special know-how, new skills, and a reconstituted system of values. The great majority of Russia's politicians lack these qualities, which is only natural given their background. Unfortunately, many do not even want to acknowledge the problems, perhaps believing that none exist. The root of this attitude is in the very low intellectual level of the newly hatched deputies, senators, and leaders of the various parties. Their lack of a basic liberal arts education and poor communication skills contrast sharply with the titles of "thinkers" and educators bestowed upon them. As a result, preposterous incompetence permeates the entire political process. Even a cursory examination of Russia's political scene provides plenty of testimony to this very sad state of affairs, an impression that is confirmed by extensive sociological surveys of the political elite. For instance, all too frequently the respondents simply dodge the questions, especially when it comes to going beyond trivial and murky statements and doing some creative thinking that can shed some light on the issue. The key indicator of this ineptitude is the politicians' inability to predict with any degree of accuracy the course of events in Russia. For instance, at the beginning of 1994, at least half of the leading politicians predicted Chernomyrdin's imminent resignation (as early as spring). Nothing of the sort ever took place. In March, 75 percent of the politicians surveyed were confident that "Yeltsin and his political opponents will not be able to reach an accord." As it turned out, a truce did come and was formally signed by all the parties involved just a few weeks after this specious prognosis.

The second drawback: the majority of Russia's political parties and their leaders lack a holistic vision and understanding of the key problems facing the country. They lack a coherent vision of a mechanism to underwrite Russia's future development. Their views resemble a cocktail of eclectic, poorly articulated, and mutually contradictory ideas. This facet of the political establishment's mind-set comes to the fore when they are asked about the future prospects of Russia's political and economic development. For instance, in assessing the social tensions resulting from the adoption of the agreement between Yeltsin and his political opponents and the subsequent analysis of its aftermath, 20 percent of them considered the possibility of a "civil war more real than before." For the leaders of the various political parties, these figures were 16 percent and 12 percent.

The aforementioned limitations suffered by Russia's political elite are certainly very serious. Even more critical, however, is the profound split among Politicians 1994 on virtually all major issues, jeopardizing the future of the country and its new political institutions. Consensus among leading politicians (or even the majority) is an exception; deep-seated conflicts are the rule. Naturally, the ratios vary depending on the issue and the formulation of the question. When presented with a dichotomous choice, the proposed alternatives differ from the ones proposed within the multiple choice framework. Nonetheless, the proposed remedies (usually no more than four or five) gravitate toward two or three diametrically opposed alternatives. Details aside, Russia's present-day political elite is still split into three major camps (just as at the inception of reforms): those vying "for something," those "opposed to something," and those advocating some kind of a compromise. Often all three groups are on par with each other; sometimes one of the two polar factions gains the upper hand. Contrary to popular belief, it is unusual for the center to come out on top. In fact, the data suggests that the position held by the center is being eroded, giving way to ever greater polarization of the pro and contra camps. Still, further empirical corroboration is required.

Basic Types of Politicians

Given the high degree of differentiation among Russia's current political elite, Politicians 1994 could be classified based on different criteria. Naturally, the criteria we want to employ should create a "stereoscopic" rather than a one-dimensional image of these diverse groups. However, the VP polling service has long been using three basic indicators in its studies of Russia's politicians: age (younger than 35, 35–55, over 55); institutional affiliation (legislative/executive branches, leaders of the various parties, military, mass media); and the general worldview and economic leanings assessed in terms of one's position along the "past-future" axis of Russia's history. Interestingly, the data reveals that the first criteria, age, is not very significant.

The second parameter, however, is significant. For instance, our data shows that the deputies tend to adhere to views different from those held by government officials; views held by the leaders of the various parties tend to differ from those held by the journalists and senior military officers. However, this criteria should be qualified, for while it works in some areas (with regard to specific alternatives) it fails when it comes to the broader issues. The aforementioned factions are conventionally grouped into three categories that are all featured in each of the three institutional groupings. This means that intergroup differentiation based on institutional affiliation is, in most cases, much less significant than inner-group differentiation. The roots of the latter are more profound, and we believe they go to the heart of the third criterion—the general worldview or the mentality of the politicians, their system of values, views regarding the future of Russia, and the means ("constructive" ideas, mechanisms) to attain the set goals.

To assess one's general outlook, empirical studies have relied on questions concerning such key areas as "the future of Russia," "Western aid," "prospects for democracy in Russia," "path of economic reform," and so on. More specific solutions were uncovered by focusing on such key phrases as "acceptable/unacceptable rate of development," "plausible/unfeasible ways to resolve the problems," and "reasonable/unreasonable price to pay for various reforms." Unfortunately, the extensive data collected by VP is poorly integrated. Nonetheless, when coupled with direct observation of the top echelon of Russia's political elite, this information edifies a number of definitive hypotheses regarding the types of politicians currently active in Russia. The spectrum, based on one's position along the past-future axis (or, more precisely, "dead-alive" axis), reveals at least four basic types of politicians (individual allegiances are less unequivocal).

Type A. Dead, posing as the living. These are the people who live in the past, prior to the events of August, 1991, and October, 1993. They are spent fuel, but they still enjoy limited support from certain segments of the population. Contrary to all logic and common sense, they choose to perceive themselves as politicians of considerable import. This group includes Mikhail Gorbachev, Anatolii Luk'ianov, Alexander Rutskoi, Victor Anpilov. The distinguishing marks of this contingent of politicians are across-the-board opposition to the government currently in power and its reform policies; nostalgia for the past (in terms of both the strategy and the programs of action); and a complete inability (bordering on fanaticism) to conduct a meaningful dialogue.

The mind-set of this group is evident in such comments as that of Anatolii Luk'ianov, excerpted from the radio broadcast *Terra Incognita* on May 28, 1994: "The split in the ranks was caused by the onslaught of anti-socialist forces . . . This plan had long been fostered by those opposed to the socialist system." On the same radio program on June 25, 1994, Alexander Rutskoi commented: "The President and his team are concocting yet another manifesto regarding the national accord. Can there ever be an accord between the murderer and the murdered, between the robber and the robbed?! . . . Can we ever come to terms with

Yeltsin? Never! Just look at what he has done to our country! There is no country in the world which tolerates such lawlessness."

Type B. Alive, but completely paralyzed by the dead. These are the people who managed to survive the events of August, 1991, and October, 1993, and who have been in the vanguard of reform. They have managed to survive despite their opposition to the victors. Presently, they are either part of the ruling elite (president, prime minister, Moscow's mayor) or part of the opposition (but not so unequivocal as type-A politicians); Vladimir Zhirinovskii is an example of the type-B opposition.

The group is distinguished by 1) active involvement in reforming the Russia of old; lack of cohesive ideas concerning the nature of the proposed reform (not to speak of a consistent and mature program of implementation); 2) adherence to the basic rules of conduct and political mind-set characteristic of the command style administrative system; unabashed antidemocratic sentiments and crude populism; 3) low intellectual level, sometimes bordering on total ignorance and obtuseness.

An example is Victor Chernomyrdin. At the government meeting on March 4, 1994, to discuss the publication by *Nezavisimaia Gazeta* of the ratings of "100 politicians" (the first time the premier surpassed the president in the poll), he stated: "Let me touch upon one critical issue, which concerns me personally as well as the government which I lead. A number of media organizations have recently embarked on a loudmouth campaign aimed at 'nabbing' the premier, at trying to concentrate all the power in his hands, at assuming too much responsibility, and even at plotting to close in on the much-coveted presidency. They have even started some kind of a rating system on this matter."

Another type-B politician is Alexander Nevzorov. On the May 14, 1994, radio broadcast of *Terra Incognita,* he stated, "It is really not difficult to understand Russia as state machinery, as a human entity composed of millions of bodies, houses, factories, plants, horses, and machines . . . This entity lives according to the rules of dignity and honor which have long been dead and buried in the West. We are a medieval, perhaps an early medieval country. We are really fooling ourselves when we boast of all this progress—all these painted steel machines in place of the former wooden ones, all these rockets in space . . . What is so special about it? We can take a spoon and throw it up in the air. A rocket is no different, except it is heavier and flies further. The most precious thing is to follow our medieval roots. We have to live by the laws of medieval times. Then our country will be all right."

Type C. Alive and trying to adopt the new ways. This group champions radical reforms; they are authors of numerous well-known programs, social designs, and initiatives. With almost unabashed favor for the president and other "old-timers," the members of this group are either part of the government or work actively with the government; very seldom, they are in "loyal opposition" to the government. The distinguishing characteristics of this group, which includes the likes of Yegor Gaidar, Gregorii Yavlinskii, Vladimir Shumeiko, Boris Fedorov, are 1) strong drive to inject new elements into the political process, including a more intellectual approach than the one perpetuated by the older generation; 2) lack of political as well as personal experience necessary to compete with their "old guard" allies, or to unseat their opponents; 3) shallow views; aplomb bordering on arrogance and cockiness; bouts of unwarranted opportunism, resulting in a poor track record and defeats at the hands of their opponents.

On the March 23, 1994, broadcast of *Terra Incognita,* Gregorii Yavlinskii stated: "Actually, everything we had proposed has, to a greater or lesser extent, been implemented. Recall the liberal '500 Day' program of reform. It is true that it was delayed and put into practice by other people. It is true that it was flawed; it was ill-suited for the time when it was inaugurated. Still, all the key facets of the program have come to fruition. It was superseded by another program dubbed 'Challenge Accepted,' a program to cooperate with the West. There was no shortage of skeptics when it came to this program! However, after only eleven months the G-7 offered us 24 billion dollars, subsequently raised to 40 billion. Once again, Russia was not prepared to take advantage of Western aid. But the fact stands—the offer was made."

On the same broadcast, Nikolai Travkin commented, "My sense of the political twists and turns has not betrayed me, except, perhaps, for the December 12 elections. The reason is simple. All my predictions are based not on some 'armchair rumination' but on concrete down-to-earth observations."

Type D. Alive and embracing the new political reality. This group still lurks in the shadows. As a rule, these people don't hold high-level positions in the government or the opposition; they eschew fanfare and demonstrations and reject seductive speeches. They prefer to act rather than talk. This group includes leaders of the various departments (Andrei Kozyrev, Andrei Kokoshin); regional officials (Boris Nemtzov); and bankers and entrepreneurs who are actively involved in politics (Vladimir Gusinskii, Valerii Neverov).

What sets this group apart are 1) pragmatism, the cornerstone of their ideology, with the motto of "get the results here and now"; 2) a high level of professionalism in their area of expertise, which allows them to introduce new models of decision making into the political process; and 3) impressive results, as compared to other groups.

Conclusion

To estimate accurately the ratio of the various groups that make up Russia's political establishment would be impossible, but a quick look at the top 100 "Olympians" suggests that types B and C dominate the list, type A enjoys a hefty share as well, and type D is stuck with a sorry number. If my impressions are correct, it will take a long time for Russia's new political institutions to mature and come into their own.

3

The Elite and the Masses in Public Opinion

Yurii Levada

One of the components of long-lasting turbulence in post-Communist Russian society is the destruction of a system of social-cultural samples and examples. At the same time, there is a crisis within elite structures and a deformation of their roles in relation to societies' "mass" structures. Elites lose significance if the "masses" fail to perceive their symbolic and instrumental function (examples of their integrative function, codes of culture, rules of behavior, and so forth). Much of the modern discussion about the moral degradation of Russian society and its deprivation of spiritual leaders, along with the disintegration and decline of the intellectual and ruling elite (who are thus deprived of public recognition), is constructed around this complex. For this reason, the nature and function of elite structures is often perceived as problematic.

One can identify elites by their professional place, by the type of their employment (occupations) in society. Accordingly, it is acceptable to speak about intellectual, political, military, economic, and cultural elites. The character of any elite structure is defined by the function it performs in society. It is also expedient to divide elite structures by the way they perform their functions in relation to society, to the "masses," and to social institutions. Hence, elite structures can be defined as social groups or strata situated in functional frameworks that adapt in appropriate ways to support those functions and structures.

Public Elite and Social Elite

A public elite consists of those actors (persons, figures, personalities) or groups, whose words and actions address society as a whole, that is, their audience, students, followers, supporters, and the public in its broadest sense. This category of the elite acts predominantly through the mass media. It includes not only professional publicists or commentators but specialists, politicians, scientists, lawyers, militaries, and so forth, as far as they act outside of professional circles and "represent themselves" to the public through the mass media. The public elite is demonstrative and able to interest, inspire, evaluate, discredit, and declare generalized examples of behavior. They offer the "common public" or unskilled audiences examples of behavior and special knowledge. Therefore, the public elite is limited to a few dozen persons and is defined by their abilities to capture mass attention, or, to express it figuratively, by the size of their podium.

The social elite are those groups and structures that operate in the field of institutionalized professional activity and provide examples of behavior, purposes, and reference points. Predominantly, professional communications and contacts serve as the means of action. The ability to set, or reunderstand, examples of behavior is connected in these structures to those in the higher social status of social-elite groups, that is, those who have a higher level of education and higher positions in the hierarchy of social management.

In each sphere of activity (or professional group), a specialized elite is formed. The field of action of this type of elite is not society but a corresponding group. The acceptance of the decisions, especially political decisions, is influenced by various groups of advisers, lobbyists, and so forth. The specialized elite can be considered a specific, closed elite structure. These formations remain outside of this analysis.

Characteristics of Crisis

There is a modern crisis of elite structures in Russian society that effects first and foremost the public elite. The elite went through a short period of flourishing in the best years of perestroika and glasnost. During those years there was an opportunity to form an unprecedented public elite structure. The elite played a unique role in the destruction of the totalitarian system. Their activities and specific character were contradictory and were connected to both the strong and the weak sides of the perestroika processes. During the period of perestroika, the vanguard of the public elite was limited to several dozen bright, popular names like Yurii Afanasiev, Anatolii Sobchak, and Gavriil Popov. The vanguard appealed to the trust of democratically settled parts of society and rendered certain influences on the actions and slogans of the Gorbachev party clique. The democratic spirit of those years, supported by the euphoria of the first steps of political liberalization (for example, glasnost and "amnesty" of "dissidents"), appeared to be a nutritious environment of mutually exclusive currents of democraticism, liberalism, nationalism, neosocialism, "neo-soil doctrines," and so forth. Ambiguous from the very beginning, relations between authority and the liberal intelligentsia elite supported one of the longest lasting and most dangerous illusions of Russian history—that of reasonable, "intellectual" despotism. There is a connection between this illusion and the prestige of "new thinking" and the hope for "scheduled" reforms in society.

During the period of perestroika, the elite acted purely as publicists (or journalists): respectable scientists and parliamentary tribunes took action before mass public audiences and influenced them exclusively as publicists. Their message was rather simple, and it became popular to express the things that had already been known and transmitted secretly in prior years. The detailed examples, particularly of economic analysis, were considerably less appreciated by the public than the very opportunity "to call a spade a spade." The publicist function and its effect on public opinion made superstars out of various individuals, including scientists, writers, deputies, professional TV commentators, and even rock singers of a new (in those times) social-critical style.

The downfall of hopes for a planned transformation from totalitarian society to democracy resulted in a reevaluation of perestroika itself along with the role of Mikhail Gorbachev and the public elite of perestroika. This was not only a period of losing hope and destroying illusions but also a time of withdrawing from the social and psychological structures and conditions that required such illusions. Having played its role, the public elite of the perestroika years inevitably lost its role as a stimulator for the public mood. Many representatives of this group are now portrayed in the mass media with a tone of disappointment in perestroika and reforms. Some of the public elite are keen on the aims and purposes of nationalism and the concepts of Great State power. Very few, however, find serious analytic work (positions) in organizations.

"New" or "Old" Elites?

In the strict sense of the word, those groups of activists who set the tone in business or authority structures may be likened with elites only insofar as the necessary traditions and "gears" of their social reproduction are taken away. It is not always possible to distinguish them from cliques, clans, or other organized groups (or the mafia, with which widespread comparisons have been made). Only some of the groups that have gained stability can be transformed in elite structures. The prospects of groups with elite claims or potential deserve detailed analysis.

At present, such groups are hindered not only by the lack of material base (financial resources, property, and so on) but also by the widespread unproductive stereotypes that characterize them. There have been many charges of corruption, connections with criminal groups, and participation in the "criminal revolution." These charges serve as one of the main supports of all political critics who use these populist arguments. About half of city dwellers interviewed in September, 1994, believed that corruption in the ruling state machine was now stronger than in Soviet times. These attributions are difficult to verify because of the weakness of the legal system and the poor quality of statistics available in relation to business corruption. From the sociological standpoint, corruption of "functionaries" (members of ruling administration) is an apparent attribute of the new elite structures, in which socially repressive control is weakened and there is an absence of normative frameworks. Thus, a high level of corruption accompanies the growth of practically all modernizing societies. Corruption is an "illness" of development.

Another stereotype of new elite structures concerns the genesis of their staff. According to numerous studies, the prevailing part of the newly formed business elite as well as elites in authority (including closed structures) derive from the *nomenklatura* of the "old" party— Soviet, administrative, or economic bodies, or their descendants, relatives, and so forth. Despite all the shocks of perestroika and reforms, the command functions remain in the hands of the old social stratum.

There are some basic objections that can be given to this viewpoint. First, there is no basis for the possibility of creating structures outside the influence and the inheritance of the old Soviet structures that dominated and monopolized all channels of social and professional advancement. The conversion (simple renaming in the beginning) of nomenklatura henchmen into "independent" politicians or owners of manufacturing companies was general and inevitable, given the history of Soviet distribution of social resources. This situation will not be a yoke on future generations.

Second, "social origin" cannot be the decisive factor for determining the activity of individuals, whatever nomenklatura post they occupied. An exaggeration of the role of origin is a methodological inheritance of primitive "class" doctrines. Vulgarized Marxism links (inseparably) people and their class group and origin. From a sociological approach, people's behavior and attributes are closely linked to the social institutions they are part of. The "acting" nomenklatura was always guided by a hierarchical structure of party domination and was supervised. The wreck of this centralized structure has changed the situation in a cardinal way. Without party guardianship, the nomenklatura is inevitably transformed into a "former" one. It is compelled to search for other reference points and norms of behavior. Conventional thinking, however, lingers, as well as the group's clan connections. But they do not in themselves create "weather." Irrespective of their social origin, the nomenklatura's political beliefs and prejudices are cast into a situation of rigid economic or political "machine" competition, and they are compelled to adapt and to act pursuant to the new rules of the political economy. Certainly, there is not a uniform and universally recognized system of "rules," especially in conditions of general instability and lack of organization, specific for the transitory stage of Russia. There are various levels of possible activity and adaptation to existing conditions, from civilized and long-term to fraudulent and short-term proclivities. The trajectory of movement of activist groups or persons between such levels determines the character of their probable status in elite structures.

The State of Social Elite: The Preliminary Remarks

An "advanced" part of society is considered to be a social elite, the basic function of which is to transfer practical, daily examples of action to the rest of society. In Soviet party times, conditions supportive of a public elite were impossible, but a social elite structure did exist. Its role was interpreted predominantly as purely technical (skilled or professional: a teacher teaches the children, a doctor treats the patients, and so forth). It was assumed that the maintenance of values integrating society is a monopoly of the ruling clique and its ideological machinery. Such a model could never be realized completely. In the conditions of the disintegration of "central" value structures, the functions of a social "periphery"—a periphery in terms of both social space and geographical space—grow and expand. The social construction of everyday life becomes more important for the people despite efforts to frighten them or to seduce them with special calls to action by the party. These acting points are reference for social norms and barriers to general social disintegration. Hence, it is very important to do an analysis of the orientations of an "advanced" social stratum in comparison to the masses. A parity of positions revealed in such a comparison provides a basis for judging the condition of the social resource base and a way of estimating the direction of vectors in the value system of the public.

The Social Elite: The Empirical Analysis

The following observations are based on research conducted by the All-Russian Center for Public Opinion Research. The most reliable sources are the longitudinal surveys of the public, which include more than 47,000 respondents. From March, 1993, until March, 1994, up to 4,000 persons were interviewed monthly. They are representative of the entire population of Russia and include 28,561 respondents. One-third of them are experts and chiefs of enterprises and divisions with average or highly specialized educations. This group represents the social elite in our empirical analysis. They include industry and transport (3,300 respondents); culture, education, medicine, and health care (3,400); management (500); and army, militia, and courts (330). Two-thirds are workers of various branches who do not possess special educations or execute managing functions ("other").

The level of education of the group of chiefs and experts appreciably differs from that of the other workers (see table 3.1). The item to pay attention to is the almost complete symmetry of the extreme parameters and the affinity of "average": the elite group consists almost exclusively of people with average and maximum level educations, in a proportion of 5:4, and "other" (the masses) has approximately the same proportion in average and lower educations.

The working population is excluded for technical reasons, particularly because of the complexity of categorizing various groups of retired persons. Except for the data mentioned above, in a number of cases information is used from later research, in particular, the summary results of four monitoring interview surveys carried out in April–July, 1994.

The Status of the Chiefs and Experts

The average income per head in a group of chiefs and experts in the survey was about 48,000 rubles for chiefs and 38,000 rubles for experts. (The estimations of their financial states are shown in table 3.2.) Thus, the chiefs and experts have both the higher-level incomes as well as a little more positive estimation of their own financial state.

The elite conception of the major difficulties of social development is demonstrated by their answers to the question, "Which problems in society disturb you most of all?" The social elite is less disturbed by "practical" problems such as prices, the deficit, and unemployment, and a little more disturbed by political and ideological problems such

Table 3.1. Education of Respondents in a Nationwide Survey, 1993–94 (percentage, N = 47,343)

	Education		
	Below average	Average	Higher
Chiefs and experts	3.9	51.8	44.3
Other	42.0	54.7	3.3

Table 3.2. Estimations of Family Financial Situation, 1993–94 (percentage, N = 28,561)

	Chiefs and experts	Masses
Very good	0.7	0.5
Good	7.9	5.1
Average	33.6	48.0
Bad	30.0	35.1
Very bad	6.5	9.2
Difficult to answer	1.3	2.1

Table 3.3. Level of Worry about Various Social Problems, 1993–94 (percentage, N = 28,561)

Problems	Chiefs and experts	Masses
Deficit of goods	14.3	19.2
Rise in prices	77.1	85.5
Unemployment	32.9	39.6
Crisis in economy	34.9	44.6
Crisis of morals, culture	40.0	22.1
Pollution	31.2	28.9
International relations	18.0	16.3
Maintenance of ideals of social validity	7.6	7.1
Weakness of power	34.5	31.2

as weakness of power and international relations (see table 3.3). The most appreciable divergence of the two distinguished groups is in their assessments of the moral and cultural crisis. But the elite and the masses show similar concerns about corruption, weakness of power, and conflicts in management.

Table 3.4. Overall View of Reforms and Life Situation, 1993–94
(percentage, N = 47,343)

	March, 1993–March, 1994			April–July, 1994		
	Social elite	Other	Total	Social elite	Other	Total
"Everything is not so bad, and it is possible to live"	11.9	7.2	8.6	15.7	9.0	9.7
"Life is difficult, but it is possible to bear"	53.3	52.6	52.6	49.5	51.2	50.8
"To bear . . . is already impossible"	29.5	30.5	32.6	28.6	32.6	32.8
Difficult to answer	5.1	5.7	5.7	6.5	7.3	6.6

Table 3.5. Attitude toward Economic Reforms, April–July, 1994
(percentage, N = 10,343)

Attitude toward economic reforms	Social elite	Other	Total
Should be continued	40.3	27.7	34.4
Should be stopped	20.8	31.0	29.0
Difficult to answer	37.9	41.2	38.8
Total	1,750	2,954	10,343

Attitudes toward Reform

Overall, social elites are appreciably more optimistic than other groups (see table 3.4). All groups find conditions "possible to bear." A minority are pessimistic. As a whole, this elite group is more supportive of the reforms than the masses. It is clear that the elite consider reforms positively.

The position of the social elite is essentially different from the mass position: the number of those who support the continuation of reforms is twice that of the other group and exceeds the number of those who hesitated to answer (see table 3.5). The share of those who refused to answer is almost identical in all groups (about 40 percent).

If it is lawful to speak about practical social support of reforms, the social elite of society are usually the first to do so. The public as a whole views reforms without enthusiasm and with little understanding of their nature and consequences. The level of uncertainty and doubt differs very little. However, the social elite have more hope for reforms. In general, the social elite cannot dominate the masses. The social elite can only advance social reforms and push the masses, with half-steps, toward accepting the reforms with optimism.

4

Crime and the Formation of a New Elite

Victor Luneev

Generally, there is a direct relationship between crime levels in a society and the degree to which morality and legality is upheld by political elites. The higher the level of crime in society, the higher the level of criminality of elite groups and vice versa.

This relationship can vary, depending on the historical, national, religious, political, and other social-cultural traditions and preconditions of legal and illegal behavior of the country. In all cases, however, it remains direct and appreciable. The strongest interrelations are registered between the criminality of the ruling (managing) elite and criminological conditions in the country as a whole. For the general public, the ruling elite serve as a positive or negative example in relationship to crime. The behavior and criminality of the elite can directly and indirectly justify illegal behavior or indifference to crime.

The criminality of the elite is not fully explained with the well-known concept of "criminality of the white collars." Edwin Sutherland, the American criminologist who invented the concept, understood it as the crimes of business managers.[1] The managers of power, the power elite, are on a much higher social plane. If we use the Sutherland approach, the crime in a sphere of power can be seen as "crime of respectable white collars" or simply "respectable criminality," as it was named by another American criminologist, Edwin Shirr.[2] However, the crimes of the political and ruling elite have high degrees of unrespectability and have much more serious consequences for society.

The most dangerous and professional forms of criminal behavior are political terrorism (violence of power) and political corruption (venality of power). These are world problems. For a long time, the international community, on behalf of the UN, has been anxious to learn about the criminality of the ruling circles, especially their corruption. The Eighth Congress of the UN on the prevention of crime and delinquency (Havana, 1990) in its resolution, "Corruption in a sphere of state management," and the document, "Practical measures for struggle with corruption," noted that the problems of corruption in state administrations have a general character and their baneful influence is felt all over the world.[3]

Statistical and sociological acknowledgment of existing interrelations between criminality of the ruling elites and general criminality is hindered because of the latent character of the criminal behavior of the ruling circles and their corporate closeness or secrecy. The hidden crimes of the officials as a whole are higher than the hidden crimes of the population; the concealment of crimes, committed by elite, is even higher. This happens despite the great attention of the mass media, political opponents, and public organizations. Even when the significant part of the population feels the criminal pressure of the ruling circles, when their venality is widespread, and when information on their crimes is statistically published, the majority of crimes remain obscure or unproved. Moreover, the criminal justice system considers no more than a thousandth of the real crimes committed by the ruling elite.

This happens because 1) the delinquencies of the ruling circles are usually connected to their administrative activities and remain confidential "matters of the state"; 2) the criminal deeds committed by the elite (as a rule) have no direct victims, nor witnesses who can publish such facts; 3) the crimes of the ruling elites in various countries are committed with a high degree of "professionalism," using intelligence for illegal purposes and for overpowering modern methods of crime protection, and hence they avert discovery and denunciation; 4) members of the ruling circles, covered by laws (even in advanced democratic countries) and by virtue of the corporate solidarity of the whole power establishment, manage to avoid their real criminal liability much more often than other citizens.

Loud periodic denunciations of highly ranked officials who have committed unlawful actions are an exception to the rule. Where they occur, such denunciations are usually forms of party struggle involving cunning public demonstrations to the people of the need for "law and order." In these cases judicial processes often are sparing in punishment and do not result in imprisonment. In authoritarian and other undemocratic transition regimes, such as in Russia, the ruling elite usually distinguishes itself by its complete inviolability. It actually operates law-enforcement bodies and courts that do not have real power to administer justice and apply the law.

Official statistical data about the criminality of political and especially the ruling elite are far from objective. Some of the information (the results of prosecutor checks from various controlling bodies, letters and complaints from citizens, messages of the mass media, investigation material not delivered to the court, and so forth) is neither systematized nor indisputable. Nevertheless, the data can be used in criminological, sociological, and political research.

Proceeding from these general provisions, I will analyze the criminality of the Russian political and ruling elite in view of the national, historical preconditions and tendencies of modern crime. This is a new problem for Russian criminological science. In the United States, England, and other countries, there are many works on the subjects of crimes committed by politicians, political corruption, and political terrorism (Oxford University research being one example).[4]

The Historical Preconditions of Criminality

In the Stalin years, a low level of penal (400–500 crimes per 100,000 in the population) and especially official crimes was registered. In 1956, for example, there were only 465 cases of bribery registered (0–2 per 100,000 of the population and about 2–3 per 100,000 officials took criminal liability for their actions). According to the Criminal Code of Russian Socialist Federation of Soviet Republics (RSFSR) in 1926 (which lasted until 1960), the criminal liability of official (service) crimes, including bribery, involving a wide circle of persons occupying constant or temporary posts in official bodies, was shouldered by the enterprises and organizations. The range of such crimes was very wide. One reason for the low level of registered official crime was the state's total control over the behavior and activity of the people. In the opinion of G. P. Fedotov, the state did not leave any corner of its soul outside of its control.[5]

Each person, regardless of service to the state, was in the intersection of many organizational components: economic, legal, organizational, ideological, social-psychological, operative, and repressive. The economic component included complete dependence of the person on the unique employer—the state. Private business activity was criminally punishable. The legal component was based on legalized primacy of the state over "right," particularly over the rights of the people, and over organizations; the so-called democratic centralism was really an all-embracing rigid centralism of power garbed in a thin veneer of democratic verbiage. Secrecy deprived people of any knowledge of real validity. The ideological component expressed the Communist identity and suppression of heterodoxy and included a social-psychological domination of pro-Communist public opinion. The latter not only was imposed from above but also had some support from the people who sincerely believed in the idea of building a better future.

Total control included the systematic tracking of people's behavior and activities. It was secret yet obvious. The repressive component integrated and crowned the total control system as a whole. It registered its activity statistically. The dynamics of the official statistics of "political criminality" can be considered one of the major indicators of the Soviet's tendency to command total control.

Political repression along with all the other components of the system of total control effectively constrained deviations from established law and order, including criminal behavior. This can be seen in the low level of criminality in the USSR, especially in the lack of crimes committed by managing officials. Mass repression compensated for the low level of crime. From official data, collected between 1917 and 1990, 3,853,900 people were accused of "political crimes" and of these 827,955 were shot.[6] However, the main weight of repressions (arrests, imprisoning in camps, dispatches) was executed by administrative order. These were not entered in the statistical list of "political crimes." The real number of repressions was considerably larger.

Analysis of these statistical numbers reveals a high correlation (R = 0.80) between crime and political repression. According to international documents, victims of uncriminalized abuse by the authorities were equated as victims of usual crimes. The abuse of authority was considered official delinquency and a crime that reflected a real and dangerous criminality in ruling circles.[7]

I use the term "ruling circles" here instead of "ruling elite." Party, state, and economic chiefs in Stalin's period can be considered elite only conditionally. They did not represent a coherent social group that independently defined political and economic processes in the country.[8] They were "the nuts and bolts" bound at various hierarchical levels of party, state, and economic authority. The horizontal connections between "ruling circles" were considered to be criminal organizations.

All of them were under the strictest interdiction and were regarded as "centers" for counterrevolutionary crime activity. Supervisors of various ranks (from the secretaries and members of the Political Bureau of the Central Committee of the Communist Party of the Soviet Union

(CPSU), to members of government, to local administrators) were more often than other citizens caught up in the machinery of mass political repressions.

In the 1920s, the share of such chiefs from the central administration alone reached 28.5 percent (1929). The violent destruction of this category of individuals and their own adaptation to the ruling regime decreased their membership to less than 1 percent in 1937. The horizontal connection of the ruling circles in this period was specific: it reflected not so much conventional motivations to succeed, as in other countries, as an aspiration to survive by diligent service to a criminal regime with absolute obedience to the higher chiefs. Adherence to the law was not important.

With the easing of total control in the mid-1950s, criminality increased and became comparable to world levels. With the disintegration of the USSR in 1991, registered criminality took an even bigger jump, increasing its absolute parameters by almost six times. Within a half year, the crime rate increased by four to five times, but even this rate was below that of developed Western countries.

In this period, the party, state, and economic elite developed. The elite were special social groups with internal, horizontal, group interests and values, capable of acting relatively independently when determining the political and economic processes in the country. Their first achievement was the emergence from under the control of repressive bodies (such as the KGB and the Ministry of Foreign Affairs, or MFA) and the conversion of these bodies, especially the KGB, into an advanced group of party and state *nomenklatura*.

These elites consistently and persistently gained wide discretionary authority and unlimited access not only to management but also to the control and actual possession of national property. Moreover, they acted beyond the control of the public as well as law and order. The criminalization of the elite required the consent of the nomenklatura. During Brezhnev's era, the overwhelming majority of the elite were criminalized. Yet their activities were barely reflected in judicial practice and criminal statistics. There were some very odious cases of stealing public funds and bribery on the part of the ministers, secretaries of regional committees, members of the Communist Party (CC), and other high officials. But these became public only when such officials had lost the trust of the members of the Political Bureau and the CC.

The psychology of "justified" embezzlement of public property was not an exception even for the General Secretary CC CPSU— Leonid Brezhnev. The dominant outlook in the country was that state property actually belonged to nobody and to everybody at the same time. Such justification was widespread among the party-state nomenklatura.

From 1956 to 1986, registered official plundering of state property increased 2.5 times, and bribery, 25 times. The absolute numbers were not very large. In 1986, there were approximately 11,408 cases of bribery and 6,639 people were accused and registered.[9] Most of the criminal liability was attributed to the lowest strata of officials. The elite remained practically untouched.

During perestroika, the total control of the state collapsed. Embezzlement of state property multiplied. Corruption of the old nomenklatura and representatives of the new elite exploded. At the same time, criminal responsibility in terms of crime statistics reduced. From 1986 to 1991, registered official plundering in the USSR decreased by 30 percent, and bribery decreased by three times. In 1992, 686 persons in Russia were accused and 3,331 cases of bribery were enlisted. Corruption was five times less than in 1986. In this period the mobile part of the party, state, and economic elite came into new power and gained control of commercial structures. They were corrupted by organized criminals transferring public funds and resources abroad and into joint-stock, private, and personal property. Data from the International Monetary Fund shows that the total sum of illegal outflow of monetary means from Russia in the early 1990s reached 50 billion U.S. dollars.[10] According to the calculations of Russian experts, owing to the illegal outflow of hard currency abroad, Russia (from 1995 on) suffered economic loss of about 100 to 150 billion dollars. Aspiring to return these vast sums of money back into the Russian economy, the State Duma discussed a decree for giving amnesty to the individuals who committed illegal deeds in connection with financial assets abroad.[11]

The outflow of hard currency continues. Under the conditions of "vague" borders between countries of the CIS and Baltic states, criminal exports of petroleum, strategic raw materials, and other goods and currency values have escalated. In 1994, the Ministry for Foreign Affairs together with the customs office revealed 14,500 crimes connected with the illegal exportation of currency and strategically important material resources.[12] Though the level of illegal exportation was twelve times greater in 1994 than it had been in the previous year, many of these deeds remained latent. None of this could have been possible without the services and abuses committed by officials who were objects of graft.

In 1994, in the sphere of the economy, 124,250 crimes were registered. There were 16,543 malfeasances, which included 4,919 cases of bribery. In 1993, 1,422 corruption cases were brought to court. Forty-three percent of these cases involved workers of ministries, committees, and the corresponding local structures; 26 percent were employees of law-enforcement bodies; 11 percent were workers of the credit and financial system; 4 percent were workers in supervising bodies; and 2 percent were deputies of Soviets at various state levels. The highest level of executive and legislative power remained untouched, though there were some criminal cases investigated. The deputies of the former Supreme Soviet, for example, completely absolved themselves of criminal responsibility. Without the consent of the Supreme Soviet, law-enforcement bodies had no right to bring a criminal case against a deputy. A vicious circle emerged: legally significant evidence could be collected only in juridical proceedings in a criminal case, but such a proceeding required the consent of those involved in the criminal case. The attempts of the general public prosecutor's office to achieve such consent concerning some deputies were rebuked. In the proposed law about the struggle with corruption, which was discussed in the Supreme Soviet, deputies considered offering some "responsibility" for crimes, but it caused them great anxiety. The deputy Bir expressed it so: "We perfectly understand that as soon as we fall under this law, we are at once deprived of a deputies' immunity. This inviolability must first of all be precisely realized."[13]

The inviolability of deputies of the acting Federal Assembly was similar,[14] and the practice continued: in 1994, 334 deputies of representative bodies of various levels committed crimes. Criminal liability was attributed to only 16 persons, or about 5 percent of the cases.

A good example was the case of the president of AO MMM (joint-stock society of Mavrodi). Mavrodi was guilty of nonpayment of large sums of taxes. Following his questionable election to the Duma, the deputies in this case did not give their consent to charge him with criminal responsibility.

The corruption and criminality of high-ranking officials in executive and legislative branches is public knowledge.[15] It was officially stated, for example, that out of 55 cases of criminality raised in the Supreme Soviet, 41 were confirmed. However, real criminal cases, in which judicial responsibility was attributed to guilty persons, were not addressed. Many public actions in the press and other mass media outlets were undoubtedly inspired by the political struggles between the representative and executive authorities and other separate groups of officials. In this conflict, each side armed itself with a weapon often used against political opponents in many other countries: the denunciation of corruption. They applied it according to a classical scheme, formulated by France A. Pishon, one of the members of an independent commission on preventative measures against corruption. Each supported measures on the prevention of corruption, preferring, however, to speak first about the crimes and corruption of the other.[16] In this case, the struggle between corrupted individuals is nothing more than a fight for power and a continuation of corruption under the aegis of a professed struggle against corruption.

This politicization of mutual denunciations reveals the truth of the Russian proverb, "There is no smoke without a fire." However, all of this was reduced to "noise" in the mass media. In 1993, the Control Department of the Russian Federation president's administration testified that it conducted 98 checks. Damage caused to the state by officials amounted to a sum of 17.2 billion rubles. Still there were no criminal cases filed against the guilty.[17] For 1994, the Control Department did not even publish a report of its activity. Officials who are accused in the press of corruption and other abuses are often not even aware of these charges and quietly continue their corrupt activity.

Modern Forms of Criminal Behavior of the Elite

The great infringement of human rights in the interest of Communist ideals and of maintaining the party-state clique, mastered by the ruling circles during Stalin's period and stagnation, was complemented by the assigning of national property for mercenary and other selfish personal ends of state officials. During perestroika and the disintegration of the Soviet Union, this timeless truth was confirmed: the largest fortunes are made during the destruction of an empire and the formation of a new state. The nomenklatura justified its customary criminal motivations by arguing that all means are good for the achievement of political purposes, or "bad is the revolutionary who at the moment of sharp struggle stops before the stability of the law."[18] All of the nation's property should belong to the managers of exalted rank, they reasoned; a state post is temporary, so it should be zealously used for gaining profit not only in salary but also in bribes, plundering, and abuses, to provide a further comfortable life for the person occupying the post.

These motivations were openly employed during the criminal putsches of August, 1991, and October, 1993, and especially during the privatization, division, and redistribution of state property; in the organization of new "public-revolutionary actions"; and in the everyday activity in power structures. Remarkably, in a period of conflict between the various branches of power at the end of 1993, none of the branches—executive, legislative, or judiciary (Constitutional Court)—maintained its frameworks of acting according to the law. Obvious contradiction in the old Constitution and other laws, adopted at the boundary of the two epochs, helped extenuate the criminality of power. The high traditional antilegitimacy and the criminality of the ruling and nonruling power elite was confirmed by the nonstop conflicts, plots, and putsches among them. All shifts and replacements of the secretaries-in-general of the Central Committee of CPSU occurred by way of plots by several members of Political Bureau. History reminds us of the arrival to power of such persons as Lenin, Stalin, Khrushchev, Brezhnev, and even Gorbachev. The attempt to displace a nationally elected head of state in post-Communist Russia through former methods, instead of through the political struggle of national elections, has not so far occurred in Russia.

The range of potential and actual illegitimacy of behavior of some groups of the Russian political elite is very broad: from arrival to power at any cost to extortion for self-benefits from the state. Here are two examples of the behavior of the deputies of the former Supreme Soviet and today's State Duma. The members of the Supreme Soviet often spoke about the pauperization of the people and the criminality of officials with executive power. Acting contrary to legislation adopted by an absolute majority of votes accepting the decision about privatization, they obtained fashionable service apartments in addition to privatized apartments as their home residences. The deputies of the State Duma, elected for two years in the transition period, rushed to make decisions on issues that affected their own financial futures rather than the urgent state problems. By the absolute majority of votes, they ratified for themselves the highest official salaries and multiple extra benefits, surrounded themselves with a half-dozen assistants each, and ensured first-class housing accommodations, personal cars with drivers, and diplomatic passports for themselves.[19] At the end of the first half-year of work, they passed practically no socially significant laws, except those legally doubtful acts related to political and economic amnesty. These decrees were attempts at political reconciliation but were, for the most part, illegal. Individuals from the criminal, political, and economic elite were given amnesty. Political amnesty was given for actions of violence conducted for political motives in August, 1991, and in May, September, and October 1993. Amnesty was also given to protect officials from their economic abuses and plundering of state-owned property.

Clearly, deputies should engage in fruitful legislative activity in the interest of the people. Their excessive attention to their own welfare when more than half the population is living in poverty is immoral.

Structure of Modern Political Elite

The structure of the political elite, including the ruling elite, is complex and constantly varies. It is formed in a public struggle between various antagonistic strata. Today, there are more than sixty parties and movements in Russia. The aspiration to survive politically and win under difficult conditions strengthens the historic criminality of the Russian (Soviet) political elite. Parties and movements are sold and purchased.[20]

The largest and most significant group of the political and ruling elite are former party, state, and economic leaders who came into new political power structures by holding a belief in democracy and reforms: Mikhail Gorbachev, Boris Yeltsin, Victor Chernomyrdin, Vladimir Shumeiko, Ivan Rybkin, Yurii Luzhkov, and others. This group had the support of a majority of the deputies of the Federal Assembly. It occupies a leading position in regional ruling circles. The representatives of this group comprise a significant part of the political elite as a whole, including the opposition and its radical wing. The instant disintegration of the Soviet Union, which transpired without a concern for the people; the attempt to preserve elite power; the avoidance of a mass international collision; the destruction of the economic base of the country; the unprecedented embezzlement of national property; and the intensification of the criminalization of most of the public sector (including the political system)—all of these matters lie heavily on the conscience of this elite group. Some of their actions can be considered criminal. They did not understand the process of gradual social evolution. They only possessed revolutionary methods: destroy the base and then, by way of violent power, ruthlessly build a better future. At the same time, they are not above making money.[21]

A significant part of the former nomenklatura formed new structures of power not in accordance with the reform convictions but by virtue of conventional conformity to habits of maintaining power. They are called "democrats by circumstances." Democracy for them, as Vladimir Bukovskii points out, means nothing more than a very controllable socialist democracy, in which the market economy means nothing else but corruption. If these people are able to create anything it will more than likely be a new Mafia in the place of the old one, a new political system that, for lack of a better word, I call "kleptocracy" from the word "kleptomania."[22] Criminality of this part of the nomenklatura was displayed in mass encroachments on state and public property and in extensive corruption. The scope of this activity has occurred in a legal vacuum and with the propaganda of legal nihilism, accompanied by the destruction of the control-auditing system and the paralysis of law-enforcement activity.

The second socially significant group of new political and ruling elite are persons from scientific and other circles of the intelligentsia, who deeply realized the illness of the former system and were aiming for democratic market transformations. These include Yegor Gaidar, Alexander Shokhin, Grigorii Yavlinskii, Sergei Shakhrai, Anatolii Sobchak, Gavriil Popov, Mikhail Poltoranin, Anatolii Chubais, and Boris Fedorov. Theoretically, this group is the most professionally prepared part of the political and ruling elite (economists, lawyers, philosophers, sociologists, and so on). Many of them have shown elements of morality while facing impossible conditions for realizing their reform ideas. The most perceptive part of the political elite, they came to the political arena in the early 1990s. There seems to be no serious basis for speaking of them in terms of criminality.

A certain part of the political and ruling elite came from opponents of the old Communist order who directly or indirectly suffered from it (former political prisoners, members of their families, dissidents, and so forth). They played an appreciable role in destroying totalitarianism and the bureaucratic system. In the political elite they are reasonably represented, but only in a limited way in the ruling elite. Very little is known of their criminal behavior.

The regional ruling elites provide another picture of the dangers presented by the new elite groups. A characteristic example is Jokhar Dudaev, who on arrival to power and in subsequent activity relied on Mafia criminal clans in the republic. The conduct of the former active dissident Zviad Gamsakhurdia should also be noted. Having gained the extreme anti-Soviet post of the president of Georgia, Gamsakhurdia not only re-created the former totalitarian regime but also exceeded its repressive qualities and guided Georgia toward nonstop civil war with vast destruction and great poverty.

5

Elite Corruption in Modern China
Explanations and a Comparison
with Contemporary Russia

Tony Carnes

Elite corruption may well be the defining political and existential issue of the late 1990s and early 2000s. Elite corruption threatens national and personal survival and provokes us to ask, what is right and what is wrong? The corruption of the elite also advances practical dilemmas for everyday life along with theoretical questions for sociologists, criminologists, and others whose purpose is to understand social life. This essay brings together the relevant sociological literature, Chinese and Asian press sources, and fieldwork done over several years into a preliminary discussion on how to understand and explain the causes and effects of elite corruption. It concludes with a reflection on the meaning of elite corruption for marketization and reform politics in China and Russia.

Definitions and Scope of Corruption

Tanwu, tanwuzui, and the metaphorical *fubai* (literally meaning "rotten" or "decay and putrefaction") are cases of malpractice in which state workers misappropriate public property by diverting funds, theft, or swindling. *Shouhui* are cases in which state workers use their official positions to extort or accept bribes.[1] However, it is unclear how often corruption cases are subsumed or double-counted within the larger category of "economic crimes" *(jingji fanzui)* or "unhealthy tendencies" *(buzheng zhi feng). Guandao* is used to identify speculation by officials (also *toujidaoba,* "profiteering"). *Tequan* (privileges) is a term used in political speeches referring to privilege-seeking by officials.

Also, as Rocca points out, the simple division of crimes between *tanwu* and shouhui is complicated by overlapping jurisdictions and wide-ranging applications. The party's Discipline Inspection Committee, the State Council's Ministry of Supervision, and the Public Prosecutor's office are all involved with judging corruption cases, with the Public Prosecutor handling the most serious cases. Many cases are also handled administratively within the state and party hierarchies. The official figures "represent only between 40 and 60 per cent of all the cases of corruption accepted by the Public Prosecutor's Office." Cases involving less than 2,000 yuan are dealt with administratively either by the superior of an accused employee or by a party organization of which the accused was a member. Further, many cases are handled through mediation by local police or informally.[2]

Definitions of corruption vary also according to whether the definer is a hard-line Communist, an authoritarian reformer, or a democratic reformer.[3] It is uncertain how much these impact the fact finding of the various agencies.

As a crumbling totalitarian state, the Chinese government and party define many things as corruption that are omitted in other politico-ideological systems. Punishable corruption offenses include giving almost any internal document ("classified") to individuals or cooperatives, "providing enterprises access to raw materials or semi-finished products," "violation of economic policy," "speculation or profiteering" (variably defined), ideological deviation, and "the nonfulfillment of duty as a government servant."[4]

We don't really know how extensive corruption has been or is. This statement is even more true concerning elite corruption. It is hard to know what to make of the claims of Chinese sources, which report that corruption cases increased between 1983 and 1987 by 700 percent and that between 1980 and 1988 economic crimes tripled. Corruption statistics in China rise and fall with government campaigns against it, changing attitudes of the Public Prosecutor and judges and changing political definitions. Many enterprises prefer to negotiate rather than report or sue. Further, "there is a long gap between the time the offence is committed and when it is discovered." "In 1988, when there seemed to be a massive increase in corruption, the number of such offenses filed for prosecution *(li'an zhencha)* with the Public Prosecutor fell by 13%."[5]

The Chinese press probably understates by claiming that the "black figure" (secret figure) is twice the official ones.[6] Observers seem to agree that there have been at least four great waves of corruption: 1) the second half of 1981 to the first half of 1982, 2) the second half of 1984 to the first half of 1985, 3) 1988, and 4) 1993–94.

In 1989 the Hong Kong press reported rumors that 70 percent of

Shanghai officials' sons were in trading companies using the back doors and that, between 1987 and 1988, members of the State Council had created 700 front companies. The Chinese Academy of Social Science found that 83 percent of the urban population believe that the *nomenklatura* are corrupt. Surprisingly, 63 percent of the nomenklatura themselves admit corruption. In 1990 a survey in Guangzhou of 80,000 *mu* (a unit of area equivalent to about one-third of an acre) of land with construction found that 58 percent was being illegally used.[7]

Presently, in most provinces you can find entire localities of officials' luxurious villas built with their probably ill-gotten booty. Guangdong cities and districts often have relatively luxurious "high official streets" and "secretary mansions." For the first four months of 1993 Deputy Procurator General Liang Guo-qing said that there were 13,729 cases of bribery and corruption.[8] Based on interviews and observations at a Public Security Station in Shanghai, I would say that the corruption rivals the tawdry atmosphere of the Brezhnev period in the USSR.

Structural Explanations of Elite Corruption

Structural explanations generally argue that elite corruption arises when the opportunities for social or economic advancement are predominantly structured by power. The more power determines life-chances, the more likely corruption will arise. As Lord Acton claimed, "Power corrupts, and absolute power corrupts absolutely." For example, after the Great Leap Forward famine, cadres were given enormous autonomous authority to raise grain quotas. This sparked ruthless self-aggrandizement and favoritism. Consequently, structuralists propose that privatization may offer "the only viable prospect of curtailing corruption in the Third World."[9]

Officials are able to take advantage through corruption because the state limits production and monopolizes certain goods and services that are then supposed to be offered at official prices that are below the market prices. Taking advantage of the official versus market price differential, officials have ready opportunities to make profits (guandao) for themselves or partners. For example, the Chinese state railways offer too little transportation at a relatively low official price. Consequently, dinner invitations and gifts to railway officials have proliferated as industrialists scramble to get enough transportation to move needed supplies, products, and employees. In 1990, during an anti-corruption struggle at Shanghai station railway, officials had to turn down 115 dinner invitations and 132 gifts.[10]

Structuralists often focus attention on the corrupt results of inter-twining power hierarchies with status structures of kin, friend, local-ity, and school ties. Imperial and contemporary Chinese governments have practiced the rule of aversion, whereby an official cannot serve in his native region. Typically, too, government manuals have warned against the problems of hiring relatives and friends.

Power bureaucratized proliferates the structural resources for cor-ruption. Bureaucracy creates anonymity for the individual, thus in-creased safety from personal responsibility for corruption. With post-Mao liberalization, the countryside experienced a proliferation of state offices and organizations, increasing the complexity and contradictions of state regulations and demands. Gaps and contradictions in the gov-ernment's laws and regulations determined typical types of economic behavior like corruption to widen the gaps or to smooth over contra-dictory laws.[11]

In Maoist China the demands on cadres and people to produce an unrealistic quota of goods often led to what sociologist Robert Merton has called "innovative" behavior, that is, corruption, when socially prescribed means did not allow achievement of the socially prescribed ends. A consequence of the Great Leap Forward's unreasonable quotas for grain, iron, and other products was that cadres ruthlessly protected themselves and their favorites through corruption.[12]

The degree of power that a state is willing or able to direct against corruption is also a factor. In the early 1960s and after 1978, corruption increased as the state relaxed its pressure on society.[13] In moves from authoritarian socialist regimes the transitional period is marked by the contradiction between bureaucratically controlled markets and looser enforcement of laws. The result is a flourishing black market.

Functional Explanations

Functional explanations of elite corruption propose that societies are social systems with inherent multiple and interdependent functional prerequisites. Some functionalists emphasize how elite corruption en-hances the functions and their interrelations within a social system. Others focus more on elite corruption's dysfunctionality to the social system in which it occurs.[14]

Functionalists face the problem of how to recognize corruption. Nye has commented on the problem of the Western analyst calling some-thing corruption that indigenous reasoning might not.[15] What is called corruption varies according to culture and whether the social structure is modern or traditional. Also, the definition of corruption can be very wide, covering everything from venality to ideological erosion.

Nye proposed an operational definition of corruption: Corruption is behavior that deviates from the formal duties of a public role because of private-regarding (personal, close family, private cliques), pecuniary, or status gains; or violates rules against the exercise of certain types of private-regarding influence. This includes such behavior as bribery (use of a reward to pervert the judgement of a person in a position of trust); nepotism (bestowal of patronage by reason of ascriptive relationship rather than merit); and misappropriation (illegal appropriation of public resources for private-regarding uses).[16]

He argues that this definition has cross-cultural merit because in non-Western societies there are typically two standards of behavior and related definitions of corruption: official formal roles are part of a modern state apparatus with Western standards against corruption attached to them; and traditional private roles with indigenous normative expectations. Of course, Nye is in the end admitting that corruption is an externalist viewpoint, at least partly, of non-Western societies.

The functional analysis of elite corruption also typically utilizes two analytical refinements. What is functional in one society (for example, a traditional society) may not be functional for another (for example, a modern one). A social crisis arises when there is a change from one type of society with a certain system role for corruption to another type of society that defines a different system role for corruption.[17] Further, elite corruption may be functional in one sector of the social system but not another.

An ambiguity in the functional modeling of elite corruption is whether it is a causal model or a categorization of corruption's systemic effects. For example, Edward Banfield sees the system creating corruption to enhance system operations.[18] On the other hand, Nye's article is a superb logical taxonomy of corruption's probable negative effects on social operations.

Those analysts who emphasize elite corruption's system-functionality point to its integration of individuals and groups into the social system. Elite corruption attaches the elites and supporters to the social system through clientalism.

Corruption can "overcome divisions in a ruling elite that might otherwise result in destructive conflict." It can bridge a gap between elite groups based on power and elite groups based on wealth. After a coup, the new leaders may be integrated into the existing upper class through corruption. Corruption eases the transition of non-elites from a traditional life to modernity by scaling down the seeming awesomeness and inhumanity of the modern system. People who are shut out of formal channels can represent their grievances and interests through informal corruptions. Because corruption allows an outlet for grievances, disputes, and social frustrations, it helps to diffuse and even resolve social conflict.[19]

Collecting the support of elites and non-elites enlarges a government's capacity to rule. In particular a new government starts off with a relatively weak and fragmented position. The leaders use corruption, among other means, to "borrow power" from others to cement alliances and to fund political parties and other activities. Corruption may even allow a revolutionary party like Mexico's PRI (Institutional Revolutionary Party) to transform itself into a stable, legitimate state by providing the functional equivalent of violence.[20]

By integrating the nation and enlarging governmental capacity, corruption also enhances economic development, which supports political legitimacy. Further, if private capital is scarce and the government lacks the taxing capacity, corruption is a source of capital formation for governmental development projects.[21]

The positive corruption school likewise argues that elite corruption enhances the integration, workings, and development of the economic sphere, either indirectly through the government, as detailed above, or directly. As corruption enables the political entrepreneur to gather political capital, so it enables the economic entrepreneur to accumulate material capital. And if elites are secure in their corruption, the capital stays at home to be invested.[22]

Entrepreneurs also use corruption to make social room for their entrepreneurial skills and activities. In China corruption can help to overcome a lingering ideological bias against market-orientated activity as well as mitigate the consequences of socialist policies and a Beijing bias against the entrepreneurs on the Southeast China coast who speak a different dialect like Cantonese or Shanghainese. Sometimes "corruption may provide the means of overcoming discrimination against members of a minority group."[23]

Finally, elite corruption may enhance the moral and religious dimensions of a society. By provoking a backlash, corruption may actually reinforce traditional relations and values while undermining secular or nontraditional threats. On the other hand, elite corruption may enhance the success of a modernizing social movement or revolution by removing barriers and degrading or transforming traditionalism through monetary exchanges.[24]

Functional analysts more often focus on the dysfunctional effects of corruption. After reviewing the possible positive and negative effects of corruption on political and social development, Nye concluded that in most cases the costs of corruption will exceed its benefits. Yang's analysis of corruption in official China concluded that Chinese officials had resolved their sociological ambiguity of being caught between impersonal, official rules and affective, personal ties by means of ultimately dysfunctional corruptions.[25]

Elite corruption upsets the functional interrelations within a social system. In traditional China, Yang says, elite corruption was the result of the overintrusion of inputs of religion, familialism, and localism into the workings of a government bureaucracy that formally resembled Weber's ideal-type. "The parties involved are either relatives or old friends, either members of the same clan or neighbors . . . There is basically no ineradicable hatred between them . . . Adjudication is based on law but reconciliation is based on the situation."[26]

Accordingly, elite corruption can be very dysfunctional for the governmental administrative and political capacities and legitimacy. It is also a sign that society's and government's enforcement mechanisms are weak.

Elite corruption can enormously drain the energies and skills of both elite and bottom-level government officials, thereby weakening administrative capacity. "[To] remain impersonal he [the official] had to combat an environmental pressure from a society in which personal relationships were not merely ethically valued but also the only medium the common people had for getting things done. The average official was unable to resist this pressure."[27] Once the official succumbs to the pressure of personal relations, then he must still use an enormous energy in servicing the relations.

In modernizing China, traditionalistic corruption at the top may have alienated more modern-orientated civil servants. Additionally, the government may feel it has to restrict programs because of fear of ineffectiveness and corruption. Corruption at the bottom level means that the power of the government to carry out its duties and actions is disbursed without intended effect.[28]

In particular corruption undermines governmental legitimacy, which sometimes also leads to political instability. In China corruption is telegraphing to the national community that it is every man for himself or that the leaders are arrogantly asserting themselves over the nation's or people's interests. On the one hand, the sense of a national community is being undermined. On the other hand, the individual leaders are being recast as egoistic actors. This delegitimation is particularly disastrous for modernizing leaders who are already putting stress on communal solidarity. In China corruption is upsetting governmental balances of power and resource sharing and causing intensifying factional fights.[29]

Elite corruption is also, it is said, dysfunctional economically. Elites who are weak or feel threatened use corruption to generate capital for Swiss or Hong Kong bank accounts and foreign investments. Corruption also distorts investments into system dysfunctional patterns. In China lower-level bureaucrats use their bribes in overconsumption like banqueting. Overinvestment is made into areas like the reconstruction of Beijing and the Shanghai Pudong development because bribes can be hidden through cost-plus contracts and credits. Chinese entrepreneurs often waste their skills in corruption efforts, a situation particularly harmful as entrepreneurial skills are in short supply. Attempts to control corruption may, paradoxically, drain even more entrepreneurial skill away from economically productive pursuits as officials and entrepreneurs struggle even harder to transact corrupt business. Finally, aid donors have become wary of investing in China.[30]

Related to its undermining legitimacy, particularly of leaders and values promoting change and progress, elite corruption undermines the religious and moral functions of society. "'Corruption and nepotism rot good intentions and retard progressive policies.'"[31] In China, elite corruption has converted officials' and common people's loyalty to the state into loyalty to personal relations. It reemphasized the habit of informal relations as an operative norm.[32] If ideological, religious, and moral elites join in the dysfunctional behavior, the legitimacy of their institutions and themselves will be threatened with degradation and delegitimization.[33]

Corruption as a Cultural Phenomenon

Most of the explanations of elite corruption considered so far do not explain very well the origins of the social context that makes corruption structurally responsive, rational, or functional (or dysfunctional). Neither do the scholars with these perspectives build in a very strong or complex analysis of the origins of values or values' systematic relations to the structural, rational, or functional social situation. The functionalist perspective comes closest, but it has other difficulties, such as how to define what is functional and an ambiguity as to whether it is categorizing results of system functioning or the origins of corrupt systems events.

At the outset of his structural-functional cost-benefit analysis, Nye recognized that he didn't have an external standard by which to define political development, cost-effectiveness, corruption, and so forth. So he proposed to use internal standards, thereby saving himself from the accusation that he was imposing arbitrary Western standards on other cultures. After disavowing political development as "rational, modern honest government" and its evaluative content, he defined "political development" in relation to internal social system workings, not in-digenous definitions. "In this author's view, the term 'political development' is best used to refer to the recurring problem of relating governmental structures and processes to social change ['modernization' in this context]." [34] Of course, this definition merely changed from an overt Western evaluative definition to a covert one of the Western social system theorist.

Likewise, with "corruption" he tried to turn to an internalist definition to save himself from charges of Western theoretical imperialism. He defined "corruption" as "behavior which deviates from the formal duties of a public role because of private-regarding . . . pecuniary or status gains." [35] He averred that since "in most less developed countries, there are two standards regarding behavior, one indigenous and one more or less Western, and the formal duties and rules concerning most public roles tend to be expressed in terms of the latter," his definition "has the merit of denoting specific behavior generally called corruption by Western standards (which are at least [therefore] partly relevant [internal] in most developing countries." [36] As far as I can see, he claimed he was going to use an internalist definition of corruption, which turned out to be the Western definition because the local governmental elites have brought Western formal bureaucracy into their countries. But the definition only applies to evaluating this one sector, not indigenous institutions.

Later he stated, "Attitudes toward corruption vary greatly. In certain West African countries, observers have reported little widespread sense of indignation about corruption . . . According to Higgins, the Indonesian attitude toward corruption (which began on a large scale only in 1954) is that it is sinful . . . Very often, traditional sectors of the populace are likely to be more tolerant of corruption than some of the modern sectors . . . Thus the hypothesis [about relative occurrences of corruption] must take into account . . . the tolerant nature of the culture." However, Nye here does not incorporate or call for the development of a more complex analysis of culture to incorporate or frame his cost-benefit analysis. It is also a little unclear why "modernized," formal structures must inherently promote the values of anticorruption. His position, however careful not to comment on native cultures, is smug and self-satisfied with his own Western formal organization and its alleged attendant values. At its best his position is one more version of closing one's mind to cultural values different from one's own immediate position, except to invoke the "other's" values as different and not applicable. From where does Nye get his assurance and why are values, definitions of corruption, and potentials for political development different among cultures? The search for answers to these questions brings us to the cultural explanation of corruption.

John Noonan, in his magisterial study of the cultural origins of an absolutist concept of "bribe," concluded, "The bribe in its origins depends on religious teaching. Reciprocity is so regularly the norm of human relations that the conception of a transcendental figure, a Judge beyond the reach of ordinary reciprocities, was of enormous importance for the idea that certain reciprocities with earthly officials were intolerable. That conception of a transcendental Judge was shaped in the ancient Near East." [37] Benjamin Nelson emphasized that this Near Eastern ethic intruded upon Europe and reached its highest impact with the Reformation. [38] Richard Hofstadter picked up the thread of the Judeo-Christian religious ethic's impact in his contrast of American politics based upon a Yankee-Protestant middle-class political ethos (a politics according to general principles) with the European immigrant political ethos (politics according to personal obligations). [39]

In China disillusionment with Maoism and reform efforts has created a prolonged "incoherence of values" and legitimation crisis and a search for a new system of values to legitimize the state and give meaning to life. [40]

Chinese and Russian Elite Corruption

In both China and Russia, elite corruption has flourished during the attempts to liberalize economically and politically. It also is fairly typical for organized crime to develop with the dissolution of an autocratic state as it is intruded upon by modernization.

Neither Russia nor China has a comprehensive and clearly defined legal conception of formal political roles and corruption. Chinese legal definitions of corruption tend to be sparse, vague, overlapping, and changeable. In Russia the still-used criminal code of October 27, 1960, has a Chapter 7 on "Official Malfeasance" with five articles (170–

74) on illegal acts but with no definitions of relevant terms and no use of the word "bribery." Article 175 mentions "giving bribes" with little specificity. Russian official statistics sometimes make improbable claims such as that registered acts of bribery declined 47 percent between 1992 and 1993. Chinese corruption statistics tend to fluctuate with regularly announced "high tides" against corruption.

Chinese and Russian elite corruptions are alike in the extraordinary amount of fraud involved. In both China and Russia, fraud and embezzlement from the state is much more pervasive nationwide and larger than elsewhere.

At first both Soviet and Chinese totalitarianism exercised the power to suppress much of the criminal corruptions in the middle and lower ranks of society. The penalties were draconian and the ideology was impressed enough on the populace to serve as a restraint. Alexander Gurov, director of the Russian Institute of Security Problems located in Moscow, has said, "a totalitarian regime destroys any rival organization."[41] Rather, large organized corruptions were only possible by the very top leaders.

However, totalitarian administrative commandism in both the USSR and the People's Republic of China (PRC) undermined senses of legality and civic morality. Politics "through the gunbarrel" or decrees is whimsical to moment and urge, and comes to be *seen* as whimsical as decrees and political campaigns contradict each other.

Further, in the USSR and PRC even normal everyday activities were ideologized and made subject to changing decrees and judgment. People not only become disillusioned by inconstant law but also exasperated that everyday normal life couldn't go on without being corrupt. Soviet corruption specialist Gurov observed, "with us, even normal activities . . . were illegal. That's why [crime] organizations have been part of our Soviet society from the beginning."[42]

As Shlapentokh has demonstrated in *Public and Private in the USSR*, the disbelief in Communism had reciprocal relation to the increasing public-private split in Soviet life. At first the dream was to abolish the bourgeois distinction between public and private. The totalitarian regime destroyed any rival organization and sought to reach into the very hearts and minds of the populace. However, the costs of controlling and then abolishing the private sphere of life were too great. Morally, people came to define the crushing of the private as repugnant and, in fact, impossible. Writers Boris Pasternak for atheists and Alexander Solzhenitsyn for believers identified the necessary and inevitable continuation of moral and spiritual values even within the bleakest of circumstances.

In practice, private interests and ideals could not be suppressed, and interests were dressed up in "public uniforms" of ideological rhetoric to manipulate the taking of public resources. In the Communist states there was not a strong distinction between the idea of my property and state property. Without the mentality or the instruments of universal law, relaxation of totalitarian control quickly led to flourishing corruption, organized crime, and their mental correlates, cynicism and venality.

The facade of revolutionary morals and legality became a covering for pilfering and gangster ethics, depending on one's social position and inclination. Totalitarianism ate away civic values and "nurtured the morality of the thief and embezzler"[43] and created the "paradox of a police state and a corrupted populace." "The average citizen felt no compunction about stealing . . . from his factory, for instance, [even though] he would never rob his neighbor."[44] In the USSR this became the accepted state of affairs in the 1960s, and in China it started to become a widespread habit during the Cultural Revolution for "revolutionary purposes," a practice that became privatized within a short time after the Cultural Revolution was declared finished (in 1976).

The increase in corruption went with a decrease in the belief in the Communist ideology. Russians and Chinese started to talk about a vacuum of values and the pervasiveness of lies and corruption. The Communist ideology was spent in its power to motivate an inner fortitude against corruption.

The totalitarian demolition of the private sphere was also economically prohibitive. The intensive and extensive instruments of repression grew until they consumed as much as 30–40 percent of Soviet national product. Laborers were demoralized. Also, the attempt to abolish the market left the regime blind to the relation of supply and demand. Costs couldn't easily be assessed across the whole nation. Attempts to overcome the valuing function of the market by huge planning bureaucracies with production and distribution based on a unified national system were very inefficient and opened up even more opportunities for corruption. The situation was overripe for a black market for pricing and distribution and eventual economic meltdown of the repressive apparatus. Lev Timofeyev bitterly complained that the black market was "the living blood circulating in a dead organism . . . The entire Soviet system—everything without exception—was nothing more than an enormous black market."[45] A new moral system grew up that allowed black market behavior within certain norms.[46]

The growing split between private and public also meant an increased demand for consumer goods for the private sphere. This demand for officially disapproved self-indulgence was also channeled into the black market. A new tacit covenant arose that the populace could engage in petty corruption as long as it didn't threaten the state with "socially dangerous" crime. Most of the Soviet people became enmeshed in the web of corruption in some way (83 percent according to one estimate).[47]

In China the party's effort to demolish the private sphere was at times even more intense and intrusive. Although nationalization of the economy was at a similar level to the Soviet Union, China attempted thought-control at a much deeper level. The moral, economic, and political costs were also high. Yet, Chinese society has gone through a much shorter period in which the distinction between public and private was suppressed.

Further, China was an agricultural state that left families intact in their surname villages. This left open the option of the party-state to allow privatization in the village while keeping much higher state control of the private and economic sphere in the city. This bought about five or six years' breathing space (1980–85) before informal privatization became rampant in the city.

The replacement of the rule by law by administrative decree led inevitably, it seems, to corruption of the center. Georgii Arbatov asked, "Who with such power at his disposal can resist temptation?"[48] Administrative decree means that the leaders can arbitrarily, within the limits of elite politics, declare certain previously condemned behavior as now okay for some.

The attempted total organization of society created an elite group that became more interested in keeping power, increasing prerequisites and corrupt receipts, and maintaining a strong organization coopting ideologies and the masses. Whether this is an example of Robert Michels's "iron law of oligarchy" or the logic of Leninist collective action (Luxembourg's criticism), the massive party-state apparently became dominated by an elite caste, what Arbatov calls "a special caste" and Volensky "the nomenklatura."[49] In China the top caste is called the "princelings" *(taizi)* or the "princelings party" *(taizi dang)*.

In both China and the USSR this arbitrariness led to constant factional fights over what (and, more important, who) is corrupt or not

corrupt this week. In early September, 1993, as part of the drama leading up to the shelling of Parliament, President Yeltsin relieved Vice
President Aleksandr Rutskoi and First Deputy Prime Minister Vladimir Shumeyko of their official duties pending resolution of charges
of malfeasance against them.[50] Of course, the political manipulation of
corruption charges was itself corruption and greatly increased cynicism and decreased the capacity of the system to reform itself.

So far, elite corruption combined with organized crime through the
distribution of state property through privatization is more common
in Russia. By the mid-1970s the diversified structure of corruption was
so obvious that the Soviet government allowed senior officials in the
USSR Procurators Office to pronounce the existence of a Soviet mafia.
Gurov claims that in his 1974 investigation he discovered a Russian
trade mafia with representation at the top of the Communist Party.[51]

In China the mafia-type gangs tend to be localized in southern
China and are not nearly as widespread as they are in Russia. The
gangs have been reentering China, concerned first with reestablishing
themselves.

Both the early Bolsheviks and Maoists recruited criminals, particularly for their help in "expropriations." In 1907 Stalin and some of
these criminals committed a bank heist in Tbilisi. Stalin like Mao was
captivated by stories of brigands, even taking his moniker "Koba"
from one.[52]

Stalin and Mao both wanted to recruit more of these tough guys
into the revolution. Mao wistfully wrote that if he could recruit enough
of these criminals he could win the revolution hands down. Some did
become party members, but most refused to "submit to the proletariat
utopia,"[53] proceeding into more crime, provoking a draconian law-
and-order reaction. In 1919 Lenin was robbed by a highwaymen gang
in Moscow and reacted with a brutal war on crime.[54] Although the
Chinese Communist Party accepted a number of gangsters, most of them
either went over to the nationalists or into business for themselves.
Mao too became ruthless against the gangs, particularly remembering
how the Green Gang exterminated the party in Shanghai.

In the Soviet Union most of the professional criminals rejected the
Communist Party and formed a criminal counterculture. The first *vory
v zakonye* (thieves-in-law) arose in the earliest Soviet years with a self-
conscious value to oppose the law of the USSR. Now the old-style *vory*
have been shoved aside by the rise of *autoritets*, who are much more
closely identified with corrupt government dealings.[55] In China the
gangs mainly went out of the country rather than underground. Yet,

through connections to relatives and regional loyalties, the gangs of China have reemerged.

In both countries organized crime has proliferated and made connections with state and party elites. The term "mafia" is not accurate for Russian groups. Traditionally, mafia are local, particularly urban, or regional phenomenon. But the Russian organized crime groups are much more pervasive in the economic, political, and social life of the country. They are not a crime problem but a social problem. The more accurate image would be to compare the Russian situation to today's Italy or to Colombia with its drug lords. In China corruption is a national problem, but so far it is not often linked to organized crime at the national level. However, over the past few years the connections of organized crime are moving higher up the social ladder. Because the Chinese administration and party are organized vertically around "sectors" *(xitong),* which operate as tacitly recognized spheres of influence of different groups of elites, organized crime could make its way to the top by moving up the xitong ladder, remaining relatively immune from central government scrutiny until it reaches the very top.

Ethnic minorities like the Caucasians, Georgians, and Chechen-Ingush are highly visible in the black market and corrupt activities. Of course, because they were minority criminals, the high visibility was translated into xenophobia and exaggerated notions of ethnic predominance in crime.

In China the mafia-type corruption isn't ethnically based but is regionally typed. Southern, particularly southern coastal, Chinese gangs are most involved. These gangs do not invoke the same xenophobia or intensity of prejudice that ethnic Russian gangs do.

Sadly, perestroika started as a way to clear away the corrupt rottenness from Soviet society. While walking in the resort Pitsunda in the early 1980s, Mikhail Gorbachev and Eduard Shevardnadze started perestroika with the despair that Soviet society was rotten to the core, that corruption was dragging the system into the mud. By 1985 Yeltsin was being threatened with death for his anticorruption campaign. The "Emergency Committee" proclaimed (hypocritically) that the August, 1991, coup d'état attempt would allow a waging of "a decisive struggle against the shadow economy [and] corruption." But while their parents were talking and demonstrating, the twenty-somethings were beginning to opt for economics in the still-illegal zones.[56]

Democratization promised legalization of a normal life and has accomplished some major aspects of this hope. However, the amount of corruption, dishonesty, violence, and irregular and erratic governmental operations has led many people since 1991 to say that the period of democracy is *bespredel* (without limits), connoting a frontier chaos. Epic gun battles in 1992–93 in Ekaterinburg merely foreshadowed "wake-up" explosions on Moscow mornings in 1994–95 as people came out to start their cars. People believe that organized crime controls all aspects of public life. In summer 1992 one-third of the residents of the Russian Far East believed that criminal structures determined the course of events in their region. In 1993 three-fourths of Ekaterinburg residents believed that their city was ruled by the mafia. In December, 1992, Yeltsin disgustedly observed, "Bribery, privatization for the sake of, and by, the nomenklatura, the plunder of natural resources and nomenklatura separatism threaten the disintegration of Russia." Even the organized criminals feel that the situation is too chaotic for the good of illegal business.[57]

Conclusion

Structural and functional theories of corruption are very helpful in thinking through the system effects of corruption and some of its causes. However, structural and functional theories lack a cultural component to aid in explaining how corruption gets defined in various ways. Some aspects of Chinese culture certainly do provide resources for justifying or immunizing oneself against the guilt of corruption.

Looking to the future, elite corruption hinders reformers and democratization by undermining the rule of law and the sense of fairness and representativeness of the government or the reformers. It also encourages particularism to flourish and divide society. If China and Russia continue to liberalize, structural factors will proliferate elite corruption and undermine marketization and democratization. More important, age-old cultural factors will corrupt even incorruptible social structures. If China and Russia are to move forward with reform, the best route would be to introduce the reform movement as the bearers of new cultural values that are militant against corruption, values that also call for concomitant structural reforms. In the short run elite corruption will continue to undermine governments (and reforming movements), but the presence of a democratic ideology against particularism born by a social movement for long-term social and cultural renewal would continually provide a fountain of legitimation, a restarting of the reform cycle.

Part 2

Elites in Post-Soviet Republics

6

Typology of
the Modern Byelorussian Elite

Vladimir Snapkovskii

The social-political ideology of the former USSR did not accept or use a concept of "elite" with reference to the structure of Soviet society. Consequently, scientific analysis of the elite was not conducted. This is also the case for the social sciences in Byelarus, where the understanding of problems related to the modern Byelorussian elite remain undeveloped. Only a limited amount of data on the elite has been collected.

Most of the research on the Byelorussian elite has been collected by foreign "Byelorussologists." For example, the serious monograph *An Algebra of Soviet Power* by American social scientist Michael Urban was published at the end of the 1980s. Urban studied the party-state ruling clique of the Byelorussian Soviet Socialist Republic in the period following World War II.[1] The mechanism for selecting the managerial staff is examined and influential party clans are identified: Vitebsk, "partisan Brest," and Gomel. The first two groups possessed political force in the 1960s and 1970s and later supervised the republic in the 1980s.

The formation of an elite group is generally a lengthy process of selecting the best representatives from a social or ethnic group. The Byelorussian national elite began to form at the beginning of the twentieth century in an epoch of national revival. Most came as the representatives of the small and average Byelorussian gentry *(shlakhta)* and the nobility. Those who came from these strata, along with the national intelligentsia of peasant origin, headed the Byelorussian nation liberation movement. The movement was peasant-*narodnik* (populist) in character. The brief period of flourishing Byelorussian national consciousness and the flourishing of the creative forces of national intelligentsia collapsed in the 1920s.

The following decade became a bloody chapter in the history of the country and the Byelorussian elite. During Stalin's *chistki* (purges, "combing-outs"), about 90 percent of Byelorussian writers and poets were arrested, and the majority of them were shot or tortured to death in prisons. Repressions spread through the majority of workers in the party-state machinery, the army, and the representatives of the Byelorussian national movement. The former chiefs of the Byelorussian National Front, who had been considered the main carriers of Byelorussian nationalism, were replaced by representatives of the *nomenklatura* from Central Russia. Stalin's repressions were directed against the thin stratum of Byelorussian political, cultural, and scientific elite. The American researcher of Byelorussia, Nicholas Vakar, confirmed that only the Byelorussian leaders who worked on the creation of Byelorussian Soviet statehood in the 1920s remained alive and free after 1939.[2]

World War II had a severe impact on the elite, with more death, physical deprivation, morale losses, and political emigration. After the war, Stalin initiated a policy of Reunification, persecutions on the creative intelligentsia, and the replacement of persons of Byelorussian nationality from the highest levels of authority. The Communist Party of Byelorussia was purged of cosmopolites and the "preachers of the harmful influence" of the West. Russians replaced both Byelorussians and Jews. Up until the end of 1948, all Byelorussian communists were relieved of their high posts and replaced by Russians. In 1951, the government of Byelorussian Socialist Soviet Republic (BSSR) consisted of thirty-three persons: twenty-two Russians, one Jew, one Georgian, and nine Byelorussians.[3]

Living through the repressions and war hardships, the creative intelligentsia became conformists and the majority completely turned away from the national idea. In the opinion of a well-known Byelorussian writer, Vasil Bykov, it was "communized" and turned into the most conformist class of society, a reliable servant of totalitarian order.[4] The characteristic features of much of Byelorussian culture, science, and arts were national nihilism, provincialism, servility, and the constant reminder of the "senior brother" ("big brother"). Very few knew the Byelorussian language.

Kremlin management determined the outlook, ideology, and political practice of the managing staff. The party was a merger of all nations and peoples in the USSR into the uniform Soviet nation. The staff was unable or unwilling to express or to assert the national interests of the

Byelorussian people. A deep denationalization of Byelorussian ethnos occurred when the Byelorussian language was replaced with Russian.

The denationalization of the Byelorussians was accompanied by a simultaneous process of advancing the interests of the Russians in management. Frequently, Byelorussians changed their nationality to Russian to facilitate upward mobility on the service ladder. According to the data of a Canadian researcher of Byelorussia, Stephan Horak, the share of the Byelorussians in the national structure of the Byelorussian Communist Party in the beginning of the 1970s was 60−65 percent, quite below the percent of Byelorussians in the republic.[5] Having analyzed the representation of Byelorussians in the political and cultural elite of the Byelorussian Republic, Horak came to the conclusion that they form an obvious minority (40 percent). Among the intelligentsia, the percentage parity (ratio) of the Byelorussians and Russians was equal. Among the worker and kolkhoz (collective farm) aristocracy, there were more Byelorussians (55 percent and 60 percent). They prevailed in groups of office and industrial workers (70 percent and 80 percent) and comprised the overwhelming majority among the peasantry (95 percent). Thus, upward mobility on the social ladder by persons of Byelorussian nationality steadily declined.

This situation developed as a natural result of the denationalization of Byelorussians and their assimilation into the closely related Russian people during the nineteenth and twentieth centuries by the Russian czarist autocracy, and then by the Soviet-managed policy of Russification. Having reached this goal of transforming the party-state ruling clique of BSSR into a reliable servant, the Union Center in the 1970s and 1980s eased (slightly) the control of the nomenklatura over the national structure. As a result, there was an increase in the share of Byelorussians among the managing staff. A review of the development of the highest strata of Byelorussian society during the twentieth century revealed that at the moment of declaring the independence of Byelarus in 1990−91, there was no developed classical political elite. Instead, there was the nomenklatura, the bureaucratic machinery, and the network of privileges that united them. The most important privilege was the monopoly of authority. From this stratum the party and state machinery began to develop a nomenklatura elite of sovereign Byelarus.

The data and conclusions presented here are some of the first attempts at understanding the problem of the Byelorussian elite. Materials from sociological and political scientific research and from publications on the problems associated with the formation of the Byelorussian political, economic, cultural, and scientific elite in the first five years of post-Communist development are analyzed.

The Political Elite

Executive authority. From August to December, 1991, in Byelarus as well as in other republics of the former USSR, redistribution of authority between the state and Party nomenklatura has taken place. The structures of the CPSU as a real authority of the Soviet-Communist system were liquidated. The authority passed out of the hands of the Soviets (Councils) and their executive bodies. However, the management of Soviet bodies was seized by the former party nomenklatura. The interests of the nomenklatura were supported and advanced by the government of Viacheslav Kebitch, who was appointed by the Supreme Soviet of the republic in May, 1990. Having lost the support of the Communist Party, the nomenklatura leaned on the new state machinery and a conservative majority in Parliament to become a "party of authority."

In four years of ruling the state, the government redistributed a significant part of the public property to the nomenklatura as private (individual) property. People called this process "grabbing." As a result, yesterday's party figures became businessmen and bankers. The ministerial council concentrated authority in its hands, pushing the obedient Supreme Soviet to the background. It reorganized the former Central Committee of the Byelorussian Communist Party and created departments and administrative structures that supervised all state and public offices from the army to the press.

In the state, the government of Kebitch hindered the development of democratic reforms and acted as a supporter for closer ties of Byelarus to Russia by the means of a uniform ruble zone and an agreement for collective safety in the Commonwealth of Independent States (CIS). No radical measures were offered for pulling the country's economy out of its deep crisis. Political will was lacking, and there were no opportunities for intellectuals. In the government there were no bright, independent actors, and any display of "self-activity" was punished. When, at the end of 1993, the chiefs of the KGB and Ministry for Home Affairs of the republic, Edward Shirkovskii and Vladimir Yegorov, put forward a plan for the reformation of authority structures, they were relieved of their posts. In his last months in power, which coincided with the beginning of the presidential campaign, Kebitch and his cronies became noted for political intrigue, moral degradation, and indecent servility before the chiefs of Russia.

The putsch of August, 1991, temporarily demoralized the nomenklatura. Only one person reached the top of state authority. Provost of Byelorussian State University, Stanislav Shushkevitch, was elected chairman of the Supreme Soviet of the Byelarus Republic in September, 1991. Despite all his words about loyalty to Kebitch, Shushkevitch supported democratic reforms, independence from Russia, and a neutral Byelarus. In the ruling establishment he was a rara avis. He won international recognition but could not achieve what he set out to do. With his slowness and absence of real political achievement, he lost the support of the representatives of the Byelorussian National Front and state deputies. As a result, under pressure from the nomenklatura, in January 1994, Shushkevitch was relieved of his power.

In the wake of the presidential elections in 1994 and the victory of Alexander Lukashenko, one nomenklatura group was replaced by another. The replacement group was less respectable and more ambitious and aggressive than the first. The presidential team does not have a distinctive ideological or political shape: they are neither liberals, nor social-democrats, nor conservatives, nor nationalists. They are not communists in a conventional sense of the word. They are pragmatists and realists. According to Shushkevitch, they are the "young wolves." They did not fit in, not in the "party of authority," the surrounding circles of Shushkevitch's power, or in the environment of the national-democratic forces. They were a group of politicians united around the president. Sometimes they were called the "old Komsomol members and young communists." It was a party-komsomol group that did not believe in the communist idea. Despite the social and political affinity of Lukashenko's team and the old nomenklatura, in 1994, the group advanced important attributes of statehood such as a constitution and a presidency. Objectively, this made the "new wolves" more serious defenders of the sovereignty of Byelarus in comparison to Kebitch's "party of authority." At the same time, the president talked about his readiness to unify Byelarus with Russia.

Lukashenko's first steps were indicative of his true intentions. It became clear that he was not going to send Kebitch's cabinet to jail or even prohibit them from service, as promised. All of the ten highest chiefs, authorized in July, 1994, by the Byelorussian Parliament, had worked before the Central Committee of the Communist Party of Byelarus, the Soviet Ministry (Ministerial Council), or its structures. The first deputies of Kebitch, Sergei Ling and Mikhail Miasnikovitch, became the deputies of the new prime minister, Mikhail Chigir.

In October, 1994, the president reformed the system of local authority, which had a great impact on the activity of the Soviets (Councils). The local bureaucracy, which had saved its positions and flourished in the times of Kebitch, did not issue public declarations of loyalty to the elected president. As a result, the president created vertical lines of authority with a significant restriction on the rights of local representative bodies. All executive authority was given to presidential structures, which were nominated from above. The Soviets (Councils) had only representative functions. Hoping to secure the loyalty of the local managing elite, however, the president did not insist that the elections for chiefs of local authority be direct.

The process of governmental formation as well as the development of the new presidential nomenklatura was finished by the end of 1994. The new presidential nomenklatura's main sources were the deputies corps; the old party-economic nomenklatura, which had not been included in the circles surrounding Kebitch; and former government officials, the separate members of which saved the key posts. The presidential circle is also composed of people who had been close to the president during his work in the Mogilev District.

The distinctive feature of the presidential team is their young age: the majority of representatives are around forty years old. This new Byelorussian ruling elite is one of the youngest in the territory of the former USSR and promises to have a long life ahead of itself in politics.

A presidential team is united by its aspirations for personal political control. But, characteristically, the people who took on the role of the intellectual elite (Dmitrii Bulakhov, Victor Gonchar, and Alexander Feduta) departed from the president. Gonchar left the post of vice premier in December, 1994, and spoke out about the atmosphere of scandal surrounding the president.

The relations between the president and the cultural and scientific elite are not very harmonious. His statement about his readiness to "unify" Byelarus with Russia (after a sharp reaction, the term "unification" was replaced by "integration"), his introduction of state bilingualism, the replacement of national symbols, and his sentiments on the inclusion of nationalism in school textbooks pushed away the support of the nationally oriented intelligentsia, who from the very beginning were skeptical of the populist promises of presidential candidates. The president prefers trips around the regions and districts, conversations in labor collectives, and performances before local authorities over meetings with the representatives of the intellectual elite. Clearly, the pragmatic presidential circles lack ideologists and bright figures from the intellectual elite.

Lukashenko came to power on a wave of national discontent for the policies of Kebitch's government. He conducted his presidential campaign without leaning on party support and portrayed a fighter-of-corruption image, so popular among the people. Given the inexperience and immaturity of the Byelorussian electorate, such tactics brought results. However, in the future, powerful support from a strong, structurally formed public movement or political party will be necessary. Results of the referendum on May 14, 1995, and parliamentary elections showed that a conglomerate of parties and groups on the left supported the president.

As a whole, the internal political situation in Byelarus up to the end of the first year of the president's term was characterized by an increase in opposition among public and political forces. The president did not manage to execute his constitutional role as a national integrator and peacemaker standing above the fight. His emotionality, impulsiveness, and political engagement for the benefit of forces on the left and the majority of the Parliament caused a backlash by the opposition's national democrats, which weakened the political stability of Byelorussian society. All of this occurred under a deepening crisis and a decrease in the standard of living for the majority of the population. This strengthened the authoritarian tendencies in the government.

Legislative authority. The twelfth convocation of Parliament acted in the period between 1990 and 1995 and appeared to be the most long-term of all legislative authorities in the former USSR. Elected in a communist epoch on the basis of nondemocratic election law, it outlived the disintegration of the USSR, the development of the CIS, "the parade of the sovereignties," and the government of Kebitch. With delays and fluctuations, under pressure from the opposition and the developments of events in the neighboring republics of the former Union, the Supreme Soviet, however, made a lot of progress for Byelarus toward sovereignty and independence. While in the other newly independent states the process of formation of a new political system was accompanied by numerous dissolutions and elections of new parliaments, in Byelarus, the Supreme Soviet continued to remain stable. The idea of an opposition in the new parliamentary elections did not materialize and was only supported in the Parliament by a few people.

In the last months, the elected national representatives, worried about their future and reelection, adopted laws that fixed for them a system of privileges. The egoistic interests of the national representatives were displayed rather vividly. These interests were used by the president, especially in April, 1995, when he pushed the issue of a referendum. He publicly promised deputies employment if they voted in his favor on the referendum and the ratification of agreements with Russia.

Some figures illustrate the structure of the Byelorussian Parliament in the twelfth convocation: in May, 1990, 328 deputies were elected, 295 (90 percent) of whom had not been previously elected in the Parliament. A radical change in the legislative body had taken place: a new group of parliamentarians, inexperienced in legislative work, came to power. Eighty-eight percent (290) of the deputies were communists who had been put forward during the period of perestroika and received the trust of the electorate.[6]

On September 1, 1991, the Supreme Soviet had 348 deputies. The largest professional groups were representatives of the state authorities (24 percent); workers in science, culture, education, and public health services (17 percent); management corps (17 percent); security personnel (defense, home affairs, KGB, Office of Public Prosecutor) and ministries (9 percent); chairmen of collective farms and director of state farms (7 percent); party personnel before the prohibition of activity of the Communist Party of Byelorussia (CPB) after the August putsch (7 percent); workers (3 percent); and engineers and technicians (2 percent). In Parliament there was a large group (50 persons) of war veterans, retirees, and the armed forces. There were also one peasant, four priests, five workers of trade unions and control organs, and three representatives of public funds.[7] Among personnel in the state organs, more than half (47 persons) were the representatives of executive authority (members of government and executive committees).

The representatives of state and party organs, security departments, management and agrarian corps, and veterans' organizations were united in the "Byelarus" faction and totaled up to 150 deputies. Kebitch controlled their votes. Later, at the collection of signatures in support of his presidential candidacy, he secured the votes of 203 deputies. By the same majority, a new constitution of the Republic Byelarus (RB) and decisions on the linkage of RB to the agreement for collective security of the states in the CIS were approved. A proposal on the referendum about preterm elections of the Supreme Soviet was rejected, and Shushkevitch was removed from his post as chairman of the Supreme Soviet.

After Lukashenko came to power, almost all of the "Byelarus" faction gave their support to the president. Only ten deputies who had been close to Kebitch and who had also resigned from their posts (but not from politics) did not support Lukashenko. By the votes of the same nomenklatura majority, the undemocratic law on the creation of vertical presidential authority and the questions surrounding the referendum offered by the president were approved. Without discussion the arrangements with Russia were ratified, and the anniversary of the October Revolution of 1917 was restored on the list of national holidays. The representatives of the opposition, uniting the Byelorussian National Front (BNF) and the Byelorussian Social-Democratic Party (BSDP), comprised the national-democratic camp in the parliamentary elite. During the presidential elections of 1994, this parliamentary wing put forward two candidates, Shushkevitch and chairman of BNF Zenon Pozniak. Together, they collected about 25 percent of the vote and were not admitted to the second round. This was a defeat for the national democrats.

The parliamentary opposition was comprised of approximately thirty persons. In 1993, ten deputies from BSDP led by Oleg Trusov began to distance themselves from it. However, deputies from BSDG voted together with the deputies from BNF and accepted joint political positions on the majority of issues. As a whole, the opposition together with the representatives of other democratic forces in the Supreme Soviet were about seventy persons.

In comparison with other groups of deputies, the activity of the opposition is distinguished by a high level of professionalism. In the beginning of 1995, twenty-eight journalists from the leading Byelorussian newspapers and foreign mass media developed a list of parliamentarians, distinguished by professionalism and an ability to express the interests of their social group. Of the list of twenty-one persons, there were eleven deputies from the opposition and three representatives from other democratic forces: Gennadii Karpenko, Stanislav Shushkevitch, and Victor Gonchar. Three (Dmitrii Bulakhov, Vladimir Gribanov, and Metchislav Grib) represented the parliamentary center and four (Vladimir Telezhnikov, Vladimir Sapronov, Gennadii Kozlov, and Victor Piskarev) the majority of the deputies corps.[8] Two-thirds of the individuals on this list are in the democratic camp.

The highest rating was received by the leaders of BNF (Zenon Pozniak, Vladimir Zablotskii, Gennadii Karpenko, Vladimir Novik, and Dmitrii Bulakhov) who occupied the first five positions. From the representatives of the parliamentary majority, the highest rating was received by Vladimir Telezhnikov, who held with Metchislav Grib the seventh and eighth places, respectively. Other deputies of the opposition among the most professional parliamentarians were Valentin Golubev, Sergei Naumchik, Oleg Trusov, and Piotr Sadovskii. Other sources of political elite formation are the leaders and activists of various parties and public movements, who at the beginning of 1995 totaled more than thirty. For today's political parties, most of which are in the process of forming, organizational weakness, small numbers, and ideological and political amorphousness are characteristic. The standard division of the left and right is not yet developed; the majority of the parties consider themselves central. The watershed line between them emerges not in socioeconomic programs but in questions about Byelorussian statehood and foreign policy. The social base of the parties is in the process of development. The most active members are from the scientific, engineering and technical, and creative intelligentsia. The ambitions of the party leaders sometimes play an excessive role in parliamentary politics.

The 1995 elections in the Parliament and the local bodies of authority promoted the formation of political blocks. The block on the right or the national-democratic forces unified the BNF, BSDG, Peasants', Christian-Democratic, and National-Democratic Parties. The block on the left includes the Communist, Socialistic, and Agrarian Parties together with other groups. The party of National Consent united with the Incorporated Democratic and Civil Parties form the centrist block. Promoted by the "party of authority," the presidential vertical and independent candidates were active participants in the preelection campaign. The election results of the higher legislative and local authorities in 1995 were important in the formation of a multiparty system in Byelarus.

The Attitude of the Population

The results of sociological surveys regularly performed by an independent institute of socioeconomic and political research enables us to analyze the attitudes of the population toward the ruling elite and various institutes of authority. In November and December, 1993, the activity of the Supreme Soviet and government received the lowest ratings: about 70 percent of the respondents rated them as "bad" and "unsatisfactory." A large part of the population pinned their hopes on an exit from the economic crisis not through government activity but with foreign investments.[9]

The survey carried out in October, 1992, revealed a decline in the trust of the electorate in relation to the deputies they elected to the Supreme and local Soviets. Only 10 percent of those interviewed would vote for the deputy of the Supreme Soviet again, and 50 percent definitely would not. Moreover, 9 percent would vote for the deputy of District Soviet and 51 percent would not; 12 percent would vote for the deputy of the regional Soviet, and 50 percent would not.[10]

In March, 1993, the attitude of the population toward the corruption at various levels of state authority was studied. More than 60 percent of respondents believed that corruption was present in the republic and about 30 percent had difficulty in replying.[11] Parliamentary commissions on corruption, under the chairmanship of Lukashenko and Sergei Antonchik, confirmed widespread metastases of corruption in the higher executive authority.

Data from the same independent institute of socioeconomic and political research allows us to see how the representatives of authority view various social and political problems. In particular, in a survey conducted in February–March, 1995, about a hundred representatives of the elite participated. Among them were the chief of administration of the president, assistant of the president for special assignments, four ministers, three chairmen of parliamentary commissions, well-known businessmen and chiefs of the state enterprises, editors of the central editions and TV, and representatives of the cultural and scientific elite. The sociologists compared the opinions of the elite and the population concerning the activity of the main institutes of authority. They revealed significant differences in their views. On a five-item scale (one being the lowest rating and five the highest) the president received from the population the highest rating (2.6), and among experts the lowest (2.1). This result demonstrated once again the populist character of the president and the critical attitude toward his policy among analysts. The Supreme Soviet received from the population an average rating of 2.1 and from the representatives of the elite, 2.4. The population pins its hopes for an end to the economic crisis on the president, while the experts assign responsibility (equally) to the president as well as all state institutes except the army, state security organs, and the judicial system.[12]

The same survey revealed both positive and negative ratings for political figures in Byelarus.[13] The first five positions (those who received the most positive ratings) were occupied by Pozniak, Lukashenko, Stanislav Bogdankevitch (chairman of National Bank of Byelarus), Shushkevitch, and Grib. The five political figures with the most negative ratings were Lukashenko, Kebitch, Shushkevitch, Bogdankevitch, and Ivan Titenkov (business manager of the presidential administration).

National Structure of the Ruling Elite

The revival of Byelorussian national statehood raises again the question of the national origin of a ruling political elite. The situation that developed in this area up until the beginning of the 1990s could not change quickly. A firm, teleological, and delicate policy was required.

The national structure of the Supreme Soviet in 1990–95 deviated from the demographic profile of Byelarus. In 1989, there were 77.9 percent Byelorussians in the country, 13.2 percent Russians, 4.1 percent Poles, 2.9 percent Ukrainians, 1.1 percent Jews, and 0.8 percent other nationalities. In the Byelorussian Parliament, there were 73.5 percent Byelorussians, 19.8 percent Russians, 3.1 percent Poles and Ukrainians, and 0.2 percent Jews.[14] Thus, the representation of Byelorussians in Parliament was 4.5 percentage points less than their share in the population of the republic, while the representation of the Russians was 6.6 points greater.

In bodies of state management, per every 100,000 of the working population, there are 3.3 percent Byelorussians, 7.8 percent Russians, and 8.2 percent other nationalities.[15] Especially problematic is the distribution of management of the army and state security. Of the eight defense deputy ministers of the Byelarus Republic, Pavel Kozlovskii was the only Byelorussian. The staff of the officers of armed forces of Byelarus included, in the beginning of 1994, 30 percent Byelorussians.[16] Appointed in 1990 as the chairman of the KGB of the USSR, E. Shirovskii was the first Byelorussian at this post during the years of Soviet power.

Among the chiefs of the special departments, there were no Byelorussians. Such a situation developed for a number of reasons. Soviet military management scattered the Byelorussian officers, as well as representatives of other nationalities, throughout the territory of the Soviet Union. Within the framework of a uniform state in all districts there was control over the circulation of the military staff. Within the KGB, the Kremlin authorities did not admit Byelorussians to the highest posts. As the formation of Byelorussian statehood proceeds, an independent internal and external policy expressing the national interests of the Byelorussian people requires an end to the skewed distribution of the national representation in managing bodies of force structures imposed by the prior totalitarian order. When there is an availability of an equal level of professionalism and personal qualities, the priority must be given to the Byelorussians.

Local Political Elite

The local political elite is formed at the district, city, and regional levels of representative and executive authority. What features are characteristic for their social portrait? In part, the answer is contained in the results of sociological research on local elite (regional chain), conducted in 1991–93.

The majority are men, 82 percent are Byelorussians, about 95 percent have higher educations, and the average age is forty-four. Their social origins are 45 percent peasants, 22 percent workers, 12 percent office workers and the intelligentsia. It is evident from these figures that the local elite does not have nomenklatura roots. More than 60 percent are people who came to authority during perestroika (reorganization). As a whole, the majority of the representatives of local authority have a left-central orientation.[17]

Very few respondents believed that local authorities did have a large influence on solving local problems. Most felt local authorities only had "some influence" or "no influence." During 1991–93, opportunities for those having local authority were reduced. So, for example, public funds did not even rank among the first ten most significant opportunities for decisions on social and economic problems. Influence on the activity of political organizations was ranked lower: 64 percent believed they had no influence, 26 percent believed some, and 6 percent believed a large influence. These results enabled us to generalize that local authority does not believe it can effectively work within the limits of their competence.

The respondents also evaluated the efficiency of local chiefs as quite low. In 1993, 46 percent and 38 percent of the respondents negatively evaluated the activity of the Supreme Soviet and government respectively, and 56 percent and 57 percent had a negative opinion concerning the work of local Soviets and their executive bodies respectively. The majority believed that chiefs of local bodies of executive authority should be elected by the inhabitants of each given region. Only 2–5 percent interviewed supported the practice of higher bodies appointing local chiefs.[18] However, similar democratic trends at the province level were canceled by the president's reform initiatives on local self government. As a result, the authoritarianism of the central authorities was strengthened even more as additional opportunities for constraining the initiatives of the local ruling elite were created.

Economic Elite

The economic elite developed from the nouveau riche in trade, banking, and industrial capital; the management (directors') corps; agriculture; and workers of the state machinery. The circles of Byelorussian enterprise are relatively weak in their financial and economic power and influence. No more than 100,000 people or 2.5 percent of the able-bodied population are engaged in business. They use only 0.5 percent of the main production assets. Of 300,000 economic actors, 80 percent exist only on paper.[19] Byelorussian businessmen are united in the Byelorussian Confederation of the Industrialists and Businessmen, the Scientific-Industrial Association, the Union of Businessmen, the Union of Businessmen and Leasers, the Byelorussian Commerce and Industry Union, and a number of other organizations.

The economic elite, as a whole, is indifferent to the ideas of national revival and independence for Byelarus. As for nationally based capital, the firms Dainova and Fiko are the only possible bright representatives. The president of Dainova, A. Paliakhovitch, believes that there are only a few firms actively conducting "a Byelorussian line." A positive shift in the direction of "Byelorussization" of business is possible if the Byelorussian language is used in advertising. Paliakhovitch points out that business circles must use the language that brings money: "The Byelorussian language does not bring money to us, rather on the contrary." As a representative of nationally based capital, he acts as if he were two people: as a businessman, he is a supporter of free movement of goods and close cooperation with Russian firms, but as a citizen of the Byelarus Republic he is for the strengthening of a national state.[20] Despite the relatively slow process of forming business in Byelarus (in comparison to the neighboring republics of the former USSR), in some branches of industry, private capital already plays an indispensable role. The firm Dainova largely provides the country's industry with metal and other strategic goods. Without the metal provided by this firm, neither the Minsk tractor factory nor the Minsk automobile factory nor many other enterprises could function. Through private structures in the republic, a significant part of footwear and sunflower seed oil, 50 percent of petroleum, and 80 percent of sugar are delivered. Taxes from business make up a significant share of the budget of some cities.[21]

In recent years, the views and ideas of the business class have become a subject of great interest to sociologists. One of the first surveys of the elite was conducted in February, 1992, by the Byelorussian service Public Opinion. One of the questions was "If government does not render effective help to businessmen, what will businessmen do?" Thirty percent of the participants of the Assembly of Business Circles of the Byelarus Republic declared that they would require the resignation of the government, 21 percent would begin to move capital to countries beyond Byelorussian borders, 16 percent would move to the shadow economy (black market), and 5 percent said they would curtail production.[22]

In October, 1992, the participants at the extended meeting of the Soviet (Council) Union of Businessmen evaluated strategies for creating conditions for business development. Ninety-seven percent negatively evaluated the governmental efforts of the Republic; 91 percent gave a negative evaluation of the Supreme Soviet; and 67 percent negatively evaluated the undertakings of the local authorities.[23] The chiefs of enterprise structures believe that the best efforts on improving the economic situation and developing private business have come as a result of actions by the unions of businessmen.

Disappointment in governmental activity increased in the spring of 1994 after the ministerial council accepted the decision to withdraw foreign exchange earnings from businessmen. The economic elite were also unhappy about the uncertainty surrounding the question of unifying the monetary systems of Byelarus and Russia. However, business circles continued to support Kebitch. The amalgamation of the governmental nomenklatura with mafiosi and corrupted economic circles expanded.

One of the most serious obstacles to the formation and development of business is corruption within offices of state authority. Surveys of businessmen conducted in 1992 revealed that the most corrupted individuals are the local authorities. The local authorities are followed by the offices of foreign trade activities and customs houses, supplier-marketing organizations, courts, the Office of the Public Prosecutor, and the militia. To a lesser degree, this illness infected the national deputies and security offices. A third of the respondents admitted that they have to solve business problems by giving valuable souvenirs or compensation to state employees. A fifth of the respondents said that their firms had to "encourage" government officers as a standard practice.[24]

A more serious obstacle for businessmen is the existing system of taxation. About 80 percent said that taxes were the main obstruction to more effective work. Sixty-three percent were unsatisfied with the state financial policy and 56 percent with the absence of reliable guaranties for free business.[25] The existence of mafia in management and trade was considered by them as a lesser harm to which they probably were already accustomed.

The survey carried out in the spring of 1994 did not reveal any appreciable political preferences of businessmen: 77 percent of those interviewed had no political engagement, 3 percent held preferences for the BNF and the same number for the democratic camp.[26] The president of the Union of the Businessmen of Republic Byelarus, Vladimir Koriagin, said in an interview that in Byelarus there are people possessing millions of dollars. By this he did not mean himself or his "brothers in the business-class" but state officers, who grew rich because of state racketeering, gaining profits from the contracts with foreign firms. The Byelorussian economic elite has already passed a stage of initial accumulation and has entered a period of active financial and economic activity and increasing capital. This process will be accompanied by the inevitable phenomena of the market economy: the crash and failure of small-sized firms, the increasing concentration of capital in large structures, the coalescence of banking and industrial capital, integration with businessmen of neighboring countries (first of all, Russia), and the creation of financial-industrial groups.

The Cultural and Scientific Elite

The budding national intelligentsia has been traumatized by the conditions in which it found itself as a result of the transition to "wild" market relations. The prestige of scientific and creative activity has sharply decreased. In terms of active engagement with the masses in politics, one part of the intellectuals left politics, appearing pessimistic, and took a convenient position of "internal emigration." Another part, though insignificant, joined the movement for revival of independent Byelorussia.

Byelorussian political and cultural elites in the 1980s were seriously small in number. In 1980, Russians dominated Byelorussian agricultural science and management: there were 2 Russians for each Byelorussian. For every 100,000 people in 1979, 5 Byelorussians were doctors of sciences, and 26 Russians were doctors. By 1989 this gap increased a little more: there were 6 Byelorussian and 33 Russian doctors per 100,000 people. In 1979, for every 100,000 persons, there were 68 candidates of sciences of Byelorussian nationality and 326 Russians. After ten years, there were 93 Byelorussian candidates of sciences for every 100,000 persons and 393 Russians. For every 100,000 persons in the adult population in 1979, there were 50 Byelorussians with higher educations and 174 Russians; by 1989, the numbers went up to 84 Byelorussians and 226 Russians.[27] Among the artists, 52 percent were Byelorussians; among the composers, 42 percent; and among high school teachers, 56 percent.[28]

How can this situation be explained? The policy of nonadmission of the national creative intelligentsia, which was conducted by the Russian autocracy in the past, and the more recent Soviet-Communist system had a negative impact on the Byelorussian intelligentsia. The examples of refusals in assignment to scientific ranks and degrees because of nationality or ethnic preference are not known, but we do know of many examples of persecution for "nationalistic" beliefs, which subjected the adherents of the national idea to repression.

The roots of this problem can be found in the peasant character of the Byelorussian nation and the peasant-narodnik Byelorussian national movement. In the years of Soviet power, science, culture, and education, especially in higher elite spheres, were created by the Russian professors' staffs and creative intelligentsia. Their contributions to the formation of the scientific and cultural potential of Byelarus were invaluable. On the other hand, these individuals brought the Russian language as well as the traditions, customs, and mentality of the Russian people. They came from Moscow, Leningrad, and other scientific and cultural centers of Russia; they were Russians, Jews, or representatives of other nationalities by origin and were not supporters of the national revival in Byelarus. They educated a young scientific and cultural elite mostly with Byelorussian nationality. A complete updating of the professional groups in the Byelorussia creative elite occurred as a result of the constant struggle of party propaganda, an absence of leaders for the national revival, and the policy of Russification and urbanization. In this way, a biased national structure of scientific and cultural elite was formed.

The major criterion for evaluating the worldviews of the cultural elite was their attitude toward Russia and toward the economic and political integration of Byelarus with the Russian cultural elite. Nationally oriented representatives of the Byelorussian creative intelligentsia critically perceive the statements of Alexander Solzhenitsyn, Dmitrii

Likhachev, Valentin Rasputin, Ilia Glazunov, and other figures in Russian culture about the historical generality of the three Eastern Slavonic peoples, the serenity of mutual relations in the past, and the necessity of further development within the framework of a unified Great Russian state. In connection with this, Vasil Bykov's statements about his deeply respected Russian colleague, Valentin Rasputin, is characteristic. The Byelorussian writer emphasizes that the political consciousness of Rasputin is to a considerable extent a product of imperial statehood—in other words, the immanent aspiration of a large nation to stand above the lesser nation. The political will of Bykov, on the other hand, is directed toward the liberation from any external power.[29]

The creative elite is the vanguard of the national revival and actively acts against the antinational policy of the ruling forces. The Eleventh Congress of the writers of Byelarus on April 27, 1994, was deeply alarmed about the intention of certain political forces to include Byelarus in the structure of Russia and condemned the agreement signed by the government of Kebitch for unifying the monetary systems of Byelarus and Russia.[30] A significant part of the cultural and scientific elite were against the intentions of President Alexander Lukashenko to include questions on new national symbols as well as questions about giving equal status to the Russian language and Byelorussian in the referendum on May 14, 1995. The presidential election campaign in 1994 and the parliamentary elections and referendum in 1995 showed a split in the Byelorussian intelligentsia. The nationally oriented part of the intelligentsia wanted to strengthen Byelorussian statehood and actively called for a policy of "Byelorussization" and for the realization of real democratic and market reforms. It voted against bills offered by the president on the referendum and supported the candidates from democratic and central blocks. Another part is quieter about, if not indifferent to, the problems of national revival and the preservation of state bilingualism and supports the president's course on the integration with Russia. They did not perceive the "radicalism" of the BNF and other national-democratic forces. They voted for the representatives of the moderate central and left forces as well as for protégés of "the Party of authority." The third part, in general, avoids participation in political campaigns, having taken a position of absenteeism and focused their activity on creative and private problems.

During the presidential campaign in 1994, the rectors of the leading Byelorussian universities called on the electorate to support Kebitch, while the representatives of the creative, nationally oriented elite supported Pozniak and Shushkevitch. Lukashenko did not enjoy the sympathies of the intelligentsia, who did not trust his populist promises. Later, the president recognized that he was an elected representative of the people, and not of the elite. His readiness for the reunion with Russia along with his statements about the Byelorussian language and national symbols did not promote close relations between state authority and the national intelligentsia.

7

The Emergence of
the Lithuanian Political Elite

Vladas Gaidys

Prior to the sixteenth century, Lithuania's ruling elite had a Lithuanian identity with local origins. The elite used the Lithuanian language and identified with the Lithuanian duchy. Subsequently, Lithuania's autonomy suffered a decline as it became more integrated with the Polish state. Advanced technology and European culture came to Lithuania from Poland. As a result, a large share of nobility lost its Lithuanian identity.

As part of the Russian empire (from the eighteenth to the twentieth century), the official bureaucracy in Lithuania consisted of Russians, but the Polish-speaking nobility and Roman Catholic priests still played an important role in state affairs. Following World War I, the independent Lithuanian state was shaped by a statehood-minded intelligentsia, many of whom were graduates of Moscow and Saint Petersburg universities. Prior to the 1926 military coup, Lithuania was a parliamentary republic dominated by the political parties of social democratic persuasion. The coup propelled to power a right-wing authoritarian regime that endured until the country lost its independence in 1940. The Red Army's occupation of Lithuania gave rise to a collaborationist elite. It consisted of underground communists (the likes of Antanas Snechkus) as well as leftist intelligentsia, who entertained many illusions typical of the then prevalent mood among the intelligentsia in many countries. Members of Lithuania's former political elite were either repressed, or they emigrated to the West. Of the 79 members of the Council of Ministers of Independent Lithuania who lived to see the Soviet invasion, 38 were executed or expelled, 37 emigrated to the West, and only 4 managed to adapt to the new circumstances.[1]

Nomenklatura in Soviet Lithuania

The period of 1944−53 witnessed a profound Russification of the government and party organs. Of the 89 individuals belonging to the top echelon of power, only 43 were Lithuanian; of the 465 members of the nomenklatura employed at the Ministry of Internal Affairs and the KGB, only 36 were Lithuanian. In 1947, the Communist Party in Lithuania "boasted" only 18 percent ethnic Lithuanians.[2] After Stalin's death, the official policy shifted toward fostering the local nomenklatura. The percentage of Lithuanians in the Communist Party rose steadily: 44 percent in 1955, 64 percent in 1965, 68 percent in 1975, and 70 percent in 1985. In 1979, 13 out of the 14 members and alternate members of the bureau of the Central Committee of the Communist Party of Lithuania were Lithuanian and only 1 was Russian. In 1981, just 1 out of 10 members of the Presidium of the Council of Ministers was Russian.

With certain qualifications, the nomenklatura was synonymous with the Soviet elite during that era. The subject has aroused much interest, including a well-known book by Mikhail Voslenskii with a special section devoted to the issue of local ethnic nomenklatura: "Ethnic republics are neo-colonies governed by the nomenklatura."[3] For the purpose of our investigation of the present-day elite, we must consider other facets of the Soviet-era nomenklatura.

The Predominance of Lithuanians

A century of foreign occupation has failed to eradicate many features reminiscent of Lithuania's former statehood. Lithuanians have managed to safeguard their ethnic identity. In spite of incentives to relocate, in 1989, only 9.4 percent of Lithuania's population was Russian. High schools and post−high school institutions conducted classes in Lithuanian. Lithuanians held key posts in management and administration of culture and science. At the same time, the realm of ideology and the institutions of oppression were firmly under Moscow's control.

One's Origins—The Criteria of Loyalty

As was the case throughout the Soviet Union, potential candidates for the nomenklatura were recruited from the ranks of the Komsomol and the Communist Party. One of the key preconditions to being admitted into the Communist Party of the Soviet Union (CPSU) was not to have any "repressed" relatives or relatives living abroad. This provision made a lot of sense, for the nonrepressed class consisted of people who did not attain a position of wealth in the formerly independent Lithuania. The Soviet regime actually granted these people an opportunity to acquire education, a good position, and a career. Naturally, these strata profess greater loyalty to the Soviet regime.

According to a survey conducted in September, 1993, 31 percent of Lithuanians claimed to have members of their families who had suffered at the hands of the Soviet regime; in 1995 the figure was 39 percent.[4] Those victimized by the Soviet regime were more prone to vote for the anticommunist parties (Lithuanian Conservatives, Sajudis), while those not afflicted by the Soviet regime were more likely to vote for the "left-wing" parties.

Moral Justification for Belonging to the Elite

In Moscow, the need to justify one's belonging to the nomenklatura was limited to the intelligentsia circles. In Lithuania, any "affiliation" with the Moscow authorities had to be justified. The cynical excuse that "you have to know how to get around" simply flopped. The most common and trivial excuse followed this line of reasoning: "someone has to do it, and we have to take advantage of the opportunity to minimize the harm for Lithuania." Even the former secretary of the Central Committee for Ideology described his "struggle" with censorship.[5] Occasionally, other explanations would crop up, such as: "Lithuania could be controlled either by the Russians or the Germans. Russians are better—they are easier to get around." In any event, the Lithuanian nomenklatura was called upon to show at least a semblance of patriotism.

Genuine Concerns

The nomenklatura certainly needed the Soviet central authorities to defend its status. But unfair divisions of the privileges, a vassal-like status, a lack of power in dealing with Moscow, and moral denigration irked the Lithuanian officialdom. The nomenklatura endeavored to live better, travel abroad, and so forth. The prospects for improving their standing within the framework of the Soviet Union and its brand of socialism were dim.

Neither true Communists nor Moscow's cronies who were part of the nomenklatura can be considered among that era's elite. The former were sidelined for failing to comprehend "the reality of the situation"; the latter were rather alienated from the mainstream.

The Restoration of Independence

Perestroika crystallized the Lithuanian national nomenklatura, segregating it from the Soviet elite. It would be an oversimplification to reduce this entire process to economic motives (the desire to rule, to control the allocation of resources, and to receive additional perks "becoming" of the elite—all without Moscow's intervention). Patriotism, in the best sense of the word, and common sense played crucial roles in the drive for independence.

At the Party Congress held in 1989, the Lithuanian Communist Party split into an independent group (which was the majority) and a group allied with the "CPSU platform." As a result, the segment of the elite loyal to the CPSU became alienated, spelling the beginning of its political end. At the same time, the independent Communist Party of Lithuania and its respective elite reached the high point of moral triumph. Following the Party Congress, the Lithuanian Communist Party's approval rating was +73 (+79 among Lithuanians and +29 among non-Lithuanians on a scale from −100 to +100).[6]

The first secretary Algirdas Brazauskas of Lithuania's Communist Party gained incredible popularity; he was named by 73 percent of respondents answering an open-ended question about which politicians represent their interests. Other secretaries of the Central Committee (formerly members of the nomenklatura as well) also received high marks—Vladimir Beriozovas (37 percent), Justas Paleckis (26 percent). The anticommunist Vytautas Landsbergis ranked seventh on the list of the most popular politicians with 12 percent. However, once it severed its ties with Moscow, the old elite encountered stiff opposition in its quest for power.

The Emergence of the Anticommunist Elite

The mass movement Sajudis, launched in 1988, was formally christened "the drive for perestroika." Lithuania's nomenklatura extended unimpassioned support for this movement, basically aligning itself with its moderate wing, which advocated a gradual transition. The radical political wing of Sajudis assembled staunch proponents of independence who were dead-set against the Soviet system.

The radical faction of Sajudis raised the following moral issues: Does the nomenklatura, which collaborated with the occupiers for fifty years, have any right to wield power? What about the rights of all those who struggled for independence over those fifty years?

The nomenklatura was hard pressed for a reasonable retort. "Let us start from scratch" did not carry much weight. Such was the background for the emergence of the counterelite (in the political, economic, and cultural sense of the word). This group was composed primarily of people who managed not to soil their reputation during the years of Soviet rule.

There was another "material" factor spurring the counterelite, namely the idea of restitution. The nomenklatura that was in power did not own land, buildings, and so forth confiscated by the Soviet regime. Thus a certain segment of the new movement did contemplate potential material gains.

The 1990 elections, won by the right-wing group headed by Landsbergis, was the straw that broke the back of the former elite. Perhaps in a more congenial environment the former elite could have transformed itself and adapted to the new circumstances, but stiff political competition left very few unfilled positions and imposed strict screening, including renouncing any affiliation with the former elite. As a result, the former elite was forced to band together and act in unison.

Post-Soviet Lithuania gave rise to a bipolar elite: the elite of the left (Algirdas Brazauskas's group) and the elite of the right (Landsbergis's group). Here, the terms "left" and "right" should be understood in the context of Lithuania: the main difference between the two camps is in their attitudes toward the past. The "left" is tolerant of the Soviet era, regarding it as an evil outside of human control; the "right" is intolerant, viewing the Soviet period as an evil perpetrated by very real and specific individuals.

The Ideological Contrast Between Left and Right

Elections held in the fall of 1992 demonstrated a strong presence of a polarized political elite on the left and on the right. The left (the Democratic Labor Party) gained 73 seats; the right (the Sajudis Coalition, Christian Democratic Party, Democrats' Party, and Association of Political Prisoners and Deportees) won 48 mandates; and the other 14 parties received only 20 mandates.

Local elections held in March, 1995, indicate that the two extreme positions have not "blurred together." Rather, we observe the pendulum effect, as the population becomes disillusioned with the incumbents. In the 1995 election, the left received 27.1 percent of the seats; the right, 49.1 percent; and 23.8 percent went to other parties.

Platforms of the Left and the Right

What distinguishes the platforms of the right- and left-wing factions in Lithuania? It is not easy to pinpoint the essential difference in the agenda or the programs of the two camps. Both are inconsistent, while the actions of the opposing parties are driven by expediency. However, let us attempt a brief explanation of the two camps' positions regarding key political and economic issues.

Assessment of the Soviet Period

Left. "To some extent everyone is guilty of collaboration, for the entire process lasted too long. The Lithuanian nation had to endure and survive, to work, and to create—even at the price of accommodating the occupiers. This period ought to be viewed from a pragmatic perspective. Communists did a lot to attain the independence we enjoy today. Our goal is national unity. Let us bury the hatchet and come together in the name of a free Lithuania. In all truth, that period was not all bad."

Right. "There is a moral aspect to everything. The guilty must be punished. Can we allow KGB agents, the party nomenklatura, and the former executioners of the Lithuanian guerrillas to govern the country? Too much evil has been perpetrated over the last fifty years. This period, full of evil lies, has penetrated everything and everyone. Only following a moral ablution can a new Lithuania be formed. We shall muster our strength from that amazing period of independence between 1918 and 1940."

Attitude Toward Russia

Left. "We have no prejudice against Russia or the Russians. Stalinism and the Soviet regime are to blame for the pain suffered by Lithuania. Nowadays, Russia itself is moving toward the market and democracy. It would be ill-advised to break off all the ties with Russia. To make claims (say, indemnity for decades of occupation) against a country such as Russia seems foolish." (It should be pointed out that since 1994—following the elections to the Russian Duma—leftists have grown much more skeptical of this stance.)

Right. "In terms of our mentality and culture we are a Western European country. Throughout the ages Russia has brought suffering upon our people. There are forces in Lithuania, not to speak of Russia itself, that entertain the thought of reviving the Russian empire. Let us also be on guard against the creeping imperialism manifest in economic handouts, mass media, lack of political fortitude on the part of our government (former members of the nomenklatura). Politics must be conducted morally, and evil must not be swept under the rug."

Return of Property

Left. "Everything has changed in the last fifty years. The former owners are trying to reclaim their lands, but houses have been built on these lands and families have spent their entire lives in them. Apartment houses are occupied by different people. How can all these be given back? Can justice be done at the expense of others?"

Right. "Private property is sacrosanct. Stolen property must be returned to its rightful owners. The government has an opportunity to do so. The conflicts can be settled in a reasonable manner. The left wants to legalize nationalization."

Agriculture

Left. "The dismantling and plundering of collective farms has ruined agriculture. Transition to privatized farming was supposed to proceed gradually. In any event, only large-scale cooperative agribusiness can support an effective use of the modern technologies needed to become competitive in the European market."

Right. "The former nomenklatura managing the collective farms is afraid of losing power and so it resists agrarian reform. These same people are into 'expropriation' of the most valuable assets, rather than 'privatization.' Private ownership of land is the key to efficient performance. Give peasants back the freedom, suspend deception and subversion, and see rural Lithuania rebound."

All these arguments are "stripped down," but they do capture the essence of the views espoused by the two camps. The watershed between the two is the attitude toward the past and its legacy. The economic programs of the two groups are not as far apart. The right is socially oriented (especially now that they are out of power and in the opposition) while the left is quite liberal in the economic sphere. Still, one would be hard-pressed to pin down who is who based on the actions of the two parties.

Nonetheless, certain sentiments bond the right with traditional right-wing views and the left with left-wing views. The right is extremely keen on the idea of statehood—that is, a free and independent Lithuania that controls its own borders, can stand up for itself, and can respond to military aggression. The left is always poking fun at these ambitions and tends to dismiss allegations of subversive activities both inside and outside Lithuania.

The Line of Demarcation Between Party Affiliations

The bipolar political elite reflects the mass psyche in its present state. Empirical studies conducted over the past five years have shown repeatedly that those polled vacillate when it comes to assessing the economic policy of the government currently in power but are very sensitive to issues pertaining to Lithuania's Soviet past.

In June, 1995, one thousand respondents were asked to rank the six most active parties of Lithuania based on a seven-point system with respect to the following criteria: "proponents of radical reform—opponents of reform"; "proponents of democracy—proponents of 'strong-handed' rule, a dictatorship"; "express the interests of the poor—close to the interests of the business-rich"; "left—right"; and "sympathetic toward the Soviet past—detest the Soviet past." The parties were not ranked far apart based on the first three criteria—the average valuation covered only 10–13 percent of the entire range. However, "the left—right" criteria showed much greater variance (parties were scattered over 50 percent of the range) as did responses regarding the attitude toward the Soviet period (43 percent of the range).

The "left—right" scale has no correlation with the "rich—poor" scale (the most "leftist" ruling Democratic Labor Party received the highest mark of 4.1 on this question, that is, members of this party were perceived as representing business interests). However, this indicator is correlated (Pearson coefficient of +0.5) with the "Soviet past." The party consisting of former Communists is perceived as empathetic toward the period under Soviet rule (the average for this indicator is 3.2), and the opposing party (supporters of Landsbergis) is perceived as detesting the Soviet past (average was 5.8).

The attitude toward the past was critically examined in the "New Baltic Barometer," a study conducted in the Baltic states in 1993 and

1995. The survey asked respondents to "evaluate the former communist regime on a scale of −100 to +100, with the highest mark of +100
and the lowest mark of −100." In 1993 the difference between positive and negative marks was +2 percent for Lithuanians, −14 percent
for Latvians, and −22 percent for Estonians. In 1995 the figures were
+3 percent, −18 percent, and −30 percent respectively. The conflict-
ing assessment of the Soviet era among the various Baltic states calls
for an explanation.

Differences in the Gravity of the Ethnic Issue

There is reason to believe that the situation in Lithuania during the
Soviet period was much better than in other Baltic states. One of the
more controversial issues of that era was mass migration of people in
the USSR. In 1989, Latvians comprised 52 percent of the Latvian population (77 percent in 1935); there were 61 percent Estonians in Estonia
(88 percent in 1934). Lithuania's population was 80 percent Lithuanian
(69 percent in 1923). Immigrants were attracted to the industrial centers of Estonia and Latvia; Lithuania remained a more agrarian country.
Also, Lithuania was experiencing a different phase of the demographic
cycle. In Latvia (as in many Western European countries), natural population growth stopped completely, but Lithuania remained one of the
leading countries in this Europe-based indicator (it was surpassed only
by Ireland, Albania, Romania, and Poland). The Latvian and the Es-
tonian peoples were threatened with demographic extinction.

Another factor was the conduct of the immigrants. According to the
1989 census, Russians living in Lithuania were ranked number one in
the USSR as far as knowledge of the local language; 37.5 percent had
working knowledge of Lithuanian (the true figures are even higher because the data pertains to the entire population, including newborns).
The same indicator was 22.3 percent for Latvia and 15 percent for Estonia (for comparison, in Kazakhstan the figure was .9 percent). In other
words, the ethnic issue was less acute in Lithuania during the Soviet
era than in Latvia or Estonia.

Cultural Differences

Lithuanians and Estonians belong to different cultural milieus. According to studies conducted by the "New Baltic Barometer" project,
Lithuanians, who were the last Western European nation to adopt
Christianity, are the most ardent Catholics. There are many atheists
among the Estonians, although the country is heavily Protestant. Latvians are somewhere in the middle.

Table 7.1. Baltic Religious Affiliations (percentage)

	Catholic	Lutheran	Ortho-dox	Other denomi-nations	Non-denomi-national believers	Atheist	Unable to respond
Latvians	24	30	2	3	13	12	16
Lithuanians	75	0	0	1	9	5	10
Estonians	0	23	3	4	20	27	23

One of the key features of Protestant culture is individualism and rationality. Liberal capitalism seems to harmonize with this type of culture. On the other hand, the encyclicals of the Vatican profess not only anti-Marxist views (at least, it does recognize private property) but also an antiliberal sentiment (in the economic domain). Catholics and Protestants tend to perceive the transition to a market-type economy (with some vestiges of nineteenth-century capitalism) differently. Catholics, it seems, perceive the current period of transformation as more repugnant and view the past in terms of the current predicament.

Access to Information

During the Soviet era, Estonians enjoyed greater access to Western sources of information, notably Finnish television. Estonians had an opportunity to acquire regular information about the global political situation as well as to assimilate the fundamentals of a market economy and democratic society. Because of their proximity to Finland, Estonians have more relatives and friends living abroad (38 percent for Estonians; 28 percent for Latvians, and 26 percent for Lithuanians).

Reform Orientation

Perhaps Lithuanians are more conservative and have a harder time coming to grips with new developments. As an affirmation, Lithuania adopted Christianity in 1387, after 200 years of struggle. Lithuanians were also quite successful in sidestepping directives issued during the Soviet era—for instance, a directive calling for an all-out planting of corn. At that time, the conservative streak was an asset. Perhaps, this cautious attitude still persists. Consider the following statistics: in April, 1990, we conducted a poll asking whether respondents would support rapid but more painful reform or a moderate, more gradual reform. Fifty-three percent of Estonians favored rapid reform, while only

23 percent of Lithuanians did. In 1992, Lithuanians elected a president whose motto was "step-by-step."

Agricultural Dominance

Lithuania is a land of farmers. Agriculture is important in all the Baltic states, but the share of the gross national product (GNP) generated by agriculture is highest in Lithuania. It was precisely in agriculture that the side effects of the reform were most pronounced. The problem is rooted not only in the economy (inefficient farms and the difficulty of competing with the West) but in society itself.

Villages in the countryside are home to many old people. Previously, collective farms assumed some responsibility for their well-being. In this regard, the communal spirit was a positive feature of the collective farms. Nowadays, an old person may well find himself all alone and helpless in an aggressively evolving society.

These historical and social features of Lithuania shed some light on the underlying reasons that allow the members of the former nomenklatura to remain a powerful force on the political scene and form a party that gained the majority in the Parliament following the 1992 elections.

Let us go back to the down-the-middle split observed in Lithuania with regard to the Soviet era. In response to the aforementioned question on the attitude toward the Communist regime (1993), the supporters of the right (Landsbergis) were highly negative, −22 percent (the difference between positive and negative answers), while those on the left (Brazauskas) were positive, +28 percent. The next two years only served to widen the gap: the assessments were −17 percent and 44 percent respectively.

The Right and the Left in the Lithuanian Parliament

The guide *Who's Who in Lithuania*[7] gives us a glimpse of the political background of the deputies. Let us distinguish two groups, one consisting of former members of the CPSU and the other consisting of those who were personally persecuted or had family members who were persecuted (see table 7.2).

The press claimed that one finds many former Communists among the most zealous supporters of Landsbergis and that many former radicals now support Brazauskas.[8] Though this inversion does take place, the actual data attests that among the right there are more of those who suffered under the Soviet regime, while the left include more of those who established themselves fairly well under the old system.

Table 7.2. Political Background of Deputies (percentage)

	"Left" deputies (N = 75)	"Right" deputies (N = 51)	Others (N = 15)
Former members of the CPSU	79	15	33
Persecuted	8	27	33

Table 7.3. Frequency of Voting for Right and Left Wing and the Hurt Suffered by Soviet Regime (percentage)

	Would vote for right wing		Would vote for left wing	
	1993	1994	1993	1994
Lithuanians hurt by the Soviet regime	21	42	24	6
Lithuanians who did not suffer at the hands of the Soviet regime	12	29	37	23

The Membership of the Political Elite

Since 1989, the Public Opinion Research Center has been posing the same question: "Which politicians in Lithuania best represent your interests?" The list of the most popular politicians is fairly consistent (see table 7.4). Barring any major political calamities (such as elections), the list remains basically the same throughout the year. It is difficult to enter the political arena, and the public is reluctant to part with its "favorite sons." In the six years spanning 1989 to 1995, five politicians figured prominently in all twenty polls: Algirdas Brazauskas, Vytautas Landsbergis, Egidijus Bickauskas, Romualdas Ozolas, and Kazimieras Antanavicius.

Algirdas Brazauskas was born in a small town in 1932 to a white-collar family. After receiving his degree from an engineering college, he worked as an engineer, then as a manager of a state construction organization, and then in the ministry. He became a secretary of the Central Committee (for economy and industry) during 1977–88 and the first secretary of the Central Committee of the Communist Party of Lithuania (CPL) during 1988–90. At the beginning of 1990 he was the chairman of the Presidium of the Supreme Soviet of Lithuania. In light of his immense popularity, he was appointed deputy prime minister following the 1990 elections. During the bloody events of 1991, he was banished from all official posts by the right-wing group. He was chair-

Table 7.4. Popularity of Lithuanian Politicians (percentage)

March, 1990	(N = 1583)	September, 1993	(N = 1062)
1. A. Brazauskas	59	1. A. Brazauskas	28
2. V. Landsbergis	45	2. V. Landsbergis	14
3. K. Prunskiene	44	3. R. Ozolas	11
4. R. Ozolas	20	4. K. Antanavicius	7
5. K. Motieka	19	5. A. Slezevicius	7
6. E. Vilkas	11	6. E. Bickauskas	7
7. E. Bièkauskas	11	7. G. Vagnorius	6
8. Z. Vaisvila	10	8. C. Jursenas	5
9. K. Antanavicius	8	9. A. Sakalas	4
10. J. Paleckis	6	10. J. Paleckis	2

June, 1992	(N = 1164)	April, 1994	(N = 1050)
1. V. Landsbergis	23	1. A. Brazauskas	23
2. A. Brazauskas	18	2. V. Landsbergis	10
3. K. Antanavicius	17	3. E. Bickauskas	10
4. G. Vagnorius	10	4. G. Vagnorius	6
5. E. Vilkas	4	5. K. Antanavicius	6
6. K. Motieka	3	6. A. Slezevicius	6
7. K. Prunskiene	3	7. R. Ozolas	5
8. E. Bièkauskas	2	8. C. Jursenas	4
9. N. Ozelyte	2	9. S. Lozoraitis	2
10. R. Ozolas	2	10. A. Saudargas	1

1995	(N = 1001)	1995	(N = 1001)
1. E. Bickauskas	21	6. K. Antanavicius	7
2. A. Brazauskas	19	7. A. Slezevicius	4
3. V. Landsbergis	15	8. A. Sakalas	3
4. R. Ozolas	11	9. C. Jursenas	3
5. G. Vagnorius	8	10. A. Saudargas	3

man of the Democratic Labor Party and was elected president in 1993. His views are in line with social democratic principles; in the context of Lithuania, this is akin to being on the left.

Vytautas Landsbergis was born in 1932 in Kaunas. His father was a famous architect; during the war he was in the Provisional Government of Lithuania, and after the war he emigrated. Landsbergis graduated from a musical conservatory and was later appointed a professor at the same institution. He is a pianist, musicologist, and an author of several books on Lithuanian composers. He was not a member of the CPSU. He is one of the founders and longtime chairmen of Sajudis. From March, 1990, until November, 1992, he was the chairman of the Supreme Council. Following his unsuccessful election bid, he became the leader of the opposition and is now the chairman of the Lithuanian Conservative Party, which represents the Lithuanian right. He is a principled politician who espouses classical right views, does not suffer from the complex of representing a small country, and hates communism with a passion.

Egidijus Bickauskas was born in 1954 in a small town. He graduated from a university law school and worked as a prosecutor; since 1980 he worked in a special division that included dissident cases. He was one of the founders of Sajudis as well as the Center Party (the party did not win any seats at the party slate balloting held in 1992). He was ambassador to Moscow from 1990 to 1992 and deputy chairman of Seimas. Well-known for his crusade against crime, he espouses social democratic views, but his popularity is difficult to explain (public opinion services have been accused of artificially inflating his rating).

Romualdas Ozolas was born in 1939 in a small town. He graduated from a university philology department and became a journalist, working for various magazines and for a publishing house as assistant editor. He aided the founding of both Sajudis and the Center Party. He was deputy prime minister from 1990 to 1991 and a Seimas deputy. He does not align himself with the left or the right, but his views are closest to right-wing social democrats. He is also a regular contributor of political articles to the most popular newspapers and television networks.

Kazimieras Antanavicius was born in a village in 1937. He graduated from an engineering college. As an engineer-economist, he worked at construction sites. In 1967 he successfully defended his dissertation and became a lecturer. In 1977, he received his Ph.D. in economics and was appointed professor and head of the department at the Economics Institute of the Academy of Sciences. He is one of the founders of Sajudis, as well as the founder of the Social Democrats Party. He has been deputy and chairman of the committee on economics. He has consistently spoken for the economically less fortunate stratum of society.

Five other politicians popular among the voters in June, 1995, were Gediminas Vagnorius, Adolfas Slezevicius, Ceslovas Jursenas, Aloyzas Sakalas, and Algirdas Saudargas.

Gediminas Vagnorius was born in a village in 1957 and graduated from a civil engineering institute. He received a Ph.D., then worked at the Academy of Sciences. He did not belong to the CPSU. He was one of the founders of Sajudis and drafted programs of economic reform. He was prime minister from January, 1991, to July, 1992. He was a close ally of Landsbergis and a leading member of the conservative party. He is also a prime minister of the opposition and is popular for his campaign to compensate the population for lost savings resulting from currency devaluation.

Prime Minister Adolfas Slezevicius was born in the countryside in 1948. He graduated from an engineering college as a mechanical engineer, taught at the vocational training school, and worked as an engineer at a milk processing plant. He was deputy minister from 1977 to 1981 and took courses in Moscow. He also worked in the Central Committee of the CPL. He was deputy minister from 1990 to 1991. In 1991, he became president of the Lithuanian-Norwegian joint enterprise (in the milk industry) and consequently became quite wealthy. In 1993, Slezevicius was appointed prime minister and elected chairman of the Democratic Labor Party.

Ceslovas Jursenas, a chairman of Seimas, was born in the countryside in 1938. A university graduate and a journalist, Jursenas worked in television and on the editorial staffs of several publications. He is a member of the Central Committee of the CPL and was active in the "divorce" of the CPL and the CPSU. He worked in government administration during 1990–91 and is now active in the Democratic Labor Party.

Aloyzas Sakalas was born in the countryside in 1931 and was sentenced for anti-Soviet activities in 1948. In 1960, he graduated from an engineering college and has taught physics at a university since 1963. He is responsible for numerous inventions and one original discovery. He did not belong to the Communist Party. He was chairman of the Social Democrats Party and Seimas deputy.

Algirdas Saudargas was born in 1948 in Kaunas. He graduated from a medical college and became a biophysicist, working at the neurosurgery laboratory. He was one of the founders of Sajudis and was foreign minister from 1990 to 1992. He is the leader of the Christian Democratic Party and was elected Seimas deputy in 1992.

All ten politicians were active during the period of Lithuanian Restoration. Three are on the left, three on the right, and four are in the middle. Not a single one endorses socialist or communist views. Social democratic parties (and various shades thereof) tend to predominate. Five were born in the countryside, all ten received higher education, six hold academic degrees, and all are ethnic Lithuanians.

Politicians' Reaction to the Survey Results

One politician's response to the survey results is typical: "I would be lying if I said I did not care about the results. But the rating does not make my work any easier. Moreover, people get jealous and sometimes try to 'step on your toes' without any apparent need to do so."[9] Fluctuations of the results are the main reason many political supporters are skeptical about the true merits of public opinion polls. On the other hand, longitudinal studies of such indicators suggest that the results of political popularity polls are a good barometer of the public's moods.

Experts

Fifteen individuals who either were employed within the Seimas system, were on the editorial staff of the mass media organizations, or knew the political elite through some other channels were polled as experts to determine who the political elite in Lithuania are. These "experts" were advised that the term "political elite" refers to people who can and do affect the course of the political process. Interviews with experts enhanced our a priori knowledge, but generally speaking, the information did not reveal anything significant that could not be found in the press. For example, no "gray eminence" (people unknown to the public who actually wield considerable political power) was uncovered. During the reign of the right (1990–92), Virgilijus Cepaitis was regarded by many as such a "gray eminence." He is a man of letters, an ideologue for the right who was involved in drafting a rather harsh law aimed at "desovietization" and "deKGBization." He was later accused of a twenty-year collaboration with the KGB.

Experts mentioned the following left-wing politicians as part of a political elite: Algirdas Brazauskas (president); Adolfas Slezevicius (prime minister); Ceslovas Jursenas (Seimas chairman); Gediminas Kirkilas (party ideologist and deputy chairman of the Democratic Labor Party who previously worked in the Communist Party); Justinas Karosas (leader of a faction of the Democratic Labor Party, university professor, and a Ph.D. in philosophy); Vytaus Petkevicius (a deputy and prominent writer who publishes a newspaper nostalgic for the days gone by); Povilas Gylys (foreign minister, Ph.D. in economics, and a professor); Leonardas Jaskelevicius (head of the Seimas budget and finance committee, who also holds a candidate of sciences degree in economics and worked at the Academy of Sciences); Juozas Bernatonis (deputy chairman of Seimas and an engineer who holds a Ph.D.).

Experts mentioned the following right-wing politicians as part of a political elite: Vytautas Landsbergis; Gediminas Vagnorius; Algirdas Saudargas; Algirdas Pataskas (a process engineer, teacher of philosophy and ethics, political prisoner, and Seimas deputy); Saulius Peceliunas (an engineer, dissident, and head of the Democratic Party faction); Alvyra Kuneviciene (a lecturer who holds a candidate of sciences degree in economics, finance minister from 1991 to 1992, and Seimas deputy); Andrius Kubilius (a physicist, university employee, leader of Sajudis, and Seimas deputy); and Saulius Saltenis (a writer, editor of the daily right-wing newspaper, and Seimas deputy).

Other key politicians include Egidijus Bickauskas; Kazimieras Antanavicius; Romualdas Ozolas; Aloyzas Sakalas (professor in physics, chairman of the Social Democratic Party, and deputy chairman of Seimas); Justas Paleckis (a social democrat and member of the Council to the President on Foreign Affairs who also worked in the Central Committee of the Communist Party of Lithuania and received diplomatic training); Valdas Adamkus (a U.S. citizen who holds a government position on environmental issues and is a potential presidential contender).

The above list of politicians generated by the opinion polls and interviews with experts is the starting point of our analysis of the key characteristics of the Lithuanian political elite.

Social background. The majority are of peasant stock. They had to climb the political ladder to reach the upper echelons of power. A small minority of the members of the elite come from educated families.

Education. All of the politicians have higher educations and many hold academic degrees. The most common educational backgrounds are economics and engineering.

The role of the former Communists. The Democratic Labor Party presently in power is dominated by former Communists. They tend to espouse social democratic views. For the most part, the occupations held by the left-wing groups are of intellectual orientation.

The role of the former dissidents. For all intents and purposes, dissidents are missing from the upper echelons of power. Perhaps the years spent in labor camps hurt their educations. Perhaps the personalities of these firm individuals are ill-suited for the positions of top-level politicians who must be able to compromise. Nonetheless, former political prisoners are active in politics: Alfonsas Svarinskas (a priest), Balys Gajauskas, Aleksandras Bendinskas (who represents the left), and Vytautas Skuodis (affiliated with the left). This group has set up a number of political organizations, but their primary focus is on the past.

Lithuanian Diaspora

There are about one million people of Lithuanian origin scattered throughout the world, mostly in the United States. Lithuanian emigrant organizations are thriving. During the restoration of independence, foreign advisors (mostly young people) assisted in the political and administrative bodies and were highly instrumental in diffusing the tension during this difficult and stressful period. Now, there are only a few prominent individuals from the West who have remained in the political arena. These people have not been particularly successful in politics, although it would seem that their education and experience would be major assets. Presumably, they are kept back by a reluctance to give up well-established positions in the United States; an unwillingness to be coerced into either the left- or the right-wing parties; a lack of understanding of the post-Communist reality; and a biased attitude toward local politicians. One exception to the rule is Valdas Adamkus, who is highly influential in Lithuania, notably among the intelligentsia. Surveys conducted in the spring of 1995 ranked him second in popularity as the potential president of Lithuania.

Interrelation Between the Political and the Economic Elite

The term "economic elite" denotes individuals influential in economic decision making at the national level and possessing their own vested economic interests. Economist-politicians are not part of this group unless they are personally involved in big business. The leading businessmen fall into the following categories:

Prominent bankers. In the evolving market economy, lending operations generate the biggest profits. Everyone from the government to small and big-time entrepreneurs need credit. The banks, which sprang up during the initial stage of privatization, represent one of the most influential vehicles of economic decision making. Such bankers as Genadius Konopliovas and Romualdas Visokavicius are well known in Lithuania because of their political involvement (manifest in TV presence and printed texts). They belong neither to the left nor to the right. They are steadfast in promoting conversion to a market economy and argue for a well-balanced policy. Their vested interest is the attainment of social and political stability.

Directors of large-scale Soviet enterprises. While many have gone public, most large-scale enterprises, inherited from the Soviet era, face a major challenge. The prices for inputs have shot up, technologies have become obsolete, and output is difficult to market. Tens of thousands of workers are threatened by possible layoffs. There are some profitable strategic ventures, including the petroleum and fertilizer industries. This group is interested in shielding the domestic market from competition with government aid; receiving subsidies (from the state or guaranteed by the state); maintaining economic ties with the Commonwealth of Independent States (CIS), which is a sizable market for the output of these industries; and acquiring cheap raw materials. Moreover, the people in charge of these enterprises belong to the older generation. It is difficult for them to learn a new language or to switch to a Western-type business mentality. Their connections are in the East; therefore they tend to cooperate with the left. This group has united under the banner of the Industrialists' Association.

Entrepreneurs involved in trade. This is a group of businessmen who have gotten rich fast (by trading in metal, oil, and alcohol). They are genuinely interested in reducing government intervention (taxes, customs, labor laws, and so forth) in the economy. They advocate libertarian notions of laissez-faire. It is not uncommon for entrepreneurs to finance the publication of books (by Friedrich von Hayek, for example), the operation of newly formed institutes (the Free Enterprise Institute), or educational institutions (the Business Academy, where tuition is $40,000 per year).[10] This group supports the Liberal Party (little known among voters) and created the Association of Entrepreneurs.

All three categories of business executives seek to influence Lithuania's economic and political life. However, the bipolar political system predicated upon the attitude toward the country's past coupled with the need to win votes among the not-so-rich majority has forced this group to veil their attempts to influence politics. Their lobbying is geared outside the party at an interpersonal and group level.

Politics and Culture

During the Soviet era, culture was within the nomenklatura's jurisdiction. Cultural figures were part of the propaganda machine and enjoyed considerable clout in the official and public eye. They also had personal, informal influence. Respect for the writers, artists, and actors among the people at large is not puzzling, but I believe it was also evident among the higher strata of society. Perhaps the particular freedom and defiance characteristic of the artistic milieu was missing from the spiritual life of the nomenklatura. In essence, the privileges extended to the artistic intelligentsia by the Soviet regime were sweetened with the very precious opportunity to exercise some form of liberated behavior and self-expression, which few people enjoyed at the time. Among this select group of Lithuanian artists who were truly part of the elite were Vytaus Petkevicius, the person who exposed that same nomenklatura; Jonas Avyzius, who wrote about the postwar tragedy that befell Lithuania; and Vytautas Zalakevicius, the author of the first film that told of the postwar struggle.

The role played by the artistic intelligentsia has changed under the new system. It lost state patronage, and many artists suffered a decline in their standard of living. The most treasured asset—the right to hold a dissenting opinion—has been devalued, for now it is available to everyone in Lithuania. Generally speaking, during the period of transition, artistic merit, the "thought in and of itself," is not in high demand. In the elitist circle of politicians and businessmen, the poet can only aspire to the role of an entertainer. Nonetheless, the political scene in Lithuania does feature many writers and poets, many of whom are members of Seimas.

In 1990, the opposing political agendas split the intelligentsia into two principal camps: Forum for Lithuania's Future (on the left) and the Lithuanian Citizens' Charter (on the right). This distinction—albeit more blurry—persists to this day. Mass media is less polarized (probably because of the liberal essence of the profession). In effect, all mass media has been liberated from government control; it has been privatized and lives off advertisements.

Editors-in-chief of all daily newspapers as well as the directors of television companies are certainly part of the Lithuanian elite. They partake in all prestigious events, possess information about all major deals and political ties, and are well aware of the officials' weak spots. It is probably impossible to "reshuffle" the membership of the government without their direct assistance. If so determined, they can cause a bank to go bankrupt.

The Extent of Corruption

The Soviet Period

For all intents and purposes, the term "corruption" was missing from the Soviet lexicon. Instead we spoke of "the pool," "friends in right places," "rustling up," and "wheeling and dealing." This sociolinguistic phenomenon merits an explanation.

"Barter," but not bribes, was an integral part of the Soviet system. A cozy employment spot could be secured by offering a state-owned apartment, a trip abroad, and so forth. And while the barter represents a more primitive (economically speaking) form of a basic monetary bribe, psychologically it is less prone to being labeled as corruption.

The phenomenon of corruption is associated with the elite rather than the rank and file. During the Soviet era the elite was primarily defined by the nomenklatura "roster" governed by its own unwritten but strict laws. Perks and mutual favors within the clan were commonplace. It seems that what distinguishes bribery is that the "goodies" had to be shared with other clan members. Moreover, transgressions were punished, and punished severely (by expulsion from the party—that is, from the nomenklatura).

There is plenty of evidence to suggest that corruption was not uniformly spread throughout the former Soviet Union. Stratification in the eastern region (that is, the "value" of the various levels of the nomenklatura pyramid), for instance, was more pronounced. In other words, higher echelons of power derived much greater personal benefits from their status than did their counterparts in the western part of the nation. In the western region, a large chunk of "Moscow's bounty" was employed for the good of the country (allocated "funds," opportunities for new construction projects, and so on).

Period of Independence

Once the independence of Lithuania was secured, the term "corruption" became a legitimate part of the Lithuanian vernacular. By the same token, the words "pull," "to rustle up," and "wheel and deal" went into limbo. The fate of these words was sealed by the emergence of market-type economic relations. The expression "through a friend" acquired a different connotation (implying useful information rather than specific goods). The implications of the word "bribe" have not changed, and the term "corruption" is reserved for cases when the privileges turn to illegal activities.

Over the last few years, bribing in Lithuania has become rampant. In a poll conducted in September, 1993, the question "Over the last few years, did you have to give a bribe ('gift') to a police or customs official?" was answered affirmatively (N=1062) by 8 percent of the respondents. The same question with respect to the officials working in the judicial bodies elicited affirmative answers from 7 percent, and with respect to doctors employed by the state-run hospitals or clinics, the figure was 26 percent. Some of the more typical incidents of bribery involve health certificates exempting one from the military draft (for twenty dollars); in Kaunas, 74 percent of the conscripts managed to acquire this health certificate.[11] Customs control is another bribe-infested nest; according to the chief prosecutor, "We could easily put someone in jail everyday of the week."[12] Assessing the extent of corruption among the political elite is even more problematic.

In February, 1994, the newspaper *Respublika* announced a contest: a reward was promised to a high-ranking official (at the level of a minister) who had not been involved in corruption or the abuse of power. Not many people responded to the challenge, and the applicants were subsequently disqualified. The newspaper implicated each one of them in the abuse of power. (See table 7.5.) Interestingly, since the stereotype of huge incomes reaped by the top echelon of power is widespread, the readers expected corruption to be much greater.

Ultimately, the transgressions committed by the contenders did not prove very serious. The reason for this is twofold: first of all, those who responded to the newspaper's challenge were certainly the more honest officials; and second, the extent of corruption is probably exaggerated in the public mind.

Moreover, many violations are hard to prove legally. In effect, not a single case of corruption in the upper echelons of power was ever fully prosecuted. For example, a case involving the chairman of the Bank of

Table 7.5. Experiment Conducted by the Newspaper *Respublika:*
Elites and Transgressions

Elite	Post	Transgression	Newspaper issue
M.V.	Former leader of the free trade unions, deputy	Received a three-room state-owned apartment in Vilna when he became the head of the unions (1990)	29
A.S.	Leader of the social democrats, deputy chairman of Seimas	Used his official car to go shopping	34, 35
K.P.	Former prime minister	Was allowed to purchase Volga automobile at a reduced price	27
V.K.	Former Minister of Public Health	Wanted to privatize his apartment (did not make it in time); wanted to set up and take charge of a department of neurosurgery (did not make it in time); had two official cars assigned to him (one at the ministry and another one at the clinic in another city)	37
G.V.	Former prime minister	Appropriated money from the budget to Catholic church and to right-wing parties and newspapers; received a free European cruise, for which he "paid" by allowing a Canadian advisor to reside in the area of government countryside houses	40, 41

Source: Respublika, February, 1994.
Note: Names of elite were fictionalized.

Lithuanian, R.V., who was charged with lending violations, was suspended; guilt was not proved of the former defense minister who was involved in "shady" operations involving an arms acquisition.

In 1995, charges of corruption within the government and the ruling party were levied daily. Still, not a single high-ranking official has been fired. There is a "white" and a "black" scenario that may help explain this paradox.

In the "white" scenario, the conversion from state ownership of property to private property always produces winners and losers. Flawed and unstable legislation calls for actions that can subsequently be interpreted as an evil scheme (if the results prove bad). Any person involved in decision making can be accused of being corrupt.

In the "black" scenario, all officials in Lithuania by their very nature are prone to corruption and are corrupt. This was particularly true during the reign of the Democratic Labor Party. Its members are bound together by nomenklatura ties; they have a majority in the Parliament; they control the government and the courts, and so have nothing to fear in the way of retribution.

The first explanation is too mild, but it does apply to most cases of corruption. The second explanation, that corruption is impossible to prove because there are forces obstructing the investigation, is too general. But our goal is not to assess the extent of corruption, we merely wish to note that there are two powerful forces in Lithuania that stifle corruption among the political elite: 1) a free press; and 2) the deep animosity between the left- and right-wing political elites.

Standard of Living

The customary lifestyle enjoyed by the former nomenklatura was no secret: there were special stores for the privileged few, government cars, hunting trips, and parties thrown at the public's expense. During the period of restoration of independence, these perks were "blackballed." People thought the lifestyle of the political elite in the newly formed state would not stand out that much, since the average standard of living and culture would be rather high.

The post-Communist reality has proved these notions wrong. The salaries received by the upper echelon of power are both too high and too low (the president's salary is about $750 per month, the minister receives $400 per month, and deputies receive $330 per month). From the standpoint of the businessmen, these wages are too low to live comfortably, thus driving officials to take bribes. Deputies and ministers believe that the private sector would have rewarded their connections and abilities much more handsomely, but they are willing to sacrifice material rewards in order to serve their country. On the other hand, relative to the very low overall standard of living (the average salary being $100 per month), the salaries of top-ranking officials— not to mention "company" cars, trips, and gifts—seem high. The general public believes that politicians strive for power because they want material benefits, not because they care about the welfare of the people.

8

The Ruling Elite of Kazakhstan in the Transition Period

Rustem Kadyrzhanov

One cannot separate a study of post-Communist Kazakhstan's ruling elite from the social context of the transition period during which the country reached its independence in 1991. This context is a complicated and contradictory social reality. The contradiction emerged as an opposing relationship between the reforms of the transition period (declared and conducted by the ruling elite, which was oriented toward the creation of a modern society in the republic)[1] and Kazakhstan's totalitarian and traditional past, which structured the transition period. The social reality of the transition period in Kazakhstan has been formed under the influence of three different yet interconnected factors: the traditional clan and tribal structure of the Kazakh ethnic group; the legacy of the former Soviet social and political system; and the new phenomenon of post-Soviet development in the republic.

Formation of the Elite

The ruling elite of modern Kazakhstan has the character of a typical post-Communist elite in the newly independent states (CIS). For the most part, the conclusions and observations concerning the Russian new elite are also relevant to the Kazakhstan elite. Both formed in the same social and political context at the close of the Soviet period and by the objective forces governing the development of these states in the post-Soviet period.

The transformation process of the Kazakhstan political elite began in 1990. At the union level such transformation began in 1989 in the course of the transference of power from communist party bodies to Soviet government bodies.

Unlike the union center and other parts of the USSR, in Kazakhstan and other Central Asian republics, political changes took place under the stern control of the *nomenklatura*. In some national republics, the local communist parties and their leaders lost Parliament and local Soviet elections along with their ruling status in society. At the same time, a quite different situation was forming in Kazakhstan.

Here, the first secretary of the Kazakhstan Communist Party, Nur-sultan Nazarbaev (as a sole candidate) was elected president of the re-public at the special session of the Supreme Soviet. In almost every area in the republic, all the positions were held by the same people who had held the posts of secretary of a local party committee or chair-man of a local soviet. Nazarbaev explained this as being the result of the high prestige of the Kazakhstan Communist Party and the harm-fulness of an artificial intensification of the separation of power between the soviet bodies and the party, which could have caused diarchy in many regions of the republic.[2]

In 1990, the Kazakh Supreme Soviet was elected by the same scheme that had been used the previous year by the Congress of People Depu-ties in the USSR (that is, through election by territorial constituencies and social organizations). In no other national republic, except Kazakh-stan, were the Parliament elections conducted through social organiza-tions that violated democratic principles. Kazakhstan authorities al-lowed such elections because the deputies from social organizations created an opportunity for controlling both nomenklatura and na-tional representatives in the legislative body.

The liberalization of social life in these years created conditions for the emergence of democratic, ecological, Kazakh, Russian, and other nationalist movements not controlled by the bureaucracy.[3] Neverthe-less, these movements and parties were not numerous and did not evoke any political mobilization of the population. However, realizing the need for adapting to the changing situation, the ruling elite began to use the slogans and phraseology of these movements and parties. More and more, the republican leadership propelled its claims for indepen-dence of Kazakhstan within the USSR, for the redistribution of powers between the union center and the republics, and for the transforma-tion of Moscow's national-cultural policy.[4] In 1989, the language law appeared. This law gave status to Kazakh as the state language and sta-tus to Russian as the interethnic communication language. In 1990, the Kazakh SSR declared its sovereignty. Subsequently, in 1991, there was growing pressure on the union leadership to close the Semipalatinsk nuclear proving ground.

The Kazakhstan ruling elite and other Central Asian elites distinguished themselves as the most procommunist and orthodox. Other national elites began to change their communist ideology to that of titular nationalism.[5] However, because of its nomenklatura nature, the ideological orientations of the Kazakhstan ruling elite were only gradually replaced.

The personnel of the ruling elite had undergone significant changes in the 1980s, during which Dinmukhamed Kunaev, who led the Kazakhstan Communist Party from 1964 to 1986, was replaced by Gennadii Kolbin, who was appointed by Moscow. In 1989, the latter was replaced by Nursultan Nazarbaev. The Kunaev elite was to a great extent "cleared" from power in the course of Kolbin's policy of struggle with "Kazakh nationalism."[6] Nazarbaev "cleared the house" of both Kunaev and the Kolbin elites and moved forward the second line of the old nomenklatura.

At that time, the Kazakhstan ruling elite used populist elements in its policy to support its own reputation as reformist. It broadened the channels of recruitment of personnel to its ranks through elections to the Parliament and by drawing into party and state bodies non-nomenklatura specialists from scientific and art circles.

A new elite group, the business elite, appeared. It was reinforced by representatives who could not hold office in executive bodies after Nazarbaev's dismissal of the Communist Party and by those persons who were authorized by the nomenklatura for entrepreneur activity.[7] The business elite consolidated its position and played a decisive role in ensuring economic privileges: creation of joint ventures, free conversion of check money to cash, privileged credits, operations with real estate, and so forth. These privileges were characterized by Olga Krishtanovskaia as "a privatization of the state by the state."[8]

In the last months of the Soviet Union, the Kazakhstan ruling elite was in a contradictory situation. On the one hand, it demanded more handouts from the union leadership. On the other, Nazarbaev realized that without subsidies from the union center, it would be very difficult to support sufficient life standards for the population. It is no mere chance that Nazarbaev was one of the most active elites in the preparation of a new union treaty and the author of numerous initiatives advanced by Kazakhstan to integrate the collapsing state.

Kazakhstan declared independence on December 16, 1991. It was the last Soviet national republic to do so after the signing of the Belovege Treaty (December 8, 1991) on the dissolution of the USSR. For Kazakhstan, this treaty was a catapult to independence.[9]

The Elite Is the Nomenklatura

Since Kazakhstan became independent, new groups (diplomatic, military, and so on), typical for an elite of any sovereign state, formed their own ruling elite. In part, these groups were reinforced by Kazakhs who worked before in central bodies of the USSR. Nevertheless, the ruling elite's composition after independence did not change.

The revolutionary period for the transformation of the elite in Kazakhstan as well as in Russia ended by 1992. In that year the authority structures of the republic formed—first of all, the executive and the judicial bodies. At the beginning of 1993, the Constitution of Kazakhstan as a sovereign state was adopted, which declared the legality of the three authority branches.[10]

Most of the power, however, belongs to the executive bodies (that is, the president's vertical structure of power and the government). The former includes the oblast *akims* and the *rajon akims*. An akim is the head of an administrative-territorial unit that has the same structure and function as the Communist Party hierarchy. By adopting the structure, function, personnel, and property of the party bodies, the current executive power has retained all the control-levers over society. Moreover, it has retained its nomenklatura nature.

As in the Soviet period, the nomenklatura seeks to strengthen its monopoly of power by controlling the legislative bodies in the center and the regions. In Soviet times such control was realized by the Communist Party; in post-Soviet Kazakhstan, executive bodies are doing this by using different democratic procedures and methods. In any case, both the Soviet and the post-Soviet forms of control over the legislative bodies can be characterized as pseudoparliamentarism, constitutionally and intrinsically nomenklatura.[11]

Attempts at keeping the Parliament independent are being initiated by a non-nomenklatura minority. This minority loses power whenever Parliament is dismissed. This happened in December, 1993, when the executive power used its nomenklatura majority in the Supreme and local Soviets to initiate a dismissal campaign from these bodies at the lower through the upper levels. In March, 1995, the Supreme Soviet, elected one year before, was again dismissed under the pretext of its nonlegitimacy because of violations of election legislation.

During almost all of 1995, there was no active Parliament. The laws were prepared by executive bodies and adopted by presidential decrees that had the force of law. At this time, the political culture of society, retained from Soviet times, was characterized by an underestimation and a lack of understanding of the role of Parliament in the process of state building. Thus, according to a survey conducted in June, 1995, by the sociological service the Hiller Institute in which 1,500 respondents in 94 rural and urban localities were interviewed, only 37 percent of the respondents did not know that there was no Parliament in the state.[12] One can explain this finding as a result of the absence of any crisis in the nation even after two dismissals of Parliament. Hence, it is evident that in post-Soviet Kazakhstan, a parliamentary elite still has not emerged.

The 1995 Constitution (which a lot of people call Nazarbaev's constitution[13]) and the referendum on the continuation of the presidential authority of Nazarbaev until the year 2000 (after the analogous referendums in Turkmenistan and Uzbekistan) have legally established a political system that has shaped the republic. The presidential form of rule declared in this constitution establishes the nomenklatura rule over executive bodies.

This type of rule is characteristic of all countries of the CIS. Comparing opinions of Kazakhstanis (1,000 respondents in 9 oblast centers in various regions of Kazakhstan) on the level of democracy in their country and in Russia, the Hiller Institute public opinion poll in the fall of 1995 revealed that 43.5 percent of respondents believed that there was no difference in democracy in Russia and in Kazakhstan; more than one-third of the respondents believed that the level of democracy in Russia was as high as that of Kazakhstan; 5.2 percent of the respondents held the opposite opinion.[14]

In the former Soviet republics, the problems of democracy have not raised the ire of the people. These societies still have not overcome their totalitarian legacy of strong paternalist emotions. According to the public opinion poll conducted by Elena Avraamova and Iosif Diskin in a number of Russian regions, 64.1 percent of industrial workers (a total of 1,380 persons) and 62.6 percent of the heads of enterprises (out of 99 respondents) believe in a paternalist model for state development. In this model, the state has to manage the economy and protect the entire population.[15] In Kazakhstan, the corresponding figures would not be lower.

The population trusts only themselves when it comes to solving problems. They do not respect those who are in power. Data from the public opinion poll conducted by the Hiller Institute in November, 1995 (in which 1,000 respondents in 9 oblast centers of Kazakhstan were questioned) confirm this lack of respect. According to the poll, 40.7 percent of people believe elites are in power to get richer; 20.7 percent say they are in power for the privileges; 11.8 percent say for the power itself; 5.6 percent say for their own glory; 5.6 percent say to realize their own capacities; 4.5 percent say to benefit the people; 5.1 percent say for other reasons; and 6 percent found the question difficult to answer.[16] This poll demonstrated the population's understanding of the evolution of the ruling elite in Kazakhstan as well as in other states of the CIS during the last decade, namely, the change of power into property.[17]

Paternalist moods in society are expressed through the attitude of the population toward the leader of the state. Data from the public opinion poll conducted by the Hiller Institute in the fall of 1994 (in which 1,200 respondents in 90 urban and rural localities of Kazakhstan were questioned) revealed the varying degrees of the people's trust for President Nazarbaev: 22.3 percent believe completely; 35.9 percent believe mostly; 28.5 percent believe somewhat; 9.7 percent do not believe completely; 1.5 percent do not trust at all; and 2.1 percent found it difficult to respond.[18]

The results of the poll of fifty experts (political scientists, public activists, and journalists) conducted by *Panorama* newspaper and the Republican center of public opinion studies are also of great interest. All experts consider President Nazarbaev the most popular politician in Kazakhstan.

Independent politicians have lesser popularity among both the experts and the population of Kazakhstan. These findings indicate that despite a big number of political parties in the republic, a real plural party system has not yet formed in Kazakhstan. High-ranking bureaucrats who have executive power are at the head of the "president parties," which declare their support for Nazarbaev's course. The oppositional parties face significant organizational and financial difficulties, and they are not able to put forward an influential political figure from their own ranks.

In view of the absence of a plural party system, the system of nomination and appointment to responsible governmental posts cannot be any different from that of the nomenklatura. The nomenklatura system is deeply rooted in Kazakhstan's political system. At the same time, the system itself hinders the formation of a real party system in Kazakhstan.[19]

In the post-Soviet period, those in head post positions are frequently replaced.[20] For example, from mid-1991 to mid-1995, three prime ministers, five ministers of economy, four foreign affairs ministers, and others were replaced. The situation is the same for heads of oblast administrative posts.

This elite circulation is not only vertical but horizontal movement: from executive bodies to the legislative, to the diplomatic elite, to the business elite, and vice versa. The ruling elite is closed for people "from the outside." There is an inner rotation of nomenklatura within the system.

In Kazakhstan, as in Russia, the second, third, and subsequent echelons of the old nomenklatura are recruited into the elite. However, Kazakhstan differs from Russia insofar as the self-reproduction of the nomenklatura (children of nomenklatura bureaucrats becoming members of various elite groups) is more significant.[21]

Despite the preservation of the nomenklatura system of the ruling elite formation in Kazakhstan, it is not completely identical with that of the Soviet period. The present method of cadre recruitment to the leading posts is certainly not perfect, and there are no clear mechanisms for cadre nomination and appointment (so characteristic of the former system). Even though the hierarchic construction of the modern Kazakhstan ruling elite has been preserved, it does not have the same outline and structure as the hierarchy of the party and state nomenklatura. For example, if in Soviet times it was possible to indicate correctly the personnel of the higher leadership of Kazakhstan (the Bureau of the Central Committee of the Kazakhstan Communist Party), today there is no such obvious organ of the state's higher leadership. Hence, it is difficult clearly to define the form of the modern ruling elite in Kazakhstan because the "neo-nomenklatura" is in a period of transition.

Ethnocracy and Clan-Tribal Elite Recruitment

In addition to the principle of nominating and appointing cadres, two other factors influence the formation of Kazakhstan's ruling elite: 1) the bi-ethnic structure of the republic's population, where Kazakhs and Russians are the largest and leading ethnic groups, while other nationalities are classified as national minorities and do not significantly influence the formation of various elites; and 2) the preservation of the traditional clan-tribal structure of the Soviet period in the Kazakh ethnic environment, along with the compatibility of this structure with the nomenklatura principle of the formation and functioning of the ruling elite.

In Soviet times, the questions surrounding the appointment of leading personnel in Kazakhstan were solved, reflecting the bi-ethnic demographic structure, by a parity principle: if the head of a body, institution, or enterprise was a Kazakh, his deputy was without fail a Russian-speaking person, and vice versa. Percentage alignment of leaders on the whole was correlated to the demographic proportions in the population. There were "Kazakh posts" connected to the status of Kazakhstan as a national republic (the chairman of the government, the chairman of the Supreme Soviet, the foreign affairs minister, the president of the republican academy of sciences, and so forth). By the same token, there were "Russian posts" (the chairman of the republican KGB, the leaders of oblasts with a dominant Russian population, such as the Karaganda oblast) in the structure of the nomenklatura.[22]

Consolidation of the Kazakh ethnic political elite and the rise of its competitive capacity led to a gradual change in the balance of Kazakhs and Russians in the party and state nomenklatura to the benefit of the representatives of the indigenous ethnic group. This transition took place from the mid-1960s to the beginning of the 1980s and was connected to the leadership of the republican communist party organization under Kunaev's leadership. The peculiarity of Kunaev's leadership was that he led the national republic with a totalitarian and tough centralized state in a period of its history when, on the one hand, there remained a very strong Russian influence and, on the other hand, the Kazakh nomenklatura had strengthened and increased its claims on power.[23] This contradiction was settled through a gradual, successive change within the parity structure of the Kazakhstan nomenklatura to the benefit of the Kazakhs.

With the rise of influence and the increase in the number of ethnic Kazakh political elites, a confederation *(zhuz)* affiliation of a person appointed to a leading position became more significant. The Kazakhs emerged in the mid–fifteenth century as a result of consolidation to the ethnic groups among Turkic-speaking tribes that inhabited the territory of modern Kazakhstan. These tribes were united into three confederations: Great, Middle, and Lesser. Great Zhuz occupies the south and southeastern parts of Kazakhstan; Middle Zhuz, the eastern, northern, and central parts of the country; and Lesser Zhuz, its southwestern and western parts.

It became more important for the higher levels of the nomenklatura system of Kazakhstan to join the clan-tribal systems and clanic solidarity. Regulation and coordination were necessary because the Kazakh part of the nomenklatura was divided into secretive zhuz groups.

These clan groups supported their members in their struggle for posts in both the regional and the republican levels, competing at the same time with other groups for higher positions in the hierarchy.

Up until 1985, the union leadership sought to regulate inter-zhuz relations in the Kazakh part of the ruling elite. They directed, for example, a representative of a zhuz to lead an oblast in a different zhuz. When Mikhail Gorbachev came to power in the Communist Party of the Soviet Union (CPSU), he apparently decided to oppress these relations. With that end in mind, Moscow dismissed Kunaev and sent Gennadii Kolbin, who had never had any relation with Kazakhstan, to lead the republic.

At that time, Kazakh clan elites grew and strengthened to the point that Kunaev's removal and the anticlan policy of Kolbin, conducted under the slogan of struggling with "Kazakh nationalism," could not weaken the clans significantly. By the end of the 1980s, the general situation in the Soviet Union was characterized by a growth of nationalism that spread to all the regions of the USSR, from the Trans-Caucasian areas to the Baltic.

With its course set on social-economic and political reforms, it was difficult for the Soviet leadership to oppose national elites. In Kazakhstan, this led to a refusal by the union leadership to accept Kolbin's policy. They recalled him to Moscow and appointed a representative of the indigenous population, Nursultan Nazarbaev, to the post of Communist Party leader.

From the very beginning of Nazarbaev's rule, two interconnected trends were strengthened under Kunaev: 1) the domination of Kazakhs among the political elite; and 2) the rise of clan-tribalism in the formation of this elite. The downfall of the Communist regime, the sharp weakening of Russian influence, the rise of Kazakh national consciousness, the sovereignty of Kazakhstan, and the cultural rehabilitation of tribalism created beneficial conditions and advantages for further consolidation of Kazakh clan elites.

National statehood in Kazakhstan and other former Soviet republics created beneficial conditions and advantages not so much for the entire titular ethnic group as for its ruling elite. As a consequence, the political regime of newly independent states is often defined as ethnocratic.[24] The ethnocratic character of the regime in Kazakhstan strengthened as the positions of Russians both in society and among the ruling elite weakened.

The collapse of the Communist system brought about the end of the system of nomination and appointment through the party bodies (the party nomenklatura). The end of this system implied the disappearance of "Russian posts" within the nomenklatura. Many of these posts disappeared along with the Communist regime. Other posts (chairman of the KGB, leaders of oblasts with the dominating Russian population, and so on) have been occupied by Kazakhs.

Further weakening of the positions of Russians in Kazakhstan was connected to the exodus of Russians and other Russian-speaking ethnic groups that began in 1992. From 1993 to 1994, the number of the Russians in Kazakhstan was reduced by 400,000.[25] Among the first emigrants from Kazakhstan were the representatives of the Russian nomenklatura at the higher, republican, and regional levels.[26] During these years, the parity principle of elite formation at all levels began to disappear.

A Sociological Portrait of the Elite

These observations and conclusions are corroborated empirically by sociological data from a study of the biographies of two generations of the Kazakhstan ruling elite, the Kunaev elite of the early 1980s and the present Nazarbaev elite.

However, a methodological note is needed. To analyze the Kazakhstan elite, we employed Olga Krishtanovskaia's method, which she suggested in her article about the Russian elite. When analyzing the transformational processes that the elite experienced during the 1980s, Krishtanovskaia distinguishes three generational cohorts of the Russian elite: cohort Brezhnev, cohort Gorbachev, and cohort Yeltsin. Every cohort is divided into "branch" elite groups, which, despite their differences in various periods, were a basis for comparing structures inherent in certain political functions.

As applied to Kazakhstan, we considered two cohorts of the elite—Kunaev and Nazarbaev. Though Kunaev ruled Kazakhstan until December, 1986, we examined his cohort only in the period from 1980 to 1982. This was the climax of his career and the period in which such trends (in the formation of Kunaev's elite) as the gradual dominance of Kazakhs in the ruling elite and increasing zhuz differentiation inside the Kazakh elite were clearly expressed.

In the branch elite groups, we consider the party-presidential structure as a single unit, even though the Kunaev cohort party structure included the members of the Bureau of the Central Committee and the heads of the departments of the House Committee (a total of 27 people). At present, the president structure corresponds to the party structure and includes the president, the vice president, the head of the presidential administration and his deputies, the heads of the administration departments and corresponding services, and a group of assistants and advisers (a total of 23 people).

In the regional elite of the Soviet period we included the first secretaries of the party oblast committees and the chairmen of the oblast executive committees (40 people). The regional elite during the sovereignty period consists of oblast akims and includes 19 people. Among branch elites of Nazarbaev's cohort we included the diplomatic elite because it is an important sphere for moving the nomenklatura cadres in horizontal and vertical directions. Hence, in total, we have examined 122 people in Kunaev's cohort and 139 people in Nazarbaev's cohort.

Besides using general sociological characteristics such as elite age and education (the characteristics suggested in Krishtanovskaia's methods[27]), we also considered the elite of Kazakhstan in terms of its national composition—Kazakhs, Russians, national minorities, and representativeness of the zhuzes in the Kazakh elite. These additional characteristics are of great importance for understanding the evolution of the Kazakh ruling elite.

In order to define the zhuz affiliation of the Kazakhs as well as other characteristics of members (not only Kazakhs) of Kunaev's cohort, we studied the questionnaires of members, candidates to membership of the Central Committee, and members of the Inspection Committee of the Kazakhstan Communist Party elected into its fifteenth congress in February, 1981. We also studied the biographies of deputies of the Kazakhstan Supreme Soviet of the tenth legislation, which had been elected in February, 1980.[28]

Unfortunately, these questionnaires and biographies did not indicate the place of birth of the person in question. This made it difficult to define zhuz affiliation for Kazakhs as well as those members of the elite who were born in the countryside. We also faced difficulties in defining the zhuz affiliation of those Kazakhs who were born in Kzyl-Orda, Torgay, and Taldy-Korgan oblasts where zhuzes intersect.

To solve these difficulties, we interviewed those people who in the beginning of the 1980s were acquainted with and worked with members of the elite. We had to use this method because access to many documents that included biographies of the former leaders of the republic was prohibited. Though errors may have emerged as a result of such indirect methods, we do not believe such possible errors significantly influenced our findings.

To study Nazarbaev's cohort, we used the book *Who's Who in Kazakhstan*, the first of its kind in the history of the republic.[29] However,

Table 8.1. Average Age of the Elite (years)

	Party-presidential structure	Govern-ment	Regional elite	Business elite	Diplo-matic elite	On the whole
Kunaev's cohort	52.1	54.0	52.0	0.0	0.0	52.7
Nazarbaev's cohort	45.5	47.2	49.1	43.7	51.3	47.6

Table 8.2. Women in the Elite (percentage)

	Party-presidential structure	Govern-ment	Regional elite	Business elite	Diplo-matic elite	On the whole
Kunaev's cohort	0.0	3.6	0.0	0.0	0.0	1.2
Nazarbaev's cohort	13.0	3.6	0.0	0.0	5.3	4.4

a number of politicians who undoubtedly belong to the ruling elite of Kazakhstan, particularly those in the president's structure, were not included in this book. To fill these gaps in our knowledge of the elite, we again used the method of interviewing because our direct requests to appropriate authorities brought no results.

As can be seen in table 8.1, Nazarbaev's cohort is on average five years younger than the previous elite. In those main elite groupings that have decisive influence on the policy of the state—the president structure and the government—one can observe even more rejuvenation, an average of seven years younger. The regional and diplomatic elites have a higher than average age because these elites include many members from the old elite (see table 8.8).

The youngest of all is the business elite. Here the average age is lower because the business elite includes only persons authorized by the nomenklatura for entrepreneur activity (those who were promoted from Komsomol bodies, science, technical intelligentsia, professors of the universities). The business elite also includes some members of the old nomenklatura who moved to business.

As one can see from table 8.2, the ruling elite in Kazakhstan is made up almost entirely of men. This was true under Kunaev and is also true of the Nazarbaev elite. The business elite is also closed to women, though there are many women in small and midsized businesses. Women can be found in the president structure, though they are not in the higher levels of this structure. Women hold positions as presidential assistants and heads of departments. In the government, as far

Table 8.3. Elite Born in the Countryside (percentage)

	Party-presidential structure	Government	Regional elite	Business elite	Diplomatic elite	On the whole
Kunaev's cohort	70.4	72.7	90.0	0.0	0.0	77.7
Nazarbaev's cohort	60.9	60.7	89.5	47.7	63.2	64.4

Table 8.4. Kazakh Elite Born in the Countryside (percentage)

	Party-presidential structure	Government	Regional elite	Business elite	Diplomatic elite	On the whole
Kunaev's cohort	91.7	82.1	100.0	0.0	0.0	91.3
Nazarbaev's cohort	68.8	71.8	92.9	47.4	66.7	69.5

back as Soviet times, there were minister posts "for women": social security and youth affairs. Within the diplomatic elite, there is one woman; she holds the authoritative post as permanent representative of Kazakhstan to the UN.

Like average age, in all elite groups the number of members born in the countryside has decreased (see table 8.3). In the regional elite, this decrease is very small, just 0.5 percent. In the central elite groups—the president's and government's—this indicator has decreased more noticeably and is somewhat lower than for the elite as a whole. This is characteristic of the diplomatic elite as well. These findings are significant for a state that has set its course for modernization of social, economic, and political systems and where the urban population (56 percent) prevails over the rural population (44 percent). If one compares the elites of Russia and Kazakhstan by place of birth, the relative number of those elites born in the countryside is three times higher in Kazakhstan; and for the business elite, the same indicator is two times higher for Kazakhstan.[30]

Overrepresentation of those members of the elite who were born in the countryside confirms our conclusion that, in Kazakhstan, the Kazakh part of the elite is formed on the basis of clan-tribal bonds. One can see from table 8.4 that Nazarbaev's cohort has decreased in terms of rural born Kazakhs as compared to Kunaev's cohort. The number of rural born Kazakhs in the Kazakh sector of the elite is higher than the proportions of rural born of all nationalities in the elite as a whole. This is due to the fact that Kazakhs are a rural ethnic group.

Table 8.5. Elite with a Degree (percentage)

	Party-presidential structure	Government	Regional elite	Business elite	Diplomatic elite	On the whole
Kunaev's cohort	29.6	20.0	12.5	0.0	0.0	20.7
Nazarbaev's cohort	43.5	34.0	10.5	36.4	31.6	31.2

At present, in Kazakhstan, 61.6 percent of Kazakhs are living in the countryside.[31] Thus, the number of rural-born Kazakhs in the Kazakh sector of the elite is higher than all rural Kazakhs in the total Kazakh population. By comparing tables 8.3 and 8.4, one can see that in all elite groups, except the business elite, the proportion of the rural-born Kazakhs in the Kazakh sector of the elite is higher than that of rural-born members of the elite for all nationalities. The exceptionally high percentage of rural-born Kazakhs in Kunaev's cohort corresponds to the low level of urbanity of the Kazakh population in the 1920s and 1930s, when the main part of this cohort was born.

High levels of education are characteristic for most elite groups. The difference between the Kunaev and Nazarbaev cohorts in terms of higher education is insignificant. The level of education in the Nazarbaev cohort is as high as the Kunaev cohort because in the latter there were a lot of people who graduated from periphery institutes of higher education, very often correspondence schools, as well as higher party schools. In Nazarbaev's cohort, many graduated from prestigious Moscow, Saint Petersburg, and other Russian universities as well as the universities of Almaty. Most recently, some members of this cohort have been trained at Western universities, corporations, and banks.

The percentage of the elite with degrees in Nazarbaev's cohort (see table 8.5) is especially high. Nazarbaev seeks to draw intellectuals into working on and compiling the reforms of the transition period. Higher education training is also high for business elites. Many top businessmen emerge from scientific and professorial circles.

The data confirms the well-known belief that the elite of the Soviet period, including the Kunaev cohort, had technocratic educations (see table 8.6). The main part (60 percent) of the members of the Kazakhstan ruling elite had engineering and agricultural educations.

At first sight, this indicator has not changed significantly since the Soviet period. Nazarbaev's elite on the whole has 58.9 percent technical educations. However, one can observe significant differences between Kunaev's and Nazarbaev's elites. The number of technocrats has

Table 8.6. Technocrats in the Elite (percentage)

	Party-presidential structure	Govern-ment	Regional elite	Business elite	Diplo-matic elite	On the whole
Kunaev's cohort	59.3	58.2	62.5	0.0	0.0	60.0
Nazarbaev's cohort	39.1	44.6	100.0	63.6	47.4	58.9

Table 8.7. Economists and Lawyers in the Elite (percentage)

	Party-presidential structure	Govern-ment	Regional elite	Business elite	Diplo-matic elite	On the whole
Kunaev's cohort	3.7	18.2	10.0	0.0	0.0	10.6
Nazarbaev's cohort	26.1	41.1	0.0	18.2	15.8	20.2

been significantly reduced in the central elite groups—that is, those in the governments and especially the president's structure. Moreover, among the regional elite, many oblast leaders were alumni of local pedagogical universities, Soviet-party schools, and so on.

The high percentage of technocrats among businessmen is owing to the large number of nomenklatura technocrats and representatives of scientific and educational institutions, a large part of which are technical. Technocrats are also predominant among the diplomatic elite, which has many former nomenklatura technocrats as well.

In the 1990s, many elites have economic and law educations. Nazarbaev's cohort has twice as many of these educated individuals as Kunaev's cohort (see table 8.7). However, technocrats are still the primary holders of high state posts. The number of economists and lawyers among the central elite groups is low when compared to the number of technocrats with law and economics educations. On the whole, economic and law educations in the current ruling elite are quite scarce for a state that has set its course for market reforms in the economy.

During Soviet times, the elite was close to those who did not have a nomenklatura past. As can be seen in table 8.8, in Kunaev's cohort, there was no one without a nomenklatura past. Only at the end of perestroika (1989–91) and afterwards was there an opportunity for those without a nomenklatura past to gain access to the elite. The best opportunities were in the business elite.

The population is not misled about the origins of the elite. A public

Table 8.8. Elite without a Nomenklatura Past (percentage)

	Party-presidential structure	Government	Regional elite	Business elite	Diplomatic elite	On the whole
Kunaev's cohort	0.0	0.0	0.0	0.0	0.0	0.0
Nazarbaev's cohort	21.7	26.8	10.5	45.5	15.8	24.1

Table 8.9. National Composition of Kunaev's Cohort (percentage)

Nationalities	Party structure	Government	Regional elite	On the whole
Kazakhs	44.4	70.9	62.5	59.3
Russians	48.1	20.0	30.0	32.7
Others	7.5	9.1	7.5	8.0

opinion poll conducted by the Hiller Institute in February, 1996, asked 1,000 respondents in ten oblast centers to answer the question "What, in your opinion, did the upper Kazakhstan business elite do before?" The responses: high-ranking state bureaucrats or party functionaries, 47.6 percent; directors of enterprises, 15.3 percent; *tsekhovik,* or representatives of the illegal economy, 12.5 percent; *vor v zakone,* or criminal authorities, 7.3 percent; Komsomol functionaries, 2.9 percent; scholars, 2 percent; other, 2 percent; difficult to answer, 10.4 percent.[32] For the most part, the current elite consists of those who moved into their power positions from the nomenklatura during the mid-1980s and early 1990s. Very few (less than 10 percent) of Nazarbaev's cohort were in the upper nomenklatura under Kunaev. The current elite comes from the second, third, and successive echelons of Kunaev's nomenklatura. Under Kunaev, they held posts as ministers' deputies, secretaries of cities, or raion party committees, directors of enterprises, and so forth.

Of great importance in the formation of the Kazakhstan ruling elite is its national composition. In Soviet times, especially in the 1950s and 1960s, the Kazakhstan elite were mainly Russians. This situation appeared to change under Kunaev. Kazakhs began to move up into leading elite positions. As tables 8.9–12 show, the party structure contained more Russians than Kazakhs.

In the sovereignty period, the Kazakhs began to dominate the ruling

Table 8.10. National Composition of Nazarbaev's Cohort (percentage)

Nationalities	Presidential structure	Govern-ment	Regional elite	Business elite	Diplomatic elite	On the whole
Kazakhs	69.6	69.5	73.6	86.5	94.7	78.8
Russians	21.7	17.9	15.8	9.0	5.3	13.9
Others	8.3	12.6	10.6	4.5	0.0	7.3

Table 8.11. Representativeness of Kazakhs by Zhuzes in Kunaev's Cohort (percentage)

Zhuz	Party structure	Government	Regional elite	On the whole
Great	41.7	40.0	28.0	36.6
Middle	25.0	48.6	52.0	41.8
Lesser	33.3	11.4	20.0	21.6

elite (see table 8.10). Kazakhs prevailed over Russians and other nationalities in all elite groups, especially within the new elites: diplomats and entrepreneurs. The government retained its national representations at its former level.

Since Soviet times, there has been almost no change in the elite in terms of Ukrainians, Germans, Tartars, Koreans, and others. Thus, the changes in national composition of the elite have occurred as a result of the redistribution of positions of Kazakhs and Russians; Kazakhs increased their representation in the elite by 20 percent, while Russians decreased by the same percentage.

Zhuz affiliation is also of great importance to the formation of the Kazakhstan ruling elite. Taking into account that, in Nazarbaev's cohort, Kazakhs make up about 80 percent of its total staff, one can conclude that this zhuz affiliation is important not only for the Kazakh part of the elite but for the elite as a whole.

Many specialists and nonspecialists believe that under Kunaev the dominant positions in the Kazakh elite included representatives of the Great Zhuz.[33] As table 8.11 shows, the Great Zhuz dominated only one elite group of Kunaev's cohort, but this group was then the most influential in Kazakhstan. In government and regional groups especially, the Middle Zhuz prevailed. The Lesser Zhuz, both in the Soviet and post-Soviet periods, was not represented in the elite. This was apparent especially in the central elite groups—the presidential and the governmental levels. Thus, during the sovereignty period, the main changes

Table 8.12. Representativeness of Kazakhs by Zhuzes in Nazarbaev's Cohort (percentage)

Zhuz	President's structure	Govern-ment	Regional elite	Business elite	Diplomatic elite	On the whole
Great	36.4	60.7	35.7	44.4	41.7	43.8
Middle	45.4	25.0	35.7	22.2	25.0	30.6
Lesser	18.2	14.3	28.6	33.4	33.3	25.6

in zhuz representation of the Kazakh elite have been the result of the redistribution of posts and positions between those who have come from the Great and Middle Zhuzes.

The number of dominant elite positions held by the Middle Zhuz during Soviet times can be explained, perhaps, by their level of Russification as compared to Kazakhs in other zhuzes. The Middle Zhuz occupies territories in Kazakhstan where the Russian population is largest. Though Kunaev, as a representative of the Great Zhuz, preferred his cotribal members, Moscow had the decisive role in cadre appointments. Moscow trusted more Kazakhs from the Middle Zhuz.

In conclusion, the Great Zhuz was dominant in the elite during the sovereignty period, and the Middle Zhuz had the secondary position. The national state of Kazakhstan has strengthened traditional clan-tribal relations throughout society, not only in the political sphere, as was the case in the Soviet period. Such conditions favor the Kazakhs of the Great Zhuz, whose relations are deep and sustain character.

9

The New Elite
in Post-Communist Uzbekistan

William Kandinov

An analysis of Uzbekistan's post-Communist elite not only enables us to understand the processes taking place in Uzbekistan but enhances our ability to forecast future sociopolitical developments in Central Asia. Three key questions must be addressed: 1) Who comprised Uzbekistan's elite under Communism and what were their positions? 2) What is the nature of the new elite and what are their politics? 3) What path will Uzbekistan take in its future development?

The Elite of Communist Uzbekistan

The Uzbek elite felt the effects of general laws that marked the development of the Soviet system. For this reason, the nature and status of the elite in Communist Uzbekistan differed little from the situation of the party-bureaucratic elite in the former Soviet Union. They had the same "ownerless" property, the same power, which was transformed into a commodity, and the same trafficking in power. Matters reached a point where money could buy the post of a high-placed party official, a chief of a regional Department of Internal Affairs, or a directorship of a sovkhoz. At the same time, the specifics of the national and religious mentality, as well as parochial and clan interests that aggravated the acute general-systemic crisis of the former Soviet Union, could not help but make themselves felt in Uzbekistan. One may recall the well-known "cotton affair" of the 1970s and 1980s. It was more commonly termed the "Uzbek affair" in Moscow official circles, with a focus on its specifically national rather than systemic character. The cotton affair meant many billions in stolen rubles for the state; it cost the lives of more than one member of the highest party and economic elite and ruined the lives of many others.

Everything was explained as the moral degradation of individual members of the top party-bureaucratic elite, lapses in educational work, and poor selection and deployment of personnel. Therefore, with the purpose of "normalizing" the situation, in the mid-1980s the republic saw an organized onslaught of the masses of party bureaucrats from the country's central regions. They replaced local functionaries, primarily at the top and middle levels of the party-economic hierarchy. Nonetheless, this did not remedy the situation but rather aggravated it. As a rule these new officials neither knew nor cared to familiarize themselves with local conditions and issues; they had no command of the Uzbek language or any conception of national traditions and customs.

The system sank further into its death throes, and the cotton affair, with its attendant circumstances (viewed against a backdrop of economic crisis), brought about an extremely tense social atmosphere in the isolated region. The situation was exacerbated by the frequent changes in appointments within the republic, the trials of members of the Uzbek elite in Moscow, and the scandalous exposés on the pages of the central press and on television. The underlying causes of Uzbekistan's societal ills were sought not in the nature of what was happening but in the symptoms and their individual manifestations. The essence of the crisis lay in the criminal nature of the system, in the doctrine upon which it was founded, and not on any basic generic, national, or internal flaw in a particular segment of the Uzbek elite.

The dynamics of post-Communist Uzbekistan's embarkment upon the course of civilized development have proven unexpectedly complicated by the absence of clear parameters or theoretical models, and by reliance on methods of trial and error, which have made Uzbekistan's future unpredictable in so many ways. The bridging of this gap and the forecast of possible scenarios represent not only a complex theoretical task but a seriously practical one. For instance, it is presently difficult to say with any certainty what the collapse of the Soviet Union holds in store for Uzbekistan, or what path of development the newly independent state shall take: Will it be yet another variety of totalitarianism, or will it become a democratic society? Will it be symbiotic— authoritarian with attributes of a market economy? Will it become yet another state based on the ideology of Islamic fundamentalism?

The Ruling Elite in Post-Communist Uzbekistan

One thing is clear: the nature of Uzbekistan's development and the direction it takes will be determined largely by the position of the elite, its interests, values, and orientation. However, is it even possible, at present, to speak of the emergence of a new elite in post-Communist Uzbekistan? If we are talking about the highest echelons of the political elite, on a personal and individual level, the answer is most probably no. There has not been a new emergence because the present-day political elite has been recruited (for the most part) from the ranks of the former party bureaucracy. The following is an explanation of "who's who" among the top political elite of present-day Uzbekistan.

Islam Karimov is the president of the republic. He is a fifty-six-year-old career politician who has passed through every echelon of the party *nomenklatura*. Karimov is, by nature, a strict pragmatist with an authoritarian style of governing, convinced of the need for strong executive power; he was an advocate of limiting parliamentary democracy during the period of transition. His university background is twofold—technical and economic, with a Ph.D. in economics. At various stages of his political career, he has held posts as Minister of Finance, chairman of the State Planning Committee, secretary of the Regional Party Committee, and secretary of the Republic's Central Committee of the Communist Party. Until his election as president in 1991, he held the post of first secretary of the Central Committee of the Communist Party. In recent years, he has rehabilitated many of the prominent members of Uzbekistan's political and economic elite who had suffered repression in the 1980s. Among these is Sharaf Rashidov, a longtime leader of the Communist Party of Uzbekistan who, after his death, was blamed for all the wrongdoings in the government.

The president displays extreme vigor and independence in matters of foreign policy. This tendency expresses itself partly in the strengthening of relations with Israel, which elicits a negative reaction on the part of Islamic Iran. Contending for the leading role in post-Soviet Central Asia, Karimov is creating (for the Uzbek political elite) an image of being the most realistic barrier to the advancement of Islamic fundamentalism. It is no accident that the West is coming ever closer to the same understanding of Uzbekistan's role in the geopolitical distribution of power in the region, which significantly raises the international authority of the republic and its leader.

Saidmukhtar Saidkasymov is the minister of Foreign Affairs and a professor with a doctorate in philosophy. Previously a department head in the Tashkent Regional Party Committee, he was later a senior official on the staff of the Central Committee of the Communist Party. Following the outlawing of the Communist Party and the disintegration of the Soviet Union, he returned to Tashkent, where he has made a brilliant career for himself.

Akil Salimov, a minister of specialized higher and secondary education, is a professor with a Ph.D. in engineering. Formerly the secretary of ideology for the Central Committee of the Communist Party, he suffered repression in the mid-1980s and was subsequently rehabilitated. Incidentally, at roughly the same time, an identical fate befell Rano Abdullaeva, Akil Salimov's successor in the post of ideology secretary, as well as the former secretary of the party's Central Committee, Inamzhon Usmankhodzhaev, and Khudoberdyev, prime minister of the republic. One could list others, but it is more important to note that until recently the logic of destruction and self-destruction inherent in a totalitarian system continued to operate at all stages of its existence. The elite was always more vulnerable than its own offspring. The system dealt ruthlessly with its own flesh and blood. This paradox has no historical parallels, neither in scope nor in refinement.

Individuals who had no ties to the party nomenklatura have begun to appear ever more frequently among the republic's top political elite. Yurii Paigin, a Russian who was recently appointed to the post of vice premier of the cabinet, should be included in this category. Previously, he worked as director of the "Uzbektekstil'mash" monopoly. Murad Sharifkhodzhaev, who has recently been promoted to the post of chairman of the State Committee for Forecasting and Statistics, may also be counted among their ranks. He is renowned in the republic as an expert economics scholar, Doctor of Sciences, and member of the Academy of Science. Prior to his appointment to this post, he was the dean of the Tashkent Institute of Finances. Yurii Sharonov, a Russian, recently filled the post of head of "Uzoptbirzhatorg" (Uzbekistan Commodity Exchange; previously, Gossnab). Lerik Akhmedov, a Crimean Tartar, a professional economics scholar, Doctor of Sciences, and professor, has in recent years headed the Ministry of Automotive Transportation. Ruben Safarov, an Armenian, a Doctor of Historical Sciences, a professor, and member of the Academy of Sciences, previously worked as a senior official in the Central Committee's party apparatus. He is also the executive editor of *Pravda Vostoka,* the republic's leading Russian-language progovernment newspaper. Thus, no matter how active the process of indigenization of the ruling elite might be, the multinational structure of the population remains visible in its ranks.

Following the abolition of the Communist Party within the republic, the party elite ceased to exist, but individuals once in its ranks now hold important posts in the presidential staff and in various government structures. There is nothing surprising in this, for there is no realistic alternative for recruiting personnel. It is not difficult to imagine the consequences of restricting access to professions on political grounds. The former political elite had a great opportunity to attract highly trained specialists. For example, in recent years, a substantial portion of the professorate and experienced former economic managers worked in the republic's Central Committee of the party. However, it is doubtful that these people, having found themselves in new circumstances, will be able to free themselves quickly from the load of stereotypes fostered by the old system. While this might complicate the regeneration of society, the old elite, having found itself at the top echelons of government power and having recognized that it has no choice, is indeed evolving. Either the old system will be transformed, together with the changes within the elite and the successful recruitment of new forces, or it will collapse and another will be created, one even more ominous and unpredictable. The legitimacy of such a hypothesis shall be illustrated.

A great deal of the power in Uzbekistan is concentrated in the hands of President Islam Karimov and members of the old political elite, much the same as before. There is only one difference: previously, the pyramid of power culminated in the leader of the party Central Committee's Politburo, whose unquestioned authority extended to all facets of society; today, the power is fully concentrated in the hands of a single person, the president. While two or three years ago, under the influence of perestroika sentiments, the republic still had a few newspapers of opposition orientation, now such dissent, let alone the recognition of any kind of opposition movement or party, is out of the question. Now that the president controls the power structure under the new circumstances, the old party elite with its characteristic mind-set only slightly modifies the trimmings, and continues to act in accordance to the previous command-administrative methods.

It is true that the president and those in his immediate circle, namely, the regional, district, and city leader-elders, as well as those working in the ministries and government agencies, come primarily from the ranks of the old party nomenklatura. The republic lacks a legal opposition, and occasional violations of human rights do occur. For these reasons, Uzbekistan belongs to that category of countries where generally accepted democratic rights are not observed. Thus, according to the well-known independent organization Freedom House, which annually publishes a report on the level of freedom accorded to the press in various countries, Tajikistan, Uzbekistan, and Turkmenistan are listed as not free, with Russia and Kazakhstan listed as partially free.

This issue merits a closer look, beyond surface manifestations and familiar stereotypes. Why is political change ignored with such determination within the republic, even though it inflicts no small damage to the international reputation of the recently established state? Could it be that the political elite is attempting to safeguard its position with the sole purpose of protecting personal and corporate interests, as was previously the case in the Soviet period? We can assume that matters are significantly more complex. The ruling political elite is fully aware that the command-administrative system, which it inherited from the Soviet Union and which continues to function, needs to be dismantled; otherwise, the country has no future. Even a basic instinct of self-preservation requires that decisive measures be taken to ensure that the tragic mistakes of the past do not repeat themselves. But how can the old system be dismantled, and with what should it be replaced? These are questions with no set answers. This problem, metaphorically speaking, presents itself as a system of equations with many economic, social, political, and emotional-psychological variables, each of which, in turn, entails its own complex subsystem. Furthermore, the experience of solving such equations, acquired over the history of civilization, may not automatically be applied to Uzbekistan. This is a result of the particular nature of Uzbekistan's sociopolitical legacy.

Uzbekistan's Economy and the Politics of the New Elite

Before becoming a part of the USSR, the territory of present-day Uzbekistan was a part of the Russian Empire included in the general-governorship of Turkestan. This spanned a period of more than one hundred years, right up to the fall of 1991. The October Revolution of 1917 forced the peoples of this region to experience the bitterness of an artificially induced interruption in the course of their historical development. In place of the czarist great-power and local national elites, which promoted the capitalist relations in the region, came the rule of the characteristically self-reproducing Bolshevik Party–bureaucratic elite.

Uzbekistan, with 21 million people, is the third most populous republic of the former Soviet Union, and also one of the poorest. The system was extremely methodical in depleting the region, so rich in terms of climate and natural resources, to the brink of exhaustion, which created an extremely tense sociopolitical situation. Twenty-five percent of Soviet gold and 60 percent of cotton fiber production came from the republic, which played the role of a raw materials appendage to the Soviet Union. The last two decades saw a steady drop in all socio-economic indicators of development. Uzbekistan increasingly lagged behind not only the industrial nations of West and East but also the vast majority of former Soviet republics. The economic crisis was exacerbated by constant social tension, which was determined by galloping structural unemployment, a drop in the standard of living, and increasing health problems. Matters were further intensified by the ecological situation resulting from a major catastrophe in the Aral Sea region and a serious depletion of farmland.

This was the general socioeconomic situation within the republic on the eve of the collapse of the Soviet Union and Uzbekistan's declaration of independence on September 1, 1991. Achieving political independence did nothing to alleviate the pressures of the social and economic crisis. It had the opposite effect, serving to aggravate the situation. It could not have been otherwise, for the old system continued to exist, and its potential for destruction, complicated by the breakdown of existing ties, mass unemployment, and financial collapse, is well known. Realizing this, the Uzbek political elite adopted a conception of post-Communist development for the state laid out repeatedly by President Karimov.

The ultimate strategic aim of this program was to create a democratic society founded upon a highly developed market economy. The president is still firm in his conviction that this goal can only be accomplished under conditions of public order and with international and social support, which is first on the agenda. While he considers private property to be as legitimate as other forms of property, he opposes moving quickly with privatization, rules out the purchase and sale of land, rejects a program of shock therapy, and insists on the implementation of gradual, stage-by-stage economic reform under strict government control. At the same time, in his opinion, the economic life of society should be free of political trusteeship in accordance with the law. While he views Islam as an important element in man's ethical and moral development, he does not condone religious fundamentalism. Underscoring the particular nature of Uzbek national and religious mentality, the president insists on the need to choose an appropriate path for its movement toward a democratic society, and actively stresses the need to maintain a secular state. The importance of the president's views on this issue become more apparent if one takes into account that religious fundamentalism poses a real threat to Uzbekistan. However, one thing is clear: looking toward the future, the scale will tip in the president's favor only if the republic sees real economic achievements. Otherwise the president might become a hostage to the fundamentalist sentiments in Uzbekistan, the position of which is unambiguous.

Karimov is not against the presence of opposition in society, but under the condition that it be constructive. While he supports Uzbekistan's independence with conviction, he also considers its economic and intellectual interests to be inseparably tied to Russia. Consequently, he has reacted negatively to the exodus of the Russian-speaking segment of the population from the republic. However, it is one matter to examine the declarations and another altogether to see how the policy is played out in real life. In this essay I investigate the nature of words and deeds and the extent to which Uzbekistan's political elite is capable of supporting the birth and development of a new system.

Recognition of the legitimacy of private property on the part of the ruling political elite of the former Soviet Union was one of the most important indicators of a new structure emerging in the very depths of the Communist system. At roughly the same time, the infallibility of the Communist Party was called into question among the ruling political elite for the first time in the history of the totalitarian system's existence, and it was declared necessary to eliminate Article 6 (concerning the leading role of the Communist Party) of the USSR's constitution. These developments, which commenced in Russia, were also echoed in Uzbekistan, but with one fundamental difference. In Russia, the legitimization of various forms of ownership and a new elite were accompanied by the emergence of a diverse assembly of political parties and movements, whereas in Uzbekistan new economic relations and the new elite never challenged the inviolability of the old political elite's position of power. In this connection, the examples of Turkey, South Korea, and China are especially informative. China draws particular attention for its ability to find a compromise between a stringent totalitarian political system and a liberal market economy. Such a symbiosis, considered illogical by the standards of Western sociology, has nevertheless secured a sustainable and high annual rate of economic growth and political stability. It has also done little to harm China's status as a great power. The problems of democracy and a market economy are no less acute for Uzbekistan.

The choice that the Uzbek political elite has made in this matter is clear: new provisional market reforms should be introduced gradually and democratic freedoms should meanwhile be limited. This has provoked disapproval and negative reactions on the part of many countries, among them the United States. An inability to accept the quality of democratic freedom in Uzbekistan is certainly understandable from the viewpoint of Western values, keeping in mind their deep attachment to democracy and, in particular, its individualistic mind-set. However, it would seem that this situation arises from the fact that U.S. public opinion has not sufficiently taken into account (with an objective analysis) the specifics of Uzbekistan. Needless to say, there can be no excuses for infringements on democratic freedoms on the part of the old political elite. But it is extremely important to understand and make sense of the leadership's policies.

The New Elite and the Development of Market Relations

The market is more than a complex economic system that demands the highest standards of professionalism from the ruling elite and a gift for dealing with questions of employment, inflation, taxes, currency, ecology, competition, poverty, and so forth. It is also a reflection of a person's makeup, his capacity to accept the laws of this harsh yet logical system at the level of traditions, customs, values, interests, needs, and wants. In other words, realizing the potential of a market economy is contingent on the extent to which the laws of this system correspond to the people's way of thinking.

The mentality of the Western capitalist society was shaped by a gradual evolutionary adaptation to naturally changing conditions of human activity. It was fortunate to avoid the trials experienced by Soviet society, whose citizens were placed under harsh social conditions. The difficulty of the situation in Uzbekistan lies in the fact that the mind-set of its people hampers their ability to adapt to the new conditions and accept the changes that accompany a market economy. The market includes private property, free enterprise, and free choice, actions determined primarily by self-interest, competition, and a limited role of the government. This is not an easy pill to swallow for someone who lacks the proper background. Special skills and habits are required, and developing these skills cannot be accomplished posthaste.

Uzbekistan has bitterly experienced totalitarianism and an economy that has known the full extent of what is meant by a system of command-distribution. Its people absorbed from birth the benefits of "leveling" *(uravnilovka)* wages contingent not upon performance but upon coming to work. They enjoyed "free" health care and did not know the pains of unemployment. If one also considers that an Uzbek household often has many children, the reasons that the market economy poses many additional and quite complex problems become even more apparent.

The New Elite and the Question of Nationality

The breakup of the Soviet Union exposed additional complex chronic ailments that contributed to the difficulties faced by the ruling elite of the sovereign Uzbekistan. First, acute ethnic conflicts between Uzbekistan and Kyrgyzstan and between the Uzbeks and Turks-Meskhi flared up almost immediately. Blood was spilled in the Fergan and Andizhan affairs, and anti-Russian sentiments grew stronger. Central Asia knew no national boundaries before Russian colonization. States were built on the basis of either dynastic or territorial principles. Under Soviet rule, Central Asia found itself divided in such a way that, given its self-determination, many people belonging to local nationalities now find themselves "aliens" and "foreigners" in the land of their ancestors. The mass exodus of Russian-speaking members of the population is a delicate subject that evokes a negative reaction on the part of the ruling elite. There are many reasons for this, but one thing is certain: this process is grounded in the reality of the situation that does not depend on the will or the conscious decisions of the people or the authorities. There are no reasons to think that anyone has consciously and purposely encouraged this migration (if only out of purely mercantile interests), for it has meant considerable economic losses for the republic. It is more likely that this abnormal phenomenon has its roots in the socialist system, which, with its planned economy and ownerless property, perverted the nature of ethnic relations. Under these conditions, a person's nationality could determine whether he or she would enjoy advantages from birth or be stigmatized for life.

At the social level, a directive economy provided the material basis to pit nations and nationalities against each other. It neither could nor desired to take into account ethnic economic interests, national–cultural specificity, and working traditions. Rather, it was assumed that the "center" knows best and that all should submit to the interests of the state as a whole. For these reasons, the question of who feeds whom arose in the Soviet Union and all its republics, which were being branded "dependent parasites" and chronic "debtors." Moscow considered Uzbekistan among this group, causing great resentment among Uzbekistan's political, scientific, and cultural elite. With time, particularly in the years of Gorbachev's perestroika, this resentment manifested itself in open official protest.

Going by Soviet statistics, one would be hard-pressed to show a link between a person's standard of living and the work he or she put in. Furthermore, it turns out that by raising legal, half-legal, and illegal redistributions to the level of common occurrence on a national scale, those republics that, according to these statistics, worked better were worse off, and vice versa. Vakhab Usmanov, a former minister of the Uzbekistan cotton-refining industry who was later executed in connection with the "cotton affair," characterized one of the mechanisms of this phenomenon in the following fashion: During his imprisonment at Lefortovo, he told his cellmates that the fate of the Soviet economy was not decided in Gosplan but in baths, restaurants, and country villas. Furthermore, all kinds of favors cost less in Moscow than in Central Asia. For example, a couple of gold trinkets given to the USSR Ministry of Light Industry, which directly oversaw the minister and his entire ministry, allowed for favorable changes in the plan registry. This reduced the plan deductions earmarked for the state treasury by millions. A great deal of direct and indirect information reflects the operation of this mechanism of redistribution at the national level; the information lurks in the statistical abstracts *The National Economy of the USSR* and *The National Economy of the Uzbek SSR,* as well as in certain other sources.

In other words, the economic policies of the old party-bureaucratic elite endorsed the development of nationalism at the state level, and this, following the collapse of the Soviet Union, nurtured bloody ethnic conflicts. Thus, the legacy that the former empire left to Uzbekistan is quite complex, and a multitude of various factors needs to be set in motion in order to overcome the past and bring the republic out of stagnation. This process is entirely contingent upon a consistently maintained backdrop of ethnic peace and public order. For this reason, sovereign Uzbekistan's ruling political elite are afraid of being drawn into internecine clashes and interethnic conflicts; they react poorly to actions on the part of the opposition and anxiously watch the events unfolding in neighboring Tajikistan and Afghanistan, where conditions are not conducive to stability in the region.

An important question arises. Should the ruling political elite of Uzbekistan sacrifice its country's social tranquillity in favor of generally accepted democratic principles? This question might seem improper, but its relevance can hardly be doubted. Obviously the post-Communist development of sovereign Uzbekistan, together with all of post-Soviet Central Asia, will be characterized in the foreseeable future by the breakdown of the old administrative-command system and the development of market relations, but with inescapable, objectively necessary restrictions placed on democratic freedoms. No matter how attractive democratic principles might be, an unbiased examination of the current situation will show that the development of democracy here is not an instantaneous, directive, and willful decision but a long and complex evolutionary process.

Sociological studies dealing with differences in the national mentality of Uzbeks and Russians, as well as many years of my own personal observations, indicate that while Russians display a marked preference for democratic forms of management on the part of administrations, Uzbeks are rather inclined toward an authoritative style of management within a collective. For Russians, the authority of management often depends more on practical qualities, while the Uzbeks prefer a priori authority in order to grant managers and administrators high status. Russians are typically prepared to criticize the administration; Uzbeks tend to strive for leadership within the collective. There is also, among the Uzbeks, a strong sense of traditional respect and honor for elders. This greatly influences the nature of relationships not only within the family and the workplace but within society as a whole. While these considerations should not be taken as absolutes, they may nevertheless serve as food for thought within the context of this investigation.

All of this requires subtle, well-thought-out action and, of course, time. Only time can transform a man's soul, his consciousness, and his stereotypes, deformed by seventy-five years of totalitarian rule. As the position of the market economy becomes stronger and the economic elite grow in both quantity and quality, the material basis for democracy will broaden. A new type of person will emerge, one who is law-abiding and tolerant of dissenting opinions, wealth, and the financial success of the diligent and fortunate business class. In this way, the feeling of envy, so deeply rooted in Soviet society, will be replaced by an inner desire to follow the example of the energetic entrepreneur, to outperform the competition, to attain better results, to show one's abilities and to realize one's potential. This will serve as a catalyst for the progress of a market economy. This will be the source from which the new economic elite in post-Communist Uzbekistan will emerge and develop. Let us consider the dynamics of development of the new elite.

The New Economic Elite

The euphoria that gripped the ruling political elite of Uzbekistan upon its declaration of independence is gradually waning. The achievement of political sovereignty has failed to alleviate the strain of economic difficulties; rather, it has intensified it. Everything turned out to be much harder than it seemed at the outset. Wealthy investors are not rushing to Uzbekistan with their money, although the country's political elite does quite a bit to attract foreign capital. For example, the republic periodically either abolishes or modifies taxes and tariffs on imported goods. Favorable conditions are created for transferring profits by either juridical or private persons out of the country. Encouraging in this respect is President Karimov's decree signed January 21, 1994, sanctioning denationalization and privatization and removing limits on the import and export of foreign hard currency and of Commonwealth of Independent States (CIS) banknotes for both the citizens of Uzbekistan and foreigners.

However, things are not so rosy. The complexity of the situation lies in the fact that these generally positive developments, which are gaining momentum within the republic, cannot help but feel the pressure of the contradictory interests of the ruling elite, which is heterogeneous in its makeup, its social status, its income, and its attitude toward property. Under these circumstances, the elite will undergo differentiation. Its more active, younger segment, confident in its abilities and professional skills, will consciously embrace the new rules of economic conduct. The new approach promises this group quite a few advantages and the ability to satisfy their ambitions. The other segment, associated with the long-entrenched method of administration under the old regime, possessed, and still retains, quite a few privileges. It still manipulates "ownerless" property, and, most important, it has tasted power. Most likely, it does not want nor will it be able to adapt painlessly to the new circumstances.

For example, the ruling political elite presently finds itself in a contradictory situation. On one hand, it does not own property, it still retains great power, and thus it is not interested in market forms. On the other hand, realizing the futility of this approach, the political elite is certainly interested in dismantling the old system. Nonetheless, its pressing concerns require it to check the pace of market reforms. Otherwise, in losing power, they will also lose their material well-being and social status. Under these circumstances, the role played by personal power is very great, and it is largely the guarantor of market reforms in Uzbekistan. Apparently, this is one of the weak links in the process that is taking place, since personal power, no matter how great, cannot take the place of legally underwritten reforms. Consequently, there is a pronounced tendency for the political and the economic elite to grow closer with newly emerging entrepreneurial structures. This certainly harms society, since bribery, abuse of power, and corruption becomes rampant. But this process is grounded in reality. As they recognize that there is no going back to the way things were, members of the ruling elite seek points of departure by shifting to new positions and adapting to the changing conditions.

The nomenklatura segment of the old economic elite finds itself in a similar predicament. This segment is the so-called director corps, which includes the heads of industrial, construction, and transportation enterprises as well as the heads of state and collective farms. Because old economic ties were disrupted by the collapse of the Soviet Union, this segment of the old economic elite has found itself in a very difficult situation. It lost the well-being, founded upon the command-distribution system, it previously enjoyed. This segment of the old elite cannot help but remember the past with a sense of longing. Even as these people receive a certain measure of economic freedom and feel the great potential that it possesses, they take on a great deal of responsibility and risk. In the past, the risks were taken at the expense of the government. Today, risk taking is often a determiner of personal well-being. To resign oneself to this position and to transform one's way of life presents psychological difficulties, not to mention the very real social and economic obstacles.

Under privatization, the owners of the republic's light industry enterprises, which account for more than half of all industrial output, fully understand that this industry's technology is hopelessly behind today's demands and impedes the manufacturing of modern and competitive products. The owner can no longer afford to just fill a warehouse, as was often the case in the past. This is not the only difficulty that checks the process of denationalization of property and discourages the old economic elite from entering into entrepreneurial activity. In the course of our study, which took place in 1992, we interviewed thirty-seven top-level officials within the republic's Ministry of Trade, including heads of various departments and directors of large state stores. These people, who represent the old trade elite, have worked in this system for many years and are well acquainted with its shadier aspects. Having been, so to say, "through thick and thin," they are all aware of the need for the privatization of trade. Nonetheless, only one in six would (at the time of the interview) be willing to invest personal funds or take out a government loan in order to organize a private enterprise. At the same time, more than half (56 percent) said that they would be willing to take this step but consider it sensible to wait for a more conducive environment. The rest (31 percent) were not prepared to take such a step.

The most significant obstacle that discourages these people from organizing private businesses is the lack of trustworthy laws to guarantee the rights of private entrepreneurs. This is the same reason that prevents former citizens, who had emigrated to the West in the last five to twenty years and achieved significant financial success, from investing their capital in Uzbekistan. Furthermore, 20 percent of the respondents also feared the responsibility and risks involved with becoming private entrepreneurs because of the high chance of bankruptcy owing to competition from state organizations and the mafia. Relatively few respondents (9 percent) mentioned market saturation or the fear that a change in power would bring about a return to the past and the repression of private businesspeople. In my opinion, this point is very important. Apparently, the idea of there being no way to return to the past is becoming securely fixed in the minds of the economic elite. Public hostility toward the business elite turned out to be the least significant (4 percent) concern of the entrepreneurs.

About one-third of those surveyed believed that civilized conditions for entrepreneurial activity will emerge in Uzbekistan in the next six to ten years; 13 percent are counting on three to five years, and 9 percent project one or two years. However, 42 percent think that such conditions will come no sooner than ten years, and almost 5 percent are inclined to believe that such a time will never come. It should be emphasized that despite many difficulties, obstacles, and doubts, private enterprise has been increasingly taking root in Uzbekistan in the last two to three years, particularly in the trade-broker domain. There has been an extensive and growing network of private stores since the process of privatization has commenced. Moreover, according to the results of a 1993 survey of 440 randomly selected individuals, the social support enjoyed by entrepreneurship and, consequently, by the new economic elite within the republic is quite encouraging. Every third respondent under age twenty-five saw opening a private business as the most dependable way of ensuring a suitable life for himself and his family. This number was only half as high for those over forty-five. Only one out of every ten respondents opposed private property as such, and one-third of those surveyed regarded themselves personally unsuited to entrepreneurship.

Uzbekistan is a republic with ancient religious traditions, and presently its people are expressing a great interest in religion, Islamic customs, and rituals. In connection with this, it is interesting to characterize Islam's attitude toward entrepreneurship and trade. Many suras in the Koran teach people to imbue their business dealings with a sense of honesty and decency. In the Kabusnam, a distinctive compilation of

Islamic ethical foundations written in the eleventh century, there are special sections dealing with how to attain wealth, how to conduct trade, how to build relations with business partners, and how to resolve financial difficulties with family and friends. These writings, interesting in and of themselves, are relevant today in shaping the ethics and psychology of entrepreneurial activity.

Sociological studies that look at the specific national characteristics of Russian and Uzbek mentality record an interesting trait. Whereas Russians tend to be oriented toward work in industry and construction, Uzbeks prefer trade, restaurants, and agriculture. Uzbek women are less inclined to work in the public sector than men. In these spheres, even under Soviet rule, there were many more opportunities to display the individual enterprises and commercial aptitudes that are so vital for conducting a market economy.

The New Elite and Democratic Prospects

For the past three or four years, there has been a move fundamentally to reevaluate the entire system of education and professional training. Practically none of the universities have retained the old program of study. Marketing and management textbooks written by top Western specialists in these fields have become standard among the students in Uzbekistan. Hayek and Friedman are well known in university auditoriums, where one may also frequently encounter foreign professors teaching lecture courses on various aspects of market economics.

A large number of young and educated people from the republic receive a higher education and undergo practical training at universities in the United States, Western Europe, and Turkey. These young people are most likely the prospective pool from which the new political and economic elite of Uzbekistan will be drawn.

How may one characterize Uzbekistan's new economic elite socially? The results of a study I conducted in 1993 offers a partial answer. This study involved a survey of 105 specialists from Tashkent, representing heads of government enterprises; joint ventures with varying forms of property, commercial structures, and cooperatives; those employed at the exchange and agent-broker offices; and owners of private stores. Of these, one-third were between the ages of 25 and 29, almost half (47 percent) were 30–39, 9 percent were 50–54, and 7 percent were under 25 years of age. Uzbeks compose almost three-quarters (74 percent) of the economic elite (of which women make up 17 percent), 7 percent are Russian, and 5 percent are Armenian. Tartars, Tadzhiks, Koreans, and Jews each make up 3–4 percent, and Ukrainians, 2 percent. Forty-three people stated that they were former members of the Communist Party.

It should be emphasized that many Russians belonging to the old economic elite still hold key positions in the economic spheres of post-Communist Uzbekistan. Among them are the directors of such major organizations as Tractor, the Almalyksk Mining-Metallurgic, the Bekabavdsk Metallurgic, and the Pod'emnik concerns. The overwhelming majority (92 percent) of those surveyed had received a higher education, with 11 percent holding higher degrees; the remainder have an uncompleted higher or secondary technical education. A high level of education does not automatically imply that members of the new economic elite possess a high level of expertise in operating a business, since many of them presently lack specialized knowledge and experience in the areas of marketing, banking, price setting, and so forth. All started either with a clean slate or, more commonly, with their economic thought already shaped by the administrative-distribution system of economic management. Interesting in this respect is the self-evaluations of the experts surveyed. Fifty-seven percent of those surveyed said they consistently feel the lack of knowledge in their field, and 21 percent emphasized that their level of expertise was entirely insufficient to run a modern enterprise. Only 22 percent of the survey participants considered themselves to be sufficiently competent in the field.

The next point is worth emphasizing, for it is indicative of a significant characteristic of the system of values governing Uzbekistan's new economic elite. In responding to the question, "Do you take the nationality of business partners or employees into consideration?" three out of four of those surveyed replied that they accord primary value to expertise, professional qualification, and the ability to achieve results, rather than to nationality. This approach to the issue is comprehensible, even natural. After all, business is business. At the same time, 15 percent of the businessmen noted that a business partner's nationality, while not decisive, does make a difference, and 10 percent indicated that they prefer doing business with members of their own nationality. This suggests that as market relations make headway into Uzbekistan, the social base of entrepreneurship widens, and the financial position and authority of the new economic elite gains momentum, the tension of interethnic conflicts will weaken and the old economic sources of nationalism and chauvinism will begin to fade.

10

The Ukrainian Political Elite
Its Features and Evolution

Nikolai Churilov

The formation of the Commonwealth of Independent States (CIS) and the subsequent disintegration of the country along national-administrative lines were two of the consequences of the USSR losing the Cold War. Ukraine's independence was achieved after the breakup of the Soviet Union but was also the result of an extended struggle by the Ukrainian political elite for independence. The national elite of other new states lacked specific strategies and tactics for moving toward independence and, consequently, resorted to ad hoc policies, which had a superficial declarative character. Many condemned the communist doctrine of the past by lowering the Soviet flag and imitating the ideology and basic features of Western governments. Under these conditions, the strategic trend among the elite of all newly formed states, including Russia and Ukraine, was to imitate the West, ostensibly to further their integration in the world community. A situation developed where the national intelligentsia and political elite pushed hard to achieve quickly the standards and norms characteristic of modern, highly developed states while ignoring the history and logic of their achievements. History teaches us that pursuing such goals requires ruling with an iron fist in order to build the institutions for which the social and political preconditions in the country do not exist.

The consequences of such policies include an increased level of social conflict, which may seriously hinder efforts to build new political structures. Some examples of social conflict are the Islamic revolution in Iran; the wave of Islamic fundamentalism in Middle Asia, formerly part of the USSR; and the increasingly strong and popular nationalistic trends in Russia today. Currently, such are the conditions in Ukraine, but in a more latent state. Ukraine has no shortage of social conflict, traditionalism, and isolationism.

The Young Ukraine Is a State Without a Political Elite

After achieving independence and sovereignty in 1991, Ukraine appeared to be the largest country in the world without a political elite. The Ukrainian political elite did not meet the standards of the modern political elite found in Western nations because of a number of circumstances: the level of political consciousness of the early Ukrainian establishment, its legislative system and general legal culture, the character of its professional experience, and its differences from the power characteristics and other elements that characterize the modern political elite of the West. More likely, this is a type of proto-elite that will be transformed over time by its new power structures, organization, and institutions. The alliance now in control consists of former "party bureaucrats" and political dissidents. This alliance cannot be considered elite by virtue of the fact that they are orientated toward serving the state instead of society.

The first group of state politicians can be referred to as the "verbal leaders." This group came to power with the help of their ability to speak convincingly. After achieving power, they piously believed in this ability and considered its force absolute. Their primary political activities consisted of discovering a critical discourse on the past, arguing with their opponents, and interacting with the electorate. At this turning point in history, society needed people who were capable of replacing the old myths and slogans with an appeal to a new ideology. Accordingly, the ruling political clique consisted of people such as the professional ideologists Leonid Kravchuk, the writer Dmitrii Pavlichek, and former dissident-journalist Viatcheslav Chornovol. However, good political leadership cannot be reduced to political recitation, just as an actor's art cannot be reduced to good articulation. Consequently, the "verbal leaders" who failed to master a whole range of political action (and, by the way, did not aspire to this) quickly lost whatever political clout they had. These leaders failed to build a new efficient economy and social structure, but they did manage to build new mythologies and ideologies.

The first leaders of independent Ukraine often credit themselves for the creation of an independent, sovereign state. Some think it is fair to say that Kravchuk, Ivan Plushtsch, Chornovol, and others, played absolutely vital roles in establishing an independent Ukraine. More likely, this is an overvaluation of the part played by the first level of leaders.

Among the members of the CIS, movements for independence progressed at equal rates, simultaneously and hence, objectively. New leaders did not have the power to hinder or advance the construction of new sovereign states.

Obviously, the leaders were not in control of the processes of state formation. Actually, it was the process itself that determined the actions and perceptions of the leaders. The leaders did not control the people, nor did they produce or implement a strategy to end the crisis. Instead, they adapted to each situation and attempted to explain what was happening. Based on their perception of the populace, they simply tried to express the chaotic and gloomy emotions the people were feeling. Unlike the skilled leaders of a modern political elite, these leaders failed to anticipate, codify, direct, or incite the interests of significant social groups. During the election campaign in 1994, it became clear that the country could not survive with the type of leadership provided by the "verbal leaders." The "verbal leaders" either left politics altogether, or tried another form of activism as *politruks* (officers for political education). They became advocates in the political arena, choosing to support various interest groups or forms of government.

Based on sociological studies conducted in 1994–95, Ukrainians widely recognized the ideologists' slogan "radical integration in Europe" as false. Based on their experiences, Ukrainians perceived their country not as a democratic society based on the European model but as a dictatorship similar to that of Latin American countries, characterized by sharp social contrasts, violence, a mafia-type elite, and widespread corruption. Hence, the initial conditions under which the new president, Leonid Kutchma, took power were not favorable.

First, proclaiming his liberalism, the president began distancing the state from managing social changes and the transformation to a new free-market economy. The state had lost control of its holdings and turned over complete control to the bureaucratic and regional offices. Populism, political intrigue, and incompetence were rampant at top levels of government. Second, according to the best data available, the laws adopted by the new congress (the Supreme Soviet of Ukraine) for regulating the national economy failed. These laws imitated those of the West and reflected the social and economic relations inherent in the Western market, relations that did not exist in Ukraine before or after independence. As a result, a discrepancy formed between the new legislation and real economic practice, with the black market gaining a strong foothold.

Third, the black market promoted violence, the criminalization of society, and the destruction of traditional morals and values. As a result of this and a number of other circumstances, such as imperfect credit and financial systems, the unbalanced economy, inflation, the significant increase in unemployment, and the manufacturing decline, the masses became discontent. The Ukrainian elite formed under extreme conditions.

The Formation and Structure of the Elite

Members of the current Ukrainian political elite lack the abilities of Western politicians who are able to integrate features of their identity (ethnic, racial, gender) with experiences outside politics and education. Today, Ukrainian politicians exhibit the obvious brand of their particular "guilds" (profession, social group, region). Let us consider when and under what conditions particular types of leaders assume power.

Leonid Kravchuk. His declared goal is the creation of new explanations, simplifications, slogans, appeals, and a new political language that replaces "building of Communism" with the key idea of waking up the Ukrainian state. In ancient times, this role was filled by shamans, priests, and cardinals who led their tribes, nations, and countries through tumultuous and dark periods. They helped people by describing their place in society and by giving them a sense of psychological well-being.

Leonid Kutchma. He considers his main mission to be the direct management of state. He is the leader of his tribe. He is also the head warrior. While he despises shamans, he must observe their rituals in order to maintain his power. It is ironic that, at one time, Kutchma was subordinate to Kravchuk and asked him to provide some kind of doctrine.

Ivan Plushtsch. His mission is to establish patriarchal-paternalist methods of management at the highest levels of government, methods characteristic of undeveloped agrarian economies. This type of leader is, to some degree, similar to the chairperson on a collective farm in Ukraine or a landowner in Sicily. The instruments of power are personal connections, knowledge of subordinates and the governing system, mutual favors, services, relationships, and favoritism. This leader dreams of inserting the model of governance used on collective farms (kolkhoz) into politics. He does not dream of making collective farms live under the principles of a particular political system. However, as the reality of political life in Russia and Ukraine demonstrate, such political leaders are unwanted by society.

Vladimir Lanovoi and Victor Pevzenik. Their mission is to create good economic, humanitarian, and other programs that solve problems thereby causing social reformation and prosperity. These leaders are distinguished by their conviction that if there is "a good program," then a marked improvement in the situation is possible in the near future. Thus, social problems are solved under specific conditions that are difficult to achieve. The politician-tutors are members of the elite under ideal social conditions. They are constantly visible and highly regarded for long periods of time, but their influence on the political process is disproportionately low.

Valentin Babitch. This is a new type of leader in Ukraine. In the previous Soviet Supreme and the president's administration, there were politician-businessmen who were able to create their own capital with the help of the bureaucracy in a totalitarian state (not in a free-market economy). They made their fortunes by creating their own "businesses" while using their powers to gain access to vital information and to disrupt any would-be competitors. These leaders did not advocate implementing business principles into politics but did attempt to impose their own interests on politics. Babitch became a political figure by purchasing opportunities, not by selling them. This is what distinguishes him from other businesspeople.

Konstantin Morozov. He almost won a role during the struggle for leadership but was unable to break into the big show. His message and his method fit his personality: clear and simple discipline and order (select those whose integrity is beyond question). That this type of politician was unpopular testifies to the fact that the main electorate does not agree with military methods of problem solving.

Alexander Moroz. He has a leftist orientation similar to that of professional politicians in the West. He tries to integrate (though not always successfully) the ideological functions of Kravchuk with the management skills of Kutchma. However, he needs Western experience in order to manage the country indirectly by using the rule of law rather than by making declarations and decrees.

The recent victory by politician-manager Leonid Kutchma is evidence of the formation of a political clique in Ukraine. The qualities that characterize these "[former] directors" [of Soviet factories] are a readiness to follow orders, a readiness to take personal responsibility, the skill for creating a hierarchical management system, the use of an "urban" or "factory" system of management (that is, depersonalized management versus using persuasion and promises), and a cynical attitude toward ideological arguments.

The Formation and Structure
of the Primary Regional Elite

Members of Ukraine's modern political elite are better understood if one considers their professional experiences, skills, and other activities rather than their political perspectives. Russian policy can be understood and predicted by analyzing the perspectives and potential actions of Moscow's central political elite. On one hand, clans such as the Arbatovs and the Gromikos constantly place their own people at the highest levels of power. On the other, smooth-talking provincial politicians, like Boris Yeltsin, are advised behind closed doors by numerous consultants and assistants.

The situation is different in Ukraine. Before the breakup of the Soviet Union, Kiev was a place where few if any politicians or activists had successful careers. Kiev was a stepping-stone for provincial leaders on their way to Moscow. But just before independence the situation in Kiev began to change. Kiev was transformed into a battleground for political power. The combatants included the local elite (some coming from the capital), clans, dynasties, and representatives from different regions. In other words, the struggle for center stage included political leaders and regional groups.

Regional representatives had the best opportunities for advancement in the political arena because they managed to capture the support of their constituents by uniting them with the right idea at the right time. So, the ideas of Ukrainian independence, sovereignty, and nation revival, to a greater degree, were promoted in the western part of the country by appealing to the people's rationality, emotions, and religious sentiments. Accordingly, the politicians in the western region of Ukraine were either more skillful or better able to express their ideas. Because they were professionals who effectively represented and backed their national idea of sacrifice, they were recognized as jealous experts of the national idea's righteousness and purity; they easily forced back the representatives of Central and Eastern Ukraine.

Their rise to power came as a result not so much of their abilities as of the merit of their ideas in the context of pro-Western sentiment.

Ideas, systems, and relations from the past returned in 1994. Again, concerns for social security, restoring economic ties with Russia, and the rising crime rate gained prominence. These concerns already had more importance than the idea of national independence. After Kutchma took control from the city of Dnepropetrovsk, he brought politicians from his home region to Kiev and gave them key posts because the eastern region was industrial and "proletarianized" and was where these concerns were initiated.

Furthermore, the power of "eastern" representatives in middle-level positions quickly increased. The regional elite, having made its way to the highest political posts, began systematically to eliminate representatives from other regions even if that elimination served no political purpose. There is a serious division in the political elite of Ukraine between the insiders and outsiders. This division is based on place of birth, residency, education, and upbringing. These factors frequently play more important roles than even professional and business relationships. This rivalry among the Ukrainian political elite is regionally restricted and is not present in southern Ukraine, including the resort districts in Crimea and Odessa. In these areas, new ideas such as hedonism, personal success, cosmopolitanism, and individualism have been imported, but there is little demand for these ideas among Ukraine's electorate. Accordingly, "the southerners" are almost completely missing from the modern central elite. In time, the situation may change. It is possible that the "eastern coloring" of the political ruling clique could be replaced by a "southern" hue.

A Functional Evaluation of the Abilities of the Forming Elite

Currently, the functions of the traditional political elite are fairly obvious. They have been well described and analyzed by both politicians and political scientists. Shifting our attention to the modern political elite of Ukraine should prove interesting and heuristically valuable. It will allow us to evaluate the elite's opportunities to develop more power. Following are discussions of the management styles being considered by the political elite.

With *direct management,* the objective is to control the main spheres of economic, political, and social life. Control is maintained through a system of the laws but includes decrees and personnel choices. Currently, the predominant politician-manager is very capable of filling this role, though there is a tendency to favor the management style that is characteristic of the state-bureaucracy. Nevertheless, the initiation of this management style should produce greater efficiency in management.

The objective of *coordination and integration* is to coordinate the efforts of various departments by prioritizing state problems. One example is coordinating the activities of different organizations for the potential use of force (Ministry of Defense, Ministry of Home Affairs, Special Services); another example is the accumulation of data and information regarding different choices for economic policies. Members of the current ruling elite are not prepared to coordinate government efforts because they are not unified by a common perspective or goal.

Sociological data indicates that there is little agreement among the Ukrainian elite on essential issues such as nuclear disarmament, Ukrainian-Russian relations, the "Crimean question," and the Black Sea fleet. Therefore, we cannot expect efficient and coordinated action or swift policy development from the fragmented elite. Moreover, the thinking of politicians in the past is best characterized as confrontational and fragmenting, not coordinating and integrative. The reorientation of political thought will be a long and painful process.

Policy review is the examination of political activities that are potential threats to the nation. The current elite has the ability to complete this task satisfactorily. However, the elite cannot be trusted to place the good of the country ahead of their own personal aspirations.

Decision making is the process of choosing the best course of action by examining various projects, analyzing political and administrative options offered by various departments, and developing policies for the realization of national interests. The elite's decision-making abilities are very poor because they lack the analytical skills necessary for modeling processes and understanding scientific search.

Forecasting and planning is the preparation of political doctrines, strategies, actions, and policies. Preparation includes analysis of potential outcomes and consequences for the short and long term. This is probably the current elite's weakest point because they are primarily interested in short-term political and economic gains.

The goal of *policy support and implementation* is to create favorable conditions (social, psychological, and financial) for the implementation of public policies. The modern elite is very capable of performing both of these tasks. There are a number of talented advisors to Leonid Kutchma who are noted for their skills in this area, including D. Tabachnik, A. Volkov, and P. Lelik.

Finally, training is a weak area for today's elite. Little attention is paid to professional preparation because today's politicians can increase their powers by making decrees and demands on their regions and by using their affiliations.

Given its poor resources and limited abilities, it remains to be seen whether or not the modern political elite of Ukraine will meet its challenges successfully. Obviously, there will be changes in personnel at the highest levels of government. This means there will be significant shifts in elite membership and, consequently, the quality of leadership in government. From this process, future opponents to existing authority will emerge.

11

The Political Elite of the Republic of Moldova

Vladimir Solonar

Many complex questions associated with the formation, development, and function of the Moldovian elite remain unanswered by Moldovian sociologists and political scientists. The reasons for this are twofold: 1) the fields of sociology and political science in Moldova are still in their infancy, and 2) the majority of social scientists interested in Moldova rely on a Marxist-Leninist methodological approach to studying society. Therefore, the reader should consider this essay as one of the first attempts at reaching a better and more accurate understanding of Moldovian political elites.

The term "elite" will be used to describe those who have access to the tools of power. The political, economic, military, and other elites are the groups of individuals who directly participate in making decisions that effect the social, economic, and political life of the country. The terms "ruling elite" and "counterelite" will also be used. Ruling elites are part of Moldova's multiparty system and are directly involved in the management of society. The counterelite also manage society and are the most politically active part of the opposition.

The Republic of Moldova appeared on the political map August 27, 1991. After the failure of the August putsch in Moscow, the Parliament accepted the decision to have the republic exit the structure of the USSR and proclaim its independence. The republic became possible because the counterelite, constituted in the conditions of reorganization (perestroika), wrested the power from the hands of the old elite. The old elite had developed under Soviet totalitarianism and had managed to ratify itself as a new authority structure.

During the Soviet "reality," any attempt to create an opposition organization was quickly impeded. The ruling elite of Moldova (within the limits determined by central authority structures) operated the society without any difficulties. The situation qualitatively changed during the democratization of society initiated by Mikhail Gorbachev. Elite positions were undermined by serious changes in the personnel structure inspired by the union center. A decisive moment came when the former first secretary of the Communist Party of Moldova Central Committee (CC CPM), Semen Grossu, was compelled to resign. He had a reputation as a conservative. He was replaced in November, 1989, with the "democrat," Petr Luchinskiy, who before had occupied a responsible post in the Central Committee of the Communist Party of Tajikistan.

Second, as Moscow departed from a principle of rigid centralized management of union republics, the Moldovian elite met with the problem of garnering acceptance for their independent decisions. While trying to maneuver and adapt to new realities, the elite nevertheless as a whole continued to supervise with its old methods. This irritated union management, which saw the supervision as a sabotage of the new political course. Simultaneously, discontent for the elite's policy grew in Moldovian society, especially among ethnic Moldovans, who witnessed the dynamic transformations in the center and in a number of other union republics.

They felt themselves suppressed by the conservatism of the local ruling elite. As a result, this elite appeared demoralized and discredited. Many representatives of the Communist elite, especially younger ones promoted to high posts during the period of reorganization, began acting as a counterelite—some according to belief, some simply for the sake of self-preservation and advancing their career. Their political weight and influence grew. In a reasonably short period of time, they managed to curtail the power of the old elite. This process began at the end of 1988 and continued until 1990. It formed in the political struggles between the supporters of the National Front of Moldova (NFM) and its opponents on problems associated with the national, social, and political emancipation of Moldova. NFM was supported by the absolute majority of Moldovans.

After the spring parliamentary elections, real authority in the republic passed from the CPM into the hands of a new deputies' corps. To be precise, it passed from the hands of the management of the Supreme Soviet of Moldova in the twelfth convocation, and generated the authority structures of the republic.

The post-totalitarian elite of Moldova could not move into the political vacuum and be ready to act. The process of the new elite's formation began at the end of 1980. Thus, in the majority of other union republics as well as at the level of a union center, the new elite was formed by two main methods. On the one hand, the old elite was transformed and grew out of the party-economic *nomenklatura* to manage the republic. On the other, it grew out of the leaders and politically active participants of the informal (using the terminology of those years) opposition in political formations.

Having been formed under these particular conditions, the new post-totalitarian elite could not have a truly open character. It was especially impossible to expect openness given its social roots and political worldview and its overall level of competence and professionalism. So, for example, those elite with a nomenklatura past, recruited among the Communist Party–economic actives and Komsomol "functionaries," brought to the new elite many of the features peculiar to political activity in the former totalitarian system.

Managing experience was actually missing in the elite that emerged from informal movements. The features of this part of the elite are low political culture, inability to search and find compromises, patience about heterodoxy, and the use of democratic structures and procedures in daily political activity. It should also be taken into account that the elite's experience in management was both positive and negative. Its attitude toward radical transformations of social, economic, and political structures was rather watchful. This faction of the new elite had not precisely formulated its priorities. While parading its rejection of Marxist-Leninist doctrines, in actuality, it rejected only a part them. The norms and rules of organizational, moral, ethical, and ideal-political structure were rejected. In turn, this new elite, which rose "from below," consisted of representatives from the creative intelligentsia of the Moldovian part of the population.

At the end of 1980, in the public consciousness of the majority ethnic group of the republic, the struggle against totalitarianism was merged into a "national revival," which was interpreted by its inspirers as a restoration of the ancient valor and freedom of the people. These national ideas were suppressed by the external and alien force of the empire (Russian, Soviet). The elite took over the role of the leaders of the national struggle and gave inflammatory speeches at political gatherings. They knew how to address the masses and win their trust. The elite were able to direct their discontent against the old political order as a way of overthrowing the old elite. In 1989, at the center of public and economic debates, the "language question" emerged. The focus of official structures and a "national-democratic opposition" was concentrated around problems concerning the reinterpretation of the historical past of Moldova and Bessarabia and the questions about decreeing state status to the Moldovian language, recognizing its roots in Romanian, and switching to the Latin alphabet system.

The elite of the national Russian minority of the republic also joined this new elite. These leaders of informal movements of Russian-speaking citizens voted against the conservatism of official authorities, especially on issues related to protection of their rights and freedoms as a national minority. The elite of the national Russian minority viewed the excessive radicalism of national-democrats, displayed in the slogan "restoration of justice," as a threat. It differed, however, in the way it reflected upon the idea of Moldovian independence, which it understood as exiting from the structure of the USSR. It is clear that the new elite, who spoke Russian, were dominant in technological areas as compared to the humanities. Among them are a large number of engineers and technical workers, as well as chiefs of large industrial enterprises, particularly those related to the military industrial complex.

The Moldovian structure of the post-totalitarian elite shared characteristics with elites in a number of other former union republics. Its distinctive features were its Moldovian national component, its nomenklatura past, and its equal multiethnic national component. In the political sphere it had an unconditionally dominant position. The reason for this is obvious: a component with a nomenklatura past could be ratified in the environment creating the new elite only by completely rejecting its ideal-political past and supporting the slogans of the movement for national emancipation. Thus, at this stage the new elite appeared in a subordinated position to the leaders of the movement. In turn, by using its moral-political superiority, the new national movement had an opportunity to manipulate those elites with a nomenklatura past. They also marginalized the elite of the national minority.

These developments are confirmed by data on the analysis of the structure of the deputies' corps and the Presidium of the Supreme Soviet of the twelfth convocation elected in spring 1990. This event was the result of the first democratic election on a multimandate basis in the history of the country. Table 11.1 shows that in the Presidium of Parliament none of the representatives of the higher level, party-economy nomenklatura were elected (that is, Workers of CC CPSU, chiefs of ministries and departments, and first secretaries and secretaries of the local committees of the CPSU). The latter made up about 14 percent of the whole deputies' corps. The share of the workers of scientific research institutes (SRI) and teachers of high schools, persons of creative professions, and journalists made up 18 percent of the

Table 11.1. The Structure of the Supreme Soviet of Moldovian Republic of the
12th Convocation and its Presidium

	Supreme Soviet in the whole (percentage)	Presidium (percentage)
Whole number of deputies	360 = 100%	22 = 100%
Moldovans	71.4	82.0
Russians	13.6	4.5
Ukrainians	8.9	4.5
Gagaus	2.8	4.5
Bulgarian	3.3	4.5
Other		
Members of the CPSU	83.9	50.0
Workers of CC CPSU	1.4	0
Chiefs of ministries and departments	1.1	0
First secretaries and secretaries of the local committees of the CPSU	10.8	0
Chiefs of the organs of Soviet power	6.9	13.6
Workers of industry and transport	15.3	0
Chiefs of the enterprises	70.9	0
Workers of agricultural industry complex	23.0	9.0
Chiefs of collective farms and state farms (sovkhoz)	81.9	50.0
Workers of scientific research institutes and universities	11.9	36.4
Workers of a sphere of national economy	4.2	0
Workers of health protection	3.3	9.0
Writers, cultural figures	6.1	13.6
Trade union figures	0.8	0
Workers of law enforcement organs	5.0	13.6
Priests	1.7	0
Military servicemen	1.4	0
Other	7.1	4.8

entire deputies' corps. In the Presidium, it equaled 50 percent. Taking into account the national structure of the management of Parliament, it is clear that the representatives of the Moldovian national component of the new elite are dominant. Remarkable is the fact that in the structure of the Presidium the share of the chiefs of bodies of Soviet authority, as well as workers of law-enforcement bodies, courts, and the public prosecutor's office, had double the representation in the whole deputies' corps. Their election was the result of the popularity of decentralization and transference of power from central structures to local bodies of authority. It also can be explained by the hopes that the people with juridical education and experience could lead efforts to create new legislation, which is the essence of a "legal" state. Finally, the nomenklatura of middle and low levels of power had the most influence and were the most represented in the new deputies' corps (23 percent). At the same time, they had their representatives in the Presidium of the Supreme Soviet.

Obviously, the new ruling elite understood that its main weakness was the absence of a strong majority in Parliament. That is why, after the parliamentary elections of 1990, the newly elected chairman of the Supreme Soviet of the twelfth convocation, Mircho Snegur (who had earlier been an officer and secretary of CC CPM; chairman of the Supreme Soviet of the Moldovian Soviet Socialist Republic since July, 1989; and a leader of the party-economy nomenklatura) regarded adapting to the new conditions and the slogans of the "informals" (dissidents) as necessary. The protégés of the NFM, including Prime Minister Mirchei Druk, were elected to the management posts in the Parliament and government. However, this peculiar bloc of "frontists" (members of NFM) and agrarians, oriented to Snegur, were the first to accept these decisions.

Contrary to their demonstrated ambitions, it became quickly apparent that the national Moldovian component of the post-Communist elite could not competently and effectively operate on a day-to-day basis and manage society. Decisions in the economic sphere, where there had been frank discussions concerning business ventures, together with excessive nationalistic eagerness in the social-political sphere (which brought ethnic relations in the republic to an extremely dangerous crisis), seriously worried the elite with a nomenklatura past. They were irritated by the fact that yesterday's uncompromising accusers and fighters against bureaucratism (the corruption of the totalitarian elite) were now the same bureaucrats who hunted for unmerited material gains and privileges.

The elite with a nomenklatura past began to lose their patience after the fall of Nicolae Ceausescu. NFM, the main political force the Moldovian national component of the new post-Communist elite depended on, departed from its initial slogans for a national-democratic movement and developed an openly pro-Romanian, unionist position, demanding an association of Moldova with Romania (July, 1990, the second congress of NFM). Taking into account the prevailing mood of the masses, who wholly supported the unionist position and the neonational part of the elite, the nomenklatura elite began to struggle for control of the main levers of power in Moldova.

In this struggle, the elite with a totalitarian past acted under the flag of independence and anti-Romanianism. The national identification question before the national Moldovian component of the new post-totalitarian elite was put forward on the wave of the "national revival" movement: who belongs to the majority ethnic group of the country— Moldovans or Romanians? This was central to how the national state would be constructed: independent of or associated with Romania. For the NFM, association with Romania, its ultimate purpose, was the major element of its ideal credo. However, public opinion revealed an extreme lack of popularity for union: it was supported by only 5–8 percent of respondents, and among ethnic Moldovans the support did not exceed 10 percent. More than 10 percent of the ethnic Moldovans would consider an association after ten to twelve years. Public mood was favorable for national emancipation under the trusteeship of Moscow and rejected the unionist perspective, ensuring mass support for the elite with a totalitarian past who were united in Parliament with a faction called "Country Life" (agrarians). Consequently, the Agrarian Democratic Party of Moldova gained control over the main levers of power.

The first appreciable success for the elite with a Communist past occurred in May, 1991. As a result of a parliamentary crisis, provoked by Snegur (since August, 1990, president of Moldova), in spite of the violent resistance of Moldovian national components, Parliament declared a vote of mistrust for Prime Minister Druk and forced him to resign. The struggle for redistribution of power among supporters of the NFM and the agrarians was interrupted in autumn 1991. After the failure of the August putsch in Moscow, the Republic of Moldova proclaimed its independence. Following the interdiction of the CPM and the deep criticism of all who were connected with the Communist past, the Moldovian public and the hetero-national elite, which were against an exit of the republic from the structure of the USSR, began to support the national Moldovian component of the post-totalitarian elite. This was evident for a short period when Snegur won the presidential elections in December, 1991, in a general vote. During the preelection campaign it became obvious that the mood of the Moldovian public was unequivocally against association with Romania. At the same time, the public supported the idea of preserving an independent Moldovian state and those political forces that defended it.

The conflict in Pridnestrov'e (in the Dnestr Region) in the spring and summer of 1992 was in many respects provoked by the NFM. The intervention of the army and resulting violence further discredited the national part of the elite. In August, 1992, under pressure from Moscow and under the initiative of Snegur, the government led by Andrei Sangeli took on the role of a government of "national consent" insofar as it included both moderate Moldovian and Russian-speaking experts as well as some members of the NFM and was predominantly "agrarian-democratic." These developments reflected the increased influence of the elite with a totalitarian past.

Having required, in December, 1992, a referendum about the independence of the republic, Snegur created another parliamentary crisis that ended when A. Moshanu (chairman of Parliament since August, 1990, and supporter of NFM policy) and three other leaders of parliamentary commissions resigned. Petr Luchinskiy was appointed chairman of Parliament while he was the ambassador of Moldova to Moscow. This internal transformation was finished in summer 1992, and the new post-totalitarian elite assumed authority at the beginning of 1993.

From the beginning of 1993 up to the elections on February 27, 1994, the authority of the elite with a nomenklatura past was in place. It achieved its organizational consolidation with the agrarian parliamentary faction and the Agrarian-Democratic Party of Moldova (ADPM).

The new elite's final triumph took place after the parliamentary elections. It supervised more than 50 percent of the deputies' mandates and had among its members President Snegur, who formed a government, recruiting only his "own people." ADPM received the legal right and opportunity to define the fate of the republic by itself.

In this way, the first internal transformation of the new post-totalitarian elite of the republic was completed. All the new comers at the top and those having an agrarian link to the party and economic nomenklatura forced the "informal" elite into the background. Simultaneously, a shift of ideological paradigms took place: the ideology of "national revival" was replaced with the ideology of independence, which was interpreted as "the embodiment of a century of aspirations of the Moldovian people." It was supposed that these aspirations could not be carried out in the structure of the Russian empire (Soviet Union) or a Greater Romania. Today, the Republic of Moldova is seen as the successor and heir to the medieval Moldovian state, a unique, authentic continuation of the cause of Stephan the Great. The lack of a common identity between Romanians and Moldovans is sometimes directly emphasized, but more often it is silently suggested. In the new Constitution of Moldova, for example, the state language is called Moldovian, and nowhere are the terms "Romanians" and "Romanian" mentioned.

The new ruling elite legitimizes its image, which it creates for itself by emphasizing its competence, pragmatism, and realism. This created conditions for an economic revival of the country. The ruling elite made some accommodations with the movements for autonomy in the Pridnestrov'e and Gagaus regions. It strengthened the civil foundation of Moldovian society by finding a compromise with the elite of the national minority.

After the parliamentary elections in 1994, the role of the elite of the national Russian minority appreciably increased. Russian-speaking leaders were in opposition to NFM's wave of nationalism. The "Unity" movement was launched to protect the interests of the national minority and to struggle for the preservation of the USSR. Since these problems could not be solved, the Gagaus and Pridestrov'e republics were formed in 1990, and the Russian-speaking leaders, who remained on the right bank of Moldova in 1990–91, were politically isolated. In time, however, they managed to develop ties to the agrarians in parliament in a common struggle against NFM's nationalism.

In the parliamentary elections of 1994, Unity acted in a bloc with the Socialist Party of Moldova (SPM, formed in 1992) and included as its members Russian-speaking activists and functionaries of average and low level in the former CPM and also pensioners. A bloc of SPM and Unity emphasized and demonstrated their special ties to agrarians. Though the hetero-national elite controlled about a third of the deputies' positions, they were not perceived as equal to the modern ruling elite. In the new parliament, a fraction of CE, a junior partner of ADPM, rendered its support on the majority of questions and lobbied to "Russian-speaking" problems. Remarkably, the CE supports independence to a greater extent than do agrarians, insisting on deepening the cooperation of Moldova within the Commonwealth of Independent States (CIS). The complexity of mutual relations between the modern ruling elite and the elite of the national minority is evident particularly in the nonadmission of the latter to main levels of authority. The ADPM conceded to them only one minister's portfolio—transport. Those managing posts in the faction CE are not "old brothers-in-arms"—that is, representatives of the old nomenklatura—but are distinguished by their involvement in the political struggle at the end of the 1980s and early 1990s, and their lack of a nomenklatura past.

The influence of the modern ruling elite on the main social, economic, and political processes is decisive. They supervise the Parliament and government and enjoy the support of the masses. In the near future, a new elite will find it very difficult to get "to the top," especially if they try to make it around "the channel of the ADPM." Obviously the new entrenched ruling elite will zealously defend the positions it won from any encroachment.

Such encroachments, however, will happen. An objective precondition is the continued deterioration of the economic situation in Moldova and, as a consequence, a further pauperization of the people. If the ruling elite cannot achieve more positive social and economic conditions and the situation worsens, it may provoke the discontent of the citizens. The disappointment in the quality of the ruling elite always benefits a counterelite.

Still, the modern counterelite is separated from the center of power and is relatively small. It also does not have any serious support in society. However, this does not mean that favorable conditions for a struggle for power will not emerge. The elections to the local authorities and the forthcoming presidential elections could prove to be just such an occasion.

Part 3

The Regional Elite in Russia

12

Elite Transformation
in the Saratov Region

Petra Stykow

One of the key issues of Russian transformation is the reconfiguration of relations between the center and the provinces. Perestroika and the subsequent political changes in post-Soviet Russia have affected the capacity to govern at every level, giving rise to a strong sense of local independence and a variety of attempts to find a "special path" of development in the regions. New regional and local opportunity structures for subnational political actors have emerged, and central agencies have subsequently lost control over the country's development.

Since 1992, transformation has shifted considerably from the central authorities to the regions. To a surprising degree, the regions have adapted the reforms to meet their specific needs and conditions.[1]

Hence, focusing on regional distinctions of the Russian transformation not only assures an empirically based description of the various facets of post-Soviet development but presents an opportunity to expose the variety of strategic options available for political actors within a given national context. If regime transformation in Russia is indeed strongly marked by "objective" economic, social, and political conditions that determine the "path dependence" of societal change, then the regional variations bear out the thesis of micro-oriented approaches to transformation processes: Objective factors, as Adam Przeworski emphasizes, "constitute, at most, constraints to that which is possible under a concrete historical situation but do not determine the outcome of such situations."[2]

This essay is the result of a case study in a Russian region directed by a research strategy focusing on political actors and their strategic behavior. Within the scope of "objective" conditions and nationally bounded patterns or traditions of political culture, regional actors and their interests, perceptions, and available resources, as well as their specific regional configuration, are of crucial importance for the peculiarities of the transformation process in the regions. In the final analysis, these are the factors that determine the relationship between continuity and change in a given politico-territorial entity, the shape of emergent and reconstructed old institutions, and actors' interaction patterns and norms.

The data on which this essay is based stems from an empirical field study in the central Russian region of Saratov during the perestroika period and the following years of reconstruction of the Russian state up to early 1995.[3] Insofar as the Saratov oblast is representative of "the majority of Russian provinces with no claim to a special path of development,"[4] it is to be expected that the research findings will reflect a rather typical regional variation of Russian transformation.

The research focuses on the regional elites as actor groups who have a decisive impact on the regional transformation process. To paraphrase G. Field et al.,[5] regional elites consist of persons or groups of persons who are able to affect regional political outcomes regularly and substantially. They are a small strata of top influentials in society whose power stems either from the positions they hold or from their public reputation. For studies of post-Soviet affairs, an elite focus is commonly applied, especially for studies of the Russian provinces where the peculiarities of the development tend to be deduced conclusively from rather "idiosyncratic" factors such as the specific shape and behavior of small leadership groups. Scholars often apply the regional elites' criterion in order to classify the Russian regions by their "degree of change" as being conservative (establishment), radical (reformist, anti-establishment), or transitional provinces.[6] Thus, it appears that the implementation of reforms at the local level is "contingent upon who governs locally, for whoever controls political power at the local level will determine how reforms are carried out and whom the beneficiaries are."[7]

This essay is less concerned with a normative evaluation of the Saratov elites' "progressiveness," its composition, or its relationship vis-à-vis "democratic" reforms. Without a doubt, the elites in the Saratov oblast are much less the "outside newcomers" in politics than persons with a professional, social, and often a political background from the "old" Soviet system. What is also clear is that their ideas about the post-Communist political system and society as well as their behavior patterns are greatly influenced by their life history.

The "new" society in Saratov is not being built by counterelites rising up from the "bottom." System transformation is, therefore, not a revolutionary breakthrough. However, the ratio of societal change and elite behavior is decisive. If the ongoing "muddling through," a stop-and-go of reforms, is to be regarded as an outcome of the specific elite configuration in the region, it at the same time forms the frames and conditions within which the elite transformation occurs.

As for the Saratov elites, it will be argued here that despite important traits of continuity, a far-reaching elite transformation has occurred. What first transpired was that the Soviet elite, ideologically unified and dominated by party functionaries, was broken up into several groups, some of which disappeared during the transformation and some of which were reorganized into "new" political or economic elites. Unlike during Soviet times, access to the elites was made possible to a certain degree by parliamentary channels of recruitment (elections), and by "nonpolitical" economic engagement out of which new elite groups then emerged. Second, the postperestroika regional elites are diversified rather than monolithic, and segmented into various competing, autonomous, but interdependent and internally incoherent sectoral groups. Third, experiencing a state of disunity and political polarization, regional elites in the Saratov oblast presently tend to bargain and cooperate, indicating that a process of "consensual unification," at least vis-à-vis the "society" and the state, is taking place. The behavior of regional elites can therefore at the same time be described as strategic, adaptive, and responsive to the changing environment. Finally, the present elite configuration creates a state of anarchy in the region, which oscillates between the threats of hierarchical regulation emerging from the Russian center and a chaotic amorphousness.

The "history of power struggle" in the Saratov region to be described below shall corroborate these theses by emphasizing the stages of elite transformation in the oblast and the emergence and behavior of different elite groups and their interactions.

The Stagnation Period

In the Saratov region at the beginning of the 1980s, about one hundred persons held the top positions in the largest or most resource-rich organizations in the society. The elite consisted of two subgroups distinguishable by their institutional affiliation. The first subgroup, the mere "political elite," was attached to the political-administrative system. It was comprised of the highest apparatchiki such as secretaries and functionaries of party apparatuses (from the province, district, and city levels), the executive branch *(ispolkomy)*, and the mass organizations.

Belonging to the second subgroup were the regional cadres of the branch ministries (managers in economics, culture, education, and so forth), the "professional elite."[8]

The Soviet elite before perestroika can be characterized as having been "ideologically unified,"[9] though to a much lesser degree than in the Stalin period. The three "pillars" of the Soviet political system— the hierarchical governance systems of both the party apparatus (with the apparatuses of the mass organizations as appendages) and the state, and the *nomenklatura* system of appointment—provided for its structural integration. This integration was widely inclusive and through the domination of the political elite—that is, the party's apparatchiki— communication and influence networks encompassed all elite subgroups. They shared a value consensus about the core assumptions of the system: elite rule of society, cognitive control, superpower status of the Soviet Union, viability of the command economy, generational change as the "natural" way to carve up the political spectrum, and bifurcation of the public and private spheres.[10]

Inasmuch as the Soviet elite at the regional level was "officially" only granted the competence to implement (and control the implementation of) *centrally* made decisions, the existence of *regional* actors *in strictu sensu* was not foreseen in the political system. The first secretaries of the Communist Party of the Soviet Union (CPSU) regional committees *(obkomy)* formally acted as representatives of the center—as "governors."[11] Hence, regional or local "top influentials" acted primarily as members of a centralized all-Union "generalized elite stratum."[12]

Though proliferated factions, interest groups, clientelist networks, and so forth existed, they were constrained by the "official" system until the initiation of the perestroika reforms. Like the Soviet system as a whole, the political system in particular left a lot of room for all kinds of formalism and shadow activities. The aforementioned "pillars" of the official political system were thwarted by informal counterparts. Thus, the regionally based Soviet elite installed efficient instruments that functioned as a quasi-autonomous actor, influencing if not central decisions then at least the extent of their regional implementation, the distribution of resources in the region, and the composition and coherence of the regional nomenklatura. Some of these instruments that allowed the regional elite to affect regional political outcomes in a profound and sustainable manner shall be characterized below by illustration of the Saratov case.

The first instrument constituted the reverse of the nomenklatura system of appointment. It could be called the "old boys network" principle and consisted of a recruitment policy where the decisive pre-requisite for having a career was gaining access to the "inner circle" of the regional authorities—that is, to make the acquaintance of regional VIPs and gain their support. The majority of the Saratovian elite was selected from a regionally based pool consisting of persons with similar (rural) origins and the same professional careers and personal contacts. The typical top influential in the *raiony* (district) of the Saratov province was born in the Saratov countryside, worked as an agronomist or agricultural engineer, and then obtained a higher education at one of the two Saratov agricultural institutes. For an urban career, the road to the top started in the regional or heavy and defense industries. This was followed by more or less steady work in medium or higher management positions at kolkhoz, sovkhoz, or construction firms (for rural careers) or at the plant. Here, one had the opportunity to become familiar with the party and state apparatchiki in the district.

At this stage a parting of ways between future apparatchiki or "professionals" occurred: either one occupied the top position at a top enterprise or one changed tracks—usually in the second half of one's fourth decade of life—to a party or state function, beginning at the raion level, often starting with a career in the state organs.[13] Thus, there were no insurmountable barriers for entry into the elite, and individual careers were constrained primarily by paths chosen and whether or not one had the proper contacts. Although the nomenklatura system was designed to control the employees of the bureaucratic apparatuses from the top, it in fact allowed apparatuses at different levels to pursue their own personnel policy through informal elite recruitment based on interpersonal relations and even to promote agents from the "bottom" to the higher levels. The regional elite was much more than a group of officeholders; it represented a network resembling a spider's web where each person was known and bound to one another, an interpersonal network whose members were linked not only by their common status and interests but also through friendship and solidarity.[14]

The old boys network principle complemented the nomenklatura system from the "bottom," that is, from the local and regional levels, providing for a mechanism of not only social advancement but elite integration as well. It thus undermined the centralized nomenklatura system in a certain sense. Atop this foundation, a second instrument for broadening the sphere of action of the regional elite emerged. It consisted of so-called localism *(mestnitchestvo)*, a phenomenon constantly criticized by the central Soviet authorities because it embodied peculiar, "special" interests of the regions, irrespective of the common "societal" interests of the Soviet Union as a whole. And while the Soviet political system did not provide formal opportunities for the representation of regional interests, given that territorial entities were only viewed as administrative bodies within a centralized system of government, localism represented "a major system of the group configuration of Soviet politics on certain issues, particularly those of an appropriations nature."[15] The institutional base of localism was the regional obkom, which acted as an locus of integration for regional elites and as an intermediary agency between them and the central decision-making apparatus in Moscow. Thus, whereas the first obkom-secretaries formally fulfilled governor functions, they acted at the same time as prefects, that is, as representatives of regional interests vis-à-vis the center.[16] "Local political machines," as durable actor coalitions based upon informal connections, emerged, enabling lower-level officials, on the one hand, "to translate broad central goals and directives into economic and political realities" and, on the other, "to support, obstruct, or ignore national directives."[17]

To sum up briefly, the Saratov elite at the end of the Soviet era was highly integrated at the regional level. This was the result not only of the effectiveness of the official Soviet integration and governance institutions in general but, in particular, of informal patterns and practices used in the pursuit and realization of regional interests such as the recruitment of regional elites through old boys networks and localism. Precisely these mechanisms provided for a certain degree of autonomy of the regional elite from the central elite, that is, the ability to influence or govern the regional development, the distribution of resources, and the implementation of central decisions in the Saratov province. Thus, the regional elite acted as much more than a mere "transmission belt" between the Politburo and regional society. The regionalization that had existed, though in a very informal sense, during the Soviet period, became the point of departure for the notorious "spontaneous regionalization" during perestroika.

The Ostrich Approach of the Old Regional Elite

Perestroika, originally perceived as a reformist project for preserving the basic elements of the existing Soviet system and increasing its efficiency, ended up digging the system's grave. The unintended consequence of the perestroika subnational elite transformation project destroyed the power system as a whole: as Lupher has pointed out, "restructuring a system in which power has been appropriated by communist officials is first and foremost a matter of modifying, diffusing, and thereby *deconcentrating* the power monopoly of the party."[18] This led to the emergence of a plurality of centers claiming decision-making competence, new loci of power that varied not only in terms of societal sectors but as territories as well. Perestroika attempts to decentralize the all-embracing power of the CPSU caused not only the intense eruption of nationalism and the collapse of the Soviet Union but the expansion of local power in the Russian periphery as well.

At first, attitudes of regional self-consciousness were expressed in the form of a "regional emancipation movement" that emerged within the context of the democratic movement in the late 1980s.[19] Later, however, parts of the regional elites became actors within the regionalization movement, yet another phenomenon that ultimately proved instrumental in sealing the disintegration of the CPSU. Several groups of the old elite at several levels survived the assault on their power from above (from the CPSU reformers at the center) and below (from the "society") either through resistance or by making it work to their own advantage. In addition, during the reform process new social groups emerged and took up privileged positions in society.

We can distinguish four stages of elite transformation in the Saratov region. The first period (from 1985 to the end of 1989) is characterized by a time-lag between changes occurring at the center and the reaction to them in the Saratov region. As Mary McAuley has observed, perestroika "was something happening in Moscow and St. Petersburg and had little relevance for everyday life" in the periphery.[20] While trends of generational change, reformer-controlled cadre turnover, and the split of the top leadership into hard-liners and soft-liners became more and more obvious at the center, the old political elite in Saratov remained widely unaffected. The reforms from above were perceived as an exogenous pressure, and the regional elite reaction was one of carrying on with "business as usual," a sort of covert resistance by formalism—that is, avoidance of behavior modification as demanded from above by doing "something without actually doing anything."[21] Appointments were characterized mostly by simple office-switching between several hierarchical levels or between party and state functions, with a few newcomers who, like their predecessors, came from the same cadre pool. The management of the major factories, the directors, were an important exception: here the generational change during the first five years of reform took on remarkable proportions. Almost half of the directors' positions of the dozen largest heavy and defense industry plants were affected. In the ministerial bureaucracies in Moscow, the perestroika reforms had a significant impact,[22] with the staff reorganization from 1985 to 1989 also encompassing the lower levels.

How the institutional elite groups experienced the reforms varied: the directors benefited from perestroika because of the growing decision-making autonomy resulting from economic reform experiments such as *khozrastchet* (self-financing) and the growing paralysis of the vertical chain of command. For those preoccupied with climbing the career ladder, changes were generally perceived as positive. Within the political elite, persons who benefited at the outset of the turbulent changes were rare. All perestroika could promise was power decentralization, a reduction of the all-embracing decision-making authority held by the party or even threats to individual careers. The hostility of regional party officials toward perestroika was therefore understandable.

The first rift in the regional elite emerged between the political elite and the directors because of different interpretations of the situation, with the former viewing it as menacing and the latter as favorable. This became most evident in how they behaved vis-à-vis the Saratov *neformaly* (the members of nonofficial organizations). The first independent political organizations emerged in Saratov at the end of 1987. As a rule, they were either cultural youth clubs or public discussion circles, primarily in search of protection against repression through organizational linkages to the *komsomol* or party committees in the large heavy and defense industry plants. However, as in the Russian province as a whole,[23] they never played a public role comparable to the Moscow or Leningrad neformaly.

In the second half of 1988, these clubs established a coordination center, began to organize public meetings and discussions about the Soviet history, and founded committees whose task was to form regional branches of the Russian opposition parties. In terms of quantity, these undertakings remained negligible,[24] but their qualitative novelty was conspicuous: for the first time, demand for change was being articulated in an organized, collective manner both from outside the party and from the bottom. The formalism strategy for repulsing change familiar to the regional party elite did not work in this situation. Whereas the management of several large plants continued, as a rule, to tolerate or even encourage (pro-perestroika) public discussions, party officialdom in Saratov was taken over by obvious hard-liners. At the end of 1988, the neformaly coordination center was dissolved, and the party media launched a campaign against the opposition. Thus, the political elite, which up until then had ignored independent political activities, chose to suppress the neformaly, which, though relatively weak, was perceived as a legitimate outside challenger to their monopoly of power.

Disintegration of the Old Elite

The second period of elite transformation in the Saratov region took place between early 1990 and August, 1991. Events like the semicompetitive elections (1989) and the abolition of the Communist Party's constitutional monopoly of power (spring 1990) were the "visible" results of the power deconcentration process. The institutional ruptures that resulted finally changed the political opportunity structure even in the province. The implications for political actors were at least threefold: the ruptures first brought about political pluralism, that is, the formal acceptance of a variety of political organizations independent of the CPSU. Second, they were indicative of a further step in the direction of the separation of powers, especially concerning the withdrawal of the party from its role of performing government functions. As an intended consequence, the Soviets became the new loci of power. Third, because the Soviet restructuring program by design strengthened regional and local competencies, the power disentanglement between the party and the state also had an impact on the regions. An action space emerged that could be captured by actors who were gaining increasingly greater independence on two fronts: from the party governance and control system and from the Moscow hierarchy.

Regional political actors actually began to acknowledge this contextual change caused both by reforms from above and pressure from the opposition at the center. Though the reaction was delayed when compared with what was happening in the Russian center, the Saratov society started transforming. The old elite disintegrated into several groups, and new groups claiming elite status emerged. The soft-liner wing of the political elite and the moderate democratic opposition entered into a strategic coalition to become challengers of the hard-liner power elite. The elections to the representative bodies, the Soviets, triggered the struggle over power in the region.

The Republican and Local Elections

The republican and local elections in March, 1990, were a catalyst for the political evolution in the Saratov region. The neformaly, representing the systemic radical opposition, remained weak after its repression in 1988. In anticipation of democratic elections, they founded several of the democratic parties in Saratov such as the Social-Democratic Party and the Christian-Democratic Union but were unable to secure a place on the electoral ballot themselves. To this day, the neformaly have yet to become influential political actors in the region. The provincial political elite, the directors of the large plants—both groups with "official" candidates nominated by the party apparatus—and the emerging moderate opposition participated in the electoral competition. All competitors made an effort to avoid open confrontation.

The differences among the competing groups became apparent during the election campaign: the party obkom's strategy of controlling the nomination process and the mass media was typical for most of the Russian provinces.[25] The top management of the large industrial defense plants chose to run in the elections because of an increasing interest in regional representation rather than because of political differences with the political elite. One of the causes for this was the reorientation of the defense and heavy industries in the region owing to the paralysis of the central ministries. Another reason for the broad participation of the directors in the regional electoral struggle had to do with how their image had changed: as the public legitimacy of the apparatchiki during perestroika declined, the professionals acquired the reputation of being the new vanguard in the transition to a socialist market economy. Thus, in the public realm, the economic elite held for a certain period of time explicit political functions.

The third competing group, the moderate opposition, consisted of single, independent candidates. Unless they were party members, they were nominated upon their own or the voters' initiative, but not by the higher party committees as had generally been the case. Such behavior was an insult to the Soviet institutional system, especially to the nomenklatura system of elite recruitment. It provoked severe criticism within the party apparatus, which had always tried to control access to the elections. A direct result of the election campaign was that the initial institutional challenge became a political one. Independent candidates who had supported "socialist" democratic reforms on behalf of perestroika ended up becoming opponents of the CPSU. The origins of the opposition were an interpersonal network within the party and consisted primarily of intellectuals who did not (yet) belong to the narrow circle of the regional elite. They regarded the new political opportunities created by perestroika as promising for the advancement of their individual political careers. This new group of political actors did not therefore represent a challenge to the political opposition. Rather, they were perestroika supporters who clashed with the party hard-liners over how they interpreted the situation. They were discontented with the immobility of the regional leadership and demanded the implementation of democratic procedures for elite recruitment as had been announced from above beginning in 1988.

The differences between these three groups were organizational in nature: while the campaign of the "official" candidates was organized by the party and the directors benefited from remarkable material and social resources given their positions as factory "masters" *(khozyainy)*, the independents bypassed official structures and organized their own elections. The programmatic differences were visible only at second glance: whereas the official candidates—both the apparatchiki and the directors—seldom mentioned reforms in their electoral propaganda—and when doing so, always within the context of a claim for "political stability"—the independents placed greater emphasis on democratization, a constitutional state, party renewal, and greater regional autonomy. Some of their candidates proclaimed support for the Union-wide "Democratic platform within the CPSU."

The election results were ambiguous. On the whole, party and state officials did rather well, suffering some defeats in the city of Saratov but claiming uncontested victories in the countryside. In the regional Soviet, the apparatchiki gained about one-third of the seats. Of the thirty-seven first *raikom* (district party committee) secretaries running in the elections, only five lost, a success rate of nearly 90 percent. The managers of the big Saratov plants emerged stronger than ever before.[26] Thus, the old elite—both their political and their economic groups—showed a remarkable capacity for survival in the regional and local elections of 1990. The cause of this had less to do with gerrymandering, numerical fraud, and malapportionment, and more to do with the "astuteness" of the apparatchiki.[27] They mobilized their voters, especially in the more conservative rural districts, and carefully picked "safe" districts, preferring those where they were able to run unopposed.

Nevertheless, a meaningful modification occurred: the nomenklatura system and its reverse, the old boys network principle of appointment, were seriously damaged. Since then, the officeholders of key positions in the center of decision making have had to acknowledge the legitimacy of the election and their accountability to the public. Thus, the institutional rupture that occurred with the realization of regional elections opened up the system of the regional elite recruitment and configuration, at least in principle.

Up until the coup in 1991, however, at first glance no serious changes appeared to have occurred at the regional level. The first party leaders in the respective areas usually became chairmen of the representative bodies, so that all the talk of "power shifting" to the soviets seemed to be nothing other than formalism. In the regional soviet, any expression of discontent remained weak and unorganized. If cleavages occurred, they took the form of clashes of interests over resource distribution between the Saratov countryside and the regional industrial cities, and were not, on the whole, political in nature. The apparatchiki group of deputies acted unanimously. Professional groups of industrial managers or workers did not represent autonomous demands until the end of 1992. The main reason for the absence of any kind of independent activities was the fact that the real power remained concentrated in the hands of the political (party-state apparatus) elite. Only in the spring of 1991 did a "democratic" deputies' group consisting of about thirty (out of three hundred) parliamentarians of the regional soviet protest the notorious ignorance of formal procedures by the soviet chairman (the first secretary of the party obkom).

The Saratov City Soviet

It was in the urban representative bodies below the regional level, especially in the Saratov city and municipal district Soviets, however, that the political struggle became critical. Here, the distribution of seats differed considerably from those of the regional soviet. Independent political actors, mostly intellectuals, were elected in much greater numbers than at the regional level.[28] Over the course of the year, processes of political differentiation took place. Parliamentary discussions encouraged the formation of new collective political frames, thereby leading to the creation of groups. The moderate opposition increased and began to mature politically.

Hence, the Saratov city soviet was transformed into an institutional realm with favorable conditions for the constitution of two antagonistic political blocs, the "democratic" opposition and the CPSU hardliners. It became the main arena for political struggle in the region up to August, 1991. Let us focus a moment on the organizational processes of the two blocs.

The opposition was the first to organize. Between the spring of 1990 and February, 1991, three parliamentary groups emerged whose programs differed in the degree of their political and "patriotic" radicalism. They tried to occupy some of the most important parliamentary committees and influence the parliamentary agenda in the Saratov city Soviet. In addition, they became the point of departure for a web of extraparliamentary activities and institutions. The parliamentary opposition first began to publish local newspapers on behalf of the respective (city and, partially, city district) soviets, attracting a much wider audience than the typewritten bulletins of the earlier neformaly. Second, the democratic deputies organized such public discussions and demonstrations as the May Day march in 1990. Third, and most significant, was the establishment of political organizations analogous to all-Russian or all-Union ones in which the deputies played a crucial role. Most of these deputies belonged to the "moderate" opposition within the CPSU. Given the Union-wide strengthening of the hard-liner wing, starting in the fall of 1990 they began to view the party as a whole as hostile to reforms. In turn, they left the party and began organizing the regional organizations of the Democratic Party, the Re-publican Party, and the movement Democratic Russia. These organiza-tions remained small and clique-like but claimed to be part of the na-tionwide democratic movement. In the spring of 1991, a final attempt at intraparty pluralization occurred with the formation of the CPSU faction Communists for Democracy. This was also reflected in the for-mation of a Saratov city soviet faction.

In the spring of 1991, the moderate opposition and the Communists for Democracy joined forces. In April, 1991, the four democratic par-liamentary groups within the Saratov city soviet organized the "Dem-ocratic faction," totaling about eighty members out of two hundred deputies. At this point, the appositional groups in Saratov began to act as a united, explicitly anti-CPSU opposition. They changed from an opposition within the system to challengers of the system. Thus, the regional opposition finally caught up with Union-wide developments. The previous time-lag between the formation of the opposition at the center and in the Saratov region had been overcome. The regional op-position could finally be clearly identified as a viable political oppo-nent of the CPSU and began to enter into open confrontation.

The organizational "outing" of the party hard-liners occurred later in the spring and summer of 1991. By this time, the old political elite was deeply divided. Interpretations of the situation, expectations for further development, and choices of survival strategies were the lines along which serious cleavages began to show.

In order to protect their basic interests even at the risk of losing mo-nopolistic control over government, parts of the nomenklatura began to contemplate what kinds of political and economic benefits were to be gained from the perestroika liberalization. They began to recognize that the employment of suppression as a strategic option vis-à-vis the opposition was too costly for their political survival.

In the political realm, the recognition of new opportunities encouraged soft-liners to enter into more or less open confrontation with the hard-liners. Adding to the political dissent were older conflicts and rivalries between different interpersonal networks in the region that up until then had lain dormant.

The possibility of moving into the emerging free economic sector became yet another option for the (state, party, and komsomol) apparatchiki, especially since the end of 1990. The fact that some of the nomenklatura opted for this route is indicative of a definitive switch in their frame of reference. They broke the logic of the communist system according to which wealth and property are linked directly to political position.[29] Apparatchiki who chose the businessman option prevented a possible loss in status through their precautionary decision of converting positional resources—material as well as social—into individual resources. Individual wealth and political positions were thereby delinked. A spontaneous privatization of party and state properties reached its first climax in the spring of 1991.

The hard-liner wing of the political elite thus became more clearly defined by the spring of 1991 and noticeably smaller in size than the former political elite in the region. The question of who actually controlled the soviets became crucial. On the one side, the party apparatus tried to control the soviets through different strategies based on the situation in the local entities: through the personal union of the soviet chairmen and the respective CPSU first secretaries, through parliamentary majorities acting on orders of the territorial party committees, or by using the party control over the executive bodies (ispolkom) to enter into confrontation with the representative bodies. On the other side, at least in Saratov city, the opposition contested the party's control over the soviets, recognizing this strategy as the legal and effective means by which to eradicate the party's power monopoly.

Unlike in the countryside, the constellation of actors in the Saratov city soviet did not clearly favor the old elite. Here, the split in the political elite took its bluntest form. The first secretary of the CPSU city committee elected as soviet chairman in 1990 changed his political persuasion over the course of the year. Motivated by rivalries within the obkom leadership, he switched to the democrats in the hopes of thereby assuring his political survival. He relinquished his function as first party secretary in the fall of 1990 in order to remain soviet chairman and began to support Yeltsin as a candidate for the Russian presidential elections in June, 1991. A strategic alliance between the soviet chairman as a party soft-liner and the democrats thus became possible. This occurred in May, 1991, and lasted until the spring of 1992.

While the actor constellation that emerged was not strong enough to withstand soviet prerogatives regarding urban policies, it was capable of preventing the CPSU obkom and city committee coalition from controlling the representative body. It forced the organizational "outing" of the hard-liners and prompted further political differentiation. In May, 1991, a faction in the Saratov city soviet emerged whose members supported the conservative Russian Communist Party of Ivan Polozkov. The faction claimed about one hundred persons, but this number was fictitious, as not all of the nondemocrats wanted to be labeled as "polozkovtsy." For this reason, in June, 1990, the management of the enterprises founded their own expert faction, and a faction of moderate centrists emerged. In the case of roll-call voting—a procedure for important questions introduced by the Democratic faction—these factions occasionally formed a coalition. More often than not, however, the hard-liners that dominated the soviets' managing committee preferred not to vote against democratic propositions in the soviet and avoided open confrontation by abstaining or absenting themselves from the sessions. In effect, the CPSU city committees' instructions to paralyze the city soviet because of its increasing autonomy were thereby heeded.

In brief, the results of this period were as follows: first, the ideologically unified soviet regional elite split. With the emergence of the moderate opposition, two disparate factions made up of different actor groups arose in the regional elite of the Saratov oblast. Among the democrats and the hard-liners, communication and influence networks were either widely interrupted or nonexistent; the disagreement between the factions on the rules of the game and the shape of the institutional system was profound. Second, "the move by some group within the ruling bloc to obtain support from forces external to it" was, as Przeworski argues, an indication of the "first critical threshold in the transition to democracy."[30] In other words, elite and political transformation in the Saratov region occurred at the point when the softliners abandoned the value consensus and structural integration of the old elite in order to enter into coalitions with the democrats. The relationship between the hard-liners, representing the power elite, and their challengers was at this point in a near state of balance.

The Emergence of an Administrative Power Elite

The August, 1991, coup destroyed by exogenous intervention the power balance (and the mutual blockade) between the opposition and the party apparatus's hard-liners in the Saratov oblast. The Committee for the State of Emergency was supported by all the official representatives of the CPSU obkom, the city committee and regional soviet leadership, as well as the conservative managing committee of the Saratov city soviet. The opposition coalition in the region benefited from the victory over communist conservatives in the center. The regional winners were those who put on a democratic face in the nationwide power struggle, even though their endogenous, regionally based resources were slighter than the potential of their adversaries.

With Yeltsin's dissolution of the party's organizations, the last pillar of the communist power monopoly fell. The emergent vacuum of organized political authority in the region was to be filled by a new state (executive) apparatus. Thus, the third stage of elite transformation in the Saratov region, lasting from the fall of 1991 to mid-1992, consisted of the struggle that took place over the shaping of regional administrative institutions and the concomitant personnel policy, in essence the emergence of a new regional power elite with control over regional decision making.

After the putsch, the anti-CPSU coalition found itself in charge of the command posts in the region. The leader of the soft-liners was appointed presidential representative in the oblast (*Predstavitel Prezidenta*) by Yeltsin, whereas the democrats focused their aspirations on the representative bodies. At the regional soviet, they partially succeeded by occupying strong positions in the new coordination committee (*malyi Soviet*). That the soviet chairman was a politically weak and inexperienced figure with a democratic image can be seen as the result of a compromise between the allied soft-liners and the democrats. The Saratov city soviet, however, was clearly dominated by the democrats. Here they were able to influence the city administration significantly up until its reorganization in early 1992. During this period, however, the democrats were unable to improve their position. They not only lacked experience and know-how but also an elaborated reform program and an institutional base to implement parliamentary decisions. So despite their dominance in the soviet, they were unable to affect political outcomes significantly.

It was the common fear of a hard-liner revenge that forged the coalition of the soft-liners and the moderate opposition, but the democrats soon began to loose cohesiveness: a more radical faction that dominated the Democratic Russia movement began to realize that relying on the soviets was a losing battle. In order to prevent a conservative rollback they became interested in installing a regime of "civilized authoritarianism." The stronger moderate wing, on the other hand, stood for "societal consensus" and "enforcement of law," preferring a strategy of appeasement vis-à-vis (potential) opponents rather than a resolute seizure of power with incalculable costs.

The main issue of the political struggle during the winter of 1991–92 was the reorganization of the regional executive power structure, that is, the transformation of the regional and local Soviet ispolkomy into state administrations. Although the initial period following the failed putsch was characterized by an upswing of party and association activities in the region, what had a decisive impact on the power restructuring was the competition between informal actors "behind the scenes" and interventions from the central authorities: with the postponement of mayoral and local council elections after the August, 1991, coup, regional political actors with power ambitions had to obtain presidential support because it was Yeltsin who appointed the regional head of administration, or governor *(gubernator)*. Another crucial figure was the Predstavitel Prezidenta, because he enjoyed numerous such rights as appointing and dismissing department heads of the local soviet executives, reorganizing these departments, and vetoing any measures passed.

All actor groups, including the two democratic factions, the Predstavitel Prezidenta clique, the directors, and even the less compromised subgroups of the conservative political elite, competed for the appointment, at first with their own candidates and later with compromise candidates chosen by group coalitions. The resources of the different actor groups, in particular their access to the presidential "decision machine," were clearly unevenly distributed. Using the strategic alliance with the democrats, the Predstavitel Prezidenta became the winner of the game. The democrats were the junior partners in this coalition. While the Predstavitel was able to exploit their anti-CPSU image in order to legitimize his claim on power, the democrats were not capable of benefiting from his interpersonal network relations. They thereby were lost in the struggle over executive power. In the spring of 1992, the struggle within the regional state apparatus was resolved via regulation from above. Top positions in the regional and Saratov city administration went to members of an interpersonal network tied to the presidential representative by their common past. All appointees had worked as top managers of the regional food industry during the Soviet period at a time when the Predstavitel Prezidenta was first secretary of the CPSU city committee. This recasting of the executive bodies in the region by the recruitment of incumbents either from this network or from the former ispolkom staff was particularly prevalent at the medium and lower levels both in the regional administration and in the rural districts.

By 1993, relatively strong and stable executive authorities had emerged. It was at this level that the power of the oblast was concentrated. The emerging administrative elite was composed primarily of individuals with either administrative or economic governmental experience in the "old" system; newcomers from the outside were in the minority. This was the result not only of the regional peculiarities of the power struggle but of the national opportunity structure. The specific path of state building in Russia, where the presidential government declared itself to be above party politics and where elections were substituted by appointments from above, was not conducive to the resolution of conflict by parliamentary means. Instead, political actors took advantage of various resources inherited from the past. What became crucial for the bargaining and coalition building taking place behind the scenes was the maintenance of interpersonal, informal relations, and reliance on clientelistic channels of access to the central authority.

Interdependence and Strategic Interactions of the Regional Elites

The Differentiation of the Regional Elite

Presently, elite transformation in the Saratov region can be characterized as a successive strategic realignment of the different elite groups that either emerged in the previous stages or have survived from Soviet times. The formation of new regional political and economic institutions has, for the most part, come to an end. Regional and local administrations have been formed and are recognized as the centers of decision making on regional issues. Political parties and pressure groups have formally been established, and national and regional elections were held in December, 1993, and in the spring of 1994. In the economic realm, the size and significance of the (state-owned) heavy industry declined, with nonstate sectors having grown and a few big multiprofile private companies having come into existence. In addition to the aforementioned elites, a group of businessmen have emerged who, given the wealth and the political influence they wield, claim an elite status.

There are at present about one hundred elites in the Saratov region, about the same number as at the end of the "stagnation" period, but with a radically different composition.[31] The political elites are made up of the regional administration, an "above-party politics" power elite consisting of different institutional interest groups (interpersonal networks) with a more or less functioning apparatus, personal and financial resources, as well as certain economic governance capabilities that are on the rise; and representatives of political organizations and intellectuals, mainly belonging to the oppositional elite, and partially involved in entrepreneurial activities. Besides different "democrats," this group includes representatives of pressure groups—for instance, the "agrarian-industrial lobby"—various cliques of new entrepreneurs, and so forth.

The economic elites represent almost half of the members of the regional elite. They include the top management (directors) of the largest, formerly state-owned enterprises now undergoing privatization. Though somewhat on the decline, this group holds an enormous economic potential and has the capacity to represent not only its "particular" interests but also the interests of its employees. They are also the top "new entrepreneurs" (businessmen), with highly fluid and important capital resources, as well as a high degree of flexibility; and the chiefs of commercial and state banks.

There are also elite groups with resources to employ force at their disposal: military and police chiefs as well as heads of the so-called mafia, interpersonal networks with economic resources and a discreet oligopoly over violence over whom the state has no control.

Strategic Interactions Under Anarchy

In recent years, no single one of the competing elite groups was able to gain absolute control of the regional government. What happened in the Saratov oblast was in part the result of interactions between the political power elite (the administrative elite) and the economic elites (the directors and businessmen). The federal government's influence was rather weak and in essence merely a resource used by the competing regional players of the game. There are not only rivalries, struggles for dominance, and even predatory competition among these groups of regional elites, but bargaining, cooperation, and coalition building as well. The situation appears anarchic. Anarchy in this context has to be understood as a social arrangement in which participants can seize and defend resources without regulation by either higher authorities or social pressures.[32] This is not "chaos" but rather a spontaneous order emerging from interactions between the different elite groups. These are, first of all, strategic; the strategies of actors are dependent upon and responsive to other actors' strategies. Strategic interactions are typical for scenarios of political discontinuity as in the

Saratov case,[33] and they can be conflictive as well as cooperative. Even if the assumption of anarchy often supposes "non-cooperative" relationships, anarchy does not in principle exclude cooperation. There are different variables to explain the evolution of cooperation in anarchic systems, but the appropriate one in the present case is the notion of strategic interdependence where "the ability of one participant to gain his ends is dependent to an important degree on the choices or decisions that the other participant will make."[34]

The main elite groups in the Saratov case are interdependent. Whereas the Soviet political elite controlled (almost) all of the economic, political, social, and other resources in the region, each of the present elite groups control a few specific types of resources but only to the extent that assures a veto position vis-à-vis other actors. The executive power structures obviously hold the strongest positions, but a good part of the economic potential, the public influence, and the access to central Russian authorities is controlled by the directors or is slowly becoming ever more concentrated in the hands of the new big businessmen. As for law and order, the state has lost its monopoly over keeping the peace. Mafia groups, often together with new entrepreneurs, have installed force oligopolies and collected taxes. The administrative elites have to keep account of the behavior of other elite groups, especially the directors and the businessmen. Exchange relations vital to each group have been established. Incumbents of the executive bodies, for example, offer subsidies, loans, tax concessions, and export/import licenses, and tolerate or promote favorable privatization decisions for economic actors who are able and willing to "pay" with (political, moral, material, social) support. All these goods of exchange are scarce and differ according to each group. The plurality of the regional elite is greater, and the reservoir of options for strategic coalition building for each elite group or faction all the more diverse, as the political power elite itself is divided into rivalries between different hierarchical levels and cliques. Thus, in addition to intra- and intergroup conflicts, unstable, conjunctural intergroup coalitions emerge.

The Organization of Conflict and Cooperation

On the surface, conflict and cooperation in the Saratov region take several institutionalized forms. The administrative elite is organized by the regional executive structures; the political opposition (democrats as well as conservatives) have founded parties; and pressure groups such as the directors have established interest associations. Since the elections in the spring of 1994, various party factions have been represented in the regional body and the Duma, where the pro-Communist "agrarian-industrials" hold more than half of the seats. However, in reality, the elite configuration and elite interactions do not correspond to the institutional structures.

Both parties as well as organized business interests (about thirty associations existed in mid-1993) have problems typical for collective actors in post-Communist Russia. The organized representation and structured aggregation of political and economic interests remain weak. Parties and associations are not only dominated by leaders but are often merely organizational "shells" of individual politicians or egocentric networks. As a rule, rivalries between politicians therefore tend to lead to the fragmentation of old organizations and the formation of new ones. Their ideological base is unstable and eclectic and does not appeal to any specific constituency. Given the popular resistance to the "partification" of politics, parties have sought to present themselves not as ideological (communist, leftist, conservative, and so on) but pragmatic, emphasizing such values as democracy and patriotism. The election platforms in 1994 contained for the most part such diffuse demands and proposals. Coherent formulations of forward-looking policies were rare. The Duma elections in late 1994, therefore, resembled more a competition between several ambitious leaders than one between social groups represented by political parties.[35]

Whereas such "procommunist" organizations as the Communist Party and the Agrarian Party are experiencing a process of relative organizational consolidation, the democrats and their leaders, having been quite strong in 1991, have lost political significance, and almost all democratic organizations are now experiencing disintegration and network rivalries.

Up until now, the regional Duma has yet to become a forum for parliamentary struggle. Rather, it continues in a role similar to that played by the regional soviet until its dissolution in the fall of 1993, where neither the soviet nor the administration worked within a political system with a "separation of powers" but worked rather as rivals, each claiming to have "all-embracing" decision-making authority in the region, similar to the competencies held by the former obkom. The regional Duma in 1995 was against the governor's power ambitions, and, unless fragmented, worked rather like a corporative political actor.[36]

The regional government is deeply divided. The old boys network that occupied the top administrative positions in 1992 has fallen apart. Meanwhile, conflicts over regional leadership exist between the governor, the vice mayor of Saratov city, and the presidential representative, each of whom receives support from interpersonal networks and temporary coalitions with other elite groups.

Thus, a good part of the political struggle occurs via informal coalition building and conflict. In order to restrict the power ambitions of the governor, the Saratov vice mayor once entered into a coalition with the Predstavitel Prezidenta, once with the Duma, and once with different groups of economic actors. The governor, on the other hand, leans on the rural administrative bodies, prefers "weak" persons in the lower administrative levels, and maintains strong connections to certain actors in Moscow. The directors, as well as the new big businessmen, support various persons in the administrations and try to influence Duma deputies or selectively promote certain political organizations.[37]

Whereas a variety of organizations and interests have been built up for the purpose of aggregating and representing specific demands, the political and functional differentiation of the political realm remains in an embryonic state. The key roles in the power play are filled by (unorganized) pressure groups rather than by political organizations. Up until now, processes of coalition building, rupture, and realignment are in persistent flux, and the results of the power struggles are unpredictable. However, the strategic behavior of the different elite groups assures a certain balance of power. The central issue of political conflict during 1994 was the hotly contested (re)casting of the gubernator's position. The group reconfiguration, bargaining, hatching of plots, and so forth that occurred, however, actually had no impact on the political system and the elite configuration. And yet, while the political conflicts remain truly inconclusive, the regional development has not been thereby blocked. The state of anarchy seems to persist, which also means that neither regulation from above nor "chaos" prevails. Hierarchical regulation of regional conflicts is just as impossible given the weakness of the central state as it is undesirable, because central interventions would not be appropriate for the interests of the region.

13

The Ruling Elite of Tatarstan
Contemporary Challenges and Problems of Adjustment

Midkhat Farukshin

Regional or local elites play an important role in the political life of any society. The elite represents a distinct and influential force in the political process. It promotes its own interests and possesses considerable resources to do so. Russian history has shown that defying the vested interests of the local elite is bound to trigger conflicts and social tension.

Local political elites also serve as the vehicle of national policy in their respective regions—a pillar in the mechanism of state operation. Normal operation of society and government is impossible without close cooperation between regional and national elites. Moreover, local political elites are a source of new blood for the national elite, predominant in the central organs of power.

The study of local political elites in Russia is a highly pertinent but little explored topic in political science and sociology. It is a broad subject since the political elite in every region of Russia has its own unique character. This essay explores the basic framework of the present-day ruling political elite in the Tatarstan Republic. Tatarstan is a political entity within the Russian Federation. The republic is located 500 miles east of Moscow; it covers an area of more than 26,000 square miles and has a population of 3.7 million people.

This essay will show that the slow pace of reforms in Tatarstan, ineffective government policy, and the membership and methods of forming the local elite provide ample evidence that the elite does not reflect the potential and the needs of the Tatarstan society. The elite is slow to respond to new social trends and is in need of a major overhaul.

Factors Defining Strengths and Weaknesses of Russia's Ruling Elites

The economic, social, and spiritual crisis of Russian society coupled with the striking inability of the federal authorities to resolve pressing problems in a timely manner bolstered the "office" of the local elites. Another factor that played into the hands of the local elites was the development of the market economy, which was accompanied by decentralization of power. The introduction of market-type relations increased the number of autonomous economic agents, including the regions, which have gained more discretion in decision making. Following the implementation of market-type levers of control, the scheme where the central authorities exercise complete control over the economy seemed absurd, especially when considering the scale of the Russian economy. The search for ethnic identity contributed to the dramatic rise in the clout enjoyed by the local political elites in the various republics of the Russian Federation. This search manifested itself in the call for greater independence from the center, for the genuine institution of national statehood, with guarantees of autonomy. Another factor leading to the ascent of the local political elite was the incessant fighting among the upper echelons of power. Local elites managed to boost their power and prestige by exploiting the internal conflicts enveloping the federal authorities. At the same time, the authorities allied themselves with their regional counterparts in order to gain the upper hand over their rivals.

The political course assumed by the leadership of Tatarstan is typical in this respect. In 1992 when the Russian leadership cast the country into shock "without therapy," Tatarstan announced a policy of "smooth transition to a market system." This meant safeguarding government-set price controls subsidized by the budget. While futile in the long run, this policy did help the republic's population weather the price shock during the first year of reform implementation. Local political elites also managed to augment their physical assets by gaining direct control over much of the previously centralized state property. For instance, prior to perestroika, 80 percent of the industrial enterprises located in Tatarstan were subordinated to the All-Union bodies; 18 percent were controlled by the Russian Federation; and only 2 percent by the republic. As a result of decentralization and the incessant drive for autonomy, Tatarstan gained administrative control over 65 percent of the state property located within its borders.

There are numerous factors limiting the administrative authority and power of local political elites. Most important is the very real trend toward centralization. No society can function properly without some degree of centralization, and this is doubly true for such a socially and ethnically diverse and populous country as Russia. Centralization imposes certain limitations on the power of the local political elite. It demands that elites exercise self-restraint. Other powerful factors that limit the authority of the local elites include the large physical and financial holdings at the disposal of the center, the center's prerogative to enact laws and administrative decrees, and the center's control over law enforcement and armed services. All these levers of control empower the center to exert strong pressure upon the regions and their local elites.

In most Russian republics, more than half of the population is not indigenous. For instance, according to the national population survey conducted in 1989, Bashkirs comprise 22 percent of the population of Bashkortostan; 43 percent of the people in the Republic of Mari-El are Maryts; 32 percent of the population of Udmurtia are Udmurts; and Tatars comprise 48 percent of the population of Tatarstan. The great majority of the nonethnic (or Russian speaking) population opts for closer ties with Russia and Russian federal authorities. These groups act directly, or via political parties/movements, and they form a broad social base that tends to support the central political elite.

Another key factor limiting the latitude of local political elites and favoring the national elite is the authoritarian-patriarchal political traditions that enjoy broad-based support among the very diverse stratum of the Russian society. Russian political culture is predicated upon rigid centralization, contempt for the law, a tendency to employ coercive means to resolve controversial issues, intolerance for dissenting or alternative points of view, and pronounced support for monism and uniformity rather than pluralism and diversity. Last but not least is the international support extended to Russia's central elite over the last few years. Fearing, and justifiably so, excessive disintegration of Russia, which could lead to chaos and spark major conflicts throughout the world (with all the ensuing economic and political consequences), the Western countries have demonstrated their support for the elite that governs the whole of Russia.

Tatarstan's Elite: Qualitative Characteristics

This investigation of Tatarstan's local political elite formed on defining the boundaries of this social entity and gathering empirical material about the individuals comprising this elite class. First of all, we must distinguish between the notions of "political elite" and "ruling elite." The former is more general; it includes the ruling elite as well as the "counterelite." The counterelite are groups that vie for power but have presently been denied and thus belong to the opposition. The following criteria may be used to delineate the political elite: 1) it consists of people in pursuit of power and professionally involved in politics; 2) these same individuals comprise a united front with a common system of values, tenets, and "rules of the game" (naturally, the interests, values, and precepts espoused by the various factions of the political elite may vary), and 3) members of the political elite are recognized as political leaders, which to a certain extent legitimizes their hold on power.

What distinguishes the ruling elite as the spearhead of the political elite is its power to make political and administrative decisions and its ability to exercise control over society's political resources. This criterion was used to define Tatarstan's ruling political elite. This group includes individuals who conduct the most important political and economic affairs at the republican and regional levels and who make decisions that affect the population of the republic at large as well as its individual regions.

Included in the political elite are the president, vice president, president's chief of staff, chairman of the Supreme Soviet of the Republic, his deputy chairmen, chief of the secretariat, prime minister, deputy prime ministers, ministers, chairmen of state committees, chief of the secretariat of the Council of Ministers, and heads of major urban and regional administrative bodies.

Deputies of the Supreme Soviet were not counted as part of the political elite. For one thing, many of these people do not work in the Parliament full-time. Moreover, decisions made by the ruling elite are easily bulldozed through the legislation. A number of top-level officials included among the local political elite are also deputies of the Supreme Soviet of the republic (recently renamed State Council).

The following parameters were incorporated in a background probe of the individuals comprising the elite: ethnic background, the nature of previous employment, social origins, sex, education, and age. The top share of the local political elite, namely 78 percent, are Tatars; others belong to different ethnic groups. Comparing these figures with the population ratios for the republic as a whole (Tatars, 48 percent; Russians, 44 percent; and others 8 percent) reveals that the ethnic composition of the ruling elite does not reflect the overall proportions of the various ethnic groups in the republic.

The great majority of the local political elite had previously worked within the *nomenklatura*. In light of the fact that in the not-so-distant past all party and government positions as well as many managerial positions were part of the nomenklatura of their respective party organs, I established that at most 8 percent of the members of the local political elite were not affiliated with the nomenklatura. Ninety-two percent of Tatarstan's ruling elite comes from the ranks of the nomenklatura. Moreover, 68 percent of this group are former party-government officials. In Russia, the second and third levels of the nomenklatura have gained power, while in Tatarstan the reigns of power are still firmly held by the top echelon.

Two-thirds of the Tatarstan elite are originally from rural areas. If we add those originally from small towns, the figure climbs to 86 percent. Naturally, these people brought with them a "village culture" that permeates all relationships within the elite. This culture features traditional customs of servility; disdain for dissent and opposition; favoritism toward people from the same milieu, especially nepotism; distrust for "strangers," particularly the urbanites and the more educated stratum of society; self-righteousness; and narcissism. This culture is antidemocratic at its very core.

Practically all the members of the ruling elite have higher educations. However, their background is heavily skewed toward the agricultural sciences. For instance, 44 percent of the elite graduated from agricultural or veterinary schools, and only 13 percent are university graduates.

The republic's elite is practically all male. Women, who are in less prestigious positions, comprise only 4 percent of the elite group. As for age, 14 percent of the elite are 30 to 39; half belong to the 40 to 49 age group; one-third are 50 to 59; and only 3 percent are 60 and over.

First in line to replace the present leaders of Tatarstan are the very same people from the villages who once assumed top-level positions. They will propagate others in their own image from the younger generation of village dwellers. The social solidarity inculcated into those of rural origin tends to be much stronger than that of the urbanites.

The Social Base of the Local Political Elite

The considerations expressed above in no way imply that the support base for the ruling elite is narrow. The elite is actually locked into a multilayered and highly diverse support base. Surveys conducted by the Center for Sociological Studies at the Supreme Soviet of Tatarstan reveal interesting information about the elite's support base. Surveys

Table 13.1. Confidence in the Top Leadership of Tatarstan as a Function of Ethnic Origin (percentage of the total number polled in each group)

Groups	July, 1993		January, 1994		November, 1994	
	Trust	Mistrust	Trust	Mistrust	Trust	Mistrust
Tatars	42	5	52	5	37	8
Russians	24	11	32	9	26	13
Others	39	6	30	9	36	8

Table 13.2. Confidence in the Top Leadership of Tatarstan as a Function of Domicile (percentage of the total number polled in each group)

Territory	February, 1992		June, 1992		June, 1993		January, 1994	
	Trust	Mistrust	Trust	Mistrust	Trust	Mistrust	Trust	Mistrust
Kazan	22	22	17	21	22	16	26	18
Other cities	30	6	28	7	26	6	40	9
Villages	38	8	38	9	52	3	56	5

were conducted in the republic's capital of Kazan, in the cities of Aznakaevo, Elabuga, Zelenodolsk, Naberezhnye Chelny, as well as in several other regions of the republic. More than two thousand people were polled and represented in terms of key social and demographic criteria (sex, age, occupation, ethnic background, and residence). The purpose of the surveys was to determine the level of confidence on the part of the population in the republic's leadership—the president, the chairman of the Supreme Soviet, and the prime minister. Since these leaders are quite typical of the local political elite, the attitude of the various population groups toward them is a good indicator of the elite's true support base. The results of the survey reveal some general trends.

The ethnic group most supportive of the local political elite are the Tatars (see table 13.1). In terms of social background and residence, the greatest share of the support base for the local political elite are the inhabitants of small towns and villages. Those who live in the capital city of Kazan (population 1,160,000) are significantly less likely to trust the Tatarstan leadership.

Looking at the social-occupational aspect of the survey, we observe that the local political elite relies on support from peasants, retirees, and managers and enjoys less support from entrepreneurs and engineering-technical professionals (see tables 13.2 and 13.3).

Table 13.3. Confidence in the Top Leadership of Tatarstan as a Function of Social Status (percentage of the total number polled in each group)

Social groups	June, 1992	July, 1993		January, 1994		November, 1994	
	Trust	Trust	Mistrust	Trust	Mistrust	Trust	Mistrust
Workers	41	22	11	35	8	24	14
Peasants	55	60	0	68	2	46	5
Service workers	47	43	6	40	7	26	13
Engineering-technical personnel intelligentsia	35	28	8	30	12	25	13
Specialists in the service sector	50	26	7	38	6	26	12
Directors, managers	0	0	0	43	4	38	8
Entrepreneurs	0	27	24	16	15	13	9
Retirees	57	49	5	55	5	48	5

Naturally, the local political elite tries to ingratiate itself with all the major population groups in order to ensure its own stability. The elite must take into account the ethnic sentiments of the indigenous ethnic Tatars, other nationalities residing in Tatarstan, as well as the common concerns shared by its ethnically diverse population. The elite must certainly heed the interests of the Russian Federation as expressed by Russia's central authorities. Any attempt to foster the interests of one group at the expense of another group may increase social tensions and result in a collapse of the image of the elite as representative of all major population groups in the republic.

Homage ought to be paid to the skillful maneuvering of the local elite and its willingness to look soberly at the situation. The ruling elite appealed to the indigenous population with slogans promoting national identity and statehood, improved legal and political status of the republic, and the revival of ethnic values and ethnic culture. Many years of deep humiliation, injustice, and infringement on their national pride made a large share of the Tatar population (outside the republic as well) support the republic's political elite.

Until very recently, the totalitarian system of the former Soviet Union openly proclaimed the "great achievements" of its ethnic-political policy. All nationalities and their respective political jurisdictions were classified into four groups: Union republics, autonomous republics, autonomous regions, and national (later called autonomous) districts (*okrug*). Vestiges of this "great feat" are still evident. The grouping based on this scheme failed to take into account the size of the ethnic group, the territory it inhabits, its economic and intellectual potential, as well as its cultural and historical traditions. The national group itself had no say in self-determination. This ranking of the various nationalities was a source of latent ethnic hostility. The assigned category completely defined the nation's political status as well as the powers delegated to it.

As a result of the injustice in the determination of the nation's political status, many ethnic groups were stripped of an opportunity to voice their concerns within the institutional framework of the Soviet political system. For instance, there was no reasonable explanation for the fact that a Union republic with a population of 1.5–2.5 million people would send thirty-two delegates to the Supreme Soviet (later the Congress of Peoples' Deputies), while an autonomous region almost twice that size, Tatarstan, was allowed to send only eleven delegates. Moreover, the Supreme Soviet (later Chamber of Nationalities), not to mention other central administrative and political organs, was comprised of representatives of the republics rather than the representatives of ethnic groups. This had major consequences on the articulation of ethnic issues.

The lack of an institutional mechanism to represent ethnic concerns dealt a particularly harsh blow to those ethnic groups deprived of "statehood" as well as those in the diaspora. The more scattered the group was, the less opportunity it had to bring ethnic issues to the attention of the authorities. For instance, only 27 percent of the almost seven million Tatars reside in the Republic of Tatarstan. This group was represented in various government and administrative republican bodies, but what about the institutions designed to convey the interests and national/cultural concerns of the remaining 73 percent? Their voices were silenced.

Erosion of the national and political status of the former autonomous republics was evident. Unlike Union entities, they lacked the right to have their own Academy of Sciences or film studios; they had to secure permission from Moscow to start a new newspaper, or build a monument on their own land, or even increase television or radio programming broadcasted in their native tongue. Disregard for the future of the Tatar nation had a profound impact upon its spiritual and cultural vitality. The most far-reaching outcome of the Soviet policy was stripping the nation of its cultural identity. The most blatant manifestation of the indifference to the fate of the Tatars was total disregard for their native language.

Highly pernicious in this respect was the curbing of the use of the Tatar language, essentially limiting its role in social and family life. The Tatar language was no longer the primary source of communication for the Tatar people. As a result, there was a widening gap between the oral or colloquial speech and the literary language. The sociolinguistic predicament of the Tatars manifested itself in the Russification of a large share of the population, particularly young people. An ever-rising percentage of the ethnic population did not know or was not fluent in its own native tongue. The number of schools that conducted classes in Tatar was on the decline as was the number of titles and the circulation of books written in the Tatar language. Consider the following statistics: in 1926, 99 percent of the Tatars called Tatar their native tongue; in 1959 the figure was 92 percent; in 1979, 86 percent, and in 1989, 83 percent. Downgrading of the Tatar language reverberated in the literature published in Tatar. The number of titles and printed copies steadily declined. In 1928, 428 book titles came out in Tatar, totaling 1.8 million copies; in 1932, the figure increased to 855 (5.9 million copies); in 1940, it dropped to 329 (4.9 million); in 1970, 195 (2.8 million); in 1980, it was 183 (2.1 million); and in 1986, 181 books were published in Tatar (1.36 million).

Flagging interest in the native tongue was a strong indicator of the "de-ethnication" that was taking place. This process challenged the very existence of the Tatar nation and violated the people's sense of ethnic identity. The lawlessness, injustice, and total disregard for the interests of the ethnic peoples living in the former autonomous republics spurred the drive for national identity and autonomy. These very tangible factors are at the root of the indigenous people's desire for autonomy, a movement supported by the local ruling elite, which made it their main battle cry.

It seems that the groups that are not part of the indigenous population and that pursue their own agenda had been attracted by the centrist policy proclaimed by Tatarstan's ruling elite, which, for all intents and purposes, conceded to remain subjects of the Russian Federation. The leadership of Tatarstan did not openly support any nationalist parties or extremist movements, allegedly acting on behalf of the local ethnos. By the same token, the leadership did not show any sympathy for the "Russian-speaking" parties and movements.

Another major reason for the broad-based support for the local political elite was the profound dismay over the socioeconomic situation in the republic. As part of the former USSR, the Tatar Autonomous Republic was politically impotent and, in effect, oppressed in terms of the socioeconomic welfare of all the nationalities there. For instance, by former Soviet as well as current Russian standards, Tatarstan has a highly developed economy. Its GNP (in 1991 prices) is estimated at about 50 billion rubles. In 1991, the per capita output of agricultural products in Tatarstan was 20.6 percent higher than the average for the Russian Federation, and industrial output was 20.3 percent higher. In 1990 with a population of only 1.26 percent of the total Soviet population, the republic's share of the USSR's national income was 1.7 percent. The per-capita annual income in Tatarstan was 2,733 rubles, as compared with 2,221 rubles for the USSR as a whole.

While Tatarstan figured prominently in terms of economic indicators, ranking in the top ten republics, territories (*krai*), and regions, it was unable to provide its multinational population with a decent standard of living. There was a large gap between production and consumption. A number of key indicators point to the fact that the standard of living in Tatarstan lagged behind the Soviet as well as the Russian average. As far as housing, medical care, telecommunications, and other components of social and cultural welfare, Tatarstan had a middle to low ranking when compared with the 89 regional units in the Russian Federation. In Tatarstan the amount of savings per capita deposited in the savings bank in 1990 was about 1,025 rubles compared with 1,147 for Russia as a whole. There were 38 passenger automobiles in Tatarstan for every 1,000 people, compared with 52 in Russia and 53 in the former Soviet Union. In the late 1980s, the Tatarstan per capita share of national income spent on consumption was 90.4 percent of the national level and 76.1 percent of the Russian Socialist Federation of Soviet Republics' (RSFSR) level. In spite of the fact that the per capita output of certain agricultural items (milk, meat) was higher in Tatarstan than in the USSR or RSFSR, the consumption of these items was actually lower. Rivaling in its total output the combined output of the three Baltic republics of Estonia, Latvia, and Lithuania, Tatarstan's budget was lower than that of each individual Baltic republic.

The public pinned its hopes on overcoming the socioeconomic injustice inflicted when Tatarstan was part of the former USSR and later RSFSR upon improving its political and legal status. The need to better the life of the people through greater autonomy in the economic and social realms seemed to echo the grievances of the entire multinational population of Tatarstan. The local elite, which upheld these concerns, gained broad-based support from the Tatarstan population.

Relationship with the Federal Authorities: A Precarious Balance

Over the last five years, the political strategy of Tatarstan's local elite was predicated upon improving the political-legal status of the republic as it pushed for greater autonomy. The idea was to expand the powers of the republic and make it more independent of the central authorities of the Russian Federation. There wasn't a political force in Tatarstan openly opposing the republic's autonomy. Naturally, different groups varied in their interpretation of the concept—ranging from minor expansion of the republic's scope of power within the framework of the Russian Federation to complete sovereignty and creation of an independent state of Tatarstan.

Within the spectrum of the political forces operating in Tatarstan, the leadership stuck to the centrist course on such issues as sovereignty and the nation's right to self-determination. This basic right laid the legal groundwork for the leadership's call for statehood and sovereignty. Nonetheless, recognizing the political and economic reality of the situation, the local elite conceded to Tatarstan's status as one of the eighty-nine subjects of the Russian Federation. The ruling elite found itself in a bind.

The primary motive behind the local elite's push for sovereignty was to liberate itself from the Russian shackles. It would be fair to say that the greatest achievement of this struggle is the previously unseen level of independence of the local elite from the Moscow authorities. While the present-day situation is a far cry from complete independence (keep in mind the powerful economic, financial, social, political, and coercive levers at the disposal of Russia), it is a major milestone in the history of the interaction between the republics and the center. In the old days, the first secretary of the Tatarstan Regional Committee of the CPSU posed as a two-faced Janus. He enjoyed tremendous power within the republic and was in effect a kind of governor-general. By the same token, this governor-general was to the center a vassal to be dumped if his presence was no longer expedient. In any event, the first secretary of the regional committee followed orders given by Moscow and was completely under Moscow's control. How things have changed! The local political elite has no superiors. It is left to its own devices and is not bashful about taking advantage of this control vacuum from above (control from below was never an effective instrument in Russia). A civilized society institutes powerful levers of control, namely the law. With an entrenched, predominantly authoritarian-patriarchal, political culture and contempt for the law, Russia has traditionally counted on a benevolent czar and a good boss.

In essence, the relationship between Tatarstan's local political elite and the federal administration revolves around the struggle for power, that is, the kind and the scope of authority delegated to each side. This perspective on the evolution of post-totalitarian Russia marks several distinct stages. During 1990–91, the local elite sought to raise the status of the Tatar Autonomous Soviet Socialist Republic to the that of an All-Union Republic—in effect, to secede from the RSFSR to be on par with other Soviet republics. This period of Tatarstan history witnessed some key political events: adoption of the Declaration of State Sovereignty, election of the Republic's first President, occasional participation of Tatarstan in the Novo-Ogarevsk negotiations. Over the course of these two years, the local political elite exploited the internal struggle between the All-Union and the Russian hubs of power, both weakened by mutual hostility and confrontations. The second period commenced with the collapse of the Soviet Union (from 1992, to October, 1993). During this time, the local political leadership attempted to secure a special status for Tatarstan. The measures undertaken by the local elite include an associative union between Tatarstan and the Russian Federation; a declaration of Tatarstan as the subject of international law; the founding of a relationship between Tatarstan and the Russian Federation upon an international treaty; and an unqualified constitutional affirmation of the precedence of republican laws over federal laws within the borders of Tatarstan.

The policy that unfolded along these lines was fueled by a number of strong political moves including the All-Republican referendum on the political status of Tatarstan (held on March 21, 1992); the adoption in November, 1992, of a new constitution, which unilaterally declared the republic as subject to international law and reaffirmed its status as a sovereign nation. The relationship with the Russian Federation was to be based on a treaty that stipulated the mutually delegated political and administrative powers. The trump card successfully played by the local elite during this period was the conflict between the legislative and the executive branches of the Russian government.

The events that took place in Moscow in October, 1993, marked the third stage of the liaison between Moscow and the local political elite. The regions were subjected to pressure by the center following the adoption of the new constitution, which effectively laid the foundation for a unitary state. This period witnessed a precarious balance between the republican political elite and the federal administration. Eventually a treaty was signed on February 15, 1994, entitled the "Delegation of Power and Separation of Administrative Authority between the Government of the Russian Federation and the Government of the Republic of Tatarstan." Appended to the treaty were twelve agreements containing additional stipulations concerning the separation of power in the various domains subject to administrative control.

The true ramifications of the treaty can be understood in the context of historical circumstances that certainly influenced the nature of negotiations (which spanned two and a half years) and the substance of the treaty. Russia's central authorities were ill-disposed toward the idea of concluding a separate agreement with Tatarstan, which they always regarded as an integral part of Russia. Also, the treaty was overshadowed by the December 12, 1993, adoption of the new Constitution of the Russian Federation, which equated national republics with territories and regions. On the other hand, the local political elite wanted the treaty ratified. From the very beginning the elite made a play for a special status for Tatarstan, opting for an associated alliance of independent republics and the Russian Federation founded upon an agreement stipulating the political and administrative powers mutually delegated by and to the parties involved. The local elite was extremely proud of the fact that it was a step, or a half-step, ahead of the other republics making up the Russian Federation and of its image as the vanguard of the independence movement. Tatarstan was the first republic to adopt the Declaration of Sovereignty and to conduct a republican referendum giving its ethnically diverse population an opportunity to voice their views on independent Tatarstan. It was also the first republic to fully incorporate the independence clause into its new constitution. At one point, the political elite of Tatarstan joined the other republics in refusing to sign the Federation Treaty, so it wanted to demonstrate its crusade for a special status by signing a separate agreement with Russia. However, the agreement remained on the back burner for quite some time.

The catalyst which jump-started the whole process was the election of the Federal Council of the Russian Federation. Under direct and indirect pressure from the local elite, Tatarstan did not hold elections in December, 1993. The elections scheduled for March 13, 1994, were also in jeopardy. As a result, the central authorities and the local leadership made a deal: Russia signs the treaty and Tatarstan holds the elections of deputies to the State Duma and the Federal Council. The treaty was signed on February 15, 1994, and the elections were held on March 13, 1994, as scheduled. This compromise served as the foundation for the temporary and precarious balance between Russia's center and the local elite. Of course, the political circumstances influenced the substance of the treaty and, even more important, its implementation.

Let us examine the treaty and other intergovernmental accords objectively. If we hail the agreements, we might become overly ecstatic. On the other hand, an outright rejection might be cause for unqualified pessimism. The title of the treaty itself raises the question of reciprocity in the delegation of powers. Should this formulation be understood to imply that prior to the treaty each side was endowed with independent authority and then decided to delegate some of its powers to the other party? Did Russia actually delegate some of its authority to Tatarstan? The answer is a resounding "no."

The treaty failed to include the most important provision championed by Tatarstan's leadership, namely the republic's autonomy. In fact, the treaty curbs certain powers granted by the current Constitution of Tatarstan. The treaty is also legally flawed since it is in direct violation of the principle of equality of all subjects of the Russian Federation—the tenet incorporated into the Russian Constitution. The treaty conflicts with the Tatarstan Constitution by omitting the associative framework as written in Article 61 of the Tatarstan Constitution and merely reinforces Tatarstan's status as one of the subjects of the federation.

The treaty also violates Article 59 of the Tatarstan Constitution, which stipulates that the republic "is independent and free to determine its own legal and political status." As we now know, things did not work out as planned. According to the same article, "laws of the Republic of Tatarstan shall have precedence within the Republic, unless they violate international agreements entered into by Tatarstan." In effect, the treaty annuls this constitutional provision. For instance, the treaty confers upon the Russian Federation and its administrative organs control over such matters as the legal framework for a common market; monetary, hard currency, credit, and tariff regulations; a judicial system; policing, criminal court, and enforcement legislation; civil, civil court, and arbitration court legislation; and so forth. As stated in the treaty, these and other laws governing the political and economic life in the Russian Federation shall be enforced in Tatarstan. Having cited the legal weight of the Russian laws, can one reasonably claim that the laws of the republic have precedence within its borders?

The treaty was politically significant as it mollified some social groups and allowed the local elite to save face. The document is largely a matter of pompous declaration, propaganda, and prestige. Considering the fact that the Russia-Tatarstan treaty was signed by the leaders of the respective executive branches, it is quite feasible that it will be invalidated by the Constitutional Court of Russia or the Russian legislative body, which already ignores this document when it designs new legislative acts.

Nonetheless, the agreed-upon provisions should not be condemned outright. If brushed-up legally and properly implemented, the treaty would extend certain benefits insofar as Tatarstan's autonomy is concerned. The treaty actually charts a new course aimed at the creation of a democratically structured federation and it contains the seeds of a highly credible idea of asymmetry in the political structure of the new Russian Federation.

As expected, the most serious obstacle to the implementation of the treaty and other intergovernment accords is the deplorable trend running through Russian history: the signing of the accords by the leadership of the Russian state is no guarantee that the accord provisions will be observed by mid- and low-level officials.

It seems Tatarstan will have to overcome a number of obstacles that impede the implementation of the treaty. First of all, the bias for centralization, which is highly pronounced among the Russian establishment, is not to be slighted. It manifests itself in the desire to amass as much power as possible while delegating very few rights and dumping many responsibilities upon the regions. Another cause for skepticism is the vested interest (primarily economic) of the Russian leadership, which goes against the grain of the treaty and other accords. In all probability, the Russian leadership will not be enthused about complying with the various agreements between Russia and Tatarstan, particularly because the bulk of day-to-day decisions will be entrusted to the middle and lower echelons of the Russian officialdom.

Last but not least, the implementation of the treaty and other intergovernment accords is complicated by the many contradictions that crept into the agreements. One example is the setup of free trade zones (FTZ) on Tatarstan soil. Purportedly within the republic's scope of authority, all the key issues (duty and tariff exemptions, partial or complete exemption from federal taxes, operation of foreign banks within the FTZ, visa regulations, and so on) are placed under the jurisdiction of the Russian Federation. It may well turn out that as the socioeconomic and political situation in Russia stabilizes, all these agreements will fall by the wayside, becoming historical relics of purely academic interest.

Prospects

An analysis of Tatarstan's future must rest upon our assessment of the progress made by the republic since the August, 1990, adoption of the Declaration of State Sovereignty. In all truth, the gains have not been impressive.

Hopes for autonomy failed to materialize since autonomy for the ruling elite did not become a goal in and of itself. This movement transformed into an expedient tool used to avoid the control exercised by the center. The implementation of political reform in the republic has slowed. There is no unified and stable mechanism of government. The third branch of the government, the judicial branch, is not fully operational. The state bureaucracy is bloated. In July, 1994, the local elite advanced a concept of reform of the representative institutions as well as for the executive and administrative bodies. Laws based upon this concept were also proposed. All these documents repudiate many democratic tenets, including a professional parliament, equality of the deputies, a multiparty election system, making the chief positions in the municipal and regional administrations elected offices, and so forth. In effect, the nomenklatura has secured a strong grip on power, at least in the foreseeable future, and set up major roadblocks en route to a democratic society.

Economic reform in Tatarstan fared no better. The republic is actually no closer to a market-type economy than it was four or five years ago. Privatization is crawling along at a snail's pace without producing the desired results. Investment opportunities for Russian and foreign investors are limited. While numerous laws and decrees are passed to encourage entrepreneurship, the elite does little or nothing to see them through. This elite is highly intolerant of outside criticism and is incapable of engaging in self-criticisms. It spouts self-righteousness and arrogance. The local ruling elites have not resolved any major economic or social problems. The economic and social welfare of the great majority of the population is declining. Output is falling while prices on foodstuffs, utilities, and housing are soaring. The price of the so-called consumer basket is rising. The average wage in Tatarstan is below the average for Russia as a whole. The group of people entitled to so-called targeted social welfare is becoming more and more narrow.

The republic has a budget deficit, and revenues continue to fall. The rising deficit puts tremendous pressure on the budget to support the policy of social welfare, which is more extensive than its Russian counterpart. All these factors serve to erode the people's support for the ruling elite. In all likelihood, popular support is not unconditional; it will be given only as long as the living conditions in Tatarstan do not deteriorate to a level significantly lower than that of Russia as a whole. If the economic situation does not improve, the popular support base for the elite will continue to erode.

Judging by the experience of the recent past, a large share of the local political elite has exhausted its potential and is incapable of carrying out an effective political and economic reform. The mentality inculcated over many years with the party-government nomenklatura was ill suited for leading the society along the path of major reform. The overriding objective and governing principle adopted by Tatarstan's elite is self-preservation—maneuvering and adopting to whatever comes their way while keeping a firm grip on the levers of control over the resource distribution system.

In the interests of the people of Tatarstan, the republic's course of development must be changed. The most pressing task is making the shift from a delayed response policy to one of well-corroborated conceptual analysis. Nonetheless, the local elite lacks a genuine program of economic recovery; nor does it envision a model of economic and political development of the republic. The elite is apprehensive of democratization, believing it poses a threat to its own authority. In short, the local elite, or at least the bigger part of it, is ill-equipped to meet the challenges of the modern era.

True reform is just as inevitable in Tatarstan as it is in Russia. However, the pace of reform is contingent upon the political elite. No real progress can be made without "rejuvenating" the ruling elite, preferably from the ranks of the younger generation. Indeed, the old nomenklatura does not want to let go and has become quite proficient at maneuvering and political camouflage. The elite intervenes in the elections because it has no confidence in the competence of the voters. At the same time, the opposition to the nomenklatura's grip on power is weak, primarily because the opposition is atomized and torn internally by the ambitions of some of its leaders. The key to Tatarstan's future is the organization of a strong and constructive opposition. Also, the entrenched mechanism of formation and succession of the political elite must be overhauled and replaced with one based on the democratic principles of government. The implementation of these measures depends on the platform offered to the voters, the political culture, and the vigor and organization of the people, particularly the urban population. The ultimate proof of any nation is in the government that the people place in control, provided, of course, the people are not coerced in any way.

14

Social Structure and Political Tenets of the New Branch of the Russian Regional Elite

Mikhail Loiberg

The new regional elite in Russia is comprised of the representatives of the legislative branch of the regional, territorial *(krai)*, and republican governments. These officials were elected (in this sense, the term "elite," as it applies to the legislators, signifies a select or an elected body) during the first half of 1994 by open or secret ballot as stipulated by the provisions of the Constitution of the Russian Federation, adopted in 1993.

Certainly, these developments represent an entirely new phenomenon in the history of the country. While local legislative bodies operated prior to the adoption of the new constitution, in effect members of these institutions were not elected but appointed by the party organs—the true authority in the USSR. Moreover, the legislative branch was not truly such because it was artificially intertwined with the executive branch within the Soviets. While voter turnout was not high, the recently held local elections to the legislature created, for the first time in Russia's history, a government branch dedicated to legislating at the regional level. As an affirmation of their newly acquired power, the local legislative branches are empowered to 1) oversee the operations of the regional administration; and 2) ratify the regional budget.

The same key functions are assigned to state legislatures in the United States as well as other local jurisdictions in democratic countries. Another feature shared by the U.S. state legislatures and the elected regional councils in Russia is the size of the local legislative bodies as determined by the regions themselves.

The scope of regional legislation depends on the membership of the legislature, which, in turn, is defined by the deputies' social and political views. This essay examines these two phenomena. The research methodology used is based on the analysis of newspapers published in sampled regions of the Russian Federation. This is not an exhaustive analysis of this level of the Russian political hierarchy. The sampling strategy was informed by the essay's objectives, namely to describe and analyze the membership and the platform of recently elected legislators in a number of the ethnically Russian regions. Given the volatile political situation in Russia, these regions play an important and unique role. For the most part, these ethnically Russian regions are not at the border of the Russian Federation and are therefore spared often sensitive international issues (unlike Stavropol or the Krasnodar krai). One set of regions in the European-Ural part of Russia that falls into the sampled category includes all regions comprising the Chernozem (Black Earth) Belt (Voronezh, Kursk, Orel, Lipetsk, Tambov, and Belgorod); certain regions of the Nechernozemnaia (Non–Black Earth) Belt adjoining them (Tula, Riazan); and the Volga region (Penza).

Historically, these regions were the cradles of the peasant revolts, particularly in 1917–18 when the burning of landowners' estates lent support for the Bolshevik coup d'état. The reason for discontent was rural overpopulation across the region. Peasants were "land-poor" and the reforms instituted by Alexander II and Piotr Stolypin failed to resolve their predicament. Significant overpopulation of these rural areas continues to be a problem, as confirmed by the statistics showing the ratio of population density for the region to its rural population. Governed by procommunist administrations, these central regions have been christened Moscow's Red Belt.

Another group of regions included in this study is the Yaroslavl and the Kostroma regions, both historically involved in trade and manufacturing. These regions do not suffer from rural overpopulation (the ratio of population density to the percentage of rural population is 22/22 for the Yaroslavl region and 13/21 for the Kostroma region). Historically, these parts of the country did not figure prominently in the consolidation of the Russian lands even though, as purported by contemporary scholarship, they were well equipped to do so. These regions make up the "Golden Ring," which features the very attractive sights of Northeastern Russia.

The last regional group in the sample is the Perm, Cheliabinsk, and Orenburg regions, which belong to the Ural part of Russia and are among the most industrialized areas in the country. These regions produce about 80 percent of the country's industrial output, or twice the total industrial production of the four regions comprising the Red Belt.

The Ural regions have now regained the role they had played for about two centuries of Russian history from the time of Peter the Great up until the epicenter of the heavy industry shifted (at the end of nineteenth and the beginning of twentieth century) to the Donetsk-Krivoi Rog zone. This sample is adequate to account for the political ramifications of the recent elections, which have fashioned a new breed of regional political elite.

The newspapers that were reviewed are *Kurskaia Pravda, Communa* (Voronezh), *Tambovskii Krai, Penzenskaia Pravda, Kostromskoi Krai, Yaroslavkii Rabochii, Kirovskaia Pravda, Permskie Vesti, Cheliabinskii Rabochi, Orenburzhie, Orlovskaia Pravda, Kommunar* (Tula), *Priokskaia Pravda* (Riazan), *Tverskie Vesti, Novaia Gazeta* (Volgograd), *Nasha Gazeta* (Ulianovsk), and a number of others.

The Social Structure of the Regional Legislators

The sociodemographic structure of the legislatures is primarily homogeneous. The regional legislative councils are almost exclusively male. Some councils do not have a single female member. The fact that the elections were free and women comprised a considerable share of the registered candidates suggests that, just as one hundred years ago, women are not regarded in the Russian province as full-fledged participants in the sociopolitical process. Women, who make up the larger share of the electorate, share these views. The Women of Russia faction born out of the December elections to the State Duma is not typical in this respect. Female legislators elected in December are nationally known, with many of them residing in Moscow. However, the average provincial voter still cannot fathom local women as political personae.

The list of candidates and onomastic analysis (the candidate's nationality was not always specified in the list) indicates that 99 percent of the members of the aforementioned legislative councils are Russians. One percent of ethnic minorities among the deputies are Jews. There is one Jewish deputy in Tambovsk and three in the Cheliabinsk Duma.

The membership of the Russian regional elite is much more diverse in terms of professional backgrounds. The legislatures of the ten regions surveyed have 306 members, representing almost every major social stratum. Eighty-four are heads of regional, city, and district government; 44 are entrepreneurs (joint stock companies and banks; 30 are heads of collective farms and agricultural cooperatives; 28 are officials employed by government bodies; 27 are medical workers; 24

are directors of state enterprises; 15 are heads of public organizations; 12 are high school staff members; 6 are staff members of higher educational institutions and scholars; 4 are workers; 3 are freelancers; 3 are heads of the local government institutions; 1 is a farmers; 1 is military personnel; 1 is a clergyperson; and 3 are temporarily unemployed.

What merits attention is that the legislative councils of all ten regions are comprised of merely two of the fourteen social strata, namely heads of the administrative bodies and local government officials. These two "omnipresent" contingents are complemented by the other fourteen, which shape the specific contours of the social structures and reflect the role and weight carried by the respective region at the national level.

The majority of those elected in 1994 to the legislative councils of the Red Belt regions are heads of local administrations (57 from Kursk, 49 from Voronezh, 32 from Tambov, and 48 from Penza). As a result, regional legislative issues can be resolved to the advantage of the executive branch. The situation in Tambov is more complex, because the heads of local administrative bodies control only about one-third of the seats. Still, if joined by the chairmen of collective farms, this group has the majority required to pass legislation. In the Kursk Regional Duma, heads of local administrative bodies have 60 percent of the seats, with 61 percent in Voronezh and 62 percent in Penza. The conditions are ripe for the "marriage" of the local executive and legislative branches. This environment explains the low percentage of local entrepreneurs (8 percent in Kursk, 5 percent in Tambov, none in Voronezh and Penza). Not a single farmer has made it to the regional dumas of the Red Belt. One can imagine the obstacles in the way of adopting legislation that supports the development of the private agricultural sector in this region.

Legislative councils in the Golden Ring tell a different story. While the percentage of the heads of local administrative bodies is not insignificant (Yaroslavl, 35 percent; Kostroma, 25 percent), it is counterbalanced by the entrepreneurs' vote (12 percent in Yaroslavl; however, if we count the seats controlled by the local intelligentsia, which frequently supports newcomers, the figure is about 30 percent). The biggest social cluster at the Kostroma Regional Duma are the entrepreneurs. If this group is split on a certain issue with the local administration, all it needs to do is secure the votes of deputies from such groups as doctors, teachers, and the staff of the higher educational institutions. An alliance of the legislative and executive branches in the regions comprising the Golden Ring is unlikely, particularly if the policy pits itself against the platform set by the president and the government of Russia.

The membership of the Kirov regional legislature includes entrepreneurs, who comprise a small group (about 4 percent); the largest faction is made up of the chairmen of collective farms (29 percent); and the heads of the administrative bodies enjoy 24 percent of the mandates. Without a doubt, the alliance (and a natural one at that) of the local administration and the leading managers of collective farms represents a decisive force in the legislative branch of what used to be the Viatsk Province. The relatively backward social infrastructure of the region has produced a unique situation: the medical profession comprises 29 percent of the regional parliament. Perhaps, this will lead to improved health care services for the population of this vast forested region.

Entrepreneurs constitute the largest faction in the legislative councils in the Ural regions (42 percent in Perm, 38 percent in Cheliabinsk, and 28 percent in Orenburg) with few seats controlled by the heads of local administrative bodies. Moreover, the executive branch in the Ural regions is very different from its Black Earth Belt counterpart. There is not a single collective farm chairman among the legislators of Cheliabinsk and Perm. The leader of the local Communists lost his election bid for the post of chairman of the Cheliabinsk Regional Duma to the head of the Regional Association of Businessmen and Industrialists.

The performance of the legislative bodies suffers as a result of its inability to operate on a consistent basis, as was initially intended. At the very least, the deputies must be given modern housing, since most of them live outside the regional seats of government (this is true of 60 percent of the deputies in Perm, 72 percent in Orenburg, and so on). The severe housing shortage in the regional centers makes it impossible to provide deputies with adequate living conditions. There are hardly any regional dumas or councils that operate on a consistent basis. Amendments to the provisions governing the session schedule for the regional dumas and councils stipulate a quota on the number of standing deputies (2/5 of the roll) and the session schedule (once every two months). All these clauses detract from the power of the local legislative branch and the regional political elite that represents this branch. This is particularly true for the speakers of the regional dumas and councils. It is one thing for the decisions to be made every day and quite another for them to be made only once every two months.

Another factor that tends to subvert the regional legislatures is the lack of political professionalism. The Russian province has not produced enough professional lawyers or other intellectuals who are at least able to carry on a dignified election campaign. It is surprising to see the passive stance assumed by the local bar, which includes at least a dozen professional lawyers.

The Political and Ideological Mind-set of the Regional Legislators

In this essay, information about the deputies is limited to a study of their ideological and political programs during the election campaigns of spring, 1995. Naturally, the political platforms depend on the local circumstances particular to the region as well as the party or social affiliations of the deputies. Still, there are certain agenda items that are shared by most regional politicians.

First of all, "global" programs concerned with the socioeconomic and political framework of the Russian society had been proposed only by the deputies belonging to the opposition parties and groups. Oftentimes, these people were communists or national-patriots who forged a kind of alliance and who advanced the same or similar slogans. By the same token, the deputies supporting the president's and the government's policies eschewed sweeping political declarations, preferring to focus on regional issues.

Second, the one item common to all political programs is the recognition of the need to provide a social safety net for retired and low-income individuals. It seems that the deputies in the regional dumas and councils did not know, just like the federal authorities, how to protect the less competitive strata of society. Yet they could not run for office without raising this issue.

The third point emphasized by all programs proposed by the present-day regional political elite is the battle cry against crime and corruption. To show their seriousness in combating crime, one proposal was to require public officials to report their income.

Russia's regional legislative elections did not feature any overt support for the policies pursued by the federal executive branch. This was a tactical maneuver on the part of the politicians forced to heed the results of the December, 1993, parliamentary elections. It did not bode well for the democratic parties. By the same token, is it not deplorable that the proponents of the democratic reforms carried out by the nationally elected president are reluctant to portray themselves as such at the local legislative elections?

The political elite of the Red Belt was vehement in its criticism of the federal policies. Following is an excerpt from an election campaign policy statement published by the newspaper *Kurskaia Pravda:*

> The country is ruled by pseudodemocrats who have managed over a relatively short period of time to:
> - dismantle a great superpower;
> - destroy industry, which took so much hard work to develop;
> - undermine the legitimacy of the Supreme Soviet;
> - defame our past;
> - drive the country into an ethnic war;
> - destroy agriculture as a public asset.

Interestingly enough, the same issue published official statistics, which indicated that the lower output by the state-owned industry was more than offset by the growing output of private ventures. The deputies in Kursk exhibited the long-forgotten communist haughtiness known in 1920s and 1930s terminology as *komchvanstvo*. On the verge of the elections, the leader of the Communists called for the immediate institution of a "broad-based government" and the reestablishment of the Soviet Union. The leitmotif of the campaign carried out by the Kursk Communists was the rebirth of Russia founded upon the principles of socialism.

The political elites of the Tambov region were even more extreme in their defiant stance. Suffice it to say that during 1993's October events in Moscow, a member of the Tambov Regional Duma and chairman of the regional council, A. Ryabov, tried to recruit a volunteer regiment to go and defend the "White House." The plan did not materialize, but this did not prevent Ryabov from winning the December election to the Federation Council. In fact, the highlight of parliamentary elections in this region was the convincing victory by the former party *nomenklatura* over democrats, who failed to win a single seat.

The Tambov regional political elite is a regional coalition (the Russia faction). This block is comprised of communists, supporters of Vladimir Zhirinovskii, and other national-patriots. It operates under the slogan, "Labor! Justice! Power to the People!" The deputies who have allied themselves with this faction (including a worker, a military serviceman, a civil worker, a teacher, and the head of an enterprise personnel department) express unequivocal support for resurrecting many facets of the social structure of the stagnation period. They also advocate instilling a genuine "Russian spirit" in the mass media. Naturally, the group is against private ownership of land and denationalization of state-owned industry. This aligns them with the chairmen of collective farms who were elected to the Duma (although they do allow for some diversity in agriculture, but with the predominance in the collective mode of farming). The latter group also champions lower taxes on agricultural items, lower interest rates on agriculture-targeted loans, parity in the prices of agricultural and industrial output, and of course, higher tariffs on imported foods.

In the Red Belt regions, the local issues have receded to the background. The megalomania on the part of the deputies of the Russia faction obviously failed to meet the expectations of the local electorate. This discontent explains the election victory of an old Jewish physician who focused on improving local health care (for instance, taking concrete steps toward insurance-based medical coverage).

The alliance (if not the unification) between the legislative and executive branches in the Red Belt regions is a fact of life. Russian sociologists have classified regional leaders into four categories: "business manager" (speaker of the Sverdlov Regional Duma Eduard Rossel), "unsuccessful democrat" (former Mordovian president Vasilii Gusliannikov), "successful democrat" (Nizhegorodsk governor Boris Nemtzov), and "old member of the nomenklatura" (speaker of the Voronezh Regional Duma and the former first secretary of the Regional Party Committee Shabanov; governor of the Orlov Region Egor Stroev). The regions of the Red Belt are predominantly ruled by the latter type. One should not dismiss the openly stated intention of the leading part of the Red Belt's ruling elite headed by Stroev to close the circle around Moscow by winning over some regions of the Non–Black Earth Belt. The Tver Region appears to be a toss-up. Its newspapers tend to snub the leaders of the democratic movements while publishing long interviews with Zhirinovskii.

The majority of the representatives in the legislatures of the Golden Ring regions tend to espouse different political and ideological tenets. For instance, in Kostroma, Zhirinovskii's party was refused a spot on the ballot (while the leader of the Economic Freedom Part, Konstantin Borovoi, was free to participate in the election campaign). Generally speaking, these regions gravitate toward the national-liberal agenda as exemplified by the program of the deputy to the Kostroma Regional Duma, Stepenov, a prominent public figure in the region, a member of the former Soviets, and the dean of the Kostroma Pedagogical Institute. As part of a comprehensive recovery program, he advocates broader powers for the local authorities, including power over the allocation of the federal budget. He seeks to increase unemployment benefits, childcare subsidies, benefits for single mothers, and so forth. He also calls for preserving the Kostroma Institution for Higher Education (currently experiencing financial distress), expediting residential construction, and creating a social safety net for the low-income strata of society. The ideological foundation of his platform is not based on socialism but is rooted in the purity and sanctity of Russia's spiritual and historical ideals.

Also indicative in this respect is the program advanced by the head of the regional administrative body in the Kostroma region, Deputy Gaikalov. His ideological starting point is the rejection of Yegor Gaidar's reform as a hoax imposed by Russia's foreign foes, whose goal is to destroy the great Russian empire, their main rival in the international arena. Gaikalov alleges that the current crisis of the Russian society stems from an all-out foreign assault in the realms of economics, morality, and culture. As a result of the separation of church and state, he argues, other religious faiths have begun to operate in Russia and the people are dumbfounded.

Programs advanced by the businessmen of these regions differ considerably from the ideology-imbued economic programs (unlike in Kursk or Tambov, here the businessmen are under the coercive pressure of the Communists). Deputy of the Kostroma Regional Duma, Morozov, is also a general director of the joint stock plywood factory, which has increased its output despite the crisis and has thus been able to assist retired persons. His program is based on a simple premise: the key to social consensus is that "we all do our job well."

Entrepreneurs (the leading force of the newly elected legislative branch) have narrowed their focus to the development of their regions. The Perm and Cheliabinsk capitalists, particularly the latter, are driven not only by the voters' concern for local and environmental issues but by the resolute attitude exhibited by the Ekaterinburg entrepreneurs who have already proposed a move to establish an independent Ural republic. Ural deputy-entrepreneurs have proclaimed their unhappiness with Ekaterinburg patronage. The chairman of the Cheliabinsk Regional Duma, Skvortsov, has announced a feasibility study for a program of recovery of the Ural regions, with the Cheliabinsk region leading the way. All the while, it maintains its status as the leading industrial region of Russia.

The situation is more complex when it comes to the "rebirth" of the Perm region. Perhaps the fact that the program is handled not by businessmen but by the local intellectuals, who formed the group, "Region," is the root of the problem. This group had proposed a rather utopian and idealized way to implement the recovery program. It seems that voters did not welcome their program of reviving Russia's Ural region: only two of the twenty-one candidates nominated by the "Region" group were elected to the Duma. On the other hand, the opposing faction, the Patriots of Russia, also failed to win the majority. In any event, the issue of recovery of the Perm region has been officially put on the table.

In summary, the regional political elite of the Red Belt and that of the Golden Ring and the Ural region represent two paradigms for the development of the European-Ural part of Russia. The Red Belt regions, led by the procommunist faction in the executive and legislative branches, pose the threat of implementing a radical change from above in order to sidetrack Russia's political course of development. On the other hand, the programs proposed by the political elite of the Golden Ring and the Ural regions are aimed at change from below. They are advocates of a gradual but steady improvement in the welfare of the population, which would ultimately mold a civilized society governed by the rule of law and based on the principles of a market economy. Currently, the two trends counterbalance each other. Perhaps the Red Belt elite will manage to close the circle around Moscow and democratic Russia before the elites of the Golden Ring and the Ural regions come to the aid of the Volga and the Ural businessmen by forging a new economic mechanism. However, we cannot rule out a contrary scenario: the Red Belt neutralizes and becomes a political force and the entire European-Ural part of the Russian Federation follows a convergent course of development. Perhaps history will repeat itself.

15

The Dominant Elites of Siberia
The Altay Region

Vladimir Shubkin

More and more experts are coming to the conclusion that the answer to the Russian political and economic future is not to be found exclusively in the Kremlin, the White House, or on Mokhovaya Street where the State Duma is now located. Certainly, the events in Moscow are both fascinating and important to consider: the open struggle between political parties, the application of heavy military equipment with leaders of various movements wandering between parliamentary tribunes, Matrosskaia Tishina and Lefortovo, the fakers of the hour whose predictions and promises would appear false tomorrow. All of this creates an image of a rough political life.

It is important, however, to understand that Moscow does not adequately reflect the entire country. In fact, many of the determining factors of Russia's success or failure occur outside Moscow in the provinces. The provinces may not have the news coverage of Moscow, but they do have a serious influence on the decisions made at the macro level and, therefore, a permanent effect. The strength of the provinces reflects the weakness of the center. The center had begun to deteriorate during Gorbachev's time and sharply worsened when Yeltsin came to power. A determining moment occurred at the end of the Soviet era. Twenty-five million Russians went abroad. The economy and infrastructure were in crisis. The volume of manufacturing dropped 60 percent. The provinces were calling for sovereignty, which created a threat of disintegration not only to the USSR but also to Russia. The entire control system of state property and state enterprises was destroyed. Slogans were now going against the Military Industrial Complex, which for years had been the apex for the scientific and technical elite. There was a sharp rise in prices and a huge differentiation of incomes within the population. The people were calling for the development of the farming system. For years, the chaos and especially the prevalence of crime only increased. As a result, the center was discredited, particularly in the eyes of the citizens of Siberia.

The national republics began to separate and increase their status. Many regions also began strengthening their independence from Moscow. They now asked: why should the center assist, both economically and politically, those Russian regions upon which the entire country depends? This question is constantly found at the forefront in the creation of the Vologda and Ural republics and in the Siberian agreement, an economic association of nineteen regions of Russia.[1] It determines much of the behavior of the elites. The easing of Moscow's authority and the strengthening of the provinces resulted in a significant increase in the role of the regional elite.

Siberia is a rather peculiar region of Russia. Its agriculture did not know serfdom. From Central Russia came millions of landowners who settled in this severe area and were accustomed to helping themselves. During the civil war, the Siberians (particularly the Western Siberians) distinguished themselves. They were independent from both the Kolchak and the army of the Central Peasant's Republic, which was headed by a simple peasant, Mamontov, from the Barnaul district, who developed the main legislative acts.[2] Such activity certainly frightened the Bolsheviks, who came there after the defeat of the Kolchak. This, for a long time, had worried the center. In 1937, the Peoples' Commissariat for Home Affairs (NKVD) decided to "accuse" Western Siberia of having an underground insurgent army.[3] After the victory of the Bolsheviks, the Siberians met with extremely rigid authority. As a rule, the management of regions and areas was nominated by the center from other regions of the country.

Moscow thought outside management would not please the local population. Kulaks and their families were exiled to the gulag during the years of collectivization. During the years of war, the largest enterprises of the Military Industrial Complex were extended. Strict control over the population of Siberia was established. Joining in the conflict with local authorities was considered extremely risky. People were worried they might simply "disappear" if they joined in the conflict with management. Self-activity of local management was displayed only when the center was in "the thaw" (that is, the regime softened and "the screw-nuts were loosened only a half-turn," yet the Siberian elite left everything the same). The center was very concerned with such a policy. When the situation was under control, the prisoners remained in their camps, exiled persons were drafted into the militia, the workers forged weapons, and the peasants produced bread. This is the way things were for many decades. The situation could not be easily changed.

The inertia of this characteristic behavior can still be seen in the elite. The ideas of self-management and independence are very important, even though, as our research reveals, they are not prevalent in Siberia. Many Siberian chiefs consider the national-territorial division obsolete. Observing the processes in Tuva, Yakutia, and Buriatia, they have come to the conclusion that such a division will prove to be the downfall of Russia. In Altai, following its split from the Gorno-Altai district (Altai Highlands district) and conversion into a republic (in order to receive certain economic advantages), moods changed and sentiments such as "Without a center we shall live better" prevailed. This is characteristic not only for the Altai region.

The idea of creating republics on the basis of an association between the areas and regions is rather popular. For example, the Krasnoiarsk region and Irkutsk district would like to unite and create the Eastern Siberian or Middle Siberian Republic. It is important to study how these ideas are distributed among different groups of the dominant elite. In this type of analysis, the important role belongs to sociologists. Rather than concentrating on the study of struggle, they become experts in exploring public opinion. Certainly, this is an easier and faster way of collecting data, especially taking into account the limitations of resources and the growth of the transport tariffs. However, such research frequently does not give an adequate picture. Another tradition in scientific literature is to consider regional elites as a whole and not divide them into types. At the same time, there are great distinctions between the elite and sometimes conflicts. Usually conflicts are latent and displayed only when the struggle intensifies.

As a rule, many local chiefs try to cut themselves off from the center. In their view, it is futile to wait for anything good to come from the center; it is better for Siberians to manage everything on their own. Such a position has a profound effect on the work of scientific employees to whom the local authorities do not provide any urgent information.

In this essay I attempt to reveal the main characteristics of the modern political and economic elite in the Altai region, using for comparison the last structure of the bureau of the Region Committee of the Communist Party of the Soviet Union (CPSU; 1991); to investigate the large-scale changes of political and economic life and the impact they have on the mobility of the elite; to study the electoral behavior of the elite during the elections in December, 1993, and in March, 1994, and discern their political positions and preferences. This will help us judge how future events will develop.

Technique and Sample

Researchers from Altai Technical University began the research procedure for this study by collecting information on the different types of the dominant elite. The following structures were distinguished:

Executives: the leading representatives of executive authority; chiefs of the Altay region and Barnaul (about twenty persons), including the head of executive authority and his deputies; managers of departments; representative of the president; and the mayor and his deputies.

Legislators: chiefs of legislative authority; members of the legislative assembly of the region and the Duma of Barnaul (chairman, deputies, and managers of commissions, a total of about twenty persons), elected in March, 1994.

Directors: chiefs of the largest state enterprises as well as those joint-stock enterprises with controlling shares owned by the state.

Businessmen: chiefs of large private enterprises, firms, and cooperative societies, including joint-stock companies that do not belong to the state.

"The Formers": former chiefs of the region—those who, in 1991, were members of the bureau of the Altai Region Committee of the CPSU. Though I have labeled them "the formers," many of them are still rather influential figures.

We planned to collect the following information on each person: his occupied post in August, 1991; October, 1993; and March, 1994; year of birth and birthplace; education; whether he remained a member of the Communist Party; whether he entered the *nomenklatura* of the Central Committee or Regional Committee of the CPSU (CC and RC CPSU); place in the management of commercial structures; role in the management of political parties and movements; outlook on the role of the center and local authority; and character of voting in December, 1993, and in March, 1994.

When data collection began, the group of sociologists from the Altai Technical University met with a number of difficulties, particularly with distinguishing directors from businessmen. They assembled data on the largest enterprises of the region, considering both private enterprises and those controlled by the state. They received the necessary data from region and city (Barnaul) committees of state property.

The researchers analyzed documents to outline a circle of people to be interviewed by telephone. They began acquiring data in the middle of March and finished in May, 1994. All key figures of local authority were interviewed: A. A. Surikov, chairman of the Region Legislative Assembly; V. A. Safronov, his deputy; L. A. Korshunov, head of the administration of the region; V. N. Bavarin, head of the administration of Barnaul, elected in April, 1994, as the head of the Barnaul Duma; H. M. Shuba, representative of the president; V. P. Kolesova, manager of the free economic zone; and directors of the largest factories, enterprises, committees, departments, and so forth.

The General Characteristics of Distinguished Groups

The representatives of the different power groups do not vary much by age, education, birthplace, and relation to the Communist Party, but they are in many respects different groups. (Table 15.1 shows the political heterogeneity of the dominant elite.) Ninety-five percent of the executives and legislators, and 78 percent of the directors of state enterprises were in the CPSU. Of these executives, 35 percent entered the nomenklatura. In addition, 26 percent of the legislators and 66 percent of the directors also entered into the nomenklatura. From the first group mentioned, all members left the Communist Party; from the second, 33 percent remained; and from the third, 22 percent kept their membership.

The "businessmen" turned out to be nonparty individuals. Businessmen were not members of the CPSU and did not enter into the nomenklatura or the Communist Party of the Russian Federation (CPRF). In contrast, all members of the bureau of Altay RC CPSU were part of the nomenklatura and "did not give up their principles." Ninety percent are members of the CPRF. The real influence of the formers cannot be described purely by statistics. They play a large role in building capital through connections and their knowledge of the people. The formers have a strong influence on the legislators. Their social and political positions are similar to those of directors of state enterprises. They are closely connected with the military industrial complex, and many have preserved close contacts with the CPRF.

Table 15.1. Characteristics of the Elite in the Altay Region (percentage)

Type of elite	Age	Higher education	Born in Altay region	Former members of CPSU	Remained in Communist Party	Nomenklatura of CC & RC CPSU
Executives	49	100	40	95	0	35
Legislators	47	100	50	95	33	26
Directors	57	100	22	78	22	66
Businessmen	53	100	50	0	0	0
Formers	54	88	44	100	90	100

Note: 90% of the formers voted on December 12, 1993, for the Communist Party of the Russian Federation (CPRF)

Age tends to be an important factor in pulling people together. Among the oldest members of the elite are the directors and formers. It would be foolish to accept the frequently expressed idea that the party nomenklatura was discredited and therefore left the scene completely. In essence, it still has a strong position. The directors, formers, and executives share a common attitude toward the transition from socialism to capitalism. Almost all of them were members of the CPSU. Such a dramatic turn for Russia (as directed from the center) has not been easy for these member of the elite to forgive.

The businessmen are an object of special interest. Born from perestroika and reforms, businesspeople are now the chiefs of various non-state (joint-stock) private enterprises. They play an active role in society and are benefiting from the opportunities of the new free market system. From the perspective of the formers, legislators, and executives, businesspeople are known (antagonistically) as the nouveaux riches. Businesspeople are also known for being closely connected to criminal structures. However, at the top of this group there is proof of legitimate growth and prosperity—highly educated individuals who before had not been members of the political or economic elite. The bitter attitudes toward the nouveaux riches will change as the business elite become stronger economically. As they accumulate more and more money and capital, their positions in the country are likely to be amplified. Soon, perhaps, the "fathers of the region" will come "with a hat," seeking financial support. Their relations with the formers and the legislators continue to lack the important quality of a good partnership, but this is also likely to change as the business elite establish more legislative and executive representation in the government.

Mobility and Political Orientations of Elite Groups

In order to define the characteristics of the modern dominant elite and understand their political position, it is important to present their mobility marked by three historical events: 1) the August, 1991, putsch; 2) the dispersal of the Supreme Soviet of the Russian Federation during the dramatic events in October, 1993; and 3) the elections in March, 1994. Our analysis is focused on the regional elites who have the ability to take high positions in the local pyramid of authority.

The most stable elites are the directors of state and non-state enterprises, firms, concerns and cooperative societies (see table 15.2). Since the August putsch, all of them have retained their status. The executives have a somewhat steady position, as about 55 percent saved their status. The formers have made a downward turn. Half of the former members of the bureau of CC CPSU have received lower posts. The most mobile group has been the legislators. Their status has varied, as it depends on the elections of the legislative assembly of the region. Now more than ever, they are less dependent on the center and more dependent on the mood and outlook of the electorate. Only 30 percent of the legislators have saved their former posts. Fierce competition now surrounds the election procedure for legislators. Apparently, however, the struggle is worth it.

The electoral behavior of the elite in December, 1993, and in March, 1994, and their attitude toward various models of management is also of interest (see table 15.3). There was a radical turn in the mood of a number of elite groups. They were disappointed with political parties as a result of the elections that took place at the time. In December, 1993, directors voted reluctantly, and in March, 1994, they generally ignored all parties. Chiefs of manufacturing lost interest in them completely. The parties lost their meaning. When respondents were asked they voted, they typically replied, "outside of parties lines and political belief"; for the responsible candidate"; "for people competent in the sphere of industry"; "for the person, rather than the party." Even more important is the way the chiefs of nonstate enterprises behaved. By December, 1993, they had already come to the same conclusion as the directors of state enterprises. The attitude taken by most businessmen was that "ties to business are more important than ties to parties; the meaning is not in parties, but in people."

Table 15.2. Mobility of the Elite in 1991–94 (percentage)

Type of elite	Dynamics of status, 1991–94			Dynamics of status, 1991–93			Dynamics of status, 1993–94		
	In-creased	Pre-served	Low-ered	In-creased	Pre-served	Low-ered	In-creased	Pre-served	Low-ered
Executives	40	55	5	25	70	5	15	80	5
Legislators	61	30	9	26	65	9	35	65	0
Directors	0	100	0	0	100	0	0	100	0
Businessmen	0	100	0	0	100	0	0	100	0
Formers	0	50	50	0	50	50	0	100	0

Table 15.3. Elite Voting Behavior, 1993–94

Type of elite	Elections in 1993 (% of votes)			Elections in 1994 (% of votes)			Supported (%)		
	The Choice of Russia	Agrarian Party	CPRF	The Choice of Russia	Agrarian Party	CPRF	Central	Both powers	Local power
Executives	68	5	0	31	8	0	37	26	37
Legislators	28	33	28	10	37	25	5	62	33
Directors	0	22	11	0	0	0	77	12	11
Businessmen	0	0	0	0	0	0	30	30	40
Formers	0	0	90	0	12	77	77	12	11

Clearly, the formers are more politically active. In December, 1993, they actively supported the CPRF, and in March, 1994, the CPRF and a party of agrarians.

All this occurred in an environment of general political apathy. The public's interest in elections fell significantly. In Barnaul, only 33 percent of the electorate participated in the city duma elections in five electoral districts (in April, 1994).

There is a considerable difference in the voting behavior of executives and that of legislators. On December 12, 1993, 70 percent of executives voted "pro-Yeltsin" and "Choice of Russia." Only 30 percent of legislators voted the same. Legislators actively voted for agrarians and communists.

Election results indicate another division of the elite electorate: the executives are primarily oriented toward the city while the legislators have an appreciable orientation to the villages.

In such a traditionally agrarian region as Altai, with its huge collective farms and state farms (many of which were created during the development of the virgin lands) that provided huge food resources for the country, the majority of elite (with the exception of the executives) believe that it is easier to break up farmland enterprises than it is to rebuild them. One of the most influential figures in the region, former first secretary of the CC CPSU Safronov went to the elections in 1994 calling for protection of the collective farm (kolkhoz) system. However, his position as the representative for the agrarian-communists deserves special attention. Let us quote his campaign leaflet entitled "My Position":

> Russia is in great trouble. The so-called radical reforms have led to the disorder of the economy, pauperism, the decline of science and culture, and the moral decomposition of society. It is necessary to stop the economic suffocation of collective farms, state farms, and state enterprises and lower taxes in the interest of manufacturers.
>
> I am against the uncontrollable rise in prices. I am for the reliable social warranty to the people of labor and, first of all, the right of labor.
>
> I say "no" to the wild market with its "shock therapy." I will do everything in my power to let the state finance the creation of a new working place, charge-free education, and medical assistance.
>
> Give the land to those who developed it!
>
> Land should not be subject to a gamble.
>
> I cannot submit to a state that is not able to protect you and me from the encroachments of criminals.
>
> I am against the Americanization of our lives, the spreading of cult violence, and the depravation of our children.
>
> The constitution, which liquidates Soviet power, divides the society between rich and poor and sets up the presidential autocracy. It should be rejected.
>
> I am a Communist and I am calling on you to renew Russia on the basis of validity, respect for labor and patriotism.

One of the key questions of this study concerns the attitudes of different types of elite toward centralism and separatism. Most of the resolute supporters of a strong state are directors of state enterprises (almost 80 percent back a powerful center). Such an attitude is quite natural considering the fact that the largest state enterprises were created for the needs of the entire country and depend on deliveries from throughout the country. The disorder of the USSR and the slogans of sovereignty make the directors long for the times when all was decided and provided by the center. They share this orientation with the former members of the bureau of the CC CPSU.

As a rule, businessmen are in direct opposition to the directors. The majority are for local self-management. The executives are split. On one hand they greatly depend on the center and should follow its political will. But on the other, they see an opportunity to expand their influence.

The divisions between the executives and legislators and between the directors and businessmen reflect the distinction between giving and receiving. The strength of the center is to a great degree determined by the perpetual struggle for a piece of the "shadow pie" (control of the shadow economy) between the central and local authorities. As the former chief of the Krasnoiarsk region, A. Tarasov, testifies, "It is necessary to have an independent and external economic policy. Not only Moscow servicemen but all of us want to live on bribe money."

Who should receive more benefits: the center or the local authorities? The answer to this question frequently depends upon one's position on the issues of sovereignty. The directors of the largest state enterprises obviously favor the center, while businessmen endorse the local authorities. The legislators act with the most care and avoid extremes. The majority of legislators want a combination of strong central power and strong local self-management. Insofar as they are elected by the population, they are less dependent on the center (5 percent favor a strong center). They are more supportive of local self-management (33 percent).

It is necessary to consider the impact of criminals and mafia structures. Criminals have taken on a new identity. They have entered the legitimate world of business, bringing with them criminal minds and corrupt business practices.

The following is a typical picture of the Siberian region. According to Aleksei Tarasov, a correspondent for *Izvestia* in Krasnoiarsk, the city is divided into eight sectors, in which 1,500 criminal groups are incorporated into five communities. In each community there are 2,000–2,500 people. They supervise all banks and markets, 90 percent of commercial structures, and 40 percent of state structures.

These are not simply gangs of racketeers but well-organized groups that are invading all levels and spheres of the economy. Resistance to these groups has been severely suppressed. In 1994, five general directors and presidents of companies were murdered within a ten-day period. The head of one of the largest trade firms in Russia, V. Tsimik, was shot and killed in the entrance of his own home.

Criminals have infiltrated all types and structures of business. The criminal gangs want to form a coalescence between criminal structures and legitimate enterprises. Criminal groups control giant corporations like Krasnoyarsk, Bratsk, Sayan Aluminum Combines, Factory of Color Metals, and Norilsk Nickel. In order to control such enterprises, one must be much more than the average crook. A great degree of experience and professionalism is certainly necessary.

Banks are not immune to criminal infiltration. Our research shows that criminal clans are well established in the Russian banking system. These clans are strictly organized and managed with a resolute hierarchy, discipline, and a rational distribution of responsibilities. Non-payments and loan defaults are often met with violence. The banks involve the gangs in strong-arming lenders. Gangs do not usually resort to pure extortion. Most of the money they receive with violent tactics stems from legal debts owed to lending institutions. Despite the number of blatant violations of law, very little has been done to combat criminal groups.

According to *Izvestia*, a collusion has developed between all levels of the hierarchy, from the district to the regional level. The first group is the bureaucracy with its experience in machine-like management. This group is united with the "new Russians" who rose to power during the 1980s and 1990s on the wave of anti-Communism. The second group is composed of the owners of legal and shadow businesses closely connected with the third group, the criminal world.[4] This relationship ranges from isolated incidents of graft to a constant cooperation between the bureaucratic elite, businessmen, and the criminal world.

In 1980, graft made up a third of all that was stolen; now it makes up more than 50 percent. Those corrupted include 42.2 percent of workers in ministries, state committees, and local management bodies; and 25.8 percent of workers in law-enforcement bodies. Eighty percent of the voting shares of companies and more than half of all capital went to criminal organizations.

The following are statistics that horrify not only the inhabitants of Russia but the entire world: there are 5,691 criminal groups in Russia; 3,000 criminal leaders; 279 "thieves-in-the-law"; 920 groups united into 155 criminal associations, and 40,000 enterprises controlled by mafia clans. Twenty billion dollars have been extracted from Russia with criminal methods and forwarded to the West for "money laundering."

Analysts point out that there are two parallel systems controlling the economy, finances, safety, social life, and policy. "One is the state, which is characterized by economic crisis, political disorder, and a steadily decreasing standard of living. The second system is organized crime: a flexible, mobile, well-structured system, providing the highest incomes, excellent protection for workers, and satisfaction of all their needs. It is easy to predict a gradual mass outflow of labor, intellectual, financial, and technological resources from the first system to the second."[5] Yeltsin was right when he warned that "organized crime aims to enter into big politics in order to receive access to the management of the state." It is highly improbable that a mafia could seize the entire country and create order. However, this is possible in a number of regions and perhaps has already happened.

An Outlook on the Future

To predict the political and economic development of any region is rather risky. Development is determined not only by the parity of local elite forces struggling for power but by the behavior of neighboring regions and the general political, social, and economic situation of the state. These forces and conditions do not give much hope to the opposition and the democrats. "This society," writes Yuri Burtin, "where production assets have been privatized, still is deprived of careful and resourceful owners. In this society, hard work is not encouraged; embezzlement of state funds and corruption prevails; officials have complete domination; and ordinary people are absolutely deprived of rights. The country is stagnant and lacks resources for self-development. It is not possible for this country to develop quietly, by normal evolutionary trends, into a normal, modern postindustrial society."[6]

The electorate has come to a similar conclusion. The Fund of Public Opinion interviewed 1,370 respondents in an all-Russian survey and found some interesting trends.[7] Respondents were asked, "Under what kind of regime would you like your children to live?" The distribution of answers was as follows: socialist, 43 percent; capitalism, 20 percent; indifferent, 16 percent; difficult to answer/hesitant, 21 percent.

It must be emphasized that in only one region did the number of respondents who selected capitalism exceed (was approximately equal to) the number of those who favored socialism. In several regions the number of those who preferred socialism was greater than the supporters of capitalism. In both Moscow and Saint Petersburg, capitalism was chosen over socialism (respectively 33 percent and 25 percent). These results once again confirm the mistake of using Moscow and Saint Petersburg as a representative view of the entire country.

Siberians are not very interested in the issues surrounding the ideological split between socialism and capitalism. They are more worried by problems such as the opportunity to work, the lack of payment for their labor, education for their children, and safety in the city streets.

One possible scenario for the development of events in Russia is backed by the pro-presidential circles that have recently connected with Choice of Russia and economic reforms (Yegor Gaidar, Anatolii Chubais and company). The popular newspaper *Moskovskii Komsomolets* reported that if Boris Yeltsin withdraws his candidacy, his support for Gaidar is assured and the chance of Gaidar winning the presidential election is estimated at above average. In the Altai region, this variant is seen differently. All types of elite (except the executives at the elections of December 12, 1993) resolutely rejected Choice of Russia and, certainly, its leader, Gaidar. It is enough to say that the directors, the businessmen, and the formers rejected this propresidential bloc on all elections. Over a period of four or five months, executive support for Choice of Russia reduced more than two times, and the support of legislators declined more than three times. All this occurred while the leaders of Choice of Russia displayed themselves with words and deeds as the people who would restore capitalism. Choice of Russia changed its name in June, 1994, to Democratic Choice of Russia, but it did not help the party. Gaidar is still the leader. He remains rather unpopular because of the deterioration of life in Russia. He is being held responsible for the poor conditions.

Another possible scenario is a return to the past. Generally, Vladimir Zhirinovskii is not listed among the dominant elite of Altai, though he has made a great deal of noise in Moscow. The formers are supported by the directors and legislators. In April, 1994, during the elections of the chairman of the regional legislative assembly, a disagreement emerged. An organizational committee was created to solve this disagreement and was headed by Safronov, the former first secretary of the Altai CC CPSU. He recommended that Surikov, former chairman of the Altai region executive committee, be elected. Later, Safronov was elected as his deputy. During an interview with the newspaper, *Altaiskaia Pravda,* Safronov noted that during his election as vice president of the legislative assembly, even "deputies who did not share my political views voted for me."[8] Before the first session of the legislative assembly, alarm in the region persisted. On the eve of the first session, a forecast of events appeared in some of the mass media predicting that the Communists and agrarians would seize high command posts in the assembly. Though this did not take place, these two parties had strong positions. The influence of the agrarians appreciably increased.

The field on which the battles between the Russian Democrats and Communists took place is now trampled. "Party tadpoles"—the parties that may have supporters in Moscow but not in the periphery—are disappearing or have disappeared. The new political movements can now appear on this field. However, much still depends on the Communists. Despite the changes, they still cling to their old names and methods. If they make an attempt at restoration, they will be confronted by the executives, who are backed by the Ministry for Home Affairs, and the army and security service. In short, a direct restoration of the past is impossible.

The third scenario ensures the development of a mixed economy. An important role is played by the social-democratic (or socialist) party. Two-thirds of the legislators voted for the Agrarian Party and for the Communists. The social-democratic orientation is acceptable for many of them. This orientation was essentially discredited by a thoughtless group in the center that often called themselves social-democrats. The directors and the businessmen (according to the last elections) appeared to be generally neutral. They do not want to go ahead with Gaidar or back with the formers. They are totally engaged in business and "grabbing." They could be a reserve for new and future movements. As for the executives, they are reasonably flexible in accepting a new ideology as long as it does not create a conflict with them and Moscow. The most conservative group is the formers, though they too have begun to look at the world more broadly (according to the elections in 1994). A considerable future change in their worldview is quite probable.

The Communist Party could eventually spilt into two parties: orthodox communists who desire restoration and social-democrats (or socialists). The latter understand that *reconquista* is impossible. They want a democratic market economy that preserves a certain number of state enterprises and strong central authority. The left socialist governments in Eastern Europe will become the models for practically all postcommunist countries. Because of its large size, its geopolitical role, and its anarchical traditions, Russia's authority will be more rigid than most Western democracies.

Part 4

Types of the Elite

16

The Orientations of
Some Elite Groups in Times of Reform

Elena Avraamova

The transformation processes now under way in Russia raise the question of the role of different social groups in times of reform. However, in previous studies, insufficient attention has been paid to the analysis of positions and expectations of social groups, in spite of their important role in the whole process. Among the various social groups, primary attention should be paid to elite groups, which influence the principal decisions on social development and determine the forms of concrete organizational measures for social and economic transformations.[1]

This study of the elites and their functional role was carried out in the framework of a theory of elites. In both totalitarian and post-totalitarian Russia, such a theory would have been discredited as incompatible with the values of real democracy. Today, however, the following statements would be unequivocally accepted: Elites can be integrated into a conception of democracy. Developing a theory of elites could enhance our knowledge of processes that characterize a society in transition. The analysis and description of transformation processes from a theory of elites has been rather rapid and organic. The reasons for this change are that 1) reforms, as often happened in the history of Russia, were announced "from the top," and this fact exactly defined the power as the main subject of transformation; and 2) the poor development of democratic foundations led to a growing misunderstanding of the roles of "the people" and "the centers of power" into whose hands all the measures of influence were concentrated.

The subject of political analyses and prognoses of the future is based on the functioning and interrelations of power holders and the specific forms they have in contemporary Russia. Elite theory is very suitable for analyses of the central political problem in Russia: are those in positions of authority really elite? Indeed, in the Russian language, the term "elite" is closely associated with such terms as "high quality" and "perfectness." The most fruitful definition (provided by Higley, Field, and Groeholt) distinguishes the elite on the basis of their participation in strategic decision making (or their ability to prevent the adoption of certain decisions).[2] Therefore, we can give the following definition of elites in Russia: groups of people either in the center or in the regions of Russia who wield power, regardless of whether they are in the government or in the opposition, the trade unions, the army, the security service, and so forth. (The classification of elite groups and their internal hierarchy will not be addressed here.)

Higley et al.'s innovation is an introduction of boundaries that distinguish the behavior of elites from non-elite groups. Elites are relatively free in their decision making as long as they do not take actions that affect the fundamental interests of the non-elite groups. This conception of elites requires the analysis of interactions within elites as well as of the links between elites and non-elite groups. The analysis of this kind of interaction should enable us to answer questions concerning the scope for possible social and political maneuvering that the Russian elites may permit themselves without fearing direct obstruction or rejection by the people.

The purpose of the sociological survey, "Transformation and Elite," carried out by the Institute for Social and Economic Problems of the Population in 1993, was to bring out and compare the viewpoints of the elite and non-elite groups on key socioeconomic problems. The following groups of respondents were studied: members of the Supreme Soviet (MSS) of the Russian Federation, which was dissolved in September, 1993 (80 percent answered the survey); where possible there is a comparison given with the results of the survey among the deputies of the Federation Council of the Federal Assembly of the Russian Federation that took place in autumn 1994; heads of regional (oblast and territory) administrations (HRA), 70 percent of which were in the survey; 99 managing directors of industrial companies (DC) in four regions in Russia (Moscow oblast, Nizhnii Novgorod, Krasnodar, and Novorossiisk); and 1,380 workers of industrial enterprises of corresponding regions of Russia whose demographic characteristics are representative of the population working in the former state sector. For the population at large, such workers are somewhat less representative, however, because it excludes some of the most active parts of the population that no longer work in the former state sector of the economy. The inclusion of the members of the former Supreme Soviet

Table 16.1. Opinions on Desired Development (percentage)

	MSS	HRA	DC	P/I
"Liberal model" of economic development (the state should guarantee individual rights, the legal basis for economic life, and minimize social support for the population)	1.3	2.6	0	3.9
"Social-democratic" model (the state regulates certain sectors of the economy and supports the poorest part of the population)	53.3	76.4	35.4	29.4
"Paternalistic" model (the state should regulate most of the economy and support all social groups of the population)	41.3	10.9	62.6	64.1
Others	4.1	10.0	2.0	2.6

Note: MSS: members of the Soviet Supreme; HRA: heads of regional administrations; DC: managing directors of industrial companies; P/I: workers of industrial companies

of the Russian Federation, the heads of regional administrations, and the managing directors of enterprises in the elites should be obvious. The reason is that they participated in the process of strategic decision making. The interactions between the legislative and executive power and between these two powers and the leaders of former state-owned industrial enterprises were dramatic at the time of the survey. These interactions were the basis of the crisis in October, 1993. Without a doubt, the relations between these three elite groups determined the character of social and economic processes in Russia in 1992–93. It should be noted that the groups mentioned do not comprise the entire Russian elite.

The purpose of this research is to bring out and compare the socio-economic and sociopolitical orientations of the aforementioned groups of respondents. Another purpose is to determine the nature of these orientations. The collected empirical information enabled us to compare the judgments and opinions given by the population with those given by the elites. On this basis, it is possible to describe the relations between elites and non-elite groups. The orientation of respondents is differentiated by their choice of three possible models of desired social and economic development. These three models are distinguished by different roles of the state in the economy (see table 16.1), because the state still has the key role in all stages of the economic development of Russia. The state is the initiator of fundamental social reforms and the main agent in carrying them out. This tradition of top-down reforms makes the distinction between the elites' assessments of the state's possibilities even sharper. The existence of elites is the result of state structures, even though they determine their position themselves.

The data in table 16.1 shows that the liberal model, which was the model for top power levels in the period of the survey,[3] did not receive much support from any of the key groups of society except, perhaps, the "ideological elite," which was not part of the survey. The choice is really between the social-democratic and paternalistic models. Members of the Supreme Soviet and heads of regional administrations prefer the social-democratic model of transformation. Leaders of enterprises and the population prefer the paternalistic model because they still consider the state as the key institution for solving major social and economic problems. In 1994, the number of allies of the "social-democratic" model among deputies of the Federation Council (the followers of the deputies of the Supreme Soviet) reached 60 percent. Correspondingly, the number of adherents of the "socialist choice" have decreased. Nevertheless, in-depth interviews revealed that the frontiers between these two models are not distinct. Paternalists appealed to the historical traditions of Russia. The character of their views is rather emotional, and rational arguments are replaced by categories of obligatory beliefs (for instance, "The state should not put everything in the hands of the people of commerce"). The arguments of the market-oriented people are addressed to both world experience and expert opinions. They also have an emotional character: "The country must not bear the dictate of the statesmen." To check the consistency of these choices concerning social development, the respondents were asked to assess variants of reform in Poland (a quick, "shock therapy" type transformation) and in China (gradual transformation) as the models of the further development for Russia. These examples are now under wide discussion in the mass media and by prominent politicians as models for the social development of Russia (see table 16.2).

Table 16.2 shows that the number of adherents of "shock therapy" in its Polish variant was higher than those who selected the liberal model. It appears that nearly 10 percent of the members of the Supreme Soviet and heads of regional administrations consider the Polish variant as the acceptable way of transforming Russia. Still, they were a minority. Nearly 25 percent consider the Chinese experience as positive and the best way out for Russia. But their opinion is not prevalent either. The majority among all groups (except HRA, many of whom refused to answer) were against borrowing any foreign models. Their development perspective of Russia requires the building of a new system of state institutions based on Russia's own experience and tradi-

Table 16.2. Support for Different Variants of Reform (percentage)

	MSS	HRA	DC	P/I
Polish variant: rapid transition to a market economy using "shock therapy" methods	9.3	10.9	4.0	6.0
Chinese variant: gradual transition to a market economy under strict government control	38.7	27.3	23.2	21.0
An original Russian variant created without borrowing foreign models	40.0	16.4	57.6	50.0
Difficult to answer	12.0	45.5	15.2	32.0

Note: MSS: members of the Soviet Supreme; HRA: heads of regional administrations; DC: managing directors of industrial companies; P/I: workers of industrial companies

tions (85 percent of the members of Parliament, 56 percent of the heads of regional administrations, 70 percent of the directors of enterprises, and 50 percent of the working population). While only 15 percent of the surveyed elite members are oriented toward the West, 25 percent of the respondents from the population are Western-oriented.

Cautious attitudes toward the West, which were replaced by emotions connected with devastation of the iron curtain, have only increased. In 1994, the deputies (adherents of the deputies of the Supreme Soviet who talked about the existence of a major threat to Russia) identified Russia as becoming a raw materials source for the West. In the opinion of many of those who were questioned, cooperation with the West brought neither sensible economic aid nor a real partnership. For most deputies, such cooperation grafted the alien "values of the free world" to the people of Russia. Earlier, this opinion was typical only for the extreme national patriots. It is now shared by more moderate representatives of elite groups. In general, it was hoped that there would be a special and unique path that would enable Russia to avoid both its transformation into a "country of shopkeepers" and the severe Chinese-inspired regulation of socioeconomic activities. Therefore, there exists a dominant group of respondents among members of Parliament and directors and among the population that has no specific model for reforms based on "desocialization" of the national economy (privatization and the reduction of foreign trade control and strict government economic regulation) and the development of "independent" individuals (people able to work as independent entrepreneurs). At the same time, there exists a significant group of respondents oriented to reducing the role of the state in the economy and to restricting social security. It can be argued that the answer to this question is determined

Table 16.3. Assessment of the Current Socioeconomic Situation (percentage)

	MSS	HRA	DC	P/I
Difficult situation, but there are some signs that it will improve	8.0	16.4	13.1	5.4
There are some signs of economic stabilization but also of growing social tensions	20.0	23.6	22.2	11.9
The economic situation is getting bad, but the social situation will not cause a disaster	32.0	32.7	24.2	21.4
The current socioeconomic situation is catastrophic	40.0	14.5	39.4	38.6
Difficult to answer	0.0	12.7	1.0	22.4

Note: MSS: members of the Soviet Supreme; HRA: heads of regional administrations; DC: managing directors of industrial companies; P/I: workers of industrial companies

by ideological, social, and cultural factors. For example, preferences for any development model strongly depend on the respondents' perception of the current socioeconomic situation (see table 16.3).

As table 16.3 demonstrates, the heads of regional administration were more optimistic, but their opinions were not shared by corporate directors and workers. However, the position of members of Parliament is characterized by a feeling of approaching catastrophe.

The members were absolutely right in perceiving the situation as catastrophic, not for the country but for their own political future. The Supreme Soviet was dissolved in October, 1993, after the unsuccessful coup d'etat and bloody battles on the streets of Moscow. Therefore, the opinions of the members of Parliament must be assessed while taking into account the rising political tensions in Russia. From table 16.4 it can be seen that the choice of transformation model, which mirrors ideological preferences, determines the assessment of the socioeconomic situation. The adherents of the social-democratic model are mostly optimistic, while adherents of paternalism are pessimistic of the socioeconomic situation. To assess the formation of sociopolitical doctrines and the adherence of different groups to the most widespread "myths" of mass conscience, the respondents were asked about the obstacles to reforms (see table 16.5).

The data shows to what extent general social-economic orientations and evaluation of the current social-economic situation are interconnected. The respondents who have restoration orientations, regardless of the elite group they represent, are inclined to negatively evaluate the changes that are taking place. Moreover, they have not abandoned the feeling of a coming catastrophe that can be prevented only by the

Table 16.4. Interaction of the Assessment of the Current Socioeconomic Situation and the Desired Model of Socioeconomic Development (percentage)

	Assessment of the current situation as a model		
	Positive	Intermediate	Negative
Adherents to the "Sociodemocratic" model			
MSS	7.3	61.9	30.9
HRA	19.0	71.5	7.1
DC	25.7	45.7	28.6
Adherents to the "Paternalist" model			
MSS	6.3	19.1	75.0
HRA	0.0	16.7	83.3
DC	6.5	46.8	45.2

Note: MSS: members of the Soviet Supreme; HRA: heads of regional administrations; DC: managing directors of industrial companies; P/I: workers of industrial companies

Table 16.5. Perceived Obstacles to Reform (percentage)

	MSS	HRA	DC	P/I
Reform does not have serious obstructions	1.3	7.3	1.0	3.2
Reform was not well designed from the beginning and does not correspond to reality	49.3	56.4	54.5	22.7
The nomenklatura is a serious obstruction	13.3	5.5	8.1	8.4
The mafia and corruption stand in the way	4.0	7.3	10.1	22.6
Separatist tendencies stand in the way	6.7	0.0	1.0	2.3
The management of the agrarian sector does not want to adapt to new economic and business practices	4.0	0.0	1.1	1.7
The inertia of the population stands in the way	14.7	10.9	6.1	10.2
In practice, there are no reforms, only imitations of reform	5.3	0.0	16.2	25.6

Note: MSS: members of the Soviet Supreme; HRA: heads of regional administrations; DC: managing directors of industrial companies; P/I: workers of industrial companies

strong state with an iron hand. The market-oriented respondents, on the other hand, often do not, or cannot, see the depth of the real problems that the Russian economy and Russian society face. They consider them only temporary and of a secondary importance. These results clearly reveal that for society, including its elite stratum, there is a mutual ideological dependency. Rationalism and pragmatism, which are currently being put forward as slogans and the titles of political parties fighting for power, have not yet become real values.

Data shown in table 16.5 illustrate that none of the respondent groups share the mass media's interpretation of reform failure.[4] Members of the Soviet Supreme, heads of regional administrations, and directors of enterprises agree to a large extent that the difficulties of implementing reform were caused by the fact that these reforms were not managed correctly and that they were remote from social and economic reality.

A significant proportion of the members of the Soviet Supreme believe that reform failure was caused by the inertia of the population. Neither the directors nor the workers support the notion that the *nomenklatura* is an obstacle to reform realization. Industrial workers have their own perception of reforms, and it is not identical to the opinions of the elite.

In the workers' view, three main obstacles to reforms have almost equal importance: poor initial design of reforms, the mafia and pervasive corruption, and the "imitation" of the reform. Most of the working population did not observe any change at their workplace during the period of transformation.

The survey of 1994 made these estimations: for about 38.8 percent of the deputies mentioned, the power of mafia, crime, and corruption is the fundamental danger to the country and the main obstacle that impedes efficient economic development. The deputies believe that regional leadership and executive power (but not the power of the center alone) can overcome the crisis. Separatist tendencies, which led to the disintegration of the former Soviet Union in 1991, are not considered to be a main barrier to economic reform. Opinions about the optimal type of economic relations with the former republics of the Soviet Union are reflected in table 16.6.

As table 16.6 reveals, economic integration based on transfer prices and inter-republican trade on the basis of world prices enjoy significant support among all elite groups. While trade among republics at world prices is favored, in reality, "wide integration" means the continuation of the practice of subsidization of other republics by the Russian Federation through maintenance of low prices on oil, gas, and electrical energy. The issues of regional transformation are very important in analyzing the priorities of social and economic development of the country (table 16.7).

Table 16.6. Types of Economic Relations with Republics of the Former USSR (percentage)

Type of relations	MSS	HRA	DC
Wide integration of the former USSR republics, common preferential tariffs and special transfer prices	36.3	43.6	41.4
Inter-republican trade on the basis of world prices, without preferences	61.3	43.7	53.5
Difficult to answer	2.4	12.7	5.1

Note: MSS: members of the Soviet Supreme; HRA: heads of regional administrations; DC: managing directors of industrial companies

Table 16.7. Opinions about Models of Regional Development (percentage)

Type of relations	HRA	DC
Export of local natural resources (oil, gas, wood, ore)	21.8	6.1
Promotion and development of regional industrial and scientific potential	45.5	66.7
Attraction of foreign investments and credits	16.4	9.1
Use of federal government investments and credits	1.8	4.0
Realization of large industrial projects in cooperation with other regions and countries of the CIS	3.6	13.1
Difficult to answer	10.9	0.0

Note: HRA: heads of regional administrations; DC: managing directors of industrial companies

Also important is that both the heads of regional administration and corporate directors are not oriented exclusively to federal subsidies and investments. Both of these key groups favor the idea that the promotion and development of locally based industrial and scientific potential is the basis of future development. The heads of regional administrations also point to the necessity of foreign investments and the export of local natural resources.

The positions of the elite and of the working population on the issue of privatization require special analysis. As far as this question is concerned, domestic economy transformation has elements of both rationalization and ideology. The different opinions of elite and non-elite groups were defined according to the consequences of privatization. Elite groups are now the most active actors in the process of privatization. The point of view of the population is the opposite: privatization will lead to the collapse of the national economy. To some extent, the population believes that privatization is carried out only for the bene-

Table 16.8. Results of Privatization (percentage)

Meaning of privatization	MSS	HRA	DC	P/I May, 1992	June, 1993
Establishing necessary conditions for effective economy	29.3	45.5	40.2	8.9	11.5
Freeing personality and raising creativity	24.0	15.1	11.1	6.8	5.3
Bringing back to the people the accumulated property	12.0	11.3	9.1	11.8	16.4
Legal pillage of national property	21.3	15.4	18.4	22.0	34.7
Loss of real moral values in the rush for material goods	4.0	3.6	9.1	13.5	9.2
Economic collapse	8.0	9.1	11.1	18.2	22.8
Difficult to answer	0.0	0.0	0.0	11.8	2.3

Note: MSS: members of the Soviet Supreme; HRA: heads of regional administrations; DC: managing directors of industrial companies; P/I: workers of industrial companies

fit of the mafia and nomenklatura. In 1992, this idea was supported by 22 percent of the population; in 1993 this figure was 35 percent. This illustrates that, so far, privatization has not yet had real economic effects and benefits for the larger strata of the population. Some respondents are even afraid that a transformation of property rights will bring down their way of life and spiritual values (table 16.8). It is widely believed that the ideological basis of the privatization process is the "liberation of the individual."[5] Only members of the Supreme Soviet pay attention to this ideological base. Most important, elite groups do not share the population's "apocalyptic" opinion about privatization as an "economic collapse" and a "pillage of national property" (57.5 percent of respondents who held this type of view used these definitions of privatization). We see here the isolation of the elite groups from their social basis, the working population. However, the elite groups are not united on the key point of privatization—the prevailing method of distributing property.[6]

Given this survey, we can speculate about the future of these elites and their ability to lead Russian society. The "real" politicians, the members of the former Soviet Supreme, have already given their answers on the key issues of socioeconomic development. The forcible

Table 16.9. Assessment of Current Leadership of Enterprises by the Leaders Themselves and Their Employees (percentage)

Opinion	Directors	Employees
Most enterprise leaders are ready to work under market conditions	33.3	18.3
In the nearest future, leaders of enterprises will be able to adapt to market conditions	32.3	29.6
In the nearest future, leaders of enterprises will not be able to adapt to market conditions	28.3	21.0
Most leaders of enterprises are against the market	6.1	15.3
No response	0.0	15.8

dissolution of the Soviet Supreme in October, 1993, and the popular support for those actions proved the unacceptability of their position for further development in Russia's future. This "historical test" gives an additional pattern to forecast for the two other surveyed elites— the heads of regional administrations and the directors of industrial companies. Indeed, the differences or conformities of their opinions with the failed model may help to estimate the viability of those groups. For directors, there was a total conformity with the population in their preferences for the "paternalistic model" (see table 16.1). The directors are also united with the population in the search for an original Russian model of transition to a market economy. The proportions of the directors and workers who see the current situation as catastrophic or close to catastrophe were also similar (see table 16.3). This means that directors may receive considerable support from their employees. However, the directors broadly diverged from the population in their perception of privatization. While the population assessed privatization mostly negatively (see table 16.8), directors supported privatization as a way to improve their legal positions and to gain access to the companies' equity. In this way, directors enjoy some support from the heads of the local administration. At the same time, the directors' willingness to acquire the companies' property and their own self-appraisal of being effective leaders of enterprises in the new market conditions were not shared by the population (see table 16.9). Directors consider themselves very "market oriented," but this opinion is not shared by the employees of their firms.

This is the present weakness of the directors' position, which will likely worsen in the near future. After the first stage of Russian privatization, 76 percent of the employees of privatized industrial companies became dominant shareholders. Now directors are searching for a way to improve their control over the companies. They want to have more control than both employee-shareholders and the "new business elite." They are looking for opportunities to invest their financial resources into real assets as a way of strengthening their political influence.

Finally, another weakness of the directors is their confrontation with the heads of regional administration. Most of the opposition originates from the directors who want to establish closer cooperation with other regions and republics of the Commonwealth of Independent States in order to realize their companies' potential manufacturing capacities. The heads of regional administration mostly rely on the capacity of the mining sectors with high export potential and try to promote a self-sufficient regional economy in order to keep their control over the material and financial flow in their regions. The position of the heads of regional administrations is more favorable. In such a semidemocratic society as present-day Russia, the heads of regional administrations are not elected but appointed by the president. Even though the heads of the regional administration should demonstrate their loyalty to the central government, they are in fact more independent from both directors and the population. In this way, the regional elite have found their own way of interpreting reforms. Their understanding of social transformation emphasizes stability and pragmatism.

Among the regional elite, consciousness of social-democratic ideas is widespread (as a middle point between proclaimed "liberal" orientations of the central government and the "paternalistic" orientations of the directors and the population). This orientation comprises such points as state regulation in key sectors of the economy and the maximum possible support for the poorest part of the population. The process of privatization was an essential factor influencing the changing orientations of the regional elite. During privatization, the regional administrations increased their influence on the redistribution of property.

This study clarified some but not all the issues concerning the establishment and development of elite groups in Russian society. Future studies should include both traditional elites (the directors and the heads of regional administrations) and the "new elites," especially private businessmen. The possibilities of fair competition and fruitful cooperation between "old" and "new" elites will ultimately determine the path and the success of the socioeconomic reforms in Russia.

17

Formation of the Business Elite in Russia

Ivan Kukolev

The transformation of the Soviet system, which began in the mid-1980s, created a new social stratum: businesspeople. The new social conditions led to a splitting of activity on the basis of "capital and labor," a polarization of income and increased stratification of society. These conditions stimulated interest in the research of varied, multiethnic problems with the formation and function of the elite.

European elitist theories were historically focused on the "power elite," the "elite of authority," and the "political elite." The definition of elite was tied to the functions of political management. In Russia, questions quickly surfaced about the degree to which an elite was independent and the determining factors of the relationship between the economic and political elite. The economic elite of Russia does not fit the conceptualizations of Western elitist theories: both classical (Pareto, Mosca, and so forth) and "neo-elitist." The need for a special study of the economic elite in modern Russia is strong, especially considering the long period of deficient capital development in Russia and the lack of conventional Western private property relations.

Generally speaking, the economic elite can be defined as the circle of people who supervise the main financial and economic structures of a country. The economic elite can be separated into two main groups: 1) the chiefs of state enterprises; and 2) the chiefs (proprietors or managers) of private structures (the business elite). The distinction between the groups is disappearing with the emergence of mass joint-stock activity in economic structures. However, the chiefs of new joint-stock companies share many of the main qualities and attributes of the former "industrial generals."

The main purposes of this research are: 1) to provide an empirical definition of the business elite in modern Russia; 2) to reveal the internal structure of the business elite and describe the groups that comprise it; and 3) to study the internal structure of the business elite and define the main trends of its evolution.

Research on Business Elites in Modern Russian Sociology

The study of elites, particularly the business elite, is for the most part in a developmental stage. In the not-so-distant past, interest in the business elite was limited to journalistic descriptions of the "new Russians." Today, serious research on the Russian elite is in progress.

Empirical research on business has isolated the characteristics, images, and "silhouettes" of this new social strata.[1] The main themes of business development in Russia are the social and demographic characteristics of businessmen, businessmen and society, and businessmen and policy. In this research, the business elite are only indirectly referred to as "big businessmen" as compared to "average" and "small" businessmen.

The first attempts to study the business elite were made in newspapers and magazines.[2] The authors and journalists were not bound by the methodological difficulties of serious sociological study when defining the business elite. They define the business elite as the "richest" part of business class. Relatively few names are identified, and these are the same names constantly discussed in the mass media. In these publications, the absence of an exact definition is easily disregarded by remarks like, "In this case we use the word 'elite' conditionally—designating . . . only a theme of research and a reasonably high level of businessmen."[3] "The most influential" businessmen in the country are often rated by writers and journalists.[4] Very frequently the published ratings have either an advertising or an image-making character.[5] In contrast, the composers of "business catalogs" not only select top businessmen but also publish information on their activity. Such information legitimizes the selection of businessmen as members of the elite.

The Theory and Study of the Business Elite

Business elites can be studied theoretically and empirically through "expert" interviews and the content-analysis of the mass media.[6] Experts refer to businessmen as representatives of various administrative structures (especially those connected with business), journalists specializing in economic themes, and leaders of political parties and associations. Experts are asked to define the most influential people in different spheres of business and to justify their choices. Each expert assigns a rating to businessmen on a weight index of their degree of influence on business. The final variant of a general rating is an outcome of a content-analysis of mass media specializing in economical problems and questions of business as well as published ratings and lists of enterprises and businessmen.

The degree of financial and economic influence of a businessman is the criterion for inclusion in the business elite. Such influence may be formal (for instance, size of a person's controllable capital) or informal (for example, place and sphere of activity, personal or corporate political authority). The necessity of the account of "personal authority" is included because of the nature of the political structure of Russia, where connections between people and membership in groups ("interiors") frequently mean more than the amount of capital. Expert interviews and content analysis of mass media rating businessmen are updated twice a year. The general list in the summer of 1995 included 563 businessmen engaged in different spheres of national business.

The first 200 positions in the rating fit the empirical definition of the business elite. To ensure the validity of this list, it was compared with other rating data. For example, up until the middle of 1994, two catalogs of the "Elite of Russian Business" were issued.[7] The first book in this series had an advertising and image-making character. Of the 127 participants in their rating list, only 14 appeared in our rating. Of the 75 businessmen mentioned in the second book, *The Golden Firms of the Year,* 39 are present in our list. A more serious rating of Russian business was made by the *Independent Newspaper (Nezavisimaia Gazeta).* This newspaper published the ratings of 50 leading businessmen in April, 1994.[8]

Press interviews of Moscow experts give a more balanced picture of Russian business, though not without some distortion. When the first 50 positions on our list were compared with the lists of the *Independent Newspaper,* there was a concurrence of 76–83 percent. In autumn 1994, one more catalog was issued. It was devoted to the Russian business elite,[9] and it used some of our materials. The concurrence of the list in the catalog with the first 86 positions on our list-rating was 66 percent.

Data Sources

The list included such information on the business elite as biographic data and various characteristics of their enterprises, politics, and other activities. The data came from informal interviews, observation, and published information about elite activity. The most complex task was scheduling and carrying out interviews with the business elite. Interviews were completed for 75–83 percent of the respondents. The information obtained was supplemented by interviews with secretaries and assistants. In only 14 percent of the cases were repeat meetings with business elites held. On each businessman, a "file" suitable for subsequent statistic processing was completed.

Formation of the Business Elite

Russian studies have made several attempts at modeling the process of free enterprise development and its relationship to the business elite. Valerii Radaev identifies four stages: zero-stage, up to 1989; first stage, 1988–89 (related to the "USSR Law on Cooperation"); second stage, 1990–91 (marked by "further legal indulgences in the field of organization and economic form-creation"); and third stage, since 1992 (impacts of mass privatization).[10]

This classification is comparable in many ways to those of Ivan Bunin.[11] In Bunin's "chronology" of business, three waves are seen: the first wave lasted until 1989 and was connected to the "Law on Individual Labor Activity"; the second wave was from 1989 to 1991; and a third wave began after August, 1991.

V. Lepekhin divides businessmen into two categories: those who came from the state sector and the new business elite.[12] The first group has a three-stage process of formation, but the second group is seen as one continuous flow. Recognizing the obvious connection between business as a whole and the business elite, I offer my own classification of stages of formation of the business elite:

Proto-Period (up until 1986–87). The main sources of the formation of free enterprise were shaped and detailed. The elite became more convex and appreciable, and displayed themselves openly in subsequent years in the party and economic *nomenklatura,* the criminal and shadow economy (black market), and individual social and economic activity. It was the time of the first economic adventurers and risk takers.

Romantic Period (from 1987 to 1993). It was a time for the active formation of free enterprise and for the emergence of a business elite as "groups of people, occupying leading social positions." During this period, restrictions on enterprise activity consistently were removed and "primary capital" was intensively formed (for example, restrictions pertaining to the differences between stock-exchange rates and state prices, the differences between world and domestic prices, and so forth). All main groups of the business elite emerged at this time.

Social and Political Stabilization Period (after 1992 and especially after the autumn of 1993). A return of the nomenklatura (first of all, the "industrial generals") occurred and was accompanied by the replacement of "romantics" from business by nearly formed financial-political groups. This led to the formation of the "party of authority."

The businessmen can also be divided into types: the red directors, old die-hards, new wavers, and party nomenklatura.[13] Such a classification does not, however, cover a number of important developments —for example, businessmen in the middle stratum, especially those with an engineering and technical education. A typology based on even more special criterion would include "losers" (will give up business), "proof" (will remain in business to the end), "grabbers" (grab resources), *"rvache"* (will return to "shadow business"), and "turncoats" (will emigrate abroad). The images of businessmen are linked to the time of their arrival in business: 1) first stage—"compelled businessman" ("adventurers," "capitalists") and "idealistic businessman"; 2) second stage—the "businessman-chief"; 3) third stage—the general picture is supplemented by "mass businessmen" and "businessmen by compulsion."[14]

This variety of businessmen can be reduced to two images: the bear and the squirrel, which reflect psychological features of organization used by the businessmen in their activities. Businessmen are also divided according to their style of life: puritans, Westerners, and little merchants.[15]

Until 1994, formation of the business elite was the result of sequential evaluation of various social strata in business as a result of social and political events. Each strata differed by its social experience and social mobility in the structure of the former USSR.

During our study of the business elite in 1992–94 Olga Krishtanovskaia and I developed two groups of elite based on a set of social-demographic characteristics (age, social origin, social education, social experience) and business attributes (time of entry in business, primary activity, sphere of interests in enterprises and business). The percentage distribution of the main groups in the business elite in 1992–94 is

Table 17.1. The Origin of the Business Elite, 1992–94 (percentages based on the first 200 people from the rating list)

Type	Beginning of 1993	Beginning of 1994	Beginning of 1995
Komsomol members	15	10	9
Physicists	24	20	19
Managers, administrators	22	14	14
Bankers	19	20	22
Directors	2	19	20
Other	18	17	16

shown in table 17.1. The emergence of the laws governing "Cooperation" and "Individual Labor Activity" opened legal channels for activity in small manufacturing that previously had been underground. The laws also ensured the inflow of the most socially mobile elements of society into free enterprise. Within the first wave of free enterprise were the Komsomol members and physicists.

Komsomol Functionaries

Almost half of the Komsomol functionaries came from families with backgrounds as office workers, engineers, and technical workers. One-third were from families of workers and peasants, and 30 percent were born and grew up in Moscow. Moreover, 30 percent lived in large industrial centers and 40 percent in small towns and agricultural districts.

Education was predominantly technical (67 percent). About a third had experience in manufacturing (30 percent in scientific research institutes). Half of them had experience working in Komsomol structures, from low-level positions to positions in the city's committees of the Komsomol Organization. Forty percent worked in the Central Committee of the Komsomol Organization. Twenty percent had experience working in international youth organizations. During their youth, they were usually leaders among the children of their age and were pugnacious, ambitious, and inclined to adventurism.

At school and in institutes, they were actively engaged in public work as members of Soviet Druzhini (Council of Group, a specific administrative organ in Soviet youth organizations in the former USSR), as members of the Komsomol committees in school, or in faculty institutes. Today, the majority of them emphasize that their participation in the Komsomol Organization and subsequently in the Communist Party (CPSU) was only a means for advancing and progressing in the existing system. In political structures Komsomol members were never engaged in particular ideological questions. Their sphere of activity, as a rule, was auxiliary: youth leisure (arranging concerts, performances of students' propaganda teams, organizing parties, arranging excursions), labor education (organization of students' building groups), sports events and tourism, and students' trade unions. These organizational skills were subsequently important to their processes in business.

After postgraduate study, work as a Komsomol instructor in district committees, or work as an instructor in a city's committee, they became "snowflakes," the name for those who worked for Komsomol organs but who officially were enlisted on a working post in the staff of some enterprise in the Komsomol organization.

The beginning of political change did not catch the Komsomol members by surprise. The initial forms of new economic activity were permitted under the guardianship of the Komsomol Organization. Komsomol members had a considerable advantage: they had experience in organizational activity and connections to the Centers of Scientific and Technical Creativity of the Youth, youth housing cooperative societies, and self-financing youth centers. The most profitable activities of that period were controlled by them (for example, cashing of public funds, public leisure activity, video marketing, and video piracy).

Komsomol members came to business in the first wave: 80 percent began their business activity in 1987–89. The average age at the moment of entry was between 30 and 32. Today the average age is 38. For Komsomol members, free choice is part of the transition from state service to private (individual) activity. They are distinguished by the initiatives in the organization of new economic forms, even though their activity was a continuation of their previous organizational and economic roles in political structures. The slogan of the Komsomol members at the end of the 1980s was "speculation always brings maximum profits." Now, Komsomol members are the heads of big holding companies, often in show business.

They also demonstrate high levels of public activity: 70 percent participate in business associations, 30 percent are advisers of state structures, and 20 percent are in legislative bodies. About 80 percent were members of the CPSU, but practically all resigned their membership between 1986 and 1988. Today, Komsomol members are true believers in the market economy.

The moral principles of this section of the business elite are pragmatism, unscrupulousness, cynicism, cruelty, and aggression. For Komsomol members, the desire to achieve prosperity by any means developed as a result of their past careerism and resourcefulness. More than half of them consider themselves believers or sympathizers of the church. Their hobbies include: watching videos, light reading, and sports (football and more recently, tennis). More than one-third have pets. Forty percent know foreign languages. Practically all are married. One-third were married twice and most of them have two children.

Physicists

The social-demographic characteristics of the physicists are similar to those of the Komsomol members. They are from an average mobile strata. Most (more than 80 percent) were born in big industrial centers. Thirty percent are from Moscow and Saint Petersburg. They are from office worker families (45 percent) and families of the nomenklatura (45 percent). About 30 percent have parents who were scientists and cultural workers. Most were in education or technical fields (85 percent), and more than 40 percent have a specialty in physics from such institutions as Moscow State University, Moscow Physical-Technical Institute, and the Moscow Engineer-Physical Institute. Some had experience in management (30 percent), and many had experience working in scientific research institutes (83 percent). Less than 14 percent had experience in political structures. Less than 30 percent joined the CPSU before 1990.

Having experienced a reasonably comfortable childhood and a high standard of living, they studied in school and displayed a propensity for exact sciences. They successfully participated in the student Olympiads of sciences. They aspired to a high level of knowledge, as promoted by their parents.

Independence and an adventurous spirit were developed early. After successfully finishing school they easily entered choice institutes; their motives were the professions of the exact sciences and a comfortable future working in the enterprises of the Military Industrial Complex. Moreover, successful study in science distanced them further from Komsomol work. During their studies, they actively participated in student expeditions, building groups, and illegal cartels *(shabashka)* in order to add extra earnings to their stipends. They also gained their first organizational experience. After their dissertations, they began teaching at an academic institution or a branch of the

Scientific Research Institute. Their average length of work was five to ten years. Physicists generally did not achieve significant successes in their careers. A typical career included moving from a laboratory assistant (during the time of study) to the chief of a laboratory, department, or some other structural division within the Scientific Research Institute. Many of them were connected with the state defense industry.

The regimented order of enterprises, labor discipline, conflicts, and other constraints oppressed the physicists. If they did not invest their time as doctoral candidates, they would leave the sciences as soon as the opportunity for independent activity arose. Eighty percent of physicists went into business at the end of the 1980s. The average age at the time of entry was 35 (it is now 40). At first, Komsomol members and physicists held similar ranks in the same structures: Centers of Scientific and Technical Creativity of the Youth and Youth Housing Cooperative Societies. However, they differed because Physicists were actively oriented to industrial applications. With enthusiasm, they engaged in repairing, constructing, and introducing new products and technologies as well as developing computer programs. Often, they tried to attain what had been forbidden by the state with its system ideas and interests.

However, after some time, they shifted from low-profit manufacturing to speculation in computers, equipment, and food production. After a sequence of organizing and reorganizing of cooperative societies, small enterprises, and various commercial structures, physicists as well as Komsomol members participated in the stock exchange (from the commodity market to the share market, from holding companies to financial-investment companies and new bank structures).

Physicists actively participate in political and business gatherings (business-*tusovka*). They are distinguished by high public activity: 70 percent participate in business associations, and 30 percent are advisers to state administrative structures. Their political sympathies include support for the center and loyalty to the authorities. They sympathize with the Party of Russian Unity and Consent, and their Party of Economic Freedom. They highly appreciate intellect, cultural refinement, and decency in relationships. Many of them are taken up with the philosophies of the past. This orientation and cultural environment of their family upbringing determined their hobbies and passions in leisure time: "heavy reading," with elements of intellectualism (Sheckly, Vonnegut, Hesse, Bulgakov, Dostoyevsky, Remarque, Hemingway, and Marcuse). They prefer classical music, and many are avid music collectors. Whenever possible, their vacation activities include tourism, mountaineering, and, now, downhill skiing and windsurfing. They are workaholics. In their private life there is an element of asceticism; they keep away from luxury and do not accept the behavior of "new Russians." Their priorities above all are based on rationalism. More than 80 percent were married once; 54 percent have one child and 35 percent have two. The transformation of the bank system of the USSR and the liberalization of economic activity gave birth to a new wave of free enterprise formation. Together with industrial managers (administrators), they went into business in 1988–91.

Managers (Administrators)

Managers had an earlier link in the management of the economy. The average age of this group is fifty-one; most were born in provincial centers (45 percent) and in regional centers and villages (40 percent). They came from families of workers and peasants (30 percent) and the service industry (45 percent). Their education is technical. They work in industry (50 percent), enterprise management and administration (70 percent), ministries (50 percent), and management of SRI (40 percent). Their nomenklatura work includes experience in economics (40 percent) and low-level structures of the CPSU (26 percent). More than 70 percent were members of the CPSU in the past. Forty percent left the CPSU when the party was terminated. Twenty-two percent received governmental awards in the USSR; 30 percent published manuscripts and books. Their childhoods were ordinary. Their families had average earnings. They studied well but not excellently. To some extent they were engaged in sports and creative activities. After school they often went into the army and then technical schools. After finishing, they worked in enterprises in order to gain a profession. A standard industrial career might proceed from foreman, to engineer, to chief of a structural division, to main expert. Their industrial activity included inventions, published works, conferences, and attempts to create new forms of organization. At a certain stage of their industrial careers, most were transferred to Moscow to a ministry or other managing body. As their careers slowed down, they usually ended up as chief of a structural division. At this stage, the managers often received additional education in economics, wrote books, and defended their dissertations.

Their professional orientations were the construction and the mining industries. The time of their entry in business was 1988–92, when they were 46–47 years old. Unlike the previous groups, the main reason for their move to business was the reorganization of state structures (60 percent) and, considerably less frequently, free choice (30 percent). Their business activity is connected with the emergence of new forms in the economy: rent enterprises, joint ventures, and commodity exchanges created by groups of manufacturers. During this period, the transformed state enterprises were, in essence, pioneers. These enterprises were in viable manufacturing areas and had managements characterized by dynamic initiative. Currently, managers are found in large financial-industrial groups, chambers of commerce and industry, and new dynamic commercial banks.

Managers do not demonstrate a high level of political activity. They give an illusion of political indifference. Their views are conservative, traditional, transient in "Russophile doctrine," and nostalgic. Yet, at the same time, they have no desire to return to the past. They actively participate in enterprise associations focused on the problems facing national business. In business relations, they adhere to a code of honor of industrial discipline characterized by a high capacity for work, decency and honesty in business contacts, interaction, and responsibility. They do not accept unscrupulousness in business and naked speculation. They are economic patriots. In leisure time, they are fond of sports involving physical strength (wrestling, boxing, heavy athletics, and weightlifting). They also read periodicals and professional literature. They are fond of Jack London and Antoine de Saint-Exupéry. Most were married once and have one child (54 percent) or two (30 percent).

The Bankers

The professional financiers of the past were employees of the USSR banking system. Ninety-five percent have high educations in finance and economics. Bankers are divided into two approximately equal groups: "the old bankers" and "the young bankers." Old bankers (average age, 53 years) predominantly head bank structures that emerged from the organization of state special commercial banks as well as "branch" banks, which were focused on the type of capital in specialized areas of the national economy. They were born in regional centers and completed their educations in financial-economic institutes. Their occupational mobility ranged from ordinary employees to branch chiefs and managers of large structural divisions in the State Bank. A financial career was not popular in the Soviet period. The level of pay for bank workers was almost two times lower than that of the industrial structures, and three to four times lower than the salaries of the Military Industrial Complex.

The reorganization of the state banking system occurred without the active participation of the old bankers. The bank structures headed by old bankers are the most stable and conservative. Young bankers have an average age of 36. Unlike their senior comrades, they did not have enough time to reach appreciable heights in the state service (the maximum level was senior economist). In many ways, they created commercial banks practically from scratch. For a short time, they focused on a clientele dealing with the export of natural resources. Young bankers are more engaged in politics and aggressively favor free choice.

Bankers were members of the CPSU and abolished their membership only after the party was terminated. Today, in general, bankers are a politically indifferent group and favor nonparticipation in politics.

Bankers attach a high meaning to the value of banks in the economic structure of the country since they are paid very highly for their own work and live a life of luxury. Their personal values include tranquillity, balance, and self-centeredness. They do not reject drinking and discussions with friends, but they do not have the merchants' dashing behavior and the bravado of "new Russians." The Soviet period had a great impact on their thinking; that is, they regard professionalism, capacity for work, and devotion to business and country as advantages. They are strongly opposed to criminal structures and work to counteract their control of financial activity. This tendency is probably connected with the high number of contracted murders of bankers. As a rule, they married once and have 2–3 children. Many consider themselves religious believers.

Directors

Directors are the youngest group in the business elite in terms of entry into business activity. They entered business at the time of mass privatization of state property in 1992. These new members of the business elite were directors of large industrial associations and later joint-stock ventures that emerged as a result of privatization. The information presented here characterizes directors at the beginning of 1995.

Directors were formerly the staff (personnel) workers in large enterprises and moved from low-level positions to the posts of deputies of the chief structural divisions. They have a higher technical education (85 percent), frequently through evening or correspondence classes (53 percent). As a result of the political events at the end of the 1980s, when the old economic nomenklatura was partially washed out from the economy and many new chiefs actively joined the political process (Mikhail Bocharov, Nikolai Travkin, Vladimir Shumeiko, and so on), directors appeared at the head of enterprises. They had an opportunity to control a considerable part of the shares of the enterprises they worked for and almost immediately became proprietors of huge industrial capital.

For the most part, the current status of the directors is a result of favorable circumstances, which they used to their utmost advantage. At the beginning of the period of political change, they were actively engaged in underground, commercial activity (leasing of premises, trade of production for low prices, and so forth). Frequently, directors go without receiving salaries for months at a time, yet they manage to purchase real estate abroad and live in luxury, forming the image of the "new Russians" all around the world. The salary of management sometimes is forty to sixty times the average salary of the enterprise workers. Knowing that this is a tricky situation, directors actively develop connections to the political establishment and new financial centers.

Elite Families

Children from elite families during the Soviet period were the sons and daughters of diplomats, trade representatives, high-ranking ministerial officials, academicians, and so forth. Their average age is now 30. Most were born in Moscow (95 percent). They were educated in international relations and international finance. Some worked in the Komsomol (38 percent) and in external economic organizations (27 percent). More than a half of them were members of the CPSU before it dissolved. They have a good knowledge of foreign languages: 23 percent know two languages, and 24 percent know more than two. As children, they attended elite schools and prestigious institutes, then held comfortable positions in elite structures, and now work abroad. As a result, they are characteristically satisfied both physiologically and spiritually. They were prepared when they entered economic structures, joint ventures, banks, and external economic associations. Their usual way of organizing business is "swapping" significant public funds either by simple transfers of money in the Charter Fund or with camouflage through credits under low interests, privileged living conditions, licenses to highly profitable activity, and so on. For example, when a bank is created, it is given rooms in a prestigious district in the building of the former state service. Suddenly there comes a profitable clientele (oil and gas, export of raw material). The bank becomes "authorized" by state structures and in a short period "enters" a group of the largest financial structures. Such is a typical scheme of having "a friend at court."

In business relations, they are not aggressive. On the contrary, they are a bit phlegmatic, infantile, and good-natured. Without support from others and without powerful material and spiritual support from the founders, they could not compete in the aggressive business world.

Free Artists

The average age of free artists is 43. They come from capitals and cities (63 percent) and regional centers (28 percent). Their social origins are generally from families of technical workers (25 percent), the creative intelligentsia (25 percent), and party workers (10 percent). They were the least socially adapted to the Soviet system, "odd, unwanted people." Usually their educations included studies at institutes with an emphasis on cultural and philosophical studies. Those who entered technical high school usually did not finish their studies and left. In the recent past, they developed a specialty; they work as *dvorniks* (street cleaners), stokers, and loaders. Such work rescued them from the charge of "sponging" and possible imprisonment. In Soviet times, they were engaged in small-sized speculation with imported goods, audio records, and so forth. Those who did not find work went to the bottom of the social scale and often developed problems with alcohol and drugs.

During the perestroika years, many of these people rushed into the business world. Being very aggressive, cunning, and unprincipled, they were often quite successful. They ascended the management of large financial empires. Their knowledge and experience of life permitted them to balance legal and illegal activity through good relations and connections to the highest levels of the establishment as well as with criminal structures.

Economic Dissidents

Economic dissidents make up the smallest group in the business elite, less than 4 percent. In this case, however, success is had "not by number, but skill." They can be characterized as self-made and goal-oriented with a durable opposition to the system.

This group is full of paradox. It consists of the people who are very popular in society and those that are absolutely unknown. Among them are the "brightest" parts of national business and the "darkest" sections of the criminal world. As former "economic dissidents" (during the Soviet period), they also do not accept much that is going on in society today. They are devoted to the ideals of the Soviet period. Patriotism is not a political slogan for them but a way of life.

Return of the Nomenklatura

If we look at the changes in the structure of the business elite (see table 17.1), it is evident that the groups most affected were the Komsomol members, physicists, and managers. Their relative number among the business elite decreased from 62 percent to 42 percent. Moreover, 15 percent either went bankrupt or emigrated, and more than half lost their business positions because of excessive engagement in politics. However, those who remained in business increased their status. Their success reveals, first of all, their high personal organizational and managing (administrative) potential, as well as their ability to adapt to varying conditions. The process of replacement will proceed for the next few years, and some groups will cease to exist. The bankers and directors are the backbone of the business elite. Bankers have a rich nomenklatura past (more than 60 percent) and have considerably strengthened their positions.

The directors have sharply expanded their presence in the business elite since the privatization of industry in 1993–94. In the first months of 1994, an active stage of "internal regrouping of forces" took place, redistributing spheres of influence. This can be called a formation of financial-political groups (not to be confused with financial-industrial groups).

Up until 1995, there were actually no large, "independent" businesses not connected with established organizations or some form of political support or shelter. This situation became widespread when political institutes formed a link with economic structures, or political economic structures, which look to politicians for support. In our research, we paid special attention to twenty of the largest financial-industrial groups in industry and numerous "pressure groups," as well as branch and regional "groups of interests."

An important question emerges: who plays the priority role in such groups, politicians or businessmen? Traditionally, the political component is thought of as playing the leading role. From our point of view, this is true only for groups that entered the party of authority or developed around the heads of administrations in the regions. This is a result of relations formed after 1991. However, more and more, "official" structures are resisting political authority, and the main role is being played by the financial component. The coming of power of such groups will mean a reduction of independence in the political establishment.

Regional Aspects

The results of the research program "Who Rules in Russia" can be illustrated by considering the developments in two regions: Krasnodar and Murmansk. These regions differ greatly in terms of climatic and social-demographic characteristics, standard of living, and the political sympathies of the population. The Krasnodar region is a populist-agrarian (separative) region, whereas the Murmansk district is a state-industrial region. Nevertheless, the processes of economic elite formation in the regions are similar. At the end of the 1980s, certain processes gave birth to a wave of formation of the new economic forms and organization. In the background of political chaos, a shift of authority in 1991 in the enterprise stratum occurred, giving rise to the regional business-elite. Regional economic generals spent more time developing in the regions than in Moscow. But the processes of forming joint-stock companies gradually changed. Up until 1995, a private (individual) business, if not inspired and powerfully supported by the administration of a region, would lose its strength and be lowered to the level of an average or small-scale business (small-scale construction, trade, and service). Regional authorities, as a rule, were former workers of the CPSU district committees or district executive committees, who in 1989–90 quit their party work and were appointed in 1991 as the heads of administration by the direct decrees of the president. Immediately, they began systematically to include in their sphere of influence the most profitable economic branches and manufacturing businesses in the region, "feeding and taming them." A differentiation occurred between a "perspective" economy and an "abandoned" economy "left to the mercy of fate," which sometimes reached 60–70 percent of the entire economy of a region.

Privatization forced the chiefs of enterprises of the abandoned economy to search for forms of influence on political processes in a united effort. As a result, the active formation of financial-political groups began. They always included the heads of administration, the mayors of the district (regional) center, vigorous chiefs of large joint-stock societies, enterprises, and associations of the enterprises.

A typical structure for a financial-political group would be three to four chiefs of executive (administrative) authorities, possessing vertical connections with federal authorities along with personal ties to these bodies; chiefs of regional branches of large federal departments

(Ministry of Home Affairs, Federal Security Service, tax police, tax inspection, Office of Public Prosecutor, military circuit); from two to four chiefs of completely controllable banks and some representatives of financial structures (from branches of Moscow banks); a deputy of the Federal Assembly and/or three or four deputies of a regional representative body (District Duma), and/or a few activists from local parties (branches of federal parties); from four to six chiefs of private commercial structures, and five to eight chiefs of large state or share enterprises; and from one to two editors of the local newspapers and an editor of a local TV channel or radio station.

In terms of the balance of forces in such groupings, the chiefs of financial and economical structures play the leading role. Besides the two or three main groups in a region, there can exist three or four more small-sized groups. These smaller groups are called free radicals. They are formed around the administration of a representative assembly, representative of the president in the area, as well as around former regional politicians. These groups, as a rule, have neither appreciable influence nor real opportunities. The role of the regional business elite has yet to emerge.

The contradictions between these groups can be both latent and open. In the Krasnodar region, the opposition between region and urban groups was ended with the removal of the mayor of Krasnodar. This, however, did not mean an unconditional victory for the region's administration. In the Murmansk district, all contradictions between groups are still in a latent condition.

To summarize the events that took place during the development of the business elite in the regions, the "romantic wave" receded and only the structures close to political circles survived. The more fortunate of the businessmen began political careers. As a rule, they lost their independence. The attempts of moderately large private structures to play an independent role have not been taken seriously by the elite or by the population. The chiefs of these private structures tended to drift to the side of established groups or groups in formation. Economic generals, on the contrary, began to play more and more substantial but split roles. The favorites among them could receive tips from authorities and grab state credits. The "unloved" among them were compelled to search for allies and to create new forms for expressing their interests.

18

The New Agricultural Elite in Post-Communist Russia
The Saratov District

Vladimir Palagin

The development of democratic tendencies in Russian society was a necessary precondition for societal change and has influenced the structure of the elite. The development of the elite class derives from specific features of social structure including stratification and the divisions that exist between particular groups. Society, in turn, gains its diverse and complex social organization partly from a well-developed elite structure in the political, economic, scientific, social, and other societal sectors. Finally, the elite are an important mechanism for articulating societal interests. The ability of different societal groups to express and promote their interests partly depends upon the ability and willingness of their elites to organize themselves into groups such as professional societies in science, culture, and different subsectors in manufacturing.

General Characteristics
of the Russian Agricultural Elite

As a group, the elite are concerned with maintaining control over decision making in regards to 1) the distribution of important values in society; 2) industrial production and economic results; and 3) the definition of parameters circumscribing their activities.

Since these individuals tend to be among society's intelligentsia and have strong feelings of responsibility toward society, they are endowed (by society) with certain privileges. Thus, the elite represent an elected and distinguished minority possessing relatively greater privileges than the common person.

This essay presents a case study of agricultural development in the

Saratov district during the post-Communist era to illustrate the relationship between the formation of the new agricultural elite and the implementation of agrarian and economic reform policies. This discussion is preceded by a description of the agricultural elite, its characteristics and structure, in the USSR.

During the Communist era, the agricultural elite differed from other elite groups in that they were formed by the branch principle. Its members included experts in agriculture with notable accomplishments in their fields; high-ranking administrators in agricultural enterprises and local branch centers; and financial experts and economists who serviced the entire agrarian industry. Charged with the responsibility of making agriculture profitable and establishing strong forward linkages with the manufacturing sector, representatives of the agricultural elite were often the sole decision makers on a broad range of activities such as economic, administrative, commercial, and financial activities in the industry.

The agricultural elites used a centralized administrative management system; this style of management was the basis for the social structure of Russian society. Many of the agricultural elite were experts who were appointed to posts and, consequently, were loyal to the central structures of management. While the agricultural elite consisted of a limited number of people, they enjoyed a broad range of privileges.

While the new agricultural elite in post-Communist Russia have enlarged their circle to include more members, many of the elites during the Communist era remain members of the elite cadre today. What has changed, however, is the context of Russian agriculture. Today, economic and agrarian reforms have given way to greater freedoms in agriculture. For example, the agricultural sector now includes different types of farms ranging from small-scale peasant farms to large farming collectives. Also, farmers now have greater freedom in managing their farms; they choose from a broad range of production enterprises and investment opportunities. Therefore, a study of the formation of the new agricultural elite at the national and regional levels must be placed in the context of economic, agrarian, and land reform as it is taking place now in Russia.

In keeping with the establishment of new social and economic relations in the post-Communist era, the new elite have modernized and have also established new relations with other classes and groups in society. Today, they have adapted to the democratic management principles accepted by the state and other societal institutions and now use modern technologies and management procedures. The new agricultural elite are currently vying for a key role in determining the strategies and tactics to be used in further reforms of the agricultural sector.

With the transformation of market relations, the agricultural elite are gradually losing the branch feature of their structure but are strengthening their relationship with the regional elite and non-elite groups. Given this, it appears likely that relations at the regional level will be very important in the formation of the post-Communist agricultural elite.

At the core of the analysis is the process of elite formation in the Saratov district, one of the largest agricultural regions in Russia. Before proceeding, it is important to understand that the economic problems in the agrarian sector are interconnected with broader social problems and that these problems have influenced the formation of new social structures at the village level. Given the importance of economic and agrarian reform in Russia and the fact that it is still relatively new, this study is timely and gives some important insights on the relationship between elite formation and agrarian reform.

In 1992–93, there were 148,700 peasants farms in the Russian Federation, averaging 42 hectares each. The following year, there were 263,300 peasant farms on 11 million hectares of land. In the Saratov district, privatization of the agricultural sector was extremely successful. Reorganization peaked in 1992 when 70 percent of all farms were reorganized. By June 1, 1994, there were 105 collective farms, 55 state farms, 157 joint-stock companies, 280 companies, and 13,000 peasants' farms (a total of 13,597 farms in the Saratov district).

Natural and geographic factors, as well as social and economic conditions, played important roles in determining the formation of joint-stock societies, companies, and privately owned farms. For example, on the right bank of the Volga River, collective and state farms have been largely preserved, while on the left bank, new forms of economic management prevail. Russian agricultural policy favors the creation of the small farm. However, peasant farming is not yet capable of leading agriculture out of its current crisis because small farms cannot achieve the same level of production as large farms owing to economy-of-scale limitations. Rather, economic transformation of the agricultural sector should preserve the state-owned collective farm as the dominant farm type because of its large productive potential. For example, the large collective farms in the Saratov district accounted for the following percentages of total district production in 1991: 99.6 percent of gross manufactured grain, 99.4 percent of sunflower seed, 71.5 percent of the vegetables, 70.6 percent of meat, 67.5 percent of milk, and 62.6 percent of eggs. At the time of this study, the district's meat industry was comprised of 24 percent big-horned cattle, 33 percent cattle, 13 percent pigs, and 15 percent goats and sheep. Personal holdings account for 0.7–3.0 percent of livestock in the Saratov district. It is important to note that the structure of production in the Saratov district is representative of other districts in Russia.

If agrarian reform is to succeed, the state must take a more active role in assisting farmers in making the transition to a market economy. One area where the state can make a significant contribution is credit. Interest rates for agricultural loans and credit was 210 percent in 1993 and 170 percent in 1996. The state should provide subsidized credit to farmers to make agriculture more financially attractive. In a sociological survey of 100 respondents in 1993–94, 20 percent responded that they wanted to work on privately owned farms, and 67 percent preferred to work on large collective farms. In 1992, the number of people wanting to work in farming dropped by over 20 percent; 22 percent wanted to work on private farms while only 45 percent wanted to work on collective farms. If farmers are not supported, the state loses their potential production, as well as the positive effects of a higher national agricultural production on other parts of the economy.

The Social Structure of Post-Communist Agricultural Elite and Non-Elite

As agrarian reform proceeds, seven main social groups in the agrarian sector can be identified: 1) chiefs of large collective state farms (0.25 percent); 2) highly qualified experts in all branches of the agrarian industry (15–20 percent); 3) farmers (2 percent); 4) businessmen (1 percent); 5) petty goods producers, managers, suppliers and distributors, and salespeople (10 percent); 6) agricultural wage laborers and artisans (60 percent); and 7) those unemployed and working part-time in the shadow economy (10 percent).

During the first stage of privatization, members of groups 1 and 2 (chiefs of large collective state farms and experts) were given capital and land in excess of that received by the other groups. Those members of groups 1 and 2 who went into farming had an unfair advantage over other farmers in succeeding in agriculture and increasing the size of their farms. Members of the third group (farmers) formed the second wave of new agricultural producers. This group received smaller lots, but most earned high incomes because of their experience, knowledge, and skills in agriculture.

Members of the fourth group, businessmen, are a new social group whose growth will take place as new service structures develop at the village level. Today, businesspeople are among the better off in their villages and are excellent candidates for forming a village middle class. Members of the fifth group (agricultural wage laborers and artisans) constitute the largest group engaged in agriculture. This social group is very mobile and will remain stable for the next few years. The sixth group (petty goods producers, managers, suppliers and distributors, and salespeople) will promote market development in their areas. With the coming of radical economic reforms, people involved in commercial subsectors such as the service, manufacturing, and retail subsectors (groups six and four) will form the basis of a qualitatively new market-oriented agricultural elite. Finally, members of the seventh group (unemployed and part-time workers) can be considered potential farmers since they are engaged in agriculture's informal economy.

The social mechanisms that are part of the agrarian reform plan have created an uneven playing field for different groups. Consequently, this situation has hastened the process of social stratification. For example, members of groups one and two, leaders and experts, were in the most advantageous situation, allowing some of them to have done very well in agriculture over the past five years. Meanwhile, the standard of living for ordinary workers in large collectives and noncommercial subsectors have declined. Similarly, while cooperators, farmers, and chiefs of the new market institutions earn more, ordinary village workers earn less. Finally, agrarian reform has reduced the number of jobs available for experts with average and higher educations. Currently, the rate of unemployment in this sector is very high, while job creation is low. Given the overriding problems of low salaries and high unemployment, feelings of insecurity and a general dissatisfaction with current conditions are on the rise among many working in the agricultural sector.

The agricultural population is becoming increasingly polarized, and differences between the classes are evident not only in property holdings but also in interests, values, and stereotypes. This process of social stratification is intimately related to the process of elite formation.

The new agricultural elite include chiefs of large collective state farms, joint-stock companies, intermediary-marketing and consumer corporations, along with businesspeople, farmers, and administration representatives. These individuals have attained levels of education and training greatly surpassing that of the average agricultural worker. For example, 80 percent of the chiefs of large collective state farms in the

Saratov district in 1994 were graduates of agricultural institutes versus only 14 percent who have had an average special or average general education. About 6 percent of the high-ranking agricultural chiefs have backgrounds in economics or the humanities. The highest-ranking economic chiefs and military servicemen have above average and specialized educations and often have had some technical training. Company and joint-stock society managers are particularly well educated, and about 90 percent of the experts in all branches of the agrarian-industrial sector have attended institutions of higher education. On the other hand, in the small-scale sector, there is a large and diverse group of former collective farm workers and machine operators whose educational backgrounds range from basic to specialized and some higher education. Many of the refugees from other republics in the Commonwealth of Independent States (CIS) are well educated and are professionals such as engineers, construction workers, doctors, and teachers.

The new agricultural elite appear to be a relatively young group. Only 2 percent of the chiefs of large collective farms are 60 years or older. The number of experts entering agriculture between the ages of 35 and 40 is on the rise. This younger group occupies key positions in joint-stock companies and in regional administrations. The average age for heads of companies, organizations, or government units is 45–50 years old.

There are very few female leaders in agriculture. In the Saratov district, for example, their number does not exceed 3 percent. Of the few existing female leaders, most run businesses in the service or marketing industry.

Political and Ideological Outlook of the New Elite

The post-Communist agricultural elite, while in favor of the current plan for economic reform and agrarian transformation, support different approaches to agricultural reform. Approximately 8 percent of the elite surveyed (as a rule, they were participants in farmers' movements) support the creation of private farms as a main directive of agrarian reform. Seventeen percent of the heads of large state collectives support the current reform plan, while 7 percent consider it useless. Among various groups in the agrarian sector (including both the elite and non-elite) that actively support farming, there are three major groups: pro-reform, 22 percent; neutral, 23 percent; and anti-reform, 38 percent.

The second group does not have a definitive attitude regarding agrarian reform and its economic and social consequences. That is, they neither oppose nor support reform while representatives of the third group absolutely oppose privatization of the agricultural sector. Among the supporters of land privatization, the strongest advocates are farmers, chiefs of state farms, and experts. The controversy surrounding the development of a land market in agriculture is closely tied to a more basic problem of economic development in Russia, namely, the definition of property rights regarding land use.

Most of the people in agriculture, including the elites, do not favor shock therapy and support moderate variants of privatization. For example, most farmers and chiefs of collective farms and joint-stock companies support state aid for agriculture and are in favor of changes in tax and credit policies. A significant number of the elite (85–90 percent) are members of the Agrarian Party, a party whose policy position closely resembles that of Russian Communists.

In 1992–95, Russian agriculture made only its first steps toward adjusting to the new economic reality in Russia. This process of adaptation will continue in the next years, bringing many changes in the behavior and attitudes of those involved in Russian agriculture.

19

The Academic Elite
in the Post-Totalitarian Period

Alexander Boronin

For many years, it was claimed that Soviet science made up between one-fourth and one-third of the world's scientific potential. In 1988, 4.2 million people were employed in research and development (R&D) and supporting services. Of these, 1.5 million were considered scientific personnel. More than half a million people (counted as scientific personnel for statistical purposes) worked in institutes of higher education (IHEs). There were 5,111 scientific institutions (including IHEs) in the country, among them 20 academies and 2,722 scientific research institutes. The collapse of the USSR and the shift to a market economy struck the R&D branch the hardest. It left science at the brink of catastrophe as a result of drastic cuts (tenfold, at least) in funding, the emigration of scientific personnel, and the declining prestige of scientific professions. The survival of science in the new environment depends not only on government policy but also on the scientific community's capacity to restructure itself. The latter would allow the R&D sector to overcome the negative tendencies acquired over the course of many years.

"Overtaking" the West had long dominated government policy on science; the formulation of that policy, the issues concerning the scientific personnel, the determination of priorities, and the distribution of resources for R&D were the prerogatives of the bureaucrats holding power.

It has long been recognized that basic research forms the foundation for creating and disseminating new scientific and technical knowledge. At the present time, society's total outlay appropriated for the intellectual framework supporting economic reproduction substantially exceeds the outlays for material reproduction. Expenditures on scientific research and pilot projects frequently exceed the amount of capital investment.[1] In 1990, however, funding for basic research in the USSR made up less than 7 percent of all expenditures on science, compared with 12 percent in the United States. There had been a marked decrease in the hiring of new personnel, and the democratic principles governing research had been weakened. This was reflected primarily in basic science. A noticeable aging of scientific personnel had taken place, conditions for young people's creative growth had worsened, and nonmaterial incentives and motivation for creative work were being undermined.

In this essay I analyze the basic laws governing the formation and performance of the scientific elite, trace its transformation in the post-totalitarian period, and explore the possibility of adaptation to the new economic environment in Russia. This particular emphasis has received practically no attention from Russian researchers. This analysis makes use of the few existing statistical materials and articles that touch on problems of scientific and technological progress, as well as specialized research on the sociodemographic situation conducted at the Pushchino Biological Research Center of the Russian Academy of Sciences.

Scientific Elite

Having transformed itself into a very complex branch, the scientific community was forced to develop a new administrative structure. The members of this structure were only partly concerned with the final product of scientific activity, notably new knowledge. As a result, two types elites, with some overlap, developed within the scientific community: one formal, one informal.

The formal elite (the scientific bureaucracy) has three basic layers: 1) the specialized staff of the central scientific administration (the most powerful layer); 2) the professional administrative apparatus of scientific institutions, which frequently takes no direct part in scientific research (this level has great influence in defining the research subject matter and working conditions for scholars); and 3) the administrative hierarchy of scientists (employed at scientific institutions) who combine research and administrative functions (directors of laboratories, groups, sectors, and so on). In this regard, according to research materials in a number of institutes, the ratio of workers fulfilling administrative functions to those directly performing research was two to three.

Along with the formal elite, Russian science is permeated by an informal elite. The informal elite is built on a network of personal connections that emerged in the process of conducting purely scientific research. Unlike the formal elite, it has an interdepartmental and interdisciplinary character and only partly overlaps with the formal elite.[2] In principle, only the formal elite is the real elite (the select minority). As Jose Ortega y Gasset writes,

> In speaking of a "select minority," the meaning of this expression is customarily distorted when we pretend to forget that the select ones are not those who arrogantly set themselves above others but those who demand more of themselves, even if those demands are excessive. Of course, the most radical step would be to divide people into two classes: those who demand much of themselves and weigh themselves down with burdens and obligations, and those who demand nothing of themselves. For the latter, life is just going with the flow, remaining whoever they are without striving to grow and develop . . . We remain to be convinced that plebeian tendencies and the oppression of the masses even in traditionally elite circles are characteristic of our time. Thus, intellectual life, which would seem to demand exacting thought, becomes the triumphal path of pseudointellectuals, the unthinking, the unthinkable, and the entirely unacceptable.[3]

The size of each elite group can only be estimated. Certainly not all directors of research subdivisions actually contribute to science at its highest level. Estimating the figures for the informal elite is even more complicated. Neither the number of doctoral dissertations, nor the total number of academic councils of scientific institutions, nor the citation indices supply reliable criteria. They contain no information about the real "eliteness" of a scientist. Nonetheless, it still seems useful to analyze the dynamics of change in the membership of the various levels of the scientific hierarchy. We shall focus upon the USSR Academy of Sciences (subsequently the Russian Academy of Sciences), where the bulk of scientific research is concentrated.

Scientific Personnel in the USSR

In 1940, 98,000 people were employed in all branches of science in the USSR. In 1950, the number increased to 162,000 people; then, in 1960, the number was 354,000; in 1970, 928,000; and in 1980, 1,373,000 people. The largest relative growth of scientific personnel for this period was between 1960 and 1962 (from 14.2 to 29.8 percent). The growth was spurred by the high-paced development of new scientific institutions. By 1970, scientific personnel made up 0.9 percent of the total number of people employed in the Soviet economy. Taken together with science-related service sectors, the figure reached 3 percent. Later, growth slowed, varying from 5.5 percent in 1974 to 0.6 percent in 1986. In 1988, total scientific personnel in the USSR numbered 1,522,000 people. There were 493,000 with Ph.D. degrees; 50,000 had post-Ph.D. degrees (equivalent to a full professorship). Of these, 12.5 percent were engaged in basic research, with 5 percent working at academic institutes, 4.5 percent in branch SRIs, and 3 percent in IHEs).[4] As of January 1, 1990, more than 250,000 people worked in institutions and organizations of the USSR Academy of Sciences. At the same time, in accordance with the Charter of the USSR Academy of Sciences (Article 15), only full members (academicians), corresponding members, and foreign members were included in the ranks of the academy. As Aleksei Zakharov writes,

> Two entirely different structures, namely a public organization with 330 members and an entire branch of the USSR's national economy, had one and the same name: the USSR Academy of Sciences. The public organization functioned on the basis of its charter. Its members, regardless of their place of employment, received life annuity from the state and enjoyed specific privileges: special medical care including sanitariums and resorts, perks in the distribution of deficit goods (cars, for example), and special food rations. One should not forget that the entire Soviet economy was structured in this fashion. There was simply no other way for the system to provide incentives.[5]

At the same time, the academy functioned as a branch in accordance with cross-departmental instructions and regulations that often overlapped with the corresponding resolutions of the Central Committee of the Communist Party and the USSR Council of Ministers. Aside from purely scientific institutions, libraries, museums, expeditions, and the like, the academy also included organizations for construction and procurement, a housing "endowment" of one thousand apartments, a maritime fleet of ten ships, sanitariums and rest homes, daycare centers, hospitals, clubs for scientists, and consumer service centers. There were 65,000 scientific workers directly involved in scientific work, 6,500 of whom held Ph.D.s and 30,000 of whom held candidate of science degrees. Moreover, 337 people were full members (academicians), and 651 (not all of whom worked on the staff of the academy) were corresponding members of the USSR Academy of Sciences. In 1990, more than 200,000 people worked at the institutions of the republics' academies of sciences. Of them, 55,000 were affiliated with science. Among the personnel of the republics' academies of sciences were 1,429 academicians and corresponding members, more than 3,000 Ph.D.s, and 25,000 with candidate of science degrees. The only republic that did not have its own academy was the Russian Federation.

The proportion of women among the scientific personnel in the Academy of Sciences was 42 percent, of whom 1,043 held doctoral degrees (16 percent of the total number of Ph.D.s) and around 10,000 held candidate degrees (33 percent of the total number). The USSR Academy of Sciences included three female academicians (0.9 percent of the total number) and 11 corresponding members (1.7 percent).

The Structure of Russia's Academic Elite

By 1992, the number of specialists involved in R&D had declined to 985,000 people, among whom, 17,400 held Ph.D.s and 111,400 were candidates of science. Moreover, the total number of people employed by scientific institutions, including auxiliary personnel, was 1,532,000. The cross-sectoral breakdown was as follows: academic sector, 186,800; IHE, 72,600; branch, 1,175,000; and factory, 97,900.[6]

The Russian Academy of Sciences brings together 445 scientific institutions, including 322 scientific research institutes. The total number of people working in scientific institutions in 1993 was approximately 144,000. The total number of scholars was 63,000.[7]

The top of the pyramid, and the actual scientific academic elite (in a formal sense), is comprised of the corresponding members and full members (academicians) of the Russian Academy of Sciences. Up until 1991, only this highest level composed the Academy of Sciences, since all others were considered employees of the academy's institutions. If one consults the USSR Academy of Sciences Charter from 1984, Article 1, the following is set out explicitly: "The USSR Academy of Sciences is the USSR's highest scientific institution, with membership comprised of the country's most outstanding scientists—citizens of the USSR"; and Article 15 states, "The USSR Academy of Sciences includes full members (academicians), corresponding members, and foreign members."[8]

This strict formal stratification of the elite was dismantled when the Russian Academy of Sciences was formed by the decree issued by the president of the Russian Federation on November 21, 1991.[9] Article 1 of the Charter of the Russian Academy of Sciences from 1993 repeats its wording verbatim: "The Russian Academy of Sciences brings together the members of the Russian Academy of Sciences—full members and corresponding members of the academy, and scientific employees of the academy's institutions."[10] Although this went practically unnoticed by the majority of scholars (as confirmed by all sociological polls), its legal significance is great. The caste system had been destroyed and formally democratized.

The top level of the academic elite consists of 1,417 scientists (560 academicians and 857 corresponding members), of whom 1,046 (437 academicians and 609 corresponding members) work directly at the institutions of the Academy of Sciences. The structure of the formal elite corresponds entirely to the system of administration in the sciences, which was adopted without changes from the former USSR Academy of Sciences.

Given this rigid formal organization, the role of the individual becomes very important. It was certain outstanding individuals who possessed organizational as well as scientific talents and created adequate conditions in several laboratories and institutes. This did yield scientific results of international repute in a number of scientific and technical fields.

The formation of the informal elite also played an important role. While it only partially overlapped with the formal elite, and despite the Soviet bureaucratic system, it brought together scientists working on par with international standards in the most disparate scientific institutions. As Zakharov writes:

> The study of networks of scientific contacts and the organization of research in a number of Moscow institutes over a period of twenty-five years shows that along with the formal (legally founded, vertical) organization, an informal (without legal basis, horizontal) organization (or self-organization) existed and continues to exist in the form of networks of systematic, personal scientific contacts. It arises as a direct byproduct of research, of the need to discuss, interpret, and evaluate ongoing and final results, as well as the need to exchange ideas, methods, and information among specialists within and outside their immediate field. It encompasses the interlaboratory, interinstitute, intercity, and international spheres of scientific contacts.[11]

Unlike the formal elite, the informal elite is not stratified and its numbers can only be tentatively determined. Among specialists in every field of science, "who's worth what" is no secret. The informal elite includes Ph.D.s as well as candidates of science, and sometimes even scientists without degrees. Understandably, the informal elite consists of profoundly knowledgeable people capable of unconventional thought. As a rule, they not only work in a scientific field but "live" science. By various estimates, such an informal elite in the academy numbers four to five thousand people.

In addition to the formal and informal elites one should include a third, emerging type of scientific elite, which can be viewed as the real elite of the future. Overlapping both of the elites mentioned above, this new elite displays a definite tendency toward partial absorption and replacement of the others. This new type of elite is comprised of certain directors of scientific research institutions, heads of laboratories, and leaders of scientific research groups who are trying to make use of new opportunities for conducting scientific work under crisis conditions. For scientific research work to maintain the current number of scientists and other personnel in research institutes, using available buildings, structures, infrastructure, equipment (much of it needs to be replaced), supply of reagents, and so forth, the funding of institutes would have to be increased at least six times as compared with the planned budget appropriations.

It is clear that only those groups of scientists, laboratories, departments, and institutes that are able to find additional sources of funding will survive. The major sources of funding for scientific work, notably basic research, are grants and contracts. There are additional means of keeping institutes afloat so as to ensure a sustainable level of basic research. These would entail such organizational changes as the development of applied research; the organization and participation of scientific workers in teaching; the organization of small business through the creation or expansion of higher educational institutions; the manufacturing of equipment, machinery, and the infrastructure for the development of agriculture, and so forth.

Promoting the integration of Russian scientists into the international scientific community is also extremely important. This calls for the development of contacts and various forms of cooperation with foreign scientists, scientific institutions, agencies, and foundations. This sort of activity should lead to the emergence of a scientific elite that will sustain itself and develop under the existing conditions.

Reforms in the Russian Academy of Sciences are progressing extremely slowly, even though several years ago its scientific institutions had already received full freedom to undertake the reorganization effort. Under these circumstances the role of the directors of the Russian Academy of Sciences' research institutes in the academic hierarchy (whether they are members of the academy or not) becomes much more important. This also applies to the heads of the institutes' research subdivisions, inasmuch as their position in the institutional and academic hierarchy is increasingly defined by whether the research units they direct have the opportunity to carry on the research.

The Elite in Scientific Research Institutes

Every young scholar in the Academy of Sciences probably dreams of becoming a corresponding member, and the boldest, of becoming an academician. This dream remains unattainable for the overwhelming majority, however, and they must be content with belonging to the elite of the respective institute. If one does not take into consideration the purely administrative-managerial sphere with its own hierarchy and system of relations, then the highest recognition of a researcher's scientific achievements in his institute is his election by his colleagues to the academic council. To be elected one must hold a degree. It also helps to have an administrative post (head of a laboratory, department, or group), although this is not a prerequisite. Scientists under 35 created the Council of Young Scientists, whose chairman was a member of the institute's academic council. During the Soviet period, the secretary of the party organization and the chairman of the labor union were without exception included in the academic council.

The party and labor union committees led a parallel existence as a sort of second layer of the institutional elite. They were built on the principle, grounded in ideology, of representing "all strata of workers," including service personnel. Thus, somebody independent of the Academic Council directly or indirectly participated in the planning and evaluation of the results of purely scientific work through the system of socialist competition and by extending or withholding support for the scientists. This institutional elite was quite dynamic and, in principle, open. Naturally, it was intended that this system would espouse and put into practice the principles upon which the socialist state is founded.

In practice, the activity of the party and labor union committees, especially in the last years of their existence, was far from uniform. It depended on the composition and mainly on the directors of these committees. Some dogmatically put into practice the demands of official policy. Others tried to minimize the evil (if not procure the benefits) inflicted by these organs. The number of potential leaders of the latter type who agreed to be chosen from among the scholars to fill these administrative positions steadily decreased with the passage of time. This was a result of disagreement with official state policy, disappointment, and the obvious detrimental effect such appointments had on their research. As a result, these posts were quite frequently taken by people pursuing purely careerist ends. All of this served to distract the scientists from their real work and complicate their lives. In general, the activities of the administration, the Academic Council, the Council of Young Scientists, the party committee, and the labor union committee created an extremely complex system of relations within the scientific community as well as a system of interrelations between the institute and the organizations to which it was subordinated.

Another avenue of forming the scientific elite was defined by the system of providing resources required for scientific research. In the 1950s and 1960s, success in many areas of experimental science depended to a large degree on a scientist's "good head and hands." Once the West began to pull away in the area of electronics and the construction of scientific instruments in the 1960s and 1970s, the availability of imported scientific equipment and reagents began to play an ever more significant role. The chances of getting this equipment depended to a certain degree on the "pull" enjoyed by the scientific-administrative chief in the state, academic, and institutional hierarchy. Some institutes were provided with modern, imported scientific equipment and reagents; for the majority of institutes, such purchases were extremely limited. This factor also facilitated the creation of elite institutes and laboratories.

Nonetheless, despite the numerous flaws in their work, it was precisely the academic councils (and especially seminars) that played a decisive role in preserving some degree of academic freedom. Without this venue, doing any science at all would have been unthinkable. The most important factor was the opportunity afforded to many scholars working in the academy's research institutions to make independent choices on the subjects and methods of their research. Moreover, there were no demands for instant results.[12] This permitted long-term research to be conducted over a period of many years and created the "surplus" of finished work that allows Russian science to exist even in the absence of subsistence-level funding.

The Top of the Elite

The Academy of Sciences turned out to be a very conservative entity with regard to changes in the elite induced by the shift to a post-Communist society. The collapse of the USSR and the emergence of new forces in the Russian academy led only to a certain expansion of the top of the elite, which consisted of members of the academy. This took place at the expense of younger scientists, whose influence on scientific progress was actually greater but who made up a sort of second echelon of the academic elite. For the most part, these people became the directors of institutes, whose formal status was already quite high. This has somewhat rejuvenated and strengthened the academy.[13]

In 1990, the USSR Academy of Sciences had approximately 6,600 scholars who held a Ph.D. (average age was 58); 30,000 candidates of science (average age was 45.6); and 26,700 scientists without higher degrees (average age was 38.2). The top of the academic community was comprised of 306 academicians and 567 corresponding members. Their average age at the beginning of 1990 was 69.5 and 63.7 respectively. Among them, 139 academicians were older than 70 and 106 were older than 75.

The Russian Academy of Sciences now has 560 academicians and 857 corresponding members, of whom 437 and 609, respectively, work in scientific institutions of the academy. This jump at the top level of the official scientific elite was the result of the merger of the USSR Academy of Sciences and the newly formed Academy of Sciences of the Russian Federation. The latter was created on the basis of a decree from the Presidium of the Supreme Soviet of the Russian Socialist Federation of Soviet Republics on January 24, 1990, as a means of strengthening the sovereignty of the Russian Federation within the USSR.[14]

The two academies were combined into a single Russian Academy of Sciences in November, 1991, almost immediately after the collapse of the USSR. This closed a nearly yearlong period of strained relations between the USSR Academy of Sciences and the leadership of the Russian Federation. For all practical purposes, continuity in the management of the academy was maintained during this time. The president of the academy was elected from among members of the scientific elite of the Ural branch of the academy. In accordance with tradition, this was done with the direct support of the country's leaders. With this move, the period of confrontation between the top of the USSR Academy of Sciences and the politicized scientific community was, for all intents and purposes, brought to a close.

The academy's charter (10) stipulates that its management is carried out by the Presidium, which includes the president, vice president, academicians, department secretaries (18), chairmen of regional departments (3), the chief academic secretary, and members of the Presidium. The number of vice presidents and members of the Presidium ("ministers without briefcases") is determined by a general meeting of the academy. As in the USSR Academy of Sciences, the Presidium is comprised of about 40 people, and, according to the charter, it can be changed by the decision of the general meeting once every five years.

Despite a desire to maintain conservative traditions, there has been an attempt to save the academy's management from the impending crisis of 1990. The result was a certain degree of democratization in the management of the Russian Academy as compared to the USSR Academy of Sciences (participation of corresponding members in presidential elections and the opportunity to nominate several candidates for a single seat).[15]

The Path to the Elite

Much like the Soviet command-bureaucratic system, the formation of the scientific elite was strictly regimented and followed the so-called career principle. This principle operated through a system of appointments, which formed a kind of "table of ranks." This table determined the material well-being and formal prestige of any scholar. In recent years, this system has undergone some insignificant changes that are perhaps best viewed as an attempt to lessen the dissatisfaction of the "high-ranking officers." Additional posts of leading and chief scientists were introduced. The latter was, in essence, intended for elderly chiefs of laboratories whose age precluded the fulfillment of their administrative duties.

The social sciences occupied a special place within the USSR Academy of Sciences. They were obligated to follow at all times the established canons of Marxism-Leninism. "The practical result of this incredible state of affairs is massive mimicry of scientific work to the point of its absolute profanation. The overwhelming majority of dissertations are produced in accordance with a template established once and for all eternity. They have no more relation to real science than does religious liturgy."[16] Luckily, the natural sciences were not as scrupulously controlled from above (with the exception of the "struggle with cosmopolitanism in science" in the 1940s and 1950s and Lysenko's battle against geneticists). But even natural sciences suffered from this strict, formal hierarchy, which perverted the system of interrelations and distorted the objective evaluation of the results.[17]

In this multi-tier hierarchy, there were only two reliable paths "upward" into the highest echelon of the academic elite: the direct, active support of some influential academicians (this was a viable alternative for those who worked closely with them) or the direct support of party and government bodies (for "special achievement"). With rare exceptions, it remained an unattainable dream for others. Their ambitions were realized at the beginning of the 1990s through the simultaneous creation of several alternative academies (natural sciences, biotechnology, oosphere, and the like). But the big-sounding title of "academician" frequently turned out to be unsupported by scientific achievements or genuine organizational work in the sciences.

The scientific hierarchy was one of the causes of mass "brain drain." For many members of the informal elite, emigration was the simplest and quickest means of raising their social status. The situation has been strikingly reminiscent of the opening of the New World, when the most enterprising representatives of various classes rushed to cross the ocean. This exodus was aggravated by the opportunity to continue research with the use of modern equipment, reagents, information systems, and so forth. In addition to earning more money, the opportunity to raise one's standard of living immediately, to live (if only in part) on par with Western standards, was also important.

Academic Elite and Social Stratification

Scientists (scholars) in the USSR who belonged to the scientific elite held a fairly high position in the social structure. In the system of "realistic communism" as defined by Alexander Zinov'ev, their position was bolstered by specific privileges and salaries. The nature of scientific work, inevitable contacts with foreign colleagues (in person or through correspondence), and methods of personnel policy permitted the Academy of Sciences to maintain fairly high standards even during the "stagnation" period. As the academician Sergei Novikov writes:

> Observation and analysis lead me to the conclusion that the community of scientists in the academy, scholars ranging from academicians to candidates of science, were influenced by the stagnation less than other related communities: the IHEs, medicine, engineering, pedagogy, agriculture, and other sciences. As a consequence, it seems that the relative value of the academy for our country has grown. It contains the greatest number of specialists in many fields who work on par with high international standards (although, unfortunately, in a number of scientific fields this percentage is, mildly speaking, not high even here).[18]

In the post-Communist period, beginning in August, 1991, the situation in the sciences changed dramatically. The elite has been re-formed and its position in the social hierarchy has fallen sharply across the board. This process continues to threaten the very existence of science, and especially basic science, in Russia. In the first place, science itself has lost its prestige. The radically altered ratio of salaries and pensions to those earned by other professions has sharply lowered the social status of scientists. In 1993, the lowest average salaries (approximately half the national average) were, in fact, in the scientific and cultural spheres. Second, major cuts in state-funded social programs, primarily housing, have eliminated one of the great incentives that once attracted young people to the academic towns.

Changes in the state system have not affected the top level of the academic elite significantly in a formal sense, but they have clearly lowered both its overall status in society and its level of financial security. To this day, however, academic titles remain quite desirable. This is also true for a number of political figures, especially those who came to the upper echelons of executive and legislative power from the network of academic institutes. Note that it was only between 1917 and 1929 that the Academy of Sciences retained its relative independence from the party-state leadership. This irritated the party to no small degree. In the spring of 1929, harsh measures were taken to bring in new scientific personnel and introduce a layer of party officials. A "purge" began. Social backgrounds, service in the pre-Revolutionary state apparatus, membership in bourgeois parties, and the like were checked.[19]

The role of party leadership in the formation of the academic elite is beyond doubt. It is enough to recall the election in 1939 of the half-literate Trofim Lysenko or chief prosecutor (provocateur and hangman) Andrei Vyshinskii as full members of the USSR Academy of Sciences. This was, however, more the exception than the rule. For the most part, true scholars with significant contributions to science were elected to the academy. Notably, personnel records indicate that over the course of forty-four years (1929–72), of the 500 newly elected full members, only 20 were directly connected to the party-government apparatus.[20] However, the party's influence cannot be thus quantified, since entire disciplines were ideologized (philosophy, sociology, economics, history, philology).

The Influence of the Scientific Elite on Basic Social, Political, and Economic Processes

The conservative streak running through the top level of the academic elite just about ensured the sharp decline in its influence in the post-Communist period. In the Soviet period, science played a prominent role, for it had to sanctify and legitimize the actions of the ruling party elite. The concept of "scientific communism" was introduced, and the social sciences became an obligatory part of every curriculum. Plans for the "implementation" of scientific achievements were under the control of the party's regional committees, and special resolutions of the Communist Party's Central Committee and the government were adopted in a number of scientific sectors. In keeping with this tradition, the academic elite—academicians Leonid Abalkin, Abel Aganbegyan, Georgii Arbatov, Andrei Sakharov, Stanislav Shatalin, Tatiana Zaslavskaia, and others—lent its authority and helped corroborate the need to reform stagnant economic and social spheres during Gorbachev's perestroika. However, their caution, their tendency toward a certain consistency of action, and their unwillingness to stake their reputations made this stratum of professionals undesirable for the new forces striving for real political power. Young economists from the second and third echelons of the Academy of Sciences began to play a more active role. They were not linked to the director corps of the party's High Committee. They were also quite ambitious, well-prepared professionally, and capable of defending their stances before any audience; they turned out to be an excellent tool for destroying the socio-economic structure of the totalitarian state. Their effectiveness exceeded all expectations. It is remarkable that the dramatic changes did not lead to complete chaos.

Representatives of the lower levels of the scientific elite (in both the academies and universities) also played an essential role in destroying the ideological and, unfortunately, the patriotic traditions that defined the mentality of the Soviet system. Significantly better informed, free-thinking, and inclined toward critical analysis, they always comprised the internal opposition to the regime. Still, they refrained from entering into open conflict with the regime, since their profession itself gave them a sense of inner freedom.

These strata provided the most active and energetic deputies to the soviets of various levels, which, until October–November, 1993, probably played the decisive role in creating a feeling of popular democracy. This served as an important psychological backdrop to a "reverse revolution" in which 10 percent of the population grew richer at the expense of the remainder.

One can ascertain that the academic scientific elite has actually held onto its position within its sphere of activity, even though its clout at the state level has fallen sharply. Respect for the Academy of Sciences among the population remains, most likely as a consequence of inertia. It is more characteristic of the generation of forty- to sixty-year-olds, whose coming of age coincided with a period when science was flourishing. Young politicians and businesspeople, living for the present, are not at all inclined to reckon with the opinions of the scientific elite.

Moreover, a significant percentage of young intellectuals who rushed into politics straight from the academy system and who know all its weaknesses "from the inside" clearly feel no respect for the academic environment that molded them and where, over the last fifteen to twenty years, intergenerational relations have become strained. This is owing primarily to the rapid growth of the USSR Academy of Sciences in the 1960s, which led to a pronounced stratification between the higher and lower levels of the scientific community, especially during the stagnation period.

Under these conditions, a corporate spirit and loyalty to the system in which they work is maintained only at the highest levels of the academy and among a small group of "honored" employees who have already advanced as far as they will. For the informal elite, whose self-assessment is high and whose prestige is determined by its personal contributions as well as its potential for future intellectual accomplishment, the current situation has opened up a number of new opportunities. These opportunities lie outside purely scientific endeavors and can even include direct participation in government structures. This, along with the opportunity to travel and work abroad, has reduced internal strife by depriving, to some degree, the bulk of scientists of their informal leaders.

20

Political Power and Science

Vladimir Zakharov

Differences between the United States, Europe, and Russia make it difficult to develop a common definition for members of the scientific elite. Professional scientists in the USSR included full and associate members of the Academy of Sciences (now, the Russian Academy); members of other academies, including medical doctors and agricultural researchers; and administrators at research institutes and prestigious schools. In Russia, there are two to three thousand people who can be considered members of the formal scientific elite. There are two important factors that characterize this group: access to important resources and control over their activities.

An informal scientific elite continues to exist in Russia. These scientists have great prestige in their respective fields. Because scientists differ in their abilities and achievements, there are hierarchies in scientific communities. In their respective fields, every scientist is very aware of who's who.

In the USSR, the formal and informal elite could not merge as is in Western countries. A career in the sciences was one of the few opportunities for people in the USSR to have a prosperous and secure life. Therefore, competition was fierce and forced some highly qualified people to seek employment outside their respective fields. On the other hand, there were some scientists who lacked either the talent or the motivation necessary to attain elite status. The formal and informal elite did not overlap; in fact, they were often in conflict. This division was well known. There has always been an interchange between the formal and informal elite that varied depending on the field and its political climate. The dynamics of this process deserve special research attention. Combined, both formal and informal elites comprised no more than 3–5 percent of the USSR's total population.

The New Government and Science

In Russia, a new government was established in January, 1991. At that time, Yegor Gaidar's appointment to the cabinet received a great deal of support from members of Russia's scientific community, especially its lower echelons. However, it has become evident that the new government does not intend to support the sciences to the same degree as the previous regime.

Government policy has and continues to have a great impact on the sciences in Russia. While the government was *gradually* reducing support in other areas, science was hit hard by the first wave of cutbacks. With high inflation, financial support for science was not a high priority. As a result, funding for the sciences was reduced at least a dozen times, if not more, in only three years. At present, the salary of the president of the Russian Academy of Sciences (RAS) is equivalent to that of a bus driver. A typical scientist in Moscow makes, on average, three to four times less than the average worker in the city. Additionally, scientists do not receive their meager salaries on a regular basis.

Experimental work and planning has been made virtually impossible owing, in part, to problems with deliveries of new equipment. Moreover, there is a lack of resources that hinders daily operations at research institutes. As a result, a number of institutes have had to close for months at a time, leaving employees jobless. Fiscal problems are such that practically no one can afford to subscribe to scientific journals published abroad. Never have Russian scientists experienced such deprivation resulting from the actions of government. Even the Bolsheviks, who disliked and feared many scientists, thought it necessary to support the development of science.

Given the current conditions, some politicians have declared that today's "occupation government" is consciously destroying Russian science. To them, however, this is not an unreasonable situation, considering the multitudes who are suffering even greater hardships in Russia. Today, approximately 0.6 percent of the gross national product is allocated to science. This percentage is less than what all other developed countries allocate to their respective science programs. Despite all the problems in the sciences, the Russian government has no difficulty in allocating large sums of money to other areas of the nation.

About New Power: The Case of Mr. A

What are the causes of the extremely negative attitudes of politicians toward science? Without an understanding of the causes, it would be impossible to devise a plan to save much of Russia's scientific elite from certain extinction. To answer this, it is necessary to know something about the nature of power in Russia today.

Currently, there is an enormous gap between those in power and ordinary Russians. This gap has grown so wide that elites who formerly were able to influence decision makers are now powerless. It is widely agreed that a revolution took place in Russia in 1990. If this is true, Russia's most recent revolution was very different from that which took place in 1917 or in France in 1789 because in those revolutions, for better or worse, the dominant class was overthrown and replaced. This was not the case at all in Russia in 1990.

In the Western press, Boris Yeltsin is known as the betrayer of communism. There are many such betrayers, the vast majority of whom are former Communist Party functionaries (especially at the middle and provincial levels). These people are now known as the "new Russians." They were positioned perfectly for the "revolution" and have adjusted quite well to life in the post-Communist regime. As an illustration, let us compare the positions of a typical "new Russian" in the old and new Russia.

For the sake of comparison we will create a fictional character called "Mr. A" (a generalization intended to illustrate my analysis). Mr. A was formerly the secretary of a regional committee. Today he is a "mover and a shaker" in his home region. He is a bank president and a chairman of the region's joint export company, which deals in raw material exports (oil, lumber, and nonferrous metals). In the old Russia, Mr. A possessed enormous formal power. He controlled party personnel in his region, lived in a beautiful apartment, was chauffeured in a luxury car, and was given access to a dacha (a summer house staffed by servants). Still, Mr. A was not very happy in his past life because his power and lifestyle could be taken away at any time. He owned very little, and his opportunities for advancement were almost nonexistent. In these respects, his position was not enviable.

During the cold war, Mr. A was responsible for the construction of arms factories in his region. This is not to say he was deeply committed to communist world domination. Actually, he had been distrustful of communism for some time. Mr. A had listened longingly to stories about life in the United States from his son who was on a diplomatic mission there. In the depths of his soul, Mr. A envied American workers because they were able to own their homes and have personal savings as a result of their hard work. He also fantasized about what he could do and buy with dollars.

In Russia today, Mr. A has no reason to envy American workers because he is rich by any measure. Mr. A has amassed considerable personal wealth in cash, property, and luxury items. Mr. A has traded formal power for property. Even though he has lost his formal power, he has retained a great deal of informal power. For example, the State Duma president is mindful of Mr. A's interests when economic issues come to a vote. Unequivocally, Mr. A was a big winner in the last Russian "pseudorevolution."

Let us examine Mr. A's attitude toward science. In prerevolutionary times, Mr. A regarded science in only one way—as necessary for its contributions to the military industrial complex (MIC). Now Mr. A's attention centers on revenues from selling raw materials abroad versus "wasting" resources on Russia's MIC and other industries. Science, it seems, has become nonessential to the rich and powerful. Worsening the situation is the fact that Mr. A had always regarded scientists with suspicion; he always felt they were capable of sedition (an attitude that is widely shared even today).

More About the New Power

Like Mr. A, many people moved from positions in government to the private sector. This produced a vacuum in the political arena that was filled by the new people from the intelligentsia. As an illustration of how this has affected Russian politics, let us consider the case of one member of the intelligentsia. We will call this fictional representation "Mr. B." In the USSR, Mr. B was an administrator in a research institute. Today, he holds a cabinet post in government where he assists a high-ranking official such as the president or prime minister. Mr. B is very influential since he has the ear of many of Russia's most powerful people and assists them with the formulation of national policies. Literally and figuratively, he walks the corridors of power.

Mr. B is not new to this type of work; it is similar to what he did as an administrator. In contrast to Mr. A, Mr. B is intelligent and well educated. He has a Ph.D., but his job does not make use of these skills. Mr. B is "politically correct" in his convictions in the sense that he is against big government. In fact, he is more fervent in this view and admires Reagan and Thatcher more than even the most extreme members of the Republican Party in the United States.

Referring to ideas they learned from foreign teachers, Mr. B and others like him think that the government should not interfere with the economy. Furthermore, they want the government to liquidate itself. Consequently, they are working to downsize the federal government in Russia as much as possible. In their view, if people are allowed to do as they will, then everything will work out just fine. People should be able to become rich any way they can. For example, they think there should be no restrictions or taxes on the export of natural resources. Mr. B believes that Russia needs rich people! And it is irrelevant whether or not wealth is acquired honestly. Russia needs an initial period of growth, of capital accumulation. He feels that Russia desperately needs a large upper class, which can be created by increasing trade. Then a period of initial growth would ensue, which, to him, is important enough to allow capitalists free reign over Russia's human and natural resources (these ideas originate from Mr. B's conventional Soviet education, during which, for a long time, he was a Marxist. It was Marx who thought there would be no honor among people at the onset of capitalism).

Mr. B and his friends have, in effect, enabled Mr. A to live a very prosperous life. While you would expect Mr. A to be grateful to Mr. B, he is unwilling to share his good fortune. Consequently, these two groups are quickly becoming adversaries. Each day, Mr. B is growing more and more envious since he receives a very modest salary. Just after the revolution, Mr. B had no ideas of revenge on the Communists. He was an idealist; he simply wanted to make Russia a better place to live.

Mr. B suffered from the naive perspective that plagued the Russian intelligentsia for one and one-half centuries (since its creation). This sickness is utopianism, the belief in a bright future that, in time, only shifts in form. The main symptoms of this illness are maximalism and the belief that swift and sharp destructive actions will immediately lead to the desired aim. Another feature of this perspective is anarchism, which is also an integral feature of the Russian mentality. Russia has produced the world's most notable theoreticians of anarchism: Mikhail Bakunin, Leo Tolstoy, Pyotr Kropotkin. Similarly, the Bolsheviks in 1917 heard the call of anarchism and utopianism. They also felt that the state is a necessary, albeit temporary, evil.

In general, there are some similarities between Mr. B and people who participated in the October Revolution that led to Bolshevism. Both considered themselves reformists, but true reform suggests thoughtful and well-considered action. This type of reform necessarily includes broad public discussion where consideration is given to all different points of view, the possible consequences of different plans, and the interests of different groups. The reforms implemented in the 1860s in Russia somehow reflected these ideals, but it was not popular to speak of them in 1991 when the reformers were much more similar to the Bolsheviks who acted "straight from the shoulder." These reformers were convinced that they knew the absolute truth, were above criticism, and needed no advice. With great wrath, they pursued only one goal: to destroy the main social institutions left in the wake of the evil empire of the past.

The reformers were destroyers who had no plans for rebuilding. They believed that the market economy would rebuild Russia. So far, the only things rebuilt are palaces. While the wealth of a nation can be found in its citizens' property, this is not the whole story.

Science and the New Power: New Comments

Mr. B was recently given the task of reforming science in Russia, something that was badly needed on a large scale. During Brezhnev's time, a number of applied research institutes ("boxes") were created for military projects. These institutes were characterized by large staffs and poor management. The informal scientific elite were almost completely missing from these institutes. Staffs consisted primarily of scientists. Institutes were generously supported by the government. In the 1980s, 4 percent of the national science program budget went to the Academy of Sciences. The rest was allocated to applied (mainly military) research institutes.

Clearly, this situation could not continue in the new Russia. Genuine reform was needed, which required consultation by experts and scrupulous planning. The first step would be to inventory all existing scientific resources and categorize them so that decisions could be made regarding military (nonusable) and nonmilitary (usable) institutes. Certainly, this would be an extremely difficult task requiring input from many different experts, including the informal scientific elite.

Another important step toward effective reform might be to initiate a national debate in the press. This could begin with the general question, "How can we reform science?" As the issue is publicly debated, the publication of confidential information such as questionable actions and the actual number of scientists would be necessary.

In the end, the discussion would provide valuable input for evaluating personnel, including a set of criteria for their selection. The criteria could be developed by independent experts and include information such as participation on expert councils, publications in international journals, the number of invitations to international conferences, and so forth. After a discussion in the press, the application of these mechanisms would have been rather straightforward.

None of this was ever accomplished. The program outlined above did not fit the spirit of the time. Then, "shock therapy" was en vogue, as one might expect from idealistic Russians who were bent on achieving a utopian society after the revolution.

Shock therapy reform seemed to have a clear objective in the industrial sector. It consisted of discontinuing financial support to state-run enterprises and privatizing (forming joint-stock companies) as quickly as possible. Also, government was downsized, as many ministries were simply liquidated. Mr. B had no time for tears because he faced so many difficult tasks.

The application of shock therapy to science was quite strange. Competition and the struggle to survive, the bases of shock therapy, took place in science in the form of searching for grants. However, a system of distribution still needed to be created. The privatization of research institutes was absolutely absurd. Only a few companies in the West can afford to fund their own research laboratories. Everywhere, the world of science is supported by government. Therefore, in Russia the radical transformation of state institutes that manage scientific research was impossible from the outset.

The main administrative institution for science, the State Committee on Science and Engineering, gained status when it was incorporated into the Ministry of Science and Technical Policy. The Academy of Sciences of the USSR also survived partly because, after existing for 269 years, it was instantly transformed into the Russian Academy of Sciences. According to this Darwinian survival of the fittest theory, the following series of events was supposed to occur (though I am aware of no one who believes it possible): Non-elite scientists will leave their areas for the private sector. A few elite scientists will survive through the lean times. After this process has reached fruition, the elites will be recognized and rewarded accordingly.

Strategy of the Formal Elite

There is now a classic example of utopian thinking that is, at the same time, dogmatic. In reality, however, something completely different is taking place. During the period of study, not one research institute closed. The Scientific Research Institute (SRI) does not just consist of employees and their salaries (sometimes paid, often not); these institutions also represent considerable value in terms of land, buildings, secondary facilities, laboratories, workshops, and vehicles. This property is considerable, and the people who control it are already acting by a known scheme; that is, if these resources are not privatized, at least they can be a source of profit. One way they could be a source of profit would be to rent portions of each facility to private interests for offices and shops. They can use them as private enterprises with the participation of foreigners. Part of the revenues could be used to support the struggling institutes by paying for electricity, water, and other miscellaneous costs. In reality, though, the bulk of the revenues is being pocketed by the managers. Today, in Russia, this sort of activity is absolutely legal. Current regulations governing private business in Russia are flawed and precipitate some very strange affairs. For example, the RAS is the sole proprietor of property and has the right to dispose of it by either renting or selling it outright. On the other hand, the RAS is a part of Russia's government and receives its budget from the Ministry of Finance. A similar situation occurs in the high schools. Student dormitories are being used as hotels, with rooms made available to the general public. It is assumed that revenues are used by the high school to pay costs. However, there are criminal elements in dormitories that are engaged in illegal activities. This is easy to criticize, but under today's conditions it is understandable for people to act in such a manner; resources are scarce and people must do what is necessary to survive.

Emigration

Emigration, as a survival strategy for Russian scientists, has attracted a great deal of media attention. Emigration is defined as a complete or partial migration from the country. This strategy has and will have nefarious consequences for Russian science. Emigration is most popular among the informal elite, except for older scientists and the active youth. The training and abilities of the informal elite are highly regarded in the West. All of Russia's informal scientific elite are known by at least one or two leading specialists in the West. Some are very well known, even famous.

Since the borders opened in 1988, Russian scientists have made many trips abroad that were financed by sponsoring institutions. Outside Russia, there are many people who hope these scientists will take either temporary or permanent positions.

Since 1991, when the new government established its policy toward the sciences, emigrations sharply increased. In the past, there were also many scientists emigrating from the USSR. Official anti-Semitic policies of the 1970s caused the first significant wave of emigrations. Mathematics were especially hard hit. However, the volume of emigration during the 1970s is minute compared with that of the last three to four years. For Russia, the latest wave of emigration has included the best scientists and caused a total catastrophe in the scientific community. It is difficult to find a university in the United States, Western Europe, or Japan without a whole group of Russian scholars and researchers. Most of these are in the fields of mathematics or physics. Also, some are chemists, biologists, and computer experts. There are even mathematics seminars in some of the best universities in the world where Russian is the only language spoken.

Some emigrants do not work at all in Russia and are content with temporary positions and traveling from place to place. Others live, for the most part, in Russia but work in the West. Both of these types of emigrants ultimately hope for permanent positions in the West.

The rapid emigration of young scientists deserves special attention. Recently the rate of emigration by middle-aged and senior scientists has slowed. This is because of a reduction in the demand for advanced personnel in Western universities. However the demand for young scientists outside Russia continues to grow. The demand is augmented by the fact that, at present, most young science students have the desire for employment in the West. If this process is not stopped, the scientific community in Russia will eventually be undermined.

Those Who Remain

It remains to be seen what will happen to the Russian scientists who do not emigrate and have not taken positions in the administrative elite. Some of the capable and active youth have ventured into the private sector. Less capable middle-aged and elderly scientists have clung to their positions in institutes. Although there is little difference between their meager salaries and unemployment benefits, at least they are guaranteed. Many of these scientists make additional income by moonlighting.

Despite chronic funding problems, none of the SRI organizations have closed. Scientists at these institutes range widely in expertise and ability. The working and living conditions for these people is remarkable. Today, they are among the most underpaid of all state employees. Even janitors who clean the subway earn more.

These scientists wish to continue their work despite these difficult conditions. Theoreticians can manage partly because they do not require laboratory facilities. Instead, they do library research, educating themselves while trying to endure these lean times. However, the mortality rate among scientists is high. While current personnel are devoted to science despite these conditions, it is unlikely they will inspire young scientists to follow their example. Instead, the next generation of Russian scientists will choose between opportunities abroad and the private sector.

Recently, a few rays of light shone on Russia's scientific community. One ray is the charitable work of George Soros on behalf of the Russian Fund for Fundamental Research (RFFR). His work has demonstrated that it is not necessary to change the government's economic policy in order to save Russian science. Sufficient measures to support science include investments of up to 3 percent of gross national production and rationally conducted reform.

The future of Russian science will be determined by economic and political developments in the near future. According to one controversial perspective, capitalism will give way to socialism, which is struggling but is still alive and dangerous. I find this idea difficult to believe. In reality, capitalism has already prevailed decisively and completely. The number of Brezhnev-type socialists in Russia is small, and they have no political future. The present and growing struggle is between the parasitic capitalism of Mr. A and others of his ilk and the more healthy "industrial" capitalists who want to develop a highly technological industry. From a sociological point of view, this is basically a struggle among former members of the Soviet elite who have split but nonetheless comprise the majority of wealthy people in Russia. The outcome of this struggle may have a decisive effect on Russian science. If Mr. A is victorious, then science is doomed. For Mr. A, science, industry, culture, and education are unnecessary; these are the natural enemies of civilization in general. If "technological" capitalism prevails, then science will have an important role and receive the stimulus necessary for its revival.

21

Women in the New Russian Elite

Tatiana Marchenko

Russia appears to be a matriarchy on the surface, but the matriarchal tendencies are actually latent and distorted. As a rule, women are decision makers, but they do not occupy the main seats of power, positions ascribed to men by the features of Russian history and welfare practices. Russia is a Eurasian country, both geographically and culturally. Traditionally, Russian women are obedient and apparently accepting of a whole host of unequal and discriminatory relations. Throughout Russian history, there has been an absence of support for women's equality.

In the USSR, an official government policy supported the participation of women in public and political spheres. In all areas of authority, quotas were implemented so that women across social and class lines could be represented. It would be false, however, to consider women as members of the elite. The female "pseudoelite" had very little if any real power in the decision-making processes and did not influence society. In the economy, women have not been leaders in the past except in "female" areas of the economy such as the light industry and trade.

With the introduction of perestroika, the state ceased to support women's participation in government, causing a considerable drop in the number of women holding political office. From 1980 to 1985, women comprised 35 percent of the Supreme Soviet. Following the 1990 elections, however, they accounted for only 8.9 percent. Today, only 5.3 percent of all national deputies are women.[1] What is happening? Are women being superseded by men who are stronger, more qualified, and more determined? Perhaps women are simply "giving up" their political offices (those nerve-racking, burdensome positions of responsibility) in favor of more "feminine" activities such as caring for their families. Perhaps now, with the introduction of certain political and economic freedoms together with the transformation of the old elite, women are preparing to reenter the scene?

During the transitional period, there were simultaneous shifts occurring in Russia's economy, society, and culture. Russia is now faced with the problem of choosing a policy regarding women in business and government. Will the new policy reinstate the former policy of state-controlled unequal "equality," or will it create a new approach based upon objective evaluations of personal merits without reference to such factors as age, gender, nationality, class, political party, and so on? With the latter, women should be able to decide for themselves whether or not to fight for a place among the elite.

The focus of this essay is women who vie for positions of power. These women are members of the political and economic elite and will have a strong influence on the development of Russian society. In this chapter, we will consider the following issues: the problems involving women in positions of power; how much power women actually have; and attitudes toward women leaders. Female elite groups are characterized by their place of origin, education, political preferences, value orientations, material welfare, and personal outlook. Based on our findings, we will analyze the evolution of female elites. Additionally, we will make some predictions and recommendations that have implications for policy development.

The empirical basis for this research consists of intensive interviews with representatives of the central political and economic elite. From March to June, 1994, twenty interviews were conducted. The respondents were drawn from Moscow's elite, including nine politicians (Parliament members, government officials, members of the presidential administration, and others), eight business leaders (heads of private-sector financial and industrial institutions and business associations), and two women who are involved in both political and economic pursuits.

This research also draws on information from statistical studies (data on women deputies in the Federal Assembly, and so forth), sociological studies, and newspaper and journal articles. The comparison of attitudes held by elite groups and women from all over Russia is based on interviews conducted by the Fund of Public Opinion in April and June, 1994.

The Status of Elite Women in Russia:
Definitions and Descriptions

In this essay, elites are defined as those who occupy management positions that give them the power and opportunity to influence the lives of others. It is difficult to know which women are members of the new elite. Sometimes this question is impossible to answer, even if we limit our discussion to only two main groups—the political and economic elite.

In this study, we consider women to be political elites if they are members of the State Duma and Soviet Federation, members of the president's administration, or political party leaders. While membership lists of various organizations are published, there is no official listing of women who occupy positions in the presidential administration.

At present, there are 69 female deputies in the Federal Assembly (11.4 percent), whereas, during the Soviet Federation there were 9 (5.6 percent). In the State Duma, there are 60 women (13.6 percent). In the federal ministries and departments, there are two women leaders. One heads the Ministry of Social Protection and the other is in charge of the Federal Migration Service. Data on the number of women in local government is not available; however, the National Report on the State of Women documents a significant reduction in the number of women in regional or territorial government in almost all 89 territories since the onset of the 1990s. In 1985, women comprised 51 percent of the deputies in small soviets. In 1993, the Moscow District Duma was 30 percent women.

Information from the business sector is more complex. There are no statistical studies regarding business ownership, membership in commercial organizations, or the managerial cadre in banks, investment funds, and so on, that focus on gender. The National Report to the 4th World Conference on the State of Women notes that women comprise only 11 percent of all the leaders in the commercial sector. However, the report does not consider the business size in its analysis. Consequently, we cannot make any conclusions regarding the membership of these women in Russia's business elite. According to estimations by experts at the State Committee on Property, the Association of Russian Banks, and the Chamber of Commerce and Industry, women are almost totally absent from the management ranks in large industrial business with the lone exception of the textile industry. Women are employed only in small to average-size banks and investment companies (experts say they are steady and reliable employees). One significant exception is that a woman holds the post of deputy acting chair of the Central Bank of the Russian Federation, an appointment she received just after the currency shocks in March, 1994.

The selection of respondents for the economic group was a subjective and complex process. The respondent pool included women bank managers, joint-stock society members, investment fund advisors, small firm owners (the number of small business enterprises is on the rise), and women who head manufacturing and trade associations. During the interviews, one peculiar detail stood out. Women leaders from small to average-size businesses participated enthusiastically and provided detailed descriptions of their business. In contrast, women from large organizations spoke reluctantly and with uncertainty. Because it was difficult to discern their type of activities, I was prone to doubt the authenticity of what women from large institutions said about their places of employment. In *Cherchez l'homme,* Galina Sillaste also wrote of this tendency. Sillaste contends that, apparently, high-ranking women in big Russian businesses are frequently window dressing for powerful male-dominated areas.[2]

There are contending points of view regarding the actual representation of women in businesses. According to one point of view, there are considerably more businesswomen than what is commonly thought. Frightened by hostile work environs characterized by frequent encounters with criminals, these women prefer to supervise the firm covertly, naming a subordinate as the puppet leader. Another point of view is essentially similar but differs in its conclusion. Some men, who do not wish to have their leadership in a firm known, name women as leaders. It was frequently mentioned that women in modern Russia are more reliable business partners because of their efficiency, reliability, and excellent managerial styles. Thus, at present, it is practically impossible to give not only a reasonable estimation of the number of women in the business elite but also an outline of the divisions within this group. However, I will attempt to describe this group on the basis of my study investigating the representatives of the proto-elite and pre-elite women leaders in business.

The influence of elite women has been rather limited in all areas of society. However, there are currently some positive changes occurring. While no women are listed among the fifty leading businesspeople in Russia (according to some of the most influential Russian politicians and businessmen), there are women listed among the top politicians.[3] In the final list of the most influential Russian politicians of 1993, there were eight women (Emma Pamfilova, Helena Bonner,

Marina Sal'e, Alevtina Fedulova, Galina Starovoitova, Sazhi Umalatova, Nina Andreieva, and Valeriia Novodvorskaia)[4] listed among the 184 leaders (4.3 percent). In the parliamentary elections in December, 1993, hundreds of leading politicians ran for office, including Pamfilova, Fedulova, and Irina Hakamada. The success that female candidates have experienced under the new open system was unexpected and suggests that women will have an increasingly greater influence in Russian politics and society in the future.

According to international norms, women who have achieved elite status are most often relegated to departments and ministries dealing with culture, public health services, and education. These positions are endowed with less power and influence in society than other ministries such as defense, commerce, and international relations. This pattern reinforces a stereotype that women should occupy positions in society that correspond to perceived "women's" interests and natural talents.[5]

These stereotypes of women are played out in the Duma where the women deputies sit in committees of the State Duma that deal with what are traditionally considered "female" issues, such as the committees for Education, Science, and Culture; Women, Families, and Youth; and those dealing with health, labor, and social support. Women from different factions and groups are represented in all structures of the Duma, including the committees on defense, safety, and international commerce. There is a large group of women from various factions who recently became members of the largest committee, which deals with the budget, taxation, banks, and finance. A woman, Irina Hakamada, who possesses a doctorate in economics, now heads the subcommittee dealing with economic policy and budgets. Thus, women continue to play subordinate roles in Russian economics and politics, but they have obviously gained some ground and continue to expand their spheres of influence.

Coordination of Women's Activities Within Elite Groups

Despite being very few in number, women in elite groups tend to remain fragmented even when they are in agreement on certain issues. For example, when asked to name an issue that united elite women, most of the respondents were unable to name one. The reasons for disunity are competition, rivalry, and a relative ignorance of other female elites, whether declared or latent. These findings suggest that while elite women might identify themselves as being members of the elite, they do not recognize other women as members or themselves as a group.

Women professionals, especially at the highest levels, identify more with those sharing common business and professional interests than with other women outside of their professions. Elite women, more than ever, are represented in a wide variety of organizations such as different political parties, movements, and public organizations. This phenomenon can be explained largely by the fact that there has been an expansion in the number of organizations in Russia. There were three hundred different women's organizations registered in the Russian Federation in 1994. Some, such as Club L and Club D in Moscow, have the brightest and most talented women in the city as members. Women's concerns and interests are expressed in the movements and clubs that they create. In general, women form clubs to gather political or social capital, create social networks, or address personal concerns or problems. Respondents often said that their motivation for joining was the desire for mutual support because "the feeling toward us in Russia is not love." It is difficult to disagree. Women leaders in Russia often provoke extreme reactions of distrust, suspicion, and criticism. "It is well-known that a woman must work one hundred times harder and more effectively to be considered equal to a man," reported a woman journalist in the central press.[6]

Ironically, the most severe critics of women are women. This makes the formation of women's support groups problematic. Support groups are very fragile, short-lived, and hindered by constant infighting and the need for wider recognition. "They are fragile, like a flower which needs constant care to keep it healthy and growing," said one woman who became a member of the Soviet Federation.

The concerns noted above are characteristic of the political elite. In contrast, the economic elite's concerns are less oriented toward social support and more toward economic interests. Women in business do not feel the malice and adversity of society to the same degree that elite women in politics do.

The results of the last Federal Assembly elections may serve as indirect indices of attitudes toward elite women. All thirteen parties and movements participating in the elections fielded women candidates for deputy positions. The largest percentage of women (20 percent) was supported by the ecological movement KEDR (cedar). The smallest (2.7 percent) was fielded by the Civil Union. The female candidates had little chance of being elected to the Duma because their names were placed near or at the end of the election bills. Consequently, no women were elected to federal district positions from the Russian Party of Unity and Consent or the Agrarian Party. Yet women represented 7.5 percent of the total registered candidates and 14 percent of those elected to federal bills during the past elections, testifying to the electorate's general preference for women over their fellow party members.

The Structure of Women's Elite Groups

In contrast to most male elites, among whom 80 percent were members of former elite and pre-elite groups,[7] elite women have made their appearance only recently and particularly since perestroika. Elite women are distinguished from their male counterparts by high vertical mobility.

Sociological studies that compare elites across national boundaries found that women have more opportunities to gain elite status during crisis periods.[8] For example, many Russian women gained elite status when Mikhail Gorbachev replaced his staff at the onset of perestroika. Additionally, there were more opportunities for women during the first congressional elections in the USSR, the Russian Socialist Federation of Soviet Republics in 1989–90, and the new Russian Parliament at the end of 1993.

The Law on Cooperation caused a major change for the business elite in 1988. At that time, skilled women (technicians and economists) were heavily recruited by cooperative societies, small business enterprises, and so forth that were engaging in new forms of economic activity. Most of these women came from simple backgrounds and should be considered "self-made," whereas, half of the male elites came from professional and well-educated families. All respondents in this study, however, attended the best schools in Russia, with many possessing doctorates in the hard sciences. The economic elite is well prepared to join the workforce because they received both academic and practical training before joining the workforce. Among the political elite, lawyers are rare.[9]

Another common feature of elite women is that most are either exceptionally or moderately beautiful regardless of age and ethnicity. With few exceptions, elite women are well groomed, elegant, stylish, and charming, each in her own way. Their average age is about 45 and coincides with that of elite Russian men. Ethnicity, however, is a major factor in determining who will attain elite political status. Slavic women can expect more support from the electorate, while non-Slavic women face great difficulties breaking into politics at the national level.

Women elites have a subdued view of the West. Most regard the West as ideal for vacationing, while some intend to send their children to Western schools. However, not one of the women respondents declared a desire to live permanently in a Western nation.

Political Preferences and Value Orientations

In spite of their diversity, most elite women are moderates on issues regarding the national government, market policy, international relations, and so forth. This finding disproves the popular idea that women leaders are inherently extreme in their views. Most elite women regret the disintegration of the USSR and would like to see better economic and political relations with the former republics. They feel that the main task today is to make Russia a stronger nation by forming a confederation based on new relations with the republics. The respondents' viewpoints demonstrate a strong solidarity with the Russian people, who in 1994 were strongly (74 percent) against the disintegration of the USSR.

Elite women regard the transition to a market economy as necessary, but they are critical of the current methods and strategies being used. They feel that these measures do not deal adequately with the problems—particularly social problems—arising from a rapidly changing market. While some political elite are concerned with the social consequences of reform, the business elite are mainly concerned with how economic policy is affecting domestic industry (that is, the burdensome tax system on small and medium-sized businesses).

In the sphere of public policy, elite and non-elite women tend to differ especially with regard to public assistance and social security. More than half of non-elite Russian women (54 percent) feel that the government should first provide a national welfare program. Surveys of women in Russia show that 71 percent do not support current reform programs and 68 percent favor a return to state price control. On the other hand, most elite women believe that the state should concentrate its efforts on insuring that people have opportunities to succeed. They believe that social welfare should serve only those truly in need, such as children, pensioners, and invalids.

Value Orientations

Elite women rank work as more important in their lives than family. Obviously, women are divided by the demands of work and home and must be flexible to meet the needs of each. However, even if a woman devotes herself to work, her family will remain a central part of her life. "I can only be happy at work if I am happy at home. When I am not happy at home, I am ineffective at work," said one informant. Data on Russian women surveyed in April, 1994, indicates that the most important daily problems concern a secure income (60 percent), food (47 percent), children (45 percent), and family (22 percent).

Prior to the initiation of reforms, Russian women named family and children as the first priority. This shift in values, while it seems to be a strong warning sign, did not affect the priority system of elite women. Most elite women reported that their main spiritual concern was good family relations. Their personal goals, however, revolved around their professional lives. Work provides these women with the opportunity for self-actualization and to contribute something to society. The importance of the latter is more prevalent among the political elite than among the economic elite.

One major change among Russian elite women is that those who had been atheists began to embrace some type of religion. They admit to believing in a higher force and a supreme being that both directs and protects them. This phenomenon can be explained by the need for women who face a great deal of stress in their professional and personal lives to find a source of support and guidance outside of the family. Religion provides these women with that type of support.

Temperament and Self-Perceptions

Elite women are pessimistic regarding the future of the Russian economy and political system. They foresee economic collapse, with many businesses going bankrupt, a general loss of management capacity in Russia, and political upheaval. On the optimistic side, they recognize a number of improvements in Russian society such as the adoption of a constitution and a multiparty system, the signing of the consent agreement, and the development of private capital. While they see the future as being difficult, elite women in general are positive about the changes to come. Therefore, elite women can be characterized as strongly self-reliant and happy, although there is great cause for dissatisfaction.

Elite and non-elite women gave strikingly different evaluations of their emotional states. The non-elites described their daily lives in terms of trepidation (53 percent), fatigue (42 percent), disappointment (37 percent), and worry over serious problems (28 percent). Elite women sometimes confessed feelings of fear, misunderstanding, and insecurity. These feelings, however, were more prevalent among the women in politics rather than those in business. Women in business said more often that they felt confident and secure. Politicians were reticent to discuss their negative feelings. One respondent reported that she was very uncertain about the future of her business and felt that she had more to lose than the average person. Many elite women consult astrologers for information before they make important decisions. Often, elite women described themselves in masculine terms: "chief," "creator," "generator," and "peacemaker." Still, more feminine descriptions prevailed: "mother," "wife," and "woman."

Elite women are not radical feminists. They reported that they preferred to be women despite the historical and culturally rooted chauvinism that makes life difficult for them, and they appreciated more female qualities such as flexibility, diplomacy, risk aversion, and balanced decision making. They respected men and almost unanimously preferred to work with male subordinates rather than female subordinates. Elite women agreed that men are better suited than they to roles in big business and the military.

Family Lifestyle

As stated above, elite women describe work as the biggest part of their lives. On average, they work twelve hours per day, including many Saturdays. Family, especially husbands, play an ambiguous role in the life of women elites. Generally, divorce coincides with a woman beginning a career in politics or business. Frequently, if a woman makes a significant career change, she will also find a new companion and friends.

All of the respondents in this study occupy roles in their families traditionally ascribed to men. Most of these women earn more money than their husbands. Only a few reported having salaries equal to their husbands'. Yet, most reported that they are still responsible for maintaining the household on a daily basis. Very few could say that their husbands made significant contributions to maintaining the home. Only a few respondents employed domestic servants. While there may be a large difference in income between elite and non-elite Russian women, they seem to have very similar responsibilities at home.

Maintaining a home requires a great deal of time and energy. For one thing, Russia is underdeveloped in terms of a household service industry. Contrary to popular belief, data indicates that women who choose to pursue careers cannot free themselves from unhappy or otherwise burdensome responsibilities at home. Almost all elite women have children and feel that they do not give their children enough attention. Obviously, in the absence of constant supervision, the children become independent early on. These children accept and acknowledge their mothers' work, and because their mothers are rarely home, they value the time they do have together. This situation produces more genial and less parental relationships between mothers and children. Most elite women reported having very few problems with their children.

Wealth and Leisure

Elite women view themselves as middle or upper middle class. This may actually be the case for Russian women in politics. Businesswomen, while they do have above-average incomes, are subjective in how they see themselves in relation to the rest of Russia's elite. For example, women real estate brokers who deal in privatized apartments and dachas do not attain the prestige or incomes of those dealing in other types of property.

Elite women spend much of their leisure time viewing educational television and reading. Most do not participate in sports or creative activities. Also, they do not have typically feminine hobbies such as knitting, sewing, and cooking, nor do they engage in activities typical of the rich and famous. Because most elite women have only recently attained high positions, their interests are dominated by professional concerns.

Future Trends in the Evolution of Elite Women

For the past few years, Russian women have made significant progress in business and politics. Presently, however, they concede that men continue to dominate in politics and business because they face fewer impediments to success. In the past, only men occupied key posts in the Komsomol and commerce. From this vantage point, men have had great opportunities to take advantage of political and market reforms, not to mention the privatization of some government assets. On the other hand, women were able to find opportunities owing to the poor economy by filling economic niches that required some expertise, an enterprising spirit, resourcefulness, and perseverance.

Women in business typically own well-established, small to medium-sized companies. In the future, these businesswomen will become "pre-elite" and will partly unite with the political elite. Today, 15 percent of women deputies in the State Duma own private businesses.

The main obstacles to increasing the status and number of elite women in Russia are the economy, poor social infrastructure, public consciousness, and a general lack of support for women. On the brighter side, women who have gained power have been very successful. They have promoted meritocractic principles (versus quota filling) to counteract conformity. In this way, Russian women will strive to reach their individual potentials. In business and politics, they will be judged based on their performance instead of being included for the sake of their gender.

Today, one cannot say that elite women play major roles in politics and business. But more are sure to come in the future. In terms of the distribution of wealth and power, women will remain second-class citizens for many years. And a Margaret Thatcher will not be arriving in the near future.

22

The Future Belongs to Me
Russian Students and Their Religious Views

Samuel Kliger

Recent changes in social status, self-perception, and religious views of Russian students are of great significance for that country. The main objectives of this essay are to analyze those changes and to show how they may affect the process of new elite recruitment. The study is based on a number of polls conducted by the International Research Institute on Value Changes (IRIVC) in Moscow in 1990–95.[1]

Social Structure and Changes in Self-Perception

According to the tradition developed by Lenin and then Stalin, Soviet society consisted of three major social classes: the working class, collective farmers, and the intelligentsia. The formula 2+1 (two major classes and a "stratum" or "layer" of intelligentsia) was the official base of almost all descriptions and analysis of social structure in the former USSR up until the early 1990s. While acknowledging the existence of other minor social groups (such as professional and educational groups, unskilled workers, and so on), Soviet scholars constantly studied the working class and its leading role in society.[2] Soviet propaganda insisted that the working class as such was a bearer of the most "progressive" values and virtues: work ethics, internationalism, atheism, family and moral values, and so forth.

Although this particular perspective did not reflect the great differentiation in society, there is no doubt that a firm social structure in Soviet society did exist. It existed not only in the form of theoretical approaches or propaganda but also as a matter of everyday life. Virtually everyone knew very clearly who was "higher" or "lower" on the social scale, and everyone was able to answer the questions "who am I" and "who's who." As Vladimir Shlapentokh mentioned in 1989, "The division of the Soviet society into two classes—superiors and subordinates—is in many ways the best key for understanding the behavior and mentality of the Soviet people."[3] With all the changes that occurred in the last few years, people are now disoriented in social space. They are no longer aware of the boundaries between social groups, and many of them have lost their former social status.

Formation of a New Young Elite

There are two major factors in the formation of the new elite: age and education. Agencies that specialized in recruiting managers and professionals for the Russian and Western companies in Moscow report that age restrictions are very tight. More than 80 percent of the companies that are seeking a manager are looking to hire someone who is under 35.[4] Social dynamics are very intensive for young people. The financial director of a midsize commercial bank was only six months ago a chauffeur. Our surveys also show that among those who placed themselves in the top quarter of society's pyramid in 1992, 62 percent are under the age of 35. For new businessmen, the tendency is much stronger: 52.4 percent of them are under the age of 35, but among those who put themselves in the top quarter, 76 percent are under 35.

The formation of the social structure in this transitional period of Russian history has some interesting features. The boundaries between social groups are so unclear that belonging to a certain class or group is no longer a matter of socioeconomic factors; rather, it is mostly a matter of belonging to an informal group and of self-perception and self-identification. To be on the top does not mean, as it did before, that one belongs to the *nomenklatura* or is a boss. Ironically, it also does not mean that one has a lot of money, is a businessman, or is a full professor. It is more of a feeling, a sense that the "future belongs to me," and since such a feeling is often a privilege of youth, it is simply a matter of age. This feeling emerged after the August, 1991, revolution against the Communists. Some studies have reflected: "Economic freedom is first of all the bonanza of energetic and active people, much more for the young than their seniors. Though there are great difficulties for building a new life, most young people . . . are rather optimistic and enjoy the vistas they see before them."[5] To be at the top simply means that one believes that one has a certain potential to ascend to the top. To be at the bottom no longer means to be an unskilled worker, collective farmer, or white-collar clerk. It means, rather, a lack of hope and time.

In general, education and especially higher education played a great role in the recruiting of the Soviet elite. Since Khrushchev's and Brezhnev's times, virtually all of the political elite was recruited from those who had completed formal higher educations. To obtain a high position in the Soviet nomenklatura in the 1970s and 1980s, it was considered desirable and even necessary to go beyond higher education and to earn a Ph.D. or other advanced degree. For millions of those who were not Communist Party members, higher education was the only way to move up through the rigid social structure.

Later, in Gorbachev's Politburo, as well as in the extended circle of his aides and advisors, there was no one without a university or institute diploma. Gorbachev himself was the only Soviet leader who graduated from one of the most prestigious schools in the USSR, Moscow State University. The intelligentsia probably was the only social group that entirely supported Gorbachev's perestroika and glasnost.[6] According to recent studies, today's political elite is younger and more educated than even Gorbachev's team. There are twice as many people with Ph.D.s in Yeltsin's inner circle than there were in Gorbachev's. The number of lawyers in the Russian parliament increased by eight times.[7] Many other elite groups—in the army, military industrial complex, culture, education, business, academia, even trade—consist mainly of people with at least a university diploma.

At the same time, the Russian system of higher education is in deep crisis. Only about 20 percent of high school students attend universities, two times less than in 1987. The number of university students dropped by almost a half-million. About 60 percent of students view their lives as meaningless and hopeless. In 1993, one out of nine students experienced permanent hunger. Seventy percent of university teachers live below the poverty level.[8] The prestige of higher education has diminished significantly; yet, higher education, especially at the Moscow State University, still plays a major role in perceptions of social status.

Our study of values in Russia shows that great and rapid changes in political and social life in the 1990s have led to an extraordinary shift in social structure as well as in self-perception. In our polls, students were asked to place themselves on a social pyramid. The social hierarchy was presented as a 20-range scale, and each individual arranged himself on one of the 20 levels according to his or her own perception. (See table 22.1.)

The general public is much lower on the social scale than the students. In 1994, only 1.7 percent of people in Moscow considered themselves on top of society, while among students the rate was 5.8 percent.

Table 22.1. Position on the Social Pyramid (percentage)

Social level	Students				General public
	1991	1992	1993	1994	1994
Upper	14.2	19.8	11.4	5.8	1.7
Upper middle	20.4	32.3	20.4	39.5	26.1
Upper lower	39.8	32.8	48.1	38.4	40.1
Lower	21.4	7.8	7.8	8.5	31.0
No answer	4.2	7.3	12.3	7.8	1.1
Total	100.0	100.0	100.0	100.0	100.0

On the other hand, only 8.5 percent of the students see themselves at the bottom of the society, almost four times less than the general public (31 percent).

The number of students on the upper level of the social pyramid has dropped almost three times from 1991 to 1994. The same is true for the lower level of society, with increasing numbers of students at the upper middle level.

We can see also a significant shift in social status between 1991 and 1992. It was the most dramatic time in the history of the perestroika period: the August, 1991, aborted coup against Gorbachev, the disintegration of the Soviet Union, and the mass euphoria of freedom and dignity. In the spring of 1991, when our poll was taken, despite the declared glasnost and perestroika, people still looked at themselves as "screws" in a huge political and ideological machine that was known as the Soviet Union. In 1992, the feeling of freedom and dignity dramatically increased in people's consciousness. The idea that "we are no longer slaves" created a great shift in the people's subjective understanding of their social positions. As a reflection of these changes in consciousness, the number of students who put themselves on the upper level of the social pyramid hit 20 percent; since then it has gradually declined.

Diminishing social status perceptions are observed among the general population as well. This is owing to the dramatic deterioration of the economy. Indeed, studies of the economic situation in Russia show that living conditions constantly became worse. For example, in the 1992 poll by Boris Grushin, 61 to 63 percent of Russians stated that their living conditions became worse during the last few months.[9]

In January–June, 1995, according to official Russian statistics, almost 64 percent of the Russian population had below-average incomes, and 20 percent of the population had a monthly income of 133,000 rubles, one-half the official poverty level. There is a widening gap between the haves and the have-nots: the richest 10 percent have 28 percent of the total income, while the poorest 10 percent have only 2.3 percent of the total income.[10]

Although the proportion of students at the upper level of the social pyramid dropped between 1992 and 1994, the number of those who perceive themselves as being on the upper middle level significantly decreased between 1992 and 1993 and then dramatically increased during 1993–94. In 1994, the number of students at the upper middle level of society was 1.5 times higher than that of the general public. Despite some fluctuations between 1992 and 1994, the upper lower level of society is more stable, and the proportion of students at that level is almost the same as the proportion of the general public. The data clearly demonstrates that students consider themselves an elite group in the new post-Communist society.

The Unfolding Ideological Drama

During the "decadence" crisis of Western civilization, the moral climate in the early period of the Soviet Union looked very attractive even to many prominent Western thinkers. In his last work, Pitirim Sorokin talked about the moral status of Russia and the rest of the world. He believed that the Soviet Union, the West, and the whole of humanity were in the greatest crisis in the history of man. This "crisis of our age," he said, threatens the very existence and, possibly, the creative mission of man on this planet. This crisis expresses itself in Russia and in the West as an appalling decline of Christianity and other institutionalized historical religions, along with their systems, dogmas, and beliefs. There is, he said, a crisis of moral commands, social institutions, and effective control over consciousness, behavior, and relationships between individuals and groups. In Russia, this decline occurred more acutely, and differently, than in the West.

Out of all cultural achievements, he continued, the moral renaissance of the Soviet population deserved a special mention. At its core, this "new ethic" was a re-creation and modification of eternal and universal moral principles, proclaimed by all great religions and ethical systems, including the Sermon on the Mount and Jesus's commandments. An affirmation for the new ethic Sorokin sought was the noticeable expression of mutual help between Soviet people and groups.

He mentioned the regeneration and growing consciousness of the division between "right" and "wrong" actions, the lowering of moral cynicism and surplus moral relativism, and the interruption of the degradation of moral values. He envisioned the guiding of the free collective ("we") united in a single vast community by mutual help, sympathy, and striving toward common great goals and responsibility. The Soviet Union, concluded Sorokin, could lead the Russian nation toward the future with hope. It would manage to become a constructive leader among all other nations and would probably continue its leading role in the following decades and, possibly, centuries.[11] Ironically, the Soviet Union did not survive even twenty-five years after Sorokin's prophecy, mostly because of its moral and ideological decline.

The entire younger generation is undergoing dramatic ideological changes. Yet in 1990, the IRIVC showed that only 6.7 percent of young adults between the ages of 18 and 41 shared the values of communism. Of those interviewed in the 18- to 26-year-old range, only 4 percent expressed devotion to communism and its values.[12]

Adam Michnik, once a leading Solidarity activist in Poland, is now editor of that country's largest newspaper, *Gazeta Wyborcza*. The newspaper expresses the common feeling in Eastern Europe and Russia: "We threw out communism, but we were left with a need for certainty. Everyone feels disoriented, looks for a guilty party, and doesn't understand what is happening."[13] Vitalii Tretiakov, the editor of *Nezavisimaia Gazeta,* in his 1994 article dismissing Solzhenitsyn as "hopelessly outdated," stated that "Nobody believes in anything anymore."[14]

Some scholars and politicians shared the belief that the flow of religious values would, to a certain extent, replace the vacuum of beliefs of the young generation. Indeed, for youth, religion seemed to be the only way out of the collapse of the official Soviet ideology.

Certainly, the values and attitudes of the real "homo soveticus" were far from the officially declared set of virtues. Some people, including the youth, seriously deviated from the moral norms of socialist society. As some scholars mentioned early in the 1980s, a life based on "high spiritual values" was being replaced by the hunt for wealth, and the principles of decency, conscience, nobility, and honesty were being replaced by egoism, cynicism, and often cruelty.[15] The degradation of the Soviet ideology started probably in the 1960s, and by the early 1990s the official ideology had practically vanished. However, no society can exist without ideology. What matters is the kind of ideology that replaces the vanished one.

The vacuum of political, economic, and moral ideals creates a demand for a new system of values, beliefs, and attitudes. Like the old
Soviet society, the newly formed Russian society is looking for an
"ideal individual." According to the Center for Humanitarian Values
of the Russian Academy of Sciences, such a "brave new man" rejects
any form of asceticism and pursues full-scale life, while consuming as
much as possible. Such a person rejects collectivism as not being based
upon private interest, and seeks individualism and/or belonging to an
elite group or a group of colleagues. He rejects altruism and strives for
self-aggrandizement at any price, even at the expense of others.[16] Although there are no clear evidences that such a "brave new man" already exists as a social type, all of Russian society is in the process of
dramatic ideological transformation.

Unfolding Religious Dramas

Religion seems to be in fashion now in Russia and in the republics
of the former Soviet Union. Probably the most impressive symbol of
it is an act of religious monumentalism, the rebuilding of the vast
nineteenth-century Cathedral of Christ the Savior, destroyed by Stalin
in 1931. The Russian Orthodox Church blessed the re-creation, but
this project is also a good symbol for the moral ambiguity of the new
Russian state. On one hand, it shows that real belief still exists in Russia. On the other, many people feel that the estimated $250 million for
the project could have been used for more utilitarian needs.[17]

Russian Orthodox believers are affected much more by rituals and
traditions than by preaching and Bible study. Youngsters like the atmosphere in church; they are excited by icons, religious holidays, and
ceremonies. A kind of residual Orthodoxy, part of the traditional culture, is still present in families evincing little religious belief.[18]

According to a 1993 poll conducted by the Russian Center of Public Opinion Study (VCIOM) based on a sample of 1,650 people representing the adult population of Russia, 45 percent consider themselves
believers (this concurs with our data) and 90 percent of them are believers in Russian Orthodox. However, only 10 percent attend church
at least once a month, and 50 percent of Russian Orthodox believers
never read the Bible.[19] Priest Innokentii states that only 3 to 5 percent
of the population attend church regularly and live within the norms
and values of Christian morality (this also concurs with our data). As
for the rest of those who consider themselves religious, their religion
has more to do with national self-identity rather than with any commitment to Christian values. For them, being Orthodox is to paint eggs

Table 22.2. Religious Attitudes (percentage)

	Students			General Public
	1992	1993	1994	1994
Are sure that God exists	22.4	36.1	47.8	38.1
Are devoted atheists	5.2	3.6	6.5	2.7
Consider themselves believers	13.5	15.7	15.9	15.9
Consider themselves believers rather than not	19.8	39.2	41.3	32.3
Agree that only a believer can be a moral person	11.5	12.0	14.0	20.5
Say religion plays a very important role in their lives	12.0	4.8	7.0	3.2

for Easter and to celebrate Christmas with a special meal. It means belonging to Russian nationality rather than having real religious commitment.[20] With all the resentment and humiliation that many Russians feel as they struggle with the question of identity, they turn to the church in search of a proud and stable life.

Our study shows that Russian students would rather acknowledge religion as culture, tradition, and a philosophical concept than as a system of values and beliefs that one should follow in life. One of the most common attitudes of students is that the strongest point of a religion is its moral laws (the Ten Commandments, for example), but that even an atheist may observe them.[21]

Religious views among students (as well as among the general public) are quite ambiguous. Although almost half of the interviewed students in 1994 were "sure that God exists," less than 16 percent decisively considered themselves believers. (See table 22.2.)

We can see four levels of religious commitment and attitude toward religion. Above all is the number of those saying they are sure that God exists. The rate of students that express this statement jumped from 22.4 percent in 1992 to 47.8 percent in 1994. After the 1991 attempted coup there was a significant increase in positive attitudes toward religion in general. The data reflect this wave of positive religious feelings. It was the time before hidden and oppressed religious groups and institutions began to emerge, when the euphoria of freedom first appeared, and when the last Soviet Parliament passed the law about freedom of conscience. Religion was in fashion after seventy years of "non-existence." In 1993, however, there was a stabilization of this process. One of the reasons was that institutionalized religion (the Russian Orthodox Church and its leaders) were accused of collaboration and cooperation with the KGB, and people became disappointed with the church and with the values traditionally associated with it. Another reason was that living conditions and the political situation started to deteriorate rapidly with the collapse of the Soviet Union, and people were forced to spend more efforts in their struggle for survival.

Although virtually half of the students express their confidence in God's existence, this reflects only an emotional attitude toward religion. To believe in God's existence, one need not do anything. It is just a philosophical concept that does not necessarily lead a person to change his or her lifestyle. This is a statement with no consequences and no obligations.

The second level of students consider themselves believers. Although the number of students who see themselves "more as believers than not" has doubled from 1992 to 1994, the rate of those who say they are definitely believers is stable and is only in a range of 13–16 percent. The statement "I am a believer" brings with it certain obligations and commitments, and that is why a much smaller number of students identify themselves as such.

The third level has to do with religion and morality. The tradition that morality goes together with religion was deeply rooted in Russian consciousness, in literature, and in philosophy. Dostoevsky expressed it sharply: If there is no God, everything is allowed and possible. The Bolsheviks reversed this idea: A person can and should be moral without God. Such a concept is still strong among post-Communist Russian youth: only 11–14 percent of the students agree that only a believer can be a moral person.

On the fourth level are those who say religion "plays a very important role" in their lives. Such a statement presumes that religion is part of their lifestyle and everyday practice. Only 5–7 percent of Moscow students are in this category.

The dynamics of religious attitudes are interesting. While the number of those who are sure that God exists and of those who are more believers than not has increased from 1992 to 1994, the number of students who say religion plays a very important role in their lives has dropped. When religion came back into fashion in 1991–92, the attitude toward it was generally positive. People did not see much difference between trust in God and religious practice. Later they realized that there is a difference, and it is much easier to express confidence in

God's existence than to practice religion on an everyday basis. To express some kind of religiosity is a culturally encouraged behavior. As one of our respondents (a 20-year-old female student) put it: "I attend the church, but it doesn't mean that I believe in God." A similar and typical answer was given in Saint Petersburg to Andrew Solomon from the *New York Times Magazine:* "I think our Orthodox religion is very beautiful, but of course I don't believe in it." [22] A few are really inspired with faith, but most come because they are looking for ideology. "It is the tragedy of our church," says one young artist in Moscow. "These people have confused doctrine with totalitarianism." [23]

In addition to Russian Orthodoxy, there are many other confessions, sects, and cults. Although Russian Jews constitute less than 1 percent of the population, Judaism also became fashionable. Yet, more than 45 percent of Russian Jews never attend synagogue, and only 4–5 percent attend regularly. Only 7.6 percent of the Jews interviewed in Moscow and Saint Petersburg (500 respondents in each city) by the Jewish Research Center in 1993 said they know the Jewish religion well; about 13 percent know Jewish traditions and customs well. [24]

Russian Jews have suffered persecution based upon their ethnic and religious identity. In addition to official oppression, they have experienced hostility from the Russians and other ethnic groups. One of the polls in 1991 revealed that more than half of the 4,200 Soviets surveyed wanted all Jews to leave the country. More than 10 percent said Soviet Jews should be moved to the Far East. [25] Even in post-Communist Russia, attitudes toward Jews remain quite negative. Lev Gudkov and Aleksei Levinson found that there are widespread assertions that Jews avoid physical labor and place money and profit above human relations. [26] Based on IRIVC studies and on the analysis of many other sources, Tony Carnes came to the conclusion that in Russia, "more than any other type of xenophobia, anti-Semitism is a powerful activator and intensifier of negative stereotypes toward other people in general." [27] After the collapse of the Soviet Union, Jewish life in the republics seemed to begin to flourish. At first glance, there were Jewish newspapers and clubs, schools and synagogues, kindergartens and yeshivas. However, various studies show that any form of Jewish activity (religious activities in particular) remains at the periphery of people's interests and value systems. A recent poll of the analytic center of the Russian Academy of Sciences reports that 53 percent of Russian Jews could not identify their religious beliefs (among ethnic Russians, only 21 percent). Twenty-three percent of Jews consider themselves atheists (among Russians, only 7 percent).[28] About 8 percent of Jews have identified themselves as confessing Judaism. Only 2.4 percent received a Jewish education and were brought up as Jews.[29]

Within the last few years, many authoritarian, New Age groups, cults, and sects of various kinds have emerged. Students and young people take part in their activities despite the fact that some of these groups are very aggressive and dangerous. During the last five years, more than 800,000 people have been damaged in different ways by the activity of these cults.[30] Today in Russia there are about thirty officially registered new sects and cults with the following common features: 1) they clearly express opposition toward the official church; 2) they believe only they are right and only they have direct contacts with God, the Virgin Mary, or with the saints; 3) they constantly refer to universal concepts such as High Cosmic Energy, Super-universal Mind, and World Harmony; 4) they promise Apocalypses soon with a transfer of their followers to the Kingdom of Absolute Light; 5) they preach extreme asceticism and poverty; and 6) they use the shaman approach in services.[31]

Broken Idols

With religion in fashion, idols and any form of authority are no longer valid in young people's consciousness. Moscow students decisively desacralize the world in favor of a rational understanding. There is no one person or social institute that can be trusted. Almost 84 percent of students (1994) stated that the Biblical commandment "Do not make an idol for yourself" literally means "Do not worship anything blindly." The second meaning of this commandment shared by 33 percent of the students is "Do not trust any leaders blindly." During the last few years, students have seen this Commandment as more and more important. (See table 22.3.)

The old stereotype that Russians do not trust anybody is unfortunately true. It is particularly true for the young people. The crisis of public confidence in leadership and authority became obvious in the former Soviet Union. It is now true not only for the political leadership in Russia, but also for bureaucratic organizations, the educational system, the health care system, the military, and many other social institutions, including the family. The level of trust and attitudes toward honesty are incredibly poor among all social groups, including the students. (See table 22.4.)

Even for one's spouse and friends there are deep suspicions. The

Table 22.3. Importance of the Second Commandment Today (percentage of students)

	1992	1993	1994
This is an extremely important Commandment and it is absolutely necessary to observe it	33	51	46

Table 22.4. Students Who Would Always Believe the Word of Honor of . . . (percentage)

	1992	1993	1994
My friend	35.4	27.7	22.9
My spouse	19.8	20.5	17.9
My teacher	14.6	12.7	6.5
A religious leader	16.7	4.8	6.0
A representative of intelligentsia	6.8	10.8	4.0
My doctor	19.8	7.2	5.0
A Russian Army officer	7.3	4.8	3.0
A KGB officer	4.7	2.4	—
My boss	1.6	1.2	0.5
A member of the Supreme Soviet (parliament)	3.6	1.8	1.0
A member of the government	5.2	1.2	0.0

sense of friendship, once deeply rooted in Russian communicative culture, particularly among young people, is gradually declining. The level of trust in one's teacher, doctor, and religious leader has dropped even more dramatically. How can one expect an effective work ethic from a person who does not even believe in the "word of honor" of her immediate boss? How can the educational system exist if only 14 percent trust their teachers' word? What kind of health care can a doctor provide who understands that 90–95 percent of his patients do not trust his advice? And how can the free-market economy be established if almost nobody trusts the government or its lawmakers?

When asked in 1994, "How do you think the world would change if everybody observed the Commandment, 'Do Not Make an Idol for Yourself'?" 10.4 percent of the students said "the world would change for the worse," compared with 3.4 percent of the general public.

Do Not Kill

When it comes to the issue of the value of human life, we can see some disturbing trends among the students (see table 22.5). Students are more likely to be for capital punishment now than they were in 1992 and 1993. They express especially cruel attitudes when considering the fate of a deformed newborn. The number of students who say the life of such a newborn can be taken is frightening. The generalization that, by human nature, people are inclined to kill is shared by only a slightly lower fraction of the student population than two years ago.

On almost every issue, students differ from the general public. These differences demonstrate not only the wide gap between generations but also the kind of moral climate that Russian society will face in a few years when today's students become the elite of society.

The concept, "human nature is genetically and originally inclined to kill," is now shared by about 8 percent of the population. Attitudes toward an "incurably ill person" as well as toward an "escaped prisoner" are especially cruel when compared to the attitudes of the general public.

When asked in 1992, "How important is the commandment, 'Do Not Kill,' for contemporary man?," 16.1 percent of the students replied that "the commandment is becoming less important today and it doesn't fit with the contemporary society." The percentage for the general public was only 2.6 percent.

Do Not Steal

Despite privatization and ongoing market reforms, the value of property is still ambiguous in the Russian value system, and particularly for students. (See table 22.6.)

There is a growing feeling that people steal more often, and that the commandment, "Do not steal," is far from being absolute. As a matter of fact, in 1994 about 6 percent of Moscow students said that the commandment does not prohibit stealing property from the very rich; 4 percent said the poor may steal in order to survive; and 9 percent stated that the commandment does not prohibit stealing from the state as long as the state is unfair to its people.

The gap between generations on the values related to property is also wide. The majority of students believe that everybody steals. They say, "most people have taken someone else's property at least once in their lifetime."

Table 22.5. Attitudes toward Human Life (percentage of students)

Complete or mostly agreed that:	1992	1993	1994
Capital punishment is admissible	54.7	48.8	58.2
A life of an incurable ill person can be taken	21.4	17.4	16.0
A newborn can be killed if he is physically deformed or mentally retarded	23.5	27.7	24.8
An escaped prisoner can be killed	22.9	—	8.0
Human nature is genetically and originally inclined to kill	25.0	16.2	17.0

Table 22.6. Attitudes toward Property (percentage of students)

Completely or mostly agreed that:	1992	1993	1994
Only the fear of being caught and punished prevents people from stealing	48.0	33.8	39.8
Believers never steal	32.8	14.4	22.9
Most people took someone else's property at least once in their life	66.7	56.6	66.7
A person who is not caught is not a thief	30.8	21.7	23.8

Here is a summary of the conclusions from this study:

• Students are probably the only social group in today's Russia who retain their relatively high social status at the top of the society, while the social structure of the society itself is rapidly and dramatically changing. Many other groups that used to enjoy officially recognized high social status in the former Soviet Union, are now considered outsiders, and vice versa.

• In an ideological vacuum, they express their interest in religion and accept religious views as long as these views do not interfere with their lifestyles. There is a four-level attitude toward religion: 1) Many students say they believe in God; 2) many fewer consider themselves believers or 3) see any connections between religion and morality, and 4) for quite a few religion plays a very important role in their lives. While more students are ready to acknowledge God's existence in the last few years, fewer of them are willing to live in accordance with religious commandments. For many students, religion is a matter of culture, national identity, traditions, and fashion. The four-level attitude toward religion describes best students' system of values.

- All idols are broken. Students do not trust anyone blindly anymore, nor do they worship anything. Even friendship—the most admirable relationship in Russia and in students' culture—is no longer a sacred cow. In 1992 more than 35 percent of students trusted their friends; in 1994—only 23 percent.

- In terms of religious values and attitudes, the new youngsters significantly differ from the general public in many respects. They are more pragmatic and money-oriented, less religious, more cruel in terms of the value of human life, and more cynical. In many other aspects of moral and social values, the younger generation, represented in our polls by students of the Moscow State University, deviates from the general public and from what was considered the "norms" of the Soviet society. For example: 1) 22 percent of the students (1992) considers a person who "believes his nation to be better than and superior to others" to be moral or moral rather than not, compared with 10.4 percent of the general public; 2) 15 percent of the students say they do not observe the commandment "Revere your father and mother," compared with only 3.6 percent among the general public; 13 percent of them said that if everyone started observing this commandment the world would change for the worse, compared with only 4.8 percent of the general public; 3) 23.5 percent of the interviewed students claimed they rather often violated the commandment "Do not commit adultery," compared with 8.5 percent of the general public; and 18.2 percent of the students said if everyone started to observe this commandment the world would change for the worse, compared to 2.6 percent of the general public.

- Because with reforms they have nothing to lose, students have a sense of a future. In an ideological free market, they buy pragmatism, and they enjoy freedom of religion rather than religion itself. They are looking forward to the pleasures of leadership in the society to come.

Epilogue

Post-Communist Elites
Who Will Guard the Guardians?

Suzanne Keller

The curtain closing on the key elites of Eastern Europe was arguably the most momentous event of the late twentieth century. The demise of elites has enormous consequences (often underestimated by democratic societies) on the functioning of society and the population as a whole. With the body politic decapitated, anomie and anarchy permeate the social atmosphere. Russian society is in a suspended state, its institutions in disarray, its idols broken. In the years since the fall of communism, the world has witnessed the fascinating, if perilous, process of a new elite phoenix struggling to rise from the ashes of the former communist system. This process has been the main focus of this book.

If I had to select one persistent refrain that was sounded by many of the authors, it would be that of the vacuum left as one set of elites abandoned the historic scene while another struggled to gain a foothold. The papers presented in this book remind us of Pareto's observation that elites lose their right to live when they lose their will to live. This loss, in the case of Russia, is a fascinating and instructive topic to explore.

The essays set themselves two ambitious goals. One was to sketch an outline of the elites of postcommunist societies by ascertaining the pattern of their social backgrounds, educations, modes of ascent, and public influence. The second was to draw out, however provisionally, the implications of these patterns for today's political, economic, and cultural landscape.

Despite variations in interests and specific aims, there was general agreement that postcommunist societies have been in a state of crisis manifested in the nature of their elites. The transitional nature of this leadership, ranging from the charismatic to the demagogic, was evident

355

in all spheres—law, politics, business, the media, and culture. Judging from the historic record, such transitional leaders are not likely to presage the permanent elite structures of the future. Still they do form a baseline against which to assess future developments.

Given the instability and unpredictability of the social and political situation, we must ask, who has been able to gain access to the top decision-making levels of society? How did they do so? And to what effect? Are these postcommunist elites relatively open to socially diverse pools of candidates or are they narrowly selective and closed? Do the members of these elites find themselves in ideological agreement on basic goals or are they at loggerheads? Admittedly, although the answers could only be provisional in this time of ferment and turmoil, the data reported in this volume provide an excellent baseline for comparative work oriented both to the historic past and to the emerging future.

The Concept of Elites

Given the dominance of Marxist thought in Eastern Europe for a good part of the twentieth century, it may be useful to point to a difference between Marxist class theory and elite theory. Lacking the concept of elites, Marxists focused instead on a larger and more inclusive ruling class.

As a result of the triumph of communism, bourgeois class rule would be overthrown, and a way would be made for a new social order and the majority rule of the people (the proletariat). This would spell the end of social exploitation and domination in the world.

Countering the Marxist class paradigm is Vilfredo Pareto's elite paradigm.[1] In this view, minority rule is an inevitable and universal feature of human societies. New elites spring up as soon as old elites expire.

Accepting Pareto's proposition that every social sector, indeed every organized social activity, is capped by an elite, the question becomes which elite to focus on. Pareto himself selected the political elite for its centrality and system power and this book's essays seem to agree with Pareto, as the ex-Soviet political elite received the lion's share of attention. This is not surprising given the historic centralization of power and the dominance of the Communist Party and Politburo in the Soviet system over its life span. Despite this focus, however, these essays did not stop at the political elite. The business elite, the agricultural elite, media elites, and the elite of crime as well as more discursive treatments of the scientific elites and regional elites are also highlighted. The notion of a single overarching elite simply cannot explain the realities of a complex, modern, market society. These realities point to a pluralism of the elites, reflecting the specialization and differentiation characteristic of the society at large. To discuss elites today one must think in multiples. For this study, this means, at the very least, the inclusion of the political, business, military, and media elites.

Closely allied to the conceptualization of elites is their operational definition, a significant point for debate in this book. The key element is where to draw the boundaries between elites and non-elites since this critically affects the portrait rendered and the conclusions drawn. When, as is often the case, there is no consistency of definition among studies, generalization becomes impossible and certainly suspect. Although the boundary problem was not fully explored, it surfaced at various points, as well it should have. How boundaries are drawn determines the kind of information to be gathered. Elites are in fact notoriously difficult to track. Like secret societies, they are among the most inaccessible elements of society, and imprecise boundaries keep them so.

There is also the matter of micro-macro scale linkage. Research on elites exhibits two points of concentration; neither are fully satisfactory. One is a focus on elites as a group. This entails a consideration of the characteristics of the top business leaders, military commanders, public idols or politicians. The individual is lost in these aggregate social profiles as one aims for the big picture. An alternative research strategy is to investigate elite individuals, in-depth; this, of course, means a loss of the big picture. Obviously, the choice of strategy depends on one's goals. Aggregate social profiles enable one to discern a general pattern of elite characteristics as to social origins, modes of selection, educational qualifications, training, and prior experience. Individual portraits, on the other hand, cannot reveal the broader pattern, but they can permit the researcher to discern the interconnections and to trace the interplay of social background, social linkages, modes of exercising authority, and success in elite performance. Both strategies are represented in these papers even though in their efforts to make sense of the nature of the societal leadership, they must work with highly uneven and incomplete data.

This prompts a more fundamental question, namely, of how to study elites when they are constantly in flux and lack stable patterns of recruitment, rewards, and tenure. Like the Heisenberg principle, it may not be possible to assess both position and change simultaneously. This is one reason for monitoring elites on a consistent, preferably continuous, basis, so as to tap into trends as they emerge.

Social Origins of Post-Communist Elites: *Nomenklatura* Still?

One matter prompting considerable discussion was that of the persistence of the previous nomenklatura elites and their infiltration into new arenas in various guises and disguises. Of course, no elite starts from a wholly clean slate. Elites carried over from a previous system are likely to retain old mind-sets, symbols, and emotional predispositions and are thus an obstacle to social change. There was some division of opinion on whether postcommunist societies were led by newly constituted elites that tapped into a variety of social and cultural backgrounds or were simply the old elites culturally enmeshed in Soviet traditions, but in new dress. Most authors leaned to the latter view, certainly for the political, business, and military elites, and doubted that they would be able to break free from the past and set forth on a new course. In the words of one author, "We human beings cannot just cut ourselves off from the decisions and deeds of our parents and grandparents," and neither can the elites.

However, there was also agreement that even if the nomenklatura traditions of the communist era persisted beyond expectations, current elites should not be viewed simply as duplicates or clones of their predecessors. More likely, they will amalgamate old and new in some fashion and should be studied with this in mind. This is where empirical data are needed to reveal how the current elites perceive the tasks assigned to them, what ideologies and goals inspire them, and whether they are likely to be a force for change or for traditionalism.

In other words, there is likely to be a complicated trade-off between the continuity provided by an experienced old guard and the thrust of inexperienced but change-oriented newcomers. Each has pluses and minuses. The first has seasoned experience but is rigid and dogmatic. The second has a fresh perspective but is less competent than the first. The continuity of old patterns comes with built-in rigidities and entrenchment, whereas the thrust toward the new is marked by risk taking and fluidity. Such tension is unavoidable during periods of transition and creates an uneasy truce between continuity and change. In the United States this problem recurs with every presidential transition as ideologies shift along with personnel.

The Social Composition of Elites

Another major focus of these essays is the question of who is represented in the current elites and whom they represent. Social representativeness is especially critical in democratic societies, and the construction of social profiles provides information about who has access to the top levels of power and to what effect. In general, the wider one's criteria of inclusion, the more diversified, heterogeneous, and democratic an elite will appear to be. Conversely, the more narrowly an elite is defined, the more exclusive and homogeneous its makeup. Hence, definitions of the elite and criteria of access greatly affect conclusions about the extent of elite representativeness. Elites are always small minorities, but the boundaries between elites and non-elites may be rigidly or loosely drawn.

All of these issues require theoretically grounded rationales without which it is not clear what information to pursue or how to interpret it. Ideally, elite analysis requires a grounding in classic theory to guide the search for meaningful information. This is not always heeded, with the result that the empirical data presented often lack historical depth and theoretical anchors, and hence data on social origins, ethnicity, education, and other dimensions of interest are offered without the rationales that would illumine their meaning.

Factionalism

Factionalism is probably inevitable in human societies and especially in directing elites. When such factionalism can be channeled and ritualized, as in the liberal democracies, its benefits outweigh its costs. That is to say, when there is a broad consensus on fundamental values and aims, factionalism will add intrigue and intensity to the social drama but not threaten the foundations of social life. However, when factions maneuver in a moral, ideological, or political vacuum, as is currently the case amidst clashes over the direction of society, then they constitute a great potential danger. Without a solid foundation in shared values and goals, the tugs and pulls of competing ideologies threaten to stifle the growth of new institutions and create a stalemate with revolutionary implications. This seems to be the case for contemporary postcommunist elites vying for positions amidst the proliferation of competing ideologies, policies, and programs, without the coping and stabilizing mechanisms of established societies.

Existing factions, representing sharply divergent worldviews, include not only the old elites battling with the elites seeking to displace them, but also competing strategies and philosophies of change captured in the familiar polarities of liberal versus conservative, radical versus reactionary, reformist versus revolutionary.

The authors of these essays offered diverse findings to support one or the other view. Alla Yaroshinskaya noted that of the fifty or so advisors and experts around Yeltsin, the old nomenklatura was not in the majority. Another larger empirical study, by Olga Krishtanovskaia, found that the contemporary top Russian business leadership was overwhelmingly from the old nomenklatura. If these differences are confirmed by ongoing research, the question then becomes whether and how the political and the economic elites can devise a unified political-economic policy when they appear to have so little in common.

Another division discussed in several of the essays involved the tension between regional power blocs as distinct from the concentrated powers at the center. In Russia, anarchic developments notwithstanding, there are strong centripetal tendencies. Nonetheless, separatist and anticentralist tendencies are notable in certain regions with their oppositional elites, who, mindful of their suppression under communism, thereby express their profound distrust in their dealings with the center. Under communism, the regional-ethnic elites were compelled to yield power to Moscow elites united by power and family connections. Thus it has been suggested that dissatisfied regional nomenklatura elites may have helped to prepare the ground for the Soviet system's collapse because of their revulsion at the corruption endemic in the central nomenklatura under communism. Along with regional elites, ethnic elites have also come to the fore and have exerted a notable influence on the politics of the center from their regional bases.

This finds some parallels to the United States. As minorities demand greater access to a central place in the political arena. All in all, according to the authors of these essays, in every postcommunist society, factionalism is rife as top elites vie for control. To avoid fragmentation, alliances across specialized elite terrains would seem to be essential, and these will undoubtedly shape the postcommunist future.

Factionalism among elites threatens the possibility of social order in a number of ways. There is the energy consumed by internecine warfare, as each faction cancels out the efficacy of the other, thereby immobilizing all. In addition, given the demise of the Communist Party and the Politburo, the societal steering mechanisms of Soviet society undermine the capacity for concerted action. When combined with the rapid infusion of newcomers without experience or a culture of leadership to guide them, the outcome is predictable: ideological and administrative stalemate.

With the elites divided, a number of classic questions emerge about what will provide the moral glue to hold the elites, as designated collective agents, and society together. How, in societies in the throes of massive ideological and institutional change, can a sense of purpose be instilled in elites that would steer them toward the general welfare and the public good? Above all, what will insure that elites serve the society and the public good rather than their own self-interest?

In this connection, the salience of the criminal elite sounded a disturbing note within the pages of this book, as more than one author considered it "the biggest danger facing Russia today." Many deplored the impact of this elite far beyond the realm of politics, permeating the general culture, human relations, and morality. "Who rules us today? Who will kill us tomorrow?" asked one author, summing up the anxieties engendered by the criminal elite in the postcommunist world.

The tragic irony, according to one of the authors, stemmed from the fact that in the Soviet past the main source of crime—large-scale, serious crime—was the state itself. The criminal elite in that sense is simply a continuation of the old system, and crime becomes part of politics as usual. When the state does not protect its citizens, the law of the jungle takes over and corruption is diffused to all levels of society. Without a firm moral code as well as a legal basis for the privatization of property, criminality and a sense of lawlessness are allowed to flourish. The idea that the criminal elite is helping to normalize society by carrying out neglected social functions did not sit well with the authors, who rejected the idea of the mafia as a positive force. At the same time, it was obvious to all that the boundaries between illegal and legal are virtually impossible to establish at this time. Some expressed fear that the criminal elite, intertwined with other elites, may be here to stay. Once in the saddle, it will become entrenched way past the point of transition. This is the dark side of the postcommunist drama.

Questions and Suggestions

These papers not only offered new information but led to new questions as well., a few of which follow. First, given that the postcommunist elites are still in the process of formation, the question arises as to whether one is really dealing with elites that do justice to the concept by their excellence of performance, their public spiritedness, their incorruptibility, or their potential for leadership. Ideally, elites should help people keep their sanity by providing some sense of orientation in the current chaotic climate. Given that chaos, some authors at the conference suggested that the term "proto-elite" is preferable to designate these transitional elites. Actually, a deep ambivalence toward current elites characterized these essays, principally because of doubts that they could in fact protect their societies from cataclysm and disaster.

A second question concerns the methods used to study elites and the characteristics focused on. The suggestive materials offered by the authors were probably the best under the circumstances, but they need to be supplemented by systematic investigations of well-defined issues and careful monitoring of significant patterns and trends. A theoretically grounded topical agenda is very much needed.

What motivates elite aspirants to seek power, honor, wealth, or fame is always a fundamental question. And what abilities and skills are needed by ambitious candidates? These direct the researcher to the human dimension of elites in conjunction with their institutional roles.

What rewards are available to the elites and how are these determined? What limits are advisable—ample enough to attract desirable candidates yet not too ample so as to distance the elites from the people they are to represent? The extent of elite privilege and self-indulgence is a measure of a society's predisposition to sustain inequality. In the present instance, the privileges of elites, when contrasted with the misery of the general population, is a distressing indicator of the widespread malaise in postcommunist societies.

Then there is the question of the extent to which the individuals in the elites are actually leaders and how this potential could be assessed. This would require reliable indicators of leadership as well as behavioral and reputational measures of elite performance.

What is the role of women in the transition to a noncommunist era? Glass ceilings exist here too, as few top elite members in politics or in business are women. The consensus in these essays seems to be that powerful or prominent women are unpopular in Russia, Poland, and other societies of Eastern Europe and are disliked by both men and women. This, too, needs elaboration.

Some suggestions for future work on postcommunist elites are in order. Good, consistent, operational definitions of elites are needed. The distinction between elites and the ruling stratum is often blurred, which muddles the discourse.

A focus on the ethnic composition of the new elites would be instructive, especially in the newly independent states where regional elites have a strong ethnic component and where ethnicity as a key criterion of recruitment and selection persists from generation to generation.

Then there is the role of the intelligentsia in politics. Its decline was noted as a critical lack to keep the elites on course and to provide a public watchdog of their performance. Generational continuities and discontinuities in social origins, ideals, and goals would help anticipate significant trends in elite formation over time and provide a basis for interpreting these.

A classic distinction in the sociological literature has been drawn between instrumental and expressive elites (first proposed by Karl Mannheim, using different terms). The first is oriented to action and the attainment of concrete social goals; the second, to less tangible objectives pertaining to public moods, morale, and states of mind that motivate the public for or against such goals. Elite analysis typically features the instrumental but neglects the expressive elites. This is regrettable since the two are interdependent in profound ways.

The recruitment and qualifications of elites have been subjects of passionate debate since Plato's time. Plato opted for a tortuous and unworkable scheme of anonymous reproduction, eugenic selection, and collective childbearing to create societal guardians of the highest moral and intellectual quality. His dubious proposals notwithstanding, Plato alerted us to a fundamental proposition that remains unchallenged: elites must be trained for morality, courage, honor, and leadership so as to assume their grand assignments. Historically, birth was the preferred criterion for elite recruitment; more recently, demonstrated merit is ideologically preferable. The preparation and training of postcommunist elites will become increasingly salient as their societies become stabilized.

There are two great afflictions of the body politic. One is the tendency of the elites toward increased control, collusion, and abuse of power. The other is disunity and fragmentation as the elites contend for hegemony. In the first case, the people suffocate for lack of freedom. In the second, people are pulled in opposite directions and thus immobilized. The latter characterizes postcommunist societies currently in their struggle to discover a common ground for action.

We should heed the warning of Martin Marger that the formation of elites in Russia or Poland or Czechoslovakia is not likely to be the same as it was in the United States. A comparative study is thus essential.

A Final Note on Entrepreneurship

Considering the current Herculean effort to transform the state-controlled societies of Eastern Europe into democratic market societies, the role of the political, economic, and cultural elites assumes supreme importance. For it is they who must provide the leadership needed for this mammoth undertaking and inspire the massive efforts and sacrifices of the population. In particular, the business elite is critical here, and one wonders whether the current postcommunist business elite is up to the economic demands made upon it.

In the emergent capitalist societies, the transformative tasks were carried out by "self-interested market men" or entrepreneurs who constituted the driving force of this economic transformation. It is they, according to Joseph Schumpeter, who possessed that special spirit for the "creative destruction" needed for that transformation.[2]

In spite of Schumpeter's pioneering efforts, little systematic work has been undertaken on entrepreneurship. Economists, in their quest for a science, tend to shun entrepreneurship, and ignore that well-documented fact that without some such dynamic force, economic take-off is unlikely.

Entrepreneurship is part of the "spirit of capitalism" that Max Weber explored in his memorable treatise.[3] That spirit does not arise automatically but must be nurtured along with whatever "shocks" are being administered to the battered societies of Eastern Europe.

As potential change agents, contemporary elites can take a lead in supporting entrepreneurial skills and institutions and thus help generate the ideological ethos of the market society to come. In Karl Polyani's words, a "market economy can only function in a market society."[4] Such a society needs a special set of institutions, including private property, contract laws, a banking system, and the cultural values of economic rationality, individualization, a profit motive, and a special calculus of success.[5] Without these defining institutions and values, a market mentality has little chance to develop, and instead we get liberated greed.

Conclusion

In general, these essays reflect a sense of apprehensiveness. The authors continue to wonder whether ex-communist societies will in fact make the transition to a market society; whether the current elites will find ways to coalesce their aims and bridge their differences; whether the hold of the nomenklatura system by which the elites were selected under communism will continue to exercise dominance, albeit in disguise, in the postcommunist era; and whether the economic, political, military, scientific, and cultural elites will not only be able to work in concert but also be effective moral leaders devoted to the public good. As the ancients understood, the influence of the leading actors in the social drama is immense, and their virtues, as well as their vices, will resonate throughout society and affect the course of collective life for generations.

Notes

Introduction

1. See Samuel Huntington, "No Exit: The Errors of Endism," *National Interest* 17 (1989): 3–11.

2. See T. B. Bottomore, *Elites and Society* (New York: Basic Books, 1964).

3. See Lowell G. Field and John Higley, *Elitism* (London: Routledge & Kegan Paul, 1980).

4. See Vilfredo Pareto, *The Mind and Society: A Treatise on General Sociology,* vols. 3 and 4, trans. Andrew Bongiorno and Arthur Livingston (New York: Dover, 1935).

5. See Gaetano Mosca, *The Ruling Class* (New York: McGraw-Hill, 1939).

6. See Suzanne Keller, *Beyond the Ruling Class* (New York: Random House, 1963).

7. Pareto, *Mind and Society,* pp. 1426–32. See Charles H. Powers, *Vilfredo Pareto* (Beverly Hills, Calif.: Sage, 1987).

8. See Robert Michels, *Political Parties,* trans. Eden Paul and Cedar Paul (New York: Dover, 1915).

9. See Michels, *First Lectures in Political Sociology,* trans. Alfred De Grazia (New York: Harper and Row, 1949), p. 106.

10. See Renzo Sereno, *The Rulers* (New York: Harper & Row, 1968), p. 31.

11. See Erich Fromm, *Escape from Freedom* (New York: Holt, Rinehart, and Winston, 1941).

12. See John Higley and Michael G. Burton, "The Elite Variable in Democratic Transitions and Breakdowns," *American Sociological Review* 54 (1989): 17–32. See Field and Higley, *Elitism,* pp. 19–20.

13. Field and Higley, *Elitism,* p. 19.

14. Ibid., p. 20.

15. See Michael Burton and John Higley, "Elite Settlements," *American Sociological Review* 52 (1987): 295, 298–99.

16. See Kenneth Maxwell, "Investigating a Tradition," *Times Literary Supplement,* December 9–15, 1988, pp. 1367–68; Ben Ross Schneider, *Politics Within the*

State: Elite Bureaucrats and Industrialization in Authoritarian Brazil (Pittsburgh: University of Pittsburgh Press, 1991).

17. See Nikolai Genov, "The Transition to Democracy in Eastern Europe: Trends and Paradoxes of Social Rationalization," *International Social Science Journal* 43 (1991): 331–41, 335–36.

18. Ibid., p. 336.

19. See Piotr Sztompka, "Trust and Emerging Democracy," *International Sociology* 11 (1989): 37–62, 44.

20. Ibid., pp. 54–55.

21. Ibid., p. 55.

22. See Victor Nee, "Social Inequalities in Reforming State Socialism: Between Redistribution and Markets in China," *American Sociological Review* 56 (1991): 267–82; Victor Nee and Rebecca Matthews, "Market Transition and Societal Transformation in Reforming State Socialism," *Annual Review of Sociology* 22 (1996): 401–35.

23. Nee, "Social Inequalities."

24. Nee and Matthews, "Market Transition," p. 412.

25. Ibid., p. 415.

26. Ibid., pp. 429–30.

27. See Olga Krishtanovskaia and Stephen White's chapter in this book. See also Ivan Szelenyi et al., eds., *Elity v Polshe, v Rosii i na Wegrzech* (Warsaw: Institut Studiow Politicznych, 1995); N. Lapina, *Formirovanie Sovremennoi Rossiiskoi Elity* (Moscow: INION, 1995); K. Mikulskii, ed., *Rossiiskaia elita: opyt sotsiologicheskogo analiza* (Moscow: Institut sotsiologii, 1997).

28. The application forms in the Soviet times for significant positions contained dozen of questions about the social origin of applicants. Among them, questions about one's parents, grandparents, spouse's parents, and several others.

29. See Egor Gaidar, "Eto reshienie-chisto politicheskoie," *Izvestia,* January 20, 1994.

30. Marx once said that to be an ideologue of shopkeepers is not necessarily to be a shopkeeper oneself. As Yurii Levada writes in the third chapter of this volume, "'social origin' cannot be the decisive factor for determining the activity of individuals, whatever *nomenklatura* post they occupied. An exaggeration of the role of origin is a methodological inheritance of primitive 'class' doctrines. Vulgarized Marxism links (inseparably) people and their class group and origin." At the same time, Vladimir Solonar, the author of the chapter on Moldova, for instance, underscores the significant influence of the old *nomenklatura* mentality on the new elite even if he describes the radical changes in the ethnic and educational composition of the elite.

31. No one in Russia can contend that former Soviet minister Victor Chernomyrdin and Anatolii Chubais behaved differently when they were in the government: both advanced the same "monetarist policy" in running the Russian economy; both tried to exploit their positions for personal enrichment; both supported some oligarches and opposed others; both were ready to use any means, including illegal, to keep their political power; and both held the masses in contempt and looked at democratic elections as a nuisance.

32. It is remarkable that on ideological issues, old apparatchiks hold the most dif-

ferent views on all major social issues, even if it is possible to discover some bias toward the high role of the state in the economy among them. For instance, in Russia we can find former apparatchiks of high status among democratic parties as well as among the most radical nationalists. The same is true with people who made their career only in post-Communist society.

33. The first chapter of this book offers much information on the origin of the new Russian elite.

34. European feudalism as it functioned in the ninth through the sixteenth centuries is probably the best historical parallel for postcommunist society in many countries. The feudal model as a particular case of the oligarchic model is much more seminal for the analysis of contemporary Russian reality. The existence of democratic institutions in Russia by itself is not a big obstacle for the application of this model as a variant of an oligarchic society to Russia because feudalism was not alien to democratic procedures extended, of course, only to oligarches themselves. There were various elections in the Middle Ages, among them the election of emperors and popes. See Vladimir Shlapentokh, "Russia as a Medieval State," *Washington Quarterly* 19, no. 1 (Winter, 1996).

35. The fluidity of the political elite is so great in Ukraine that one of the contributors to this book, Nikolai Churilov, even contends that his republic does not have a political elite in the classical meaning of the term.

36. It is remarkable that corruption among the elites is almost totally ignored in the most recent sociological books on elites in Western societies. See, for example, Robert Lerner, Althea Nagai, and Stanley Rothman, *American Elites* (New Haven: Yale University Press, 1996); Eric Carlton, *The Few and Many: A Typology of Elites* (Aldershot, England: Scholar, 1996).

37. See World Bank, *The State in a Changing World* (New York: Oxford University Press, 1997); see also John Heller, "World Bank Thumbs Robber Capitalism," *Moscow Tribune,* August 27, 1997.

38. See James Buchanan, "Rent Seeking and Profit Seeking," in *Toward a Theory of the Rent Seeking Society,* ed. James Buchanan, Robert Teleostan, and Gordian Bullock (College Station: Texas A&M University Press, 1980), p. 3.

39. See William Mitchell and Michael Manger, "Economic Models of Interests Groups: An Introductory Survey," *American Journal of Political Science* 35 (1991): 525; Glenn Parker, *Congress and Rent Seeking Society* (Ann Arbor: University of Michigan Press, 1996), p. 22. See also Buchanan, Tollison, and Tullock, *Toward a Theory of the Rent Seeking Society;* Anne Krueger, "Economists' Changing Perceptions of Government," in *Comparative Economic Systems: Models and Cases,* ed. Morris Bornstein (Burr Ridge, Ill.: Irwin, 1994), pp. 86–89.

40. The cases of the election of criminals in Russia as deputies of regional and national legislatures and in particular as mayors of big cities were typical for the Russian political landscape by the end of the 1990s. See Victor Luneev, *Prestupnost XX veka* (Moscow: Norma, 1997). See also his chapter in this book.

41. See Olga Krishtanovskaia, "V Chikh Rukakh Sobstvennost," *Argumenty I Fakty* 14 (April, 1997).

42. See Glenn Parker, *Congress and Rent Seeking Society* (Ann Arbor: University of Michigan Press, 1996), p. 22.

   Leading corporations in Russia in 1997 include financial empires such as Most, headed by Vladimir Gusinskii; Logovaz, headed by Boris Berezovskii;

Menatep, headed by Boris Khodorkovskii; Oneksimbank, headed by Vladimir Potanin; and Stolichnyi Bank, headed by Alexander Smolenskii.

Gasprom is another well-known corporation, often referred to as the cash cow. Its market capital consists of tens of billions of dollars, with sales approaching $20 billion. Gasprom's gross profits exceed $3 billion, and it employs nearly 400,000 people.

For data on the concentration of capital in the Russian economy see Goskomstat Rossii, *Rossiiskii Statisticheskii Ezhegodnik 1996* (Moscow: Logos, 1996), p. 499.

By the end of the 1990s, it was admitted in Moscow that Gasprom is under the special protection of Premier Minister Chernomyrdin, who was a former boss of this corporation and who, by all accounts, had a great deal of valuable stock in this company. Furthermore, Chernomyrdin's two sons openly worked for Gasprom (*Izvestia,* January 5, 1997).

First Deputy Chubais and a few other high officials were linked to Oneksimbank, which, by using a variety of tricks (noninterest loans, excessively high honorariums, and other methods) provided them with various perks. Facts discovered by the media (which served the interests of the rivals of Oneksimbank) led to a huge political scandal in Moscow in the second half of 1997 (see *Novaia Gazeta,* November 17 and December 1, 1997; and *Moskovskie Novosti,* November 11, 1997; *Moskovskii Komsomolets,* December 17, 1997).

43. See Aristotle, *The Politics and the Constitution of Athens* (Cambridge, England: Cambridge University Press, 1884), p. 57.

44. *Krysha* is a "normal" institution and a persistent part of Russian post-Communist life as it is in most former Soviet republics. In the opinion of my Russian business acquaintances, there is no force in the country able to destroy it since a criminal gang in one area will almost immediately be replaced by another gang when eliminated. See Shlapentokh, "Russia as a Medieval State."

45. See Luneev, *Prestupnost XX veka,* pp. 337–446.

46. For more about the collaboration of criminals and law enforcement agencies in Orel, see Alexander Vasinskii, "Thieves and Procurators," *Izvestia,* December 9, 1997.

47. Stanislav Govorukhin, *Velikaia Kriminal'naia Revoliutsiia* (Moscow: Andreevskii Flag, 1993), p. 126; see also Stephan Handelman, *Comrade Criminal* (New Haven: Yale University Press, 1997); and J. Michael Waller and Victor J. Yasmann, "Russia's Great Criminal Revolution: The Role of the Security Services," *Journal of Contemporary Criminal Justice* 11, no. 4 (December, 1995). Russian Radio, November 15, 1997.

48. For example, Gennadii Koniukhov was elected mayor of the midsized city, Leninsk-Kuznetsk, in Kuzbass. In Krasnoiarsk, an individual with an even darker past, named Bykov, was elected to the regional duma. He collected more votes than all other deputies. Terentiev, with four pending criminal cases, was elected as mayor of Artem, a city in the Maritime Territory (*Izvestia,* November 14, December 10, 11, 25, 1997). In Nizhnii-Novgorod (March, 1998) Andrei Klimentiev, an individual with a significant criminal record, was elected as mayor, though the president insisted on the annulment of the election result (see *Russkii telegraf,* April 2, 1998; *Moskovskii Komsomolets,* April 4 and 7, 1998).

Even in the elections of the local duma in Moscow, "many individuals with criminal pasts" participated, as was noted by Moscow journalist Mikhail Shevelev (see "Teni Zabytykh Vyborov," *Moskovskie Novosti,* December 21,

1997). For more about the role of criminals in the election in Novosibirsk, see Valerii Vyzhutovich, "Poslednii Vagon s Severa," *Izvestia,* December 18, 1997; about the election in Krasnoiarsk, see Grigorii Kakovkin, "Tak golosuiut Obmanutyie," *Izvestia,* December 17, 1997.

As an example of how criminal organizations control local administrations, see how local Mafias run a district in the Tula region (Sergei Zhdakaiev, "Perestreliaem Vsekh," *Izvestia,* January 13, 1998).

49.   Vladimir Mikhailenko, "Tenevoie Gosudarstvo," *Nezavisimaia Gazeta,* July 24, 1997.

50.   By 1991, the murders of businesspeople, political officials, and journalists were considered regular phenomena in Russia, Ukraine, Kazakhstan, Georgia, and several other postcommunist countries. In Russia, for instance, between 1995 and 1996, roughly two hundred bankers and businesspeople, along with dozens of journalists, were murdered. None of these murders, which had been well publicized in the media, was solved, and no one was brought to justice. By 1997, violent crime and murder in Russia no longer attracted much public interest. The media's coverage of violent crime was minuscule compared to the coverage in 1992–94. The murder by the hired gun of the vice governor of Petersburg and chairman of the State Property Committee of Mikhail Manevich, in August of 1997, only attracted public interest for a few days, after which the story was completely forgotten, along with the murders of several other prominent businesspeople (*Moskovskie Novosti,* August 31, 1997; *Segodnia,* August 19, 1997).

51.   The data related to Russia are typical for many postcommunist countries. According to data provided by Nikolai Kovalev, head of the Federal Security Service (FSB, formerly the KGB), each of the two thousand commercial banks in Russia has its own security service. Some of the private security services are comparable in size and composition to the regional office of the FSB. In 1997, Igor Sundiev, vice president of the Russian Criminological Association, contended that "in Russia, it is difficult to find banks which do not have criminal roofs" (Sundiev, "Krov I Nerv Kriminalnogo Mira," *Literaturnaia Gazeta,* August 27, 1997).

The financial complex Most, for example, has a private army for its protection. One of the army's commanders was none other than General Philip Bobko, former deputy of the KGB.

52.   At the same time, bodyguarding is becoming a very popular profession in the postcommunist world. According to some sources, there are no less than one million bodyguards in Russia. Hiring private bodyguards is already a deeply rooted custom for the elites in postcommunist countries. Bodyguards trail their masters everywhere, including the bathroom.

See Vladimir Semichastnyi, "Mne Nesterpimo Bolno," *Zavtra* 25 (1997).

53.   For example, since the first free election, the Kremlin has kept the Russian parliament in permanent fear of disbandment. In 1993, the Kremlin not only dissolved the parliament but shelled the parliamentary building, killing more than one hundred people. The president wanted to oust the parliament even earlier, in March 1993, when it threatened impeachment; the effort failed because Yeltsin's enemies could not garner the necessary number of votes. Alexander Korzhakov recounts in his book when, in March 1993, the Russian parliament came within inches of voting to impeach President Yeltsin. At this time, Yeltsin ordered his retinue to prepare the arrest of the entire parliament in the case of impeachment. What is more, he planned to use chemical gases to

smoke the deputies out of the building. Fortunately for the deputies, the impeachment vote never came. Similarly, in the election year of 1996, Yeltsin had no intention of leaving the Kremlin and was prepared to take any action to insure his continued presidency. According to Korzhakov, in the summer of 1996, Yeltsin and Prime Minister Victor Chernomyrdin seriously debated canceling the presidential election. Alexander Korzhakov, *Boris Yeltsin: Ot Rassveta Do Zakata* (Moscow: Interbuk, 1997), pp. 156–200. See also Konstantin Mikulskii, et al., "Biznes-elita," *Segodnia,* February, 1996.

54. For more about the distribution of the Russian media among major oligarches, see Yurii Zainashev's article, "The Fourth Power Is Becoming the Second Oldest Profession" (*Moskovskii Komsomolets,* August 12, 1997). One of the oldest and most respected newspapers, *Izvestia,* fell victim to oligarchic take over. Oneksimbank, a leading financial monopoly, bought out the stock and became the owner of the newspaper. Since Vladimir Potanin, the head of this bank, supported Anatolii Chubais in his struggle against Boris Berezovskii, the editor of *Izvestia* was replaced because he published materials denouncing Chubais as well as Chernomyrdin. The new owners openly ousted the chief editor, Igor Golembiovskii, in August, 1997; about the scandal, see *Novaia Gazeta,* August 18, 1997; *Ogoniok* 31 (1997): 26–27. Since the time of the scandal, the newspaper has published only articles praising the government.

55. Mikhail Afanasiev, "Golos Grazhdanskogo Obshchestva Stanovitsia Vse Tishe," *Izvestia,* December 25, 1997.

56. In April, 1998, many deputies in the Russian parliament openly voted for Yeltsin's candidate for premier minister only because in the case of its rejection the president promised to dissolve the duma, which for deputies meant the loss of their position in Moscow along with its many perks (see *New York Times,* April 25, 1998).

57. See one of the most recent works on this debate: Boris Paramonov, "Historical Culture," in *Russian Cultures at the Crossroads,* ed. Dmitry Shalin (Boulder: Westview, 1996), pp. 11–40.

58. Vasilii Aksenov, a famous Russian-American writer, described his meeting with a successful young Russian who wanted to see Russia only as a superpower and, with repressed anger, rejected the famous writer's suggestion that Russia should look for greatness not in international confrontation but in the development of its economy and in the well-being of its citizens and culture (Vasilii Aksenov, "Novogodnie Zaroki," *Moskovskie Novosti,* January 4, 1998).

59. See *Literaturnaia Gazeta,* January 28, 1998. Vasilii Aksenov noted this almost sudden change of tone in Moscow. Russians went from being delighted about everything in America to ridiculing the American way of life from every angle—from food, clothing, and cars to morals and human relations (Aksenov, "Nostalgia or Shizofrenia," *Moskovskie Novosti,* November 9, 1997).

60. See *VTSIOM* 6 (1994): 50. See also *Moskovskie Novosti,* October 2, 1994.
     Only 7 percent of the Russians responded positively in the spring of 1994, only a few months after the election of the new parliament, to the statement, "the parties in the Parliament reflect the interests and views existing in society." See *VTSIOM* 4 (1994): 13.

61. Oleg Poptsov, a prominent writer and politician, noted, "a murdered banker or entrepreneur does not arouse public compassion" (see "Iz Nichego v Nikuda," *Literaturnaia Gazeta,* December 10, 1997).

62. See C. Wright Mills, *The Power Elite* (New York: Oxford University Press,

1959); Robert A. Dahl, *Democracy, Liberty, and Equality* (Oslo: Norwegian University Press, 1986); William G. Domhoff, *The Power Elite and the State: How Policy Is Made* (New York: Aldine De Gruyter, 1990).

Chapter 1

An earlier version of this paper was presented to the International Congress for Central and East European Studies at Warsaw in August, 1995. It draws in part upon the Soviet Elites Project based at the University of Glasgow, which is supported by the U.K. Economic and Social Research Council and directed by Evan Mawdsley and Stephen White.

1. See Vilfredo Pareto, *Treatise On General Sociology* (New York: Harcourt, Brace, Jovanovich, 1935). See *Argumenty i Fakty* 35 (1994): 2 (popularity of USSR), and 23 (1993): 2 (communists still in power). In an April, 1995, survey, 67 percent of Russians gave a positive evaluation to the old Soviet system of government, compared with 26 percent who evaluated the present regime in the same way; see Richard Rose, *New Russia Barometer IV: Survey Results* (Glasgow: Centre for the Study of Public Policy, 1995), pp. 42–43.

2. On the Communist Party in the Czech Republic, see Zdenka Mansfeldova, "The Emerging New Czech Political Elites" (Madrid, April, 1994). On Poland, see, for instance, Adam Pogorecki, "The Communist and Post-Communist Nomenklatura," *Polish Sociological Review* 106, no. 2 (1994): 111–23. See also Jacek Wasilewski, ed., *Konsolidacja Elit Politycznych 1991–1993* (Warsaw: Instytut Studiow Politicznych, 1994); Wasilewski, "The Crystallization of the Post-Communist and Post-Solidarity Political Elite," in *After Communism*, ed. Edmund Wnuk-Lipinski (Warsaw: Institute of Political Studies, 1995), pp. 117–33; Wnup-Lipinski and Wasilewski, "How Much Communism Is Left With Us?," *Politicus*, August, 1995, pp. 39–44; and Ivan Szelenyi et al., eds., *Elity w Polsce, w Rosji i na Wegrzech* (Warsaw: Instytut Studiow Politicznych, 1995).

   On Gorbachev and Yeltsin elites, see David Lane and Cameron Ross, "The Changing Composition and Structure of the Political Elites," in *Russia in Transition*, ed. David Lane (London: Longman, 1995), p. 68. Up to 80 percent of local functionaries were the same as they had been in the Soviet period, according to *Rossiiskaia Gazeta*, March 4, 1992, p. 2. Yeltsin himself claimed there was less continuity at the national level. See *Izvestia*, March 27, 1992, p. 7. A comparison between the "old" and "new" elites is presented in B. V. Golovachev et al., "Formirovanie Praviashchei Elity v Rossii," *Ekonomicheskie i Sotsial'nye Peremeny: Monitoring Obshchestvennogo Mneniia* 6 (1995): 18–24; it is less directly concerned with continuity than the present study but notes that about 40 percent of elite members had been born into *nomenklatura* families (p. 21).

   N. S. Ershova, "Transformatsiia praviashchei elity Rossii v usloviiakh sotsial-nogo pereloma," in *Kuda idet Rossiia?* ed. T. I. Zaslavskaia and L. A. Arutyunian (Moscow: Interpraks, 1994), pp. 151–55, reports that "over 60 percent" of the former *nomenklatura* still occupied elite positions (p. 154). See Thomas A. Baylis, "Plus ca change? Transformation and Continuity Amongst East European Elites," *Communist and Post-Communist Studies* 27, no. 3 (September, 1994): 315–28. *Nezavisimaia Gazeta*, December 3, 1992, p. 5.

3. For a more general treatment that emphasizes elite cohesion, see John Higley and Jan Pakulski, "Revolution and Elite Transformation in Eastern Europe," *Australian Journal of Political Science* 27, no. 1 (March, 1992): 104–19; and Higley and Pakulski, "Elite Transformation in Eastern Europe and Russia" (paper presented to the Sixteenth Congress of the International Political Sci-

ence Association, Berlin, August, 1994). See also Hellmut Wollmann, "Change and Continuity of Political and Administrative Elites from Communist to Post-Communist Russia," *Governance* 6, no. 3 (July, 1993): 325–40.

4. An alternative reputational approach is available in David Lane, "Gorbachev's Political Elite in the Terminal Stage of the USSR: A Reputational Analysis," *Journal of Communist Studies and Transition Politics* 10, no. 1 (March, 1994): 104–16, and idem., "Political Elites Under Gorbachev and Yeltsin in the Early Period of Transition: A Reputational and Analytic Study," in *Patterns in Post-Soviet Political Leadership,* ed. Timothy Colton and Robert C. Tucker (Boulder, Colo.: Westview, 1995).

5. The investigations are as follows: (i) "Kto pravit Rossiei? (Issledovanie elity Rossiiskoi provintsii)," 1994; (ii) "Lidery Rossiiskogo biznesa," 1992–94; (iii) "Rossiiskaia politicheskaia elita," 1993; (iv) "Sobstvennost' v Rossii," 1993; (v) "Material'nyi uroven zhizni v Moskve i Rossii," 1993; (vi) "Politicheskie partii i tsentry vliianiia Rossii," 1992–93; (vii) "Politicheskaia elita Brezhnevskoi formatsii," 1991–93; (viii) "Vliiatel'nye liudi pri Gorbacheve i Yel'tsine," 1992; (ix) "Obshchestvennoe mnenie o bogatykh i bogatstve," 1992; (x) "Biznes i reformy," 1992; (xi) "Byvshie sotrudniki KGB v novoi roli predprinimatelei," 1992; (xii) "Biznes i politika," 1992; (xiii) "Stsenarii politicheskikh izmenenii v Rossii," 1992; (xiv) "Rossiiskie menedzhery," 1991; (xv) "Komanda Yel'tsina," 1991; (xvi) "Sovetskie millionery," 1991; (xvii) "Novaia sovetskaia elita," 1990; and (xviii) "Administrativnaia sistema i ee sub-ekty," 1989–92. Sponsorship for these studies was obtained from a variety of agencies including the Administration of the President of Russia, the French defense ministry, the U.K. Economic and Social Research Council, Columbia University, and the newspapers *Delovoi Mir* and *Moskovskie Novosti.*

6. Our principal biographical sources include *Izvestia TsK KPSS* 8 (1990): 8–61, 10, 28–61, 11, and 32–62; *Deputaty Verkhovnogo Soveta SSSR: Odinnadtsatyi sozyv* (Moscow: Izvestia, 1984); *Sostav tsentral'nykh organov KPSS, izbrannykh XXVI s'ezdom partii. Spravochnik* (Moscow: Politizdat, 1982) (a corresponding volume for the 27th Congress is available in the Centre for the Preservation of Contemporary Documentation, Moscow); A. S. Barsenkov et al., *Politicheskaia Rossiia segodnia,* 2 vols. (Moscow: Moskovskii rabochii, 1993); Vladimir Pribylovskii, *Kto est' kto v rossiiskoi politike,* 3 vols. (Moscow: Panorama, 1993); N. Poroshina, *Kto est' kto v Rossii i v blizhnem zarubezh'e: Spravochnik* (Moscow: Novoe Vremia, 1993); V. N. Berezovskii and V. V. Cherviakov, eds., *Sto partiinykh liderov: kratkii biograficheskii spravochnik* (Moscow: RAU Press, 1993); *Elita rossiiskogo biznesa,* rev. ed. (Moscow: Darin, 1994); I. Bunin et al., *Biznesmeny Rossii: 40 istorii uspekha* (Moscow: Oko, 1994); P. Gazukin and V. Pribylovskii, eds., *Pravitel'stvo Rossiiskoi Federatsii: biograficheskii spravochnik* (Moscow: Panorama, 1995); *Vlast'. Deputaty Gosudarstvennoi Dumy. Kratkii biograficheskii spravochnik,* 4 parts (Moscow: Institut sovremennoi politiki, 1994); Jeanne Vronskaya and Vladimir Chuguev, *Kto est' kto v Rossii i byvshem SSSR* (Moscow: Terra, 1994); A. S. Barsenkov et al., *Federal'noe sobranie Rossii. Sovet Federatsii. Gosudarstvennaia Duma* (Moscow: Fond Foros, 1995); and V. S. Bondarev, ed., *Kto est' kto i pochemu. Politicheskaia elita Rossii v portretakh* (Moscow: Skriptorii, 1995).

7. See for instance Michael Voslensky, *Nomenklatura: Anatomy of the Soviet Ruling Class* (London: Bodley Head, 1984).

8. For a discussion of the changing composition of the Central Committee and what Robert Daniels described as the "job slot" system, see Evan Mawdsley,

"Portrait of a Changing Elite: CPSU Central Committee Full Members, 1939–1990," in *New Directions in Soviet History,* ed. Stephen White (Cambridge: Cambridge University Press, 1991), pp. 191–206.

9. T. H. Rigby, *Political Elites in the USSR* (Aldershot, England: Edward Elgar, 1990), ch. 4; V. G. Sirotkin, "Nomenklatura (zametki istorika)," *Vestnik Akademii nauk SSSR* 6 (1990): 12–26; T. P. Kozhikhina and Yu. Figatner, "Sovetskaia nomenklatura: stanovlenie, mekhanizmy deistviia," *Voprosy Istorii* 7 (1993): 25–38; and O. T. Dzhavlanov and V. A. Mikheev, *Nomenklatura: evoliutsiia otbora* (Moscow: Luch, 1993).

10. A full listing of the positions that were included in the national party *nomenklatura* is now available in the party archives: see "Tsentr po khraneniiu sovremennoi dokumentatsii," Moscow, *fond* 89, *perechen'* 20 document 77, August 7, 1991.

11. Voslensky, *Nomenklatura,* pp. 213ff.

12. See Mervyn Matthews, *Privilege in the Soviet Union* (London: Allen and Unwin, 1978); and Il'ia Zemtsov, *Chastnaia zhizn' sovetskoi elity* (London: Overseas Publications Interchange, 1986). The party's own investigation into privilege was reported to the Central Committee in December, 1990: *Materialy Plenuma Tsentral'nogo komiteta KPSS 10–11 dekabria 1990 goda* (Moscow: Politizdat, 1991), pp. 86–95.

13. *Moskovskie Novosti,* April 24, 1988, p. 7.

14. Trotsky's views on this subject were most fully set out in *The Revolution Betrayed* (New York, 1937).

15. Ligachev was reported to have used this term by the director of the Centre for the Scientific and Technical Creativity of Youth attached to the Badman district committee of the CPSU, Anabolic Churgel'. For his assistance with this part of our discussion we are indebted to A. Pavliukov; we have also drawn upon interviews for the Soviet Elites Project with former Komsomol first secretaries Victor Mishin and Victor Mironenko.

16. Bunin et al., *Biznesmeny Rossii,* pp. 35–36, 141, 199–200 (Zatulin was also chairman of Rossiiskii Broker), and 170. A recent investigation found that 7 percent of young entrepreneurs had emerged from the Komsomol apparatus: *Moskovskaia Pravda,* November 5, 1995, p. 2.

17. For the Central Committee's resolution see V. N. Sungorkin and I. A. Savvateeva, comps., *Firma pri gorkome* (Moscow: Molodaia gvardiia, 1990), p. 222; for their purposes see *XX s"ezd Vsesoiuznogo Leninskogo Kommunisticheskogo Soiuza molodezhi, 15–18 aprelia 1987 goda: stenograficheskii otchet,* 2 vols. (Moscow: Molodaia gvardiia, 1987), vol. 1, p. 65. *Dokumenty TsK VLKSM, 1987* (Moscow: Molodaia gvardiia, 1988), pp. 64–67; for the establishment of the All-Union Coordinating Council, see *Sobranie postanovlenii pravitel'stva SSSR (otdel pervyi)* 20 (1987): art. 76. *Dokumenty i materialy II plenuma TsK VLKSM* (Moscow: Molodaia gvardiia, 1987), pp. 38–41.

18. *Dokumenty TsK VLKSM, 1988* (Moscow: Molodaia gvardiia, 1989), pp. 187; *Sobranie postanovlenii pravitel'stva SSSR (otdel pervyi)* 29 (1988): art. 81. For the text of the Law on Cooperatives as adopted, see *Vedomosti Verkhovnogo Soveta SSSR* 22 (1988): art. 355 (at p. 383). *Dokumenty TsK VLKSM, 1989* (Moscow: Molodaia gvardiia, 1990), p. 205; *Dokumenty i materialy XXI s"ezda Vsesoiuznogo Leninskogo Kommunisticheskogo Soiuza molodezhi, 11–18 aprelia 1990g* (Moscow: Molodaia gvardiia, 1990), pp. 28, 40–41.

19. Churgel' interview.

20. This account is based upon the testimony of Vladimir Shcherbakov, whose father took particular responsibility for "grain business" with the United States within the USSR.

21. Here and elsewhere we have drawn upon the studies conducted for "Lidery Rossiiskogo biznesa."

22. Zatulin discussed his own career in Bunin et al., *Biznesmeny Rossii*, pp. 199–206; he was "very grateful" for the experience he acquired working in the Komsomol headquarters (p. 200).

23. On Bukato, see *Kommercheskie banki Rossii. Spravochnik*, 2 vols. (Moscow and New York: Intelbridge, 1995), vol. I, p. 411; on Dubenetsky, see N. Poroshina, *Kto est' kto v Rossii i v blizhnem zarubezh'e*, p. 222. This section also draws upon the "Lidery Rossiiskogo biznesa" investigation.

24. Bunin et al., *Biznesmeny Rossii*, pp. 169–70; *Kommercheskie banki*, vol. I, pp. 388–91. For a discussion of these changes see Juliet Ellen Johnson, "The Russian Banking System: Institutional Responses to the Market Transition," *Europe-Asia Studies* 46, no. 6 (1994): 971–96, and *Delovye Liudi* 55 (April, 1995): 6–94.

25. For an overview of the contemporary Russian elite, see Vladimir Berezovskii's articles in *Svobodnaia mysl'* 1 (1993): 56–65; 2 (1993): 93–105; and 9 (1994): 67–86. Eberhard Schneider, "The Downfall of the Nomenklatura and the New Russian Elite" (paper presented to the 16th Congress of the International Political Science Association, Berlin, August, 1994), concentrated upon the parliamentary elite.

26. This account is based upon "Kto pravit Rossiei," part 1: "Krasnodarskii krai."

27. Kvantrishvili was assassinated on April 5, 1994: see *Izvestia*, April 7, 1994, pp. 1–2.

28. Some of these data were first presented in Ol'ga Krishtanovskaia, "Staraia nomenklatura na novyi lad," *Obshchestvennye nauki i sovremennost'* 1 (1995): 51–65.

29. See, for instance, *Sovetskoe gosudarstvo i pravo* 9 (1989): 18–19, and *Narodnyi deputat* 2 (1990): 38.

30. Andrei Grachev, *Dal'she bez menia. Ukhod Prezidenta* (Moscow: Progress-Kul'tura, 1994), p. 9.

31. Erszebet Szalai as quoted by Bill Lomax in Gordon Wightman, ed., *Party Formation in East-Central Europe* (Aldershot, England: Edward Elgar, 1994), p. 178.

32. Boris Kagarlitsky, *The Disintegration of the Monolith* (London: Verso, 1992), pp. 50–51.

33. Quoted in Jacqueline Hayden, *Poles Apart: Solidarity and the New Poland* (Dublin: Irish Academic Press, 1994), p. 33.

34. Trotsky, *Revolution Betrayed*, pp. 253–54.

35. For some preliminary discussions of elite patterns at the local level see, for instance, "Elita Peterburga," *Nevskoe vremia*, November 12, 1994, p. 4, and November 18, 1994, p. 5; A. Magomedov, "Politicheskie elity v rossiiskoi provintsii," *Mirovaia ekonomika i mezhdunarodnye otnosheniia* 4 (1994): 72–79; and, on Tatarstan, D. V. Badovskii et al., "Transformatsiia politicheskoi elity Rossii," *Politicheskie issledovaniia* 6 (1994): 42–79.

Chapter 4

1. K. H. Edin, "Iavliautsia li prestuplenia liudei v belykh vorotnichkakh prestupleniem?" in *Sotsiologia prestupnosti* (Moscow, 1966), pp. 45–59.

2. M. Edvin, *Nashe prestupnoe obshchestvo. Sotsialnye I pravovye istochniki prestupnosti v Amerike* (Moscow: Progress, 1977), p. 219.

3. "Prakticheskie mery borby s korruptsiei: Rukovodstvo, podgotovlennoe sekretariatom OON, A/Conference," 144/8, May 29, 1990. "Vosmoi kongress OON po preduprezhdeniu prestupnosti I obrashcheniu s pravonarushiteliami," Gavana, Kuba, August 27–September 7, 1990, OON, New York, 1991, p. 150.

4. A. J. Meidenheimer, M. Johnston, and V. T. Levine, eds., *Political Corruption* (New Brunswick, N.Y.: Transaction Books, 1989).

5. G. P. Fedotov, *Rossia, Evropa I My* (Paris, 1973), p. 65.

6. "Lubianka otkryvaet svoi arkhivy," *Rossiiskaia Gazeta,* April 17, 1993.

7. V. V. Luneev, "Politicheskaia Prestupnost," *Gosudarstvo I Pravo* 7 (1994): 107–27; "Deklaratsia osnovnykh printsipov I pravosudia v otnoshenii zhertv prestuplenii I zloupotreblenii vlastiu: Sedmoi kongress OON po preduprezhdeniu prestupnosti I obrashcheniu s pravonarushiteliami," August 26–September 6, 1985, OON, New York, 1986, p. 71.

8. O. G. Miasnikov, "Smena praviashchikh elit: konsolidatsia ili vechnaia skhvatka," *Politicheskie Issledovania* 1 (1993): 52–53.

9. *Prestupnost I pravonarushenia v SSSR* (Moscow, 1991, 1992, 1993, 1994).

10. V. Klimov, "Delo o propavshikh milliardakh," *Rossiiskaia Gazeta,* April 13, 1995.

11. *Rossiiskaia Gazeta,* January 28, 1995.

12. "Loviat chashche, a ubivaiut po-prezhnemu," *Rossiiskaia Gazeta,* February 23, 1995.

13. *Vedomosti s'ezda narodnykh deputatov I Verkhovnogo Soveta,* 25 (1990); *Delovoi mir,* May 4, 1993.

14. *Rossiiskaia Gazeta,* May 12, 1994.

15. A. Rutskoi, "Prestupnost-mina pod reformy," *Rossiiskaia Gazeta,* March 5, 1993; N. I. Makarov, "Korruptsia," *Sovietskaia Rossiia,* September 4, 1993; *Rossiiaskaia Gazeta,* February 17, 1994.

16. L. M. Kolodkin, *Frantsia ob'iavliaet voinu korruptsii: Sostoianie zakonnosti I borba s prestupnostiu I korruptsiei* (Moscow, 1993), p. 211.

17. "Korruptsia-bolezn gosudarstvennaia. Interviu s nachalnikom Kontrolnogo upravlenia Prezidenta RF A.Iliushenko," *Izvestia,* February 5, 1994.

18. V. I. Lenin, *Polnoe sobranie sochinenii,* vol. 36 (Moskva: Gos. izd-vo polit. lit-ry, 1960), p. 504.

19. *Rossiiskaia Gazeta,* January 29, 1994.

20. A. Kozyreva, "Preiskurant dlia partii," *Rossiiskaia Gazeta,* April 11, 1995.

21. B. Fedorov, "Krupneishee 'delo' stoletia," *Izvestia,* March 21, 1995.

22. "Dissidenty v Moskve. Diskussii," *Sotsiologicheskie issledovania* 10 (1993).

Chapter 5

This essay's operational definition of elite is state administrators and party members at or above the provincial level and other actors defined by the state or party as at or above the provincial level. This definition is one widely used and understood in China.

1.   *Renmin Ribao* (People's Daily), January 24, 1988.

2.   *Law and Politics Tribune* 5 (1989): 37–45. *Survey of World Broadcasts,* August 13, 1990, 0841, B2/6. Both as cited by Jean-Louis Rocca, "Corruption and Its Shadow: An Anthropological View of Corruption in China," *China Quarterly* 130 (June, 1992): 407. Personal observations in 1981–1991 in Lung Village and Shanghai.

3.   See especially Richard Levy, "Corruption, Economic Crime, and Social Transformation Since the Reforms: The Debate in China," *Australian Journal of Chinese Studies* (Fall, 1994). I thank Richard Levy for allowing me to see an advance copy of his article and for the many fine leads it gave me.

4.   Rocca, "Corruption and Its Shadow," p. 405.

5.   On the lack of rural corruption statistics, see John Burns, *Political Participation in Rural China* (Berkeley: University of California Press, 1988), p. 159. *Law and Politics Tribune* 5 (1989): 37–45, as cited by Rocca, "Corruption and Its Shadow," p. 406.

      Every year for a few months the government campaigns against corruption. In these months the number of corruption cases shoots up. After Tiananmen in 1989, the government felt it had to launch a stronger campaign than usual with a corresponding increase in corruption cases. Cf. *Renmin Ribao* (People's Daily), June 30, 1989. In June, 1993, another corruption campaign was launched. Cf. *China Daily,* June 11, 1993. *Guangming Daily,* June 18, 1993. Barbara Sands argues that corruption has not increased significantly but has become a bandwagon for other issues. Barbara Sands, "Decentralizing an Economy: The Role of Bureaucratic Corruption in China's Economic Reforms," *Public Choice* 65 (1990): 85–91. Rocca, "Corruption and Its Shadow," p. 402–403.

6.   *Faxue* (Law) 2 (1987): 28–30, as cited by Rocca, "Corruption and Its Shadow."

7.   *Jiushi niandai* (The Nineties) 1 (1991): 80–81. *Jingbao* 8 (1989): 46–48; 12 (1989): 56–57. See the list of companies in "Gang of Princelings," *Asia, Inc.* 4, no. 1 (January, 1995): 32–33. James Dorn, "The Depoliticization of Economic Life in China," *Cato Journal* 8, no. 3 (Winter 1989): 599. *Fazhi Ribao* (The Journal of Law), December 10, 1990, p. 1, as cited by Rocca, "Corruption and Its Shadow," p. 415.

8.   *Fazhi Ribao* (The Journal of Law), December 10, 1990, p. 1, as cited by Rocca, "Corruption and Its Shadow," p. 415.

9.   Cf. Richard Baum and Frederic Teiwes, *Ssu-Ch'ing: The Socialist Education Movement of 1962–1966* (Berkeley: University of California Press, 1968), pp. 55–56. Robin Theobald, *Corruption, Development, and Underdevelopment* (Durham: Duke University Press, 1990).

10.   *Fazhi Ribao,* December 5, 1990, p. 1, as cited by Rocca, "Corruption and Its Shadow," p. 409. *Survey of World Broadcasts,* August 28, 1990, 54, B2/2. Also on Jinan, Shantung railways see *Fazhi Ribao,* November 12, 1990, p. 1–2. Both as cited by Rocca, "Corruption and Its Shadow," p. 409. In December, 1994, Zhengzhou city's deputy station chief was sentenced to bribes for renting out scarce cargo space. Zhengzhou is an important transportation hub.

11.   James Coleman. *The Asymmetric Society* (Syracuse: Syracuse University Press, 1982), p. 9–30; Burns, *Political Participation in Rural China,* p. 163; cf. Dorn, "Depoliticization," p. 599.

12. Baum and Teiwes, *Ssu-Ch'ing,* p. 55–56. Cp. Marshall B. Clinard, *Corporate Ethics and Crime* (Beverly Hills: Sage, 1983). In interviews with 68 retired middle-management executives of Fortune 500 corporations, Clinard found that middle-level managers blamed corruption on top management's too high demands that could only be met by breaking the law.

13. Burns, *Political Participation in Rural China,* p. 153.

14. A collection surveying positive and negative views of the functionality of corruption can be found in Wei Haoben, ed. *Perplexing Thoughts: On the Spot Reports on "Hot Questions" in Society* (Kunhuozhong de Sisuo: Shehui 'Redian Wenti' Jishi; Hangzhou: Tuanji chubanshe, 1989), pp. 23–38.

15. J. S. Nye, "Corruption and Political Development: A Cost-Benefit Analysis," *American Political Science Review* 22 (1968): 419.

16. Ibid.

17. Cf. ibid., p. 419 n. 11.

18. Edward Banfield, *Political Influence* (Glencoe, Ill.: Free Press, 1961), p. 315, and *City Politics.* (1963; rpt., New York: Vintage Books, 1966).

19. Nye, "Corruption and Political Development," 420; Edward Shils, *Political Development in the New States* (The Hague, 1962), p. 385.

20. So offers Martin Needler as cited by Nye, "Corruption and Political Development," p. 421.

21. Nye, "Corruption and Political Development," p. 419.

22. Ibid., pp. 426, 424.

23. Ibid, pp. 426, 420.

24. Ibid., p. 417, quoting Max Gluckman, *Custom and Conflict in Africa* (Oxford: Oxford University Press, 1955), p. 135; Georg Simmel, *The Philosophy of Money* (London: Routledge Kegan Paul, 1978).

25. Nye, "Corruption and Political Development," p. 427. C. K. Yang, "Some Characteristics of Chinese Bureaucratic Behavior," in *Confucianism in Action,* ed. David S. Nivison and Arthur F. Wright (Stanford: Stanford University Press, 1959), p. 158. Yang concluded that in order to attempt to deal with corruption successfully the Chinese official kept a total wall between his official and personal lives, localized the area in which personal relations played a part, gave money to relatives out his own pocket, and kept a careful surveillance and control over his relatives and close associates.

26. Yang, "Some Characteristics of Chinese Bureaucratic Behavior."

27. Yang, "Some Characteristics of Chinese Bureaucratic Behavior," p. 157.

28. Nye, "Corruption and Political Development," pp. 423, 426.

29. Yang, "Some Characteristics of Chinese Bureaucratic Behavior," p. 149. Yang believes that arrogance was built into the Chinese social structure and encouraged self-righteous corruption. Nye, "Corruption and Political Development," p. 422.

30. Nye, "Corruption and Political Development," pp. 422, 424–425, 427.

31. Ibid, p. 417, quoting Ronald Wraith and Edgar Simpkins, *Corruption in Developing Countries* (London: Allen and Unwin, 1963), p. 11–12.

32. Yang, "Some Characteristics of Chinese Bureaucratic Behavior p. 149, 159.

33. Johnston conceptualizes the situation as short-term, objective interests versus long-term, perceived inequality and injustice. Michael Johnston, "Corruption,

Inequality, and Change," in *Corruption, Development, and Inequality: Soft Touch or Hard Graft?* ed. Peter M. Ward (London: Routledge, 1989), p. 13–37.

34. Nye, "Corruption and Political Development."

35. Ibid, p. 419.

36. Ibid.

37. John T. Noonan, *Bribes* (Berkeley and Los Angeles: University of California Press, 1984), p. xx.

38. Benjamin Nelson, *The Idea of Usury* (Chicago: University of Chicago Press, 1969).

39. Richard Hofstadter, *The Age of Reform* (New York: Knopf, 1955), p. 9.

40. Cp. James T. Myers, "Modernization and 'Unhealthy Tendencies,'" *Comparative Politics* 21 (January, 1989): 206f.

41. Quoted by Stephen Handelman, *Comrade Criminal* (New Haven: Yale University Press, 1995), p. 56. Handelman says his book was inspired by Gurov.

42. Ibid., p. 3.

43. Ibid., pp. 182, 275.

44. Valery Chalidze, *Criminal Russia: Essays on Crime in the Soviet Union,* trans. P. S. Falla (New York: Random House, 1977), p. 168. Also cf. Gregory Grossman, "Second Economy: Boon or Bane?" *Berkeley-Duke Occasional Papers on the Second Economy of the USSR* 11, no. 2 (1987).

45. Lev Timofeiev, *Russia's Secret Rulers,* trans. Catherine A. Fitypatrick (New York: Knopf, 1992), pp. 98–99.

46. Maria Los, "Internal Norms of the Second Economy," in *Privatization and Entrepreneurship in Post-Socialist Countries,* ed. Bruno Dallago, Gianmaria Ajani, and Bruno Scancelli (New York: St. Martin's, 1992), pp. 111–24.

47. William A. Clark, *Crime and Punishment in Soviet Officialdom Combatting Corruption in the Political Elite, 1965–1990* (Armonk, N.Y.: M. E. Sharpe, 1993), p. 73.

48. Georgii Arbatov, *The System: An Insider's Life in Soviet Politics* (New York: Random House, 1992), p. 250.

49. Ibid.; Michael Voslensky, *Nomenklatura: Anatomy of the Soviet Ruling Class,* trans. Eric Mosbacher (London: Badley Head, 1984).

50. Julia Wishnevsky, "Corruption Allegations Undermine Russia's Leaders," *Radio Free Europe/Radio Liberty Research Report,* September 17, 1993, pp. 16–22. Evidently, the anti-Yeltsin forces were preparing their own anticorruption strike just before Parliament was dissolved. See the interview with Sergev Filatov, Yeltsin's chief of staff, in *Argumenty i fakty* 39 (1993).

51. Arkady Vaksberg, *The Soviet Mafiya,* trans. John Roberts and Elisabeth Roberts (London: Weidenfeld and Nicolson, 1991), p. 45. Handelman, *Comrade Criminal,* p. 56. For the types and extent of the various *"mafiyas,"* cf. Vaksberg, *Soviet Mafiya,* and Maria Los, *Communist Ideology, Law, and Crime: A Comparative View of the USSR and Poland* (London: Macmillan, 1988), pp. 155–61.

52. Allan Bullock, *Hitler and Stalin: Parallel Lives.* (New York: Knopf, 1993), p. 35. Chalidze, *Criminal Russia,* p. 22.

53. Handelman, *Comrade Criminal,* p. 35.

54. George Leggett, *The Cheka: Lenin's Political Choice* (Oxford: Clarendon, 1981), p. 239.

55.   Alexander Gurov, *Organizovannaia prestupnost ne mif a realnost* (Organized
        Crime: Not Myth, But Reality) (Moscow: Faculty of Law of the People's Univer-
        sity, Znanie, 1992). Ministerstvo vnutrennikh del (Ministry of Internal Affairs)
        internal circulation document cited by Handelman, *Comrade Criminal,* p. 55.

56.   Boris Yeltsin, *Against the Grain,* trans. Michael Glenny (London: Jonatan Cape,
        1990) pp. 88−107. Cf. Vladimir Brovkin, "First Party Secretaries: An Endan-
        gered Soviet Species," *Problems of Communism* 39 (January−February, 1990):
        15−27. Handelman, *Comrade Criminal,* p. 189.

57.   Interfax, 7/5/92. Tass, 6/7/93. Fourteen percent of Ekaterinburg police also
        believed the city was ruled by the *mafiya.* Yeltsin quoted in *Delovyie Liudi*
        (*Business people;* newspaper), December, 1992. Handelman, *Comrade Criminal,*
        p. 17.

Chapter 6

1.   Michael E. Urban, *An Algebra of Soviet Power: Elite Circulation in the Byelo-
        russian Republic, 1966−1986* (Cambridge, England: Cambridge University
        Press, 1989); A. Ageev, "Formirovanie politicheskoi elity v poslestalinskii
        period," *Belarusskaia Minuushchyna* 4 (1994): 22−23.

2.   Nicholas Vakar, "Likuidatsia Belorusskofo natsionalizma," *Spadchyna* 6 (1992):
        19.

3.   Ivan Kasiak, ed., *Byelorussia: Historical Outline* (London: Byelorussian Central
        Council, 1989), p. 297.

4.   "My-aposhnia. Za nami chargo," *Literatura imastatstva* (March 12, 1993).

5.   Stephan Horak "Byelorussia: Modernization, Human Rights, and Nationalism,"
        Canadian Slavonic Papers 16, no. 3 (1974): 403−23.

6.   *Zvezda,* May 18, 1990.

7.   *Narodnyie Deputaty respubliki, Belarus.* Dvad-tsatyi Sozyv, Minsk, 1992.

8.   *Narodnaia gazeta,* March 25−27, 1995.

9.   *Zvezda,* March 19, 1995.

10.   *Kakoi my vidim Nashu Belarus.* Dannyie Sotsiologicheskikh oprosov 1980−93
        (Minsk: Belorusskaia Sluzhba obshchestvennogo mnenia, 1993), part 1, p. 36.

11.   Ibid.

12.   *Zvezda,* March 31, 1995.

13.   *Svobada,* April 7, 1995.

14.   See *Narodnyie Deputaty Respubliki, Belarus.*

15.   "Blinkovskii, Dva mentaliteta naroda Respubliki Belarus" (materials of the in-
        ternational conference "Osnovnyie voprosy sotsial—noi politikii khoziaistvo-
        vania v Belarusii I sosednikh gosuedarstvakh," Minsk, February 17−20, 1996),
        p. 105.

16.   *Zvezda,* March 18, 1994.

17.   *Prava I obiazannosti mestnoi vlasti Respubliki Belarus na etape eie refomirova-
        nia, Analitiches—Kaia Zapiska kafedry filo sofsko—ekonomichigkofo fakulteta*
        (Minsk: Belorussian State University, 1993).

18.   Ibid.

19.   S. I. Paulau, *Chelovek: Pradpry malnasts, kiravanne, pynak* (Minsk: Uradzhai,
        1994), p. 50.

20.   "Tsi pryiduts fundatary?" *Spadchyna* 5 (1992): 2−4.

21.   "Dziarzhava zausedy byla dpennym gaspada—rom," *Literatura I mastatsia,* September 11, 1994.

22.   *Kakoi my vidim nashu Belrus,* p. 12.

23.   Ibid், pp. 18–19.

24.   D. A. Peshko and V. A. Dadalko, *Mechanism formirova-nia korrumpurovannykh structur, nauchingi tsenta marketingovykh issledovanii* (Minsk: Jarmita, 1994), p. 16.

25.   *Kakoi my vidim nashu Belarus* (1993–94), part 2, 1994, pp. 33–35.

26.   Ibid., part 2, p. 33.

27.   *Narodnaia Gazeta,* June 20, 1993.

28.   Blinkovskii, Sochinenia, p. 105.

29.   *Narodnaia Gazeta,* May 13, 1992.

30.   *Literatura I mastatstava,* April 29, 1994.

Chapter 7

1.   Algirdas Banevicius, *111 Lietuvos valstybes 1918–1940 politikos veikeju* (Vilnius, Lithuania: Knyga, 1991).

2.   Vytautas Titinis, *Sovietine Lietuva ir jos veikejai. Enciklopedija* (Vilnius: 1994), p. 77.

3.   M. Voslenskii, *Nomenklatura Gospodstvuushchii class Sovietskogo Souza* (Moscow: Sovietskaia Rossia, 1991).

4.   Richard Rose and William Maley, *Nationalities in the Baltic States: A Survey Study* (Glasgow: University of Strathclyde, Centre for the Study of Public Policy, 1994), p. 59; Richard Rose, *New Baltics Barometer II: A Survey Study* (Glasgow: University of Strathclyde, Centre for the Study of Public Policy, 1995), p. 47.

5.   Lionginas Sepetys, "Tas nelemtas duetas: rasytojas ir cenzura," in *Rasytojas ir cenzura,* ed. by Algirdas Sabonis and Saulius Sabonis (Vilnius: Vaga, 1992), p. 375.

6.   Vladas Gaidys, "LKP situacijos dinamika," *Politika* 10 (1990): 20–23.

7.   Vaclovas Paulauskas, ed., *Kas yra as Lietuvoje, 1993. Dabartiniu Lietuvos valstybes veikejo biografinis zinynas* (Vilnius: Politika, 1993).

8.   *Respublika,* February 22, 1994, p. 3.

9.   *Lietuvos Aidas,* April 14, 1994, p. 1.

10.   *Respublika,* January 5, 1994, p. 16.

11.   *Lietuvos Rytas,* April 19, 1994, p. 40.

12.   *Respublika,* February 9, 1994, p. 3.

Chapter 8

1.   On the aims of the transition period in Kazakhstan, see N. A. Nazarbaev, "Strategia stanovlenia, razvitiia Kazakhstana kak suverennogo gosudarstva," *Kazakhstanskaia Pravda,* May 16, 1992.

2.   Nursultan Nazarbaev, *Bez pravykh, levikh* (Moscow: Molodaia gvardiia, 1991).

3.   Shirin H. Hunter, "Nationalist Movements in Soviet Asia," *Current History* 69, no. 549 (October, 1990): 328.

4.   Nazarbaev, *Bez pravykh, levikh,* pp. 192–94, 222–24.

5. R. F. Abazov, "Islamskoie vozrozhdenie v tzentre noaziatskikh novykh nezavisimykh gosudarstvakh," *Polis* 3 (1995): 66.

6. For the first time, the term "Kazakh nationalism" was used at the official level in the resolution of the Central Committee of the CPSU on the December, 1986, events in Almaty. See *Pravda,* July 16, 1987.

7. The term "authorized businessmen" was used by O. Krishtanovskaia in her article, "Finansovaia oligarkhia Rossii," in *Izvestia,* January 10, 1996.

8. O. V. Krishtanovskaia, "Transformatsiia staroi nomenklatury v novoi rossiiskoi elite," *Obshchestvennye nauki I sovremennost* 1 (1995): 58.

9. M. B. Olcott, "Central Asia's Catapult to Independence," *Foreign Affairs* 71, no. 3 (1992): 108–30.

10. *Kazakhstan Respublikanskaia Konstitutsia,* (Almaty, Kazakhstan, 1993), p. 85 (in Kazakh).

11. M. S. Voslenskii, *Nomenklatura: Gospodstvuushchii klass v Sovetskom Souze* (Moscow: Sovetskaia Rossia, Oktiabr, 1991), p. 358.

12. *Karavan,* November 10, 1995, p. 9.

13. V. Ardaev, "V Kazakhstane narodu predstavlen proekt konstitutsii 'pod Nazarbaeva,'" *Izvestia,* August 3, 1995, p. 2.

14. *Karavan,* October 13, 1995, p. 7.

15. E. Avraamova and I. Diskin, "Sotsialnyie transformatsii elity," *Obshchestvennyie nauki I sovremennost* 3 (1994): 21, table 3.

16. *Karavan,* December 22, 1995, p. 3.

17. Krishtanovskaia, "Transformatsiia staroi nomenklatury," p. 60.

18. *Karavan,* October 7, 1994.

19. Sh. Karabaev. "Zhiviot li soglasiie v mnogopartiinom dome? Etnosotsialnaia structura obshchestvenno-politicheskikh dvizhenii v perekhodnyi period," *Mysl* 7 (1993): pp. 42–45.

20. *Karavan-blitz,* October 30, 1995, p. 3.

21. *Kazakhstanskaia Pravda,* November 21, 1995, p. 4.

22. A. Galiev, et al., *Mezhnatsionalnyie otnosheniia v Kazakhstane: etnicheskii aspekt Kadrovoi politiki* (Almaty, Kazakhstan: Institut razvitiia Kazakhstana, 1994), p. 38.

23. M. B. Olcott, *The Kazakhs* (Stanford, Calif.: Hoover Institution Press, 1987), p. 240–56.

24. A. G. Zdravomyslov and C. Ia. Matveeva, "Mezhnatsionalnyie konflikty v postsovietskom prostranstve," *Vestnik Rossiiskoi Akademii nauk* 65, no. 7 (1995): 586.

25. *Kazakhstanskaia Pravda,* July 8, 1995, p. 2.

26. O. Bibikova and V. Shchennikov, "President Kazakhstana Nursultan Nazarbaev," *Aziia I Afrika segodnia* 7 (1995): 4.

27. Krishtanovskaia, "Transformatsiia staroi nomenklatury."

28. *Onynshy sailangan Kazak SSR Zhogargy Sovetinin deputattary-Deputaty Verkhovnogo Soveta Kazakhskoi SSR desyatogo sozyva* (Alma-Ata: Izdaniie Prezidiuma Verkhovnogo Soveta Kazakhskoi SSR [na Kazakhskom I russkom yazykakh]).

29. *Kto est kto v Kazakhstane* (Almaty, Kazakhstan: Karzhy-karazhat, 1995), p. 144.

30.　Krishtanovskaia, "Transformatsiia staroi nomenklatury," p. 62 (table 3).

31.　M. Kh. Asylbekov and A. B. Galiev, "Sotsialno-demograficheskiie protsessy v Kazakhstane (1897–1992)," in *Istoria Kazakhstana s drevneishikh vremion do nashikh dnei (ocherk)* (Almaty, Kazakhstan: Dauir, 1993), p. 404.

32.　*Karavan,* February 23, 1996, p. 2.

33.　A. M. Khazanov, *Underdevelopment and Ethnic Relations in Central Asia in Historical Perspective* (Boulder, Colo.: Westview, 1994), p. 148.

Chapter 12

1.　Rossiiskii Souz promyshlennikov I predprinimatelei, Ekspertnyi Institut, *Edinstvo reformy I reforma edinstva* (Moskow: Rossiiskii Souz promyshlennikov I predprinimatelei, Ekspertnyi Institut, 1992).

2.　Adam Przeworski, "Some Problems in the Study of the Transition to Democracy," in *Transitions from Authoritarian Rule: Comparative Perspectives,* ed. Guillermo O'Donnell, Philippe C. Schmitte, and Laurence Whitehead (Baltimore and London: Johns Hopkins University Press, 1986), pp. 47–63.

3.　The members of the project team are affiliated with the sponsor of the research project, the working group Institutional Transformation in the New German Länder of the Max-Planck-Gesellschaft, and with the Department of Social Sciences of the Humboldt University, both in Berlin. The Russian partners are from the Institute of World Economy and International Relations of the Russian Academy of Sciences.

　　　The empirical data was collected during 220 narrative interviews and 150 standardized questionnaires with leading representatives of the local administration, politics, security apparatus, economy, media, and social organizations in the Saratov region conducted in April, 1993; October, 1993; and May, 1994. Additional data was compiled through analyses of regional newspapers, from official documents of the executive and representative bodies, as well as from parties and associations from 1988 to 1995.

4.　A. Magomedov, "Politicheskie elity rossiiskoi provintsii," *Mirovaia ekonomika I mezhdunarodnie otnosheniia* 4 (1994): 72–79.

5.　G. Field, et al., "A New Elite Framework for Political Sociology," *Revue européenne des Sciences sociales* 88 (1990): 149–82.

6.　Joel C. Moses, "Soviet Provincial Politics in an Era of Transition and Revolution, 1989–91," *Soviet Studies* 44, no. 3 (1992): 479–509; A. Magomedov, "Politicheskie elity rossiiskoi provintsii," *Mirovaia ekonomika I mezhdunarodnie otnosheniia* 4 (1994): 72–79; Jeffrey W. Hahn, "Local Politics and Local Power in Russia: The Case of Yaroslavl," *Soviet Economy* 7, no. 4 (1991): 322–42; Mary McAuley, "Politics, Economics, and Elite Realignment in Russia: A Regional Perspective," *Soviet Economy* 8, no. 1 (1992): 46–88.

7.　Hahn, "Local Politics," p. 323.

8.　The size of the regional elite given here is based on approximations. I combined a positional approach (following the *nomenklatura* register in the region) with a reputational one (data obtained from interviews). Thus, I identified as belonging to the party or state elite the top position holders at the regional level (secretaries/chairmen and department chiefs of the party *obkom,* the mass organization apparatuses, and the *ispolkom*), the first secretaries of the party *raikomy,* and the chairmen of the *raion ispolkomy.* I assumed about fifty persons as being part of the economic elite because of their status as directors of

the major heavy and defense plants in the region and the largest factories of local industry, and ten to twenty persons as belonging to the intellectual elite.
All these elite persons were of course registered in the *obkom nomenklatura* list
or similar lists at higher levels of the party hierarchy. But it is obvious that
the regional elite identified is only the tip of the *obkom nomenklatura* iceberg,
which probably consisted of about 1,500–2,000 individuals. Peter Rutland,
The Politics of Economic Stagnation in the Soviet Union (Cambridge: Cambridge
University Press, 1993), pp. 35–36.

9. Lowell G. Field, John Higley, and Michael G. Burton, "A New Elite Framework
for Political Sociology," *Revue européenne des Sciences sociales* 88 (1990): 155.

10. Peter Rutland, *The Politics of Economic Stagnation in the Soviet Union* (Cambridge: Cambridge University Press, 1993), pp. 12–16.

11. Ibid.

12. Kenneth Jowitt, "Soviet Neotraditionalism," *Soviet Studies* 35, no. 3 (1983):
275–97.

13. This was how all the secretaries of the Saratov *obkom* in 1989—except one
former philosopher—reflected on their careers. The career ladder, therefore,
was open-ended. Thus, the position of the first secretary of the Saratov party
obkom generally proved to be a good starting point for a career in the central
party or state apparatus in Moscow up until the late period of perestroika.

14. In American Sovietology beginning in the 1970s a wealth of literature appeared about clientelistic and nepotistic networks in Soviet politics that described the "informal" side of the political system, the elite composition, and
the power relations in the USSR in terms of "patronage" and "neotraditionalism." See, e.g., John P. Willerton, "Reform, the Elite and Soviet Center-Periphery Relations," *Soviet Union/Union Soviétique* 17, nos. 1–2 (1990): 55–94; T. H.
Rigby and Bohdan Harasymiw, *Leadership Selection and Patron-Client Relations
in the USSR and Yugoslavia* (London: Allen & Unwin; Jowitt, Kenneth, 1983).

15. In a recent essay, Michael Brie and I characterized localism and departmental-
ism (the aggregation and articulation of "special" sectoral interests) as systems
of elite interaction in a more detailed fashion and tried to examine their functioning as "regimes," i.e., a specific type of coordination between different
bargaining actors, by testing the possibility and utility of adapting the regime
concept used in the field of International Political Economy to our research
field. Michael Brie and Petra Stykow, "Regionale Akteurkoordinierung im
russischen Transformationsprozeß," *Arbeitspapiere AG TRAP* 2 (1995).

16. Peter Rutland, *The Politics of Economic Stagnation in the Soviet Union* (Cambridge: Cambridge University Press, 1993).

17. John P. Willerton, "Reform, the Elite and Soviet Center-Periphery Relations,"
Soviet Union/Union Soviétique 17, nos. 1–2 (1990): 55–94.

18. Marc Lupher, "Power Restructuring in China and the Soviet Union," *Theory
and Society* 21, no. 5 (1992): 665–701.

19. Ibid., p. 684.

20. Mary McAuley, "Politics, Economics, and Elite Realignment in Russia: A Regional Perspective," *Soviet Economy* 8, no. 1 (1992): 50.

21. Michael E. Urban, "Conceptualizing Political Power in the USSR: Patterns of
Binding and Bonding," *Studies in Comparative Communism* 18, no. 4 (1995):
221.

22.   Rutland, *Politics of Economic Stagnation,* p. 208.

23.   McAuley, "Politics, Economics, and Elite Realignment," pp. 46–88.

24.   The coordination center was founded by five discussion clubs, each ranging between five and twenty members. The most popular public functions in the fall of 1988 were the "Bukharin readings" with about two to three hundred participants.

25.   Comparing the electoral behavior of regional elites in three Russian cities, McAuley also found this strategy in Perm and Arkhangel'sk, whereas in St. Petersburg the *obkom* tried to change the rules of the game and strengthen their own positions by associating themselves with conservative top leaders ("Politics, Economics, and Elite Realignment, p. 59).

26.   Among the seventeen regional deputies for the Russian parliament, there were six industrial or agricultural top managers (but only three apparatchiki from the party-state apparatuses). In the regional Soviet, top and mid-level managers hold approximately the same proportion of seats as the apparatchiki— about 30 percent.

27.   Hahn, "Local Politics," p. 328.

28.   In the Saratov city soviet both the manager and the intellectual occupational groups were superior in numbers to the apparatchiki. In some of the municipal district soviets, the party and state officials were represented even less, by only 15 percent of the deputies. The soviets could not therefore be described as "oppositional" per se, but the opportunities to control their activities by the party apparatus were clearly restricted.

29.   Robert A. Dahl, *Polyarchy* (New Haven, Conn.: Yale University Press, 1971).

30.   Przeworski, "Some Problems," pp. 47–63.

31.   Through the analysis of an opinion poll conducted by a Saratov research group and my own questionnaire presented to 160 influential persons in the region, we identified 106 persons as belonging to the regional elite: 57 political elite (31 administrative incumbents, 26 organizational leaders and intellectuals); 45 economic elite (29 directors, 12 businessmen, 4 bank chiefs); 4 elites with violent resources at their disposal (2 military and police chiefs, 2 mafiosi).

32.   Jack Hirshleifer, "Anarchy and Its Breakdown," *Journal of Political Economy* 103, no. 1 (1995): 26–52.

33.   Gary Marks, "Rational Sources of Chaos in Democratic Transition," in *Reexamining Democracy: Essays in Honor of Seymour Martin Lipset,* ed. Gary Marks and Larry Diamond (Newbury Park, Calif.: Sage, 1992), pp. 47–69. Marks characterizes the state of political discontinuity as follows: "(a) The institutions of the existing regime fail to regularize and contain political activity but become themselves a locus of political struggle; (b) political power is contested by two or more groups, each of which is composed of actors having heterogenous preferences or incomplete information about the responses of other actors in the same group; and (c) choices made within one group influence the choices of the other group" (p. 48).

34.   Robert Axelrod, *The Evolution of Cooperation* (New York: Basic Books, 1984); Hirshleifer, "Anarchy and Its Breakdown," pp. 26–52. Thomas C. Schelling, *The Strategy of Conflict* (Cambridge, Mass.: Harvard University Press, 1960).

35.   Sergei Ryzhenkov, "Itogi vyborov v Saratovskuiu oblastnuiu dumu," *Politicheskii monitoring* 5, no. 28 (1994): 103–11.

36. Sergei Ryzhenkov, "Ustav Saratovskoi oblasti I zakon o mestnom samou-pravlenii v Saratovskoi oblasti," *Politicheskii monitoring* 10, no. 33 (1994).

37. The pressure on the decision makers is camouflaged in part by their acting on behalf of political organizations. Whereas the businessmen have thus far been unsuccessful in their attempts at forming parties and associations, the directors, also having failed to establish their own party, have formed both an entrepreneurs' association and an "embedded organization," claiming thereby to have united all "constructive" regional actors. See Petra Stykow, "Formen der Repräsentation von Wirtschaftsakteuren in Rußland: Eine Fallstuie" *Arbeitspapiere AG TRAP 94/7* (Berlin: Max-Planck-Gesellschaft, Arbeitsgruppe Transformationsprozesse, 1994).

Chapter 15

The research for this essay was executed with support from the Russian Fund of Fundamental Researches. I wish to express my thanks to the group of sociologists from Altai Technical University: Ivan Polzunov, A. Udodenko, E. Mikshina and V. Melekhina.

1. The Siberian agreement is an association of the republics of Altai, Buryatia, Tuva, and Hackassia; the region of Krasnoiarsk; the areas of Irkutsk, Kemerovo, Novosibirsk, Omsk, Tomsk, Tiumen, and Chita; and the independent districts of Aginsk-Buriat, Ust-Ordinsk, Buryat, Evenk, Taymir, Khanti-Mansiisk, and Yamalo-Nenetzk. *Moskovskie Novosti* 21 (1995).

2. S. P. Zalygin, *Solenaia Pad* (Moscow: Sovetskii Pisatel, 1965).

3. U. N. Shubkin, "Svidetelstvo o smerti," *Sotsiologicheskii Journal* (1994).

4. *Izvestia,* July 20, 1994.

5. *Izvestia,* June 11, 1994.

6. *Moskovskii Komosmolets,* June 9, 1994.

7. *Obshchaia Gazeta,* April 27, 1995.

8. *Moskovskie Novosti* 21 (1995).

Chapter 16

1. See Elena Avramova and Diskin Josef, "Sotsial'nye Transformatsii I Elity" (Social Transformations and Elites), *Obshchestvennye Nauki I Sovremennost'* 4 (1993): 25–38.

2. See John Higley, Lowell Field, and Knut Groeholt, *Elite Structure and Methodology: A Theory with Application to Norway* (Oslo: Universitetstorlaget; New York: Columbia University Press, 1976).

3. Yurii A. Levada, "Elita I Massy v Obshchestevnnom Mnenii," *Economic and Social Changes: Monitoring of public opinion* 6 (1994).

4. Luis D. Nelson, Ludmila B. Babaeva, and Rustem O. Babaev, "Perspectivy Predprinimatelstva i Privatizatsii v Rossii: Politika i Obshchestvennoe Mnenie" (Perspectives of Entrepreneurship and Privatization in Russia: Policy and Public Opinion), *Sociologicheskie Issledovaniia* 1 (1993).

5. See John Higley and Grigory Pakulski, "Revolution and Elite Transformation in Eastern Europe," *Australian Journal of Political Sciences* 27 (1992): 3–27.

6. See Levada, "Elita I Massy v Obshchestevnnom Mnenii"; Nelson, Babaeva, and Babaev, "Perspectivy Predprinimatelstva i Privatizatsii v Rossii," pp. 57–76.

Chapter 17

1. I. M. Bunin, "Sotsialnyi portret melkogo I srednego predprinimatelstva v Rossii," *Polis* 3 (1993): 149–54; V. Gimpelson, "Novie rossiisko Predpriniroatelstvo: istochniki formirovania I strategii sotsialnogo zazvitia," *Mirovaia ekonomika I mezhdunarodnye otnoshenia* 6 (1993): 31–32; Z. M. Grishchenko, L. G. Novikova, and I. N. Lapsha, "Sotsialnyi portret predprinimatelia," *Sotsiologicheskie issledovania* 10 (1992): 53–61; V. V. Radaev, "Novoie Rossiiskoe predprinimatelstvo v otsenkakh ekspertov," *Mir Rossii* 3 (1996): 36–54; V. V. Radaev, "O nekotorykh chertakh normativnogo povedenia novykh Rossiiskikh predprinimatelei," *Mirovaia ekonomika I mezhdunarodnye otnoshenia* 1 (1994): 94–107; V. V. Radaev, ed., *Stanovlenie novogo Rossiiskogo predprinimatelstva* (Moscow: Institut Ekonomiki, RAN, 1993); M. O. Shkaratan, *Fenomen predprinimatelia: Interpretatsii poniatii,* in Radaev, *Stanovlenie Novogo Rossiiskogo Predprinimatelstva,* pp. 198–247; N. I. Veselkova, "Neformalizovannoe interviu," *Sotsiologicheskii Journal* 3 (1994): 103–109.

2. *Novoye Russkoye slovo* (New York), November, 1992; *Delovoi Mir,* July 18, 1992, pp. 6–7; *Delvoi Mir,* February 22, 1992, p. 16; *Ekonomika I zhinm* 43 (October, 1993): 24; *Stolitsa* 25, no. 135 (1993): 24–26; *Sovietskaia Rossia,* February 6, 1993, p. 4; *My* (We) 2 (January, 1993): 6; *Izvestia,* September 7, 1984; *Delovye Liudi,* January, 1985, p. 66–74; "Darin-93," *Elita Rossiskogo Biznesa* (Moscow: ACMO-Press, 1993).

3. "Darin-93," p. 67.

4. *Delovoi Mir,* February 22, 1992, p. 16; *Stolitsa,* 25, no. 135 (1993): 24–26: *My* (We) 2 (January, 1993): 6; *Delovye Liudi,* January, 1995, p. 66–74; *Nezavisimaia Gazeta,* September 30, 1994, p. 1; *Vozrozhdennaia Elita Rossiiskogo biznesa* (Moscow, 1994); I. M. Bunin, *Biznesmeny Rossii: 40 istorii uspecha* (Moscow: OKO, 1994).

5. "Darin-94," *Elita Rossiiskogo biznesa* (Moscow: ACMO-Press, 1994); *Nezavisimaia gazeta,* April 26, 1994, p. 1, and January 24, 1995, p. 2; M. Frybes, "Les Nouveax Entrepreneurs D'Europe D'Est," *L'Autre Europe* (1992).

6. Since 1992, under the direction of Olga Krishtanovskaia, complex study of the business elite has been carried out.

7. *Nezavisimaia Gazeta,* April 26, 1994, p. 1, and January 30, 1994, p. 1.

8. *Nezavisimaia Gazeta,* September 30, 1994, p. 1.

9. *Nezavisimaia Gazeta,* January 24, 1995, p. 1.

10. V. V. Radaev, ed., *Stanovlenie novogo Rossiiskogo predprinimatelstva* (Moscow: Institut Ekonomiki RAN, 1993), p. 56–58.

11. Bunin, *Sotsialnyi portret melkogo I srednego predprinimatelstva v Rossii;* S. A. Belanovskii, *Metodika I technika fokusirovannogo interviu* (Moscow: Nauka, 1994).

12. *Delovye Liudi,* December, 1994, p. 38.

13. V. Gimpelson, "Novoie Rossiiskoe predprinimatelstvo: istochniki formirovania I strategii sotsialnogo Razvitia," *Mirovaia ekonomika I mezhdunarodnye otnoshenia* 6 (1993): 31–32.

14. Z. M. Grishchenko, L. G. Novikova, and I. N. Lapsha, *Sotsialnyi portret predprinimatelia* (Moscow: Sotsiologicheskie issledovania, 1992), p. 53–61; Bunin, *Sotsialnyi portret melkogo I srednego predprinimatelstva v Rossii,* pp. 149–54; Veselkova, *Neformalizovannoe interviu.*

15. Radaev, *Novoie,* pp. 36–54; *Novaia Ezhednevnaia Gazeta,* September 14, 1994, p. 3.

Chapter 19

1. S. Iu. Glaziev, *Teoria dolgosrochnogo tekhniko-ekonomicheskogo Razvitia* (Moscow: Vladar, 1993).

2. G. Diumenton, "Povyshenie effektivosti organizatsionnykh struktur NII," *Vestnik Rossiiskoi Akademii Nauk* 63, no. 12 (1993): 1067–75.

3. Jose Ortego y Gasset, "Vosstanie mass," *Estetika, Filosofia kultury* (Moscow: Iskusstvo, 1991), pp. 309–50.

4. V. Z. Kelle and S. A. Kugel, eds., *Nauchnye Kadry SSSR: dinamika, struktura* (Moscow: Mysl, 1991), p. 52.

5. A. Zakharov, "Demokraticheskaia oppozitsia v protsesse sozdania Rossiiskoi Akademii Nauk," *Rubezhi* 1 (1995): pp. 111–48.

6. *Nauka Rossii: 1993* (statisticheskii sbornik) (Moscow: Tsentr issledovanii I statistiki nauki, 1994).

7. *Kratkii sbornik statisticheskokh svedenii o Rossiiskoi Akademii Nauk* (Moscow, 1993), p. 20.

8. *Ustav Akademii Nauk SSSR,* Moscow, 1984.

9. Ukaz Prezidenta RSFSR "Ob organizatsii Rossiiskoi Akademii Nauk," Moscow, November 21, 1991.

10. *Ustav Rossiskoi Akademii nauk,* Moscow, 1993.

11. A. Zakharov, "Demokraticheskaia, Oppozitsia v protsesse sozdania Rossiiskoi Akademii nauk" *Rubeszi* 1 (1995): 111–48.

12. S. R. Mikulinskii, et al., eds., *Shkoly v nauke* (Moscow: Nauka, 1977).

13. V. Ginzburg, "Demokratia po-akademicheski," *Izvestia,* April 15, 1990.

14. "Ob uchrezhdenii Akademii Nauk Rossiiskoi Federatsii," *Ukaz Prezidiuma Verkhovnogo Soveta RSFSR,* January 24, 1990; "O Dalneishei rabote po organizatsii Rossiiskoi Akademii Nauk," *Postanovlenie Verkhovnogo Sovieta RSFSR,* February 16, 1991.

15. S. Novikov, "Vybirat, a ne soglasovyvat," *Izvestia,* April 6, 1990.

16. I. Bestuzhev-Lada, *Prognoznoe obosnovanie sotsialnykh novovvedenii* (Moscow: Nauka, 1993), p. 233.

17. V. Glezer, "Tvortsy ili deltsy buedet opredeliat budushchee nashei nauki?" *Izvestia,* June 6, 1990; V. Chromov, "Pered zestkim vyborom stavit sovremennogo uchitelia itvetsgavsgaua ajadenua," *Izvestia,* September 4, 1990.

18. S. Novikov, "Vybirat, a ne soglasovyvat," *Izvestia,* April 6, 1990.

19. V. Orel, "Bitva so zdravym smyslom," *Vestnik Rossiiskoi Akademii Nauk* 64, no. 6 (1994): 366–75.

20. *Akademia Nauk SSSR: Personalnyi sostav,* books 1 and 2 (Moscow: Nauka, 1984), p. 478.

Chapter 21

1. *The National Report to the Fourth World Conference on the Situation of Women: Actions in the Interest of Equality, Development and the World* (Moscow: Proekt, 1994), p. 5.

2.   Sillaste, G. "The Nature of the Female Elite and Its Characteristics in Russia: Social Sciences and Today's World," *Cherchez l'homme* 1 (1994): 120.

3.   Service of the Study of Public Opinion, *Vox Populi* 3; "The Russian Economic and Political Elite: Fifty of the Most Influential Men in the Country," *Nezavisimaia Gazeta,* April 26, 1994.

4.   *Nezavisimaia Gazeta,* January 6, 1994.

5.   C. Epstein and R. L. Coser, eds., *Access to Power: Cross-National Studies of Women and Elites* (Boston: Allen and Unwin, 1981), p. 6.

6.   T. Khudiakova, "Female Names in a Large Policy," *Moskovskie Novosti,* November 25, 1993, p. 8.

7.   N. Ershova, "Transformation of the Russian Elite During a Social Crisis," *Where Russia Is Going* (Moscow: Interpraks, 1994), pp. 153–55.

8.   Epstein and Coser, *Access to Power,* p. 6.

9.   "The Composition of Women Deputies in the Federal Assembly" (analytical notes from the Ministry of Social Welfare of the Russian Federation).

Chapter 22

I wish to express my deep gratitude to Professor Tony Carnes for his generous contribution in collection, analysis, and thoughtful interpretation of the data used in this essay.

1.   The International Research Institute on Value Changes (IRIVC) is an independent, not-for-profit organization that was established in 1990 by a few American and Russian scholars (including the author) in New York. Its main goal has been to study the ongoing changes in moral values and religious attitudes during the unprecedented transition of the Soviet Union's totalitarian regime to a post-Communist social formation. Since its inception, IRIVC has conducted a number of polls in Russia. The IRIVC inauguration study is known as project "Changing Values in a Changing World: The Ten Commandments in Soviet People's Consciousness and Behavior." The polls were based on face-to-face interviews conducted in Moscow in spring 1990 (N=458), 1991 (N=500), 1992 (N=497), 1993 (N=492), 1994 (N=409), and in fall 1992 (N=600) in Dalnegorsk, Primorskyi Krai (two hundred miles north of Vladivostok). In each of the Moscow polls, a randomly selected sample of the population was taken. It was based on a sample of addresses selected from the recent complete list of Moscow streets. Estimated sampling error is plus or minus 5 percentage points.
    Students of the Moscow State University comprise the second target group of the study. Two hundred students were interviewed in 1991; 192 in 1992; 166 in 1993; and 201 in 1994. The third target group is new Russian businessmen. They were interviewed in 1992 (N=210), 1993 (N=202), and 1995 (N=198). The fourth group studied was that of criminals randomly selected from about 2,500 prisoners of a Russian criminal prison five hundred miles east of Moscow. In 1992, 221 of them were interviewed; in 1993, 198. Data from Moscow population surveys and student surveys are incorporated in this essay. See also Tony Carnes and Samuel Kliger, "Religion and Moral Values in Russia: Transition to the Post-Communist Era," in *Religion, Mobilization, and Social Action,* ed. Anson Shupe and Bronislaw Misztál (Westport, Conn., London: Praeger, 1998), p. 158.

2.   L. A. Gordon and A. K. Nazimova, *Rabochii klass SSSR: tendentzii I perspektivy sotzialno-ekonomicheskogo razvitiia* (Moscow: Nauka, 1985); *Rabochii klass I*

nauchno-tekhnicheskii progress (Moscow: Nauka, 1986); E. D. Igitkhanjan, I. Ju. Petrushina, and F. R. Philippov, "Industrialnyi otriad trudiashchikhsia," *Sociologicheskie Issledovaniia* 3 (1990): pp. 3–12.

3. Vladimir Shlapentokh, *Public and Private Life of the Soviet People: Changing Values in Post-Stalin Russia* (New York: Oxford University Press, 1989), p. 217.

4. *Novoye Russkoye Slovo* (Russian Daily), July 31, 1995, p. 5 (with references to *Kommersant*).

5. Shlapentokh, Vladimir, "Russia One Year After August 1991," *Dalhousie Review,* September 28, 1992, pp. 1–2.

6. *V Svoem otechestve proroki? Publitzistika perestroiki: luchshie avtory 1988 goda* (Moscow: Knizhnaia Palata, 1989).

7. Valerii Neznamov, "Lisy i l'vi Rossiiskoi elity," *Novoye Russkoye Slovo* (Russian Daily), August 12, 1994.

8. Nikolay Zlobin, "Plemia m ladoe, Strashnoe," *Novoye Russkoye Slovo* (Russian Daily), March 3, 1995, p. 14.

9. *Mir Mnenii I Mneniia o Mire* 9 (1992): 4 (the monthly publication of Vox Populi services led by Professor Boris Grushin).

10. *Novoye Russkoye Slovo* (Russian Daily), August 3, 1995, p. 5 (based on ITAR-TASS information of official statistics).

11. Pitirim Sorokin, "The Essential Characteristics of the Russian Nation in the Twentieth Century," *Annals of the American Academy of Political and Social Science* 370 (March, 1967): 99–115.

12. Samuel Kliger and Paul De Vries, "The Ten Commandments as Values in Soviet People's Consciousness," in *Religious Policy in the Soviet Union,* ed. Sabrina Petra Ramet (New York: Cambridge University Press, 1993), pp. 187–205.

13. *U.S. News & World Report,* October 4, 1993, p. 42.

14. Dorina Elliot, "Solzhenitsyn Goes Home," *Newsweek,* June 6, 1994, p. 41.

15. V. Semenov, "Kurs na uskorenie," *Voprosy Filosofii* 5 (1985): 33.

16. Andrei Turkov, "Will the Soviet Man Cease to Be Soviet?" *Novoye Russkoye Slovo* (Russian Daily), September 29, 1993, p. 5.

17. Steven Erlanger, *New York Times,* September 26, 1995.

18. Cf. John Dunstan, "Soviet Schools, Atheism, and Religion," in *Religious Policy in the Soviet Union,* ed. Sabrina Petra Ramet (New York: Cambridge University Press, 1993), p. 173.

19. "Who Reads the Bible," *Izvestia,* June 4, 1993.

20. Priest Innokentyi, "The Orthodox Church in Russia," *Novoye Russkoye Slovo* (Russian Daily), June 3, 1994.

21. Cf. Lev Adler, "Molodezh veruuschaya i neveruuschaya," *Vecherniaia Kazan,* January 16, 1995.

22. Andrew Solomon, "Young Russia's Defiant Decadence," *New York Times Magazine,* July 18, 1993, p. 22.

23. Ibid.

24. Vladimir Shapiro and Valerii Chervyakov, *What Does It Mean: "To Be a Jew?"* Linear distribution of survey results in Moscow and Saint Petersburg, Jewish Research Center, Moscow, 1993.

25. *New York Post,* September 26, 1991, p. 9.

26. Lev Gudkov and Aleksei Levinson, "Attitudes Toward Jews," *Sociological Research,* March–April, 1994, p. 64.

27. Tony Carnes, "Anti-Semitism in Russia, 1992–1995" (paper presented to the American Association for the Sociology of Religion, Washington, D.C., August, 1995).

28. Shapiro and Chervyakov, *What Does It Mean: "To Be a Jew?"*

29. *Novoye Russkoye Slovo* (Russian Daily), February 24, 1995, p. 11 (based on a *Jerusalem Post* report).

30. Dmitrii Bykov, "Tanetz Sviatogo Vitta" (The Dance of St. Vitta), *Novoye Russkoye Slovo* (Russian Daily), July 20, 1994, p. 11.

31. Ibid. See also Carnes and Kliger, "Religion and Moral Values in Russia," pp. 143–45.

Epilogue

1. Vilfredo Pareto, *The Mind and Society,* 4 vols. (New York: Harcourt Brace, 1935).

2. Joseph Schumpeter, "Comments on a Plan for the Study of Entrepreneurship," in *The Economics and Sociology of Capitalism,* ed. R. Swedberg (Princeton: Princeton University Press, 1991).

3. Max Weber, *The Protestant Ethic and the Spirit of Capitalism* (London: Allen and Unwin, 1976).

4. Karl Polayni, *The Great Transformation* (Boston: Beacon, 1975).

5. Suzanne Keller and David Jacobson, "Creating a Market Society in Eastern Europe: The Missing Ingredient" (unpublished manuscript, 1994).

Contributors

Elena Avraamova is senior fellow at the Institute of Social and Economic Problems of Population in Moscow.

Alexander Boronin is director of the Biological Institutes in the Russian Academy of Sciences in Moscow.

Anthony Carnes is chair of the Department of Sociology, King's College, New York.

Nikolai Churilov is director of the polling firm SosIs in Kiev, Ukraine.

Boris Doktorov is an independent researcher and consultant, an associate research fellow of the St. Petersburg branch of the Institute of Sociology, Russian Academy of Sciences, St. Petersburg, Russia.

Midkhat Farukshin is chair of the Department of Political Science, Kazan University. Kazan, Russia.

Vladas Gaidys is director of the Public Opinion Research Center, Institute of Philosophy, Science, and Law in Vilnius, Lithuania.

Boris Grushin is the founder and director of the polling firm Vox Populii in Moscow.

Rustem Kadyrzhanov is chair of the Department of Political Science, Institute of Philosophy, Kazakh Academy of Sciences in Kazakhstan.

William Kandinov is the former chair of the Department of Sociology, Tashkent University, Tashkent, Uzbekistan.

Suzanne Keller is professor of sociology at Princeton University in Princeton, New Jersey.

Samuel Kliger is director of the New York Association for New Americans in New York City.

Olga Krishtanovskaia is Chair of the Department of Elite Studies, Institute of Sociology, Russian Academy of Sciences, Moscow.

Ivan Kukolev is a fellow at the Institute of Sociology, Russian Academy of Sciences in Moscow.

Yurii Levada is director of the All Russian Center for Public Opinion in Moscow.

Mikhail Loiberg is a professor at Open University in Moscow.

Victor Luneev is a professor at the Institute on State and Law in Moscow.

Tatiana Marchenko is senior fellow at the Institute of Social and Economic Problems of Population in Moscow.

Vladimir Palagin is head of Agricultural Management, Engels District, Saratov Region, Russia.

Vladimir Shlapentokh is a professor in the Department of Sociology at Michigan State University.

Vladimir Shubkin is chair of the Institute of Sociology, Russian Academy of Sciences, Moscow.

Vladimir Snapkovskii is chair of the Department of International Relations, Byelorussian State University, Minsk, Belarus.

Vladimir Solonar is head of the Human Rights Committee, Moldovan Parliament, Kishiniev, Moldova.

Petra Stykow is a professor at Humboldt University, Berlin, Germany.

Christopher Vanderpool is chair of the Department of Sociology at Michigan State University.

Stephen White is a professor in the Department of Politics, University of Glasgow.

Vladimir Zhakarov is director of the Landau Institute of Physics and a member of the Russian Academy of Sciences, Moscow.

Index

Eastern European Studies

Stjepan G. Meštrović, *Series Editor*

Cigar, Norman. *Genocide in Bosnia: The Policy of "Ethnic Cleansing."* 1995.

Cohen, Philip J. *Serbia's Secret War: Propaganda and the Deceit of History.* 1996.

Gachechiladze, Revaz. *The New Georgia: Space, Society, Politics.* 1996.

Gibbs, Joseph. *Gorbachev's Glasnost: The Soviet Media in the First Phase of Perestroika.* 1999.

Knezys, Stasys, and Romanas Sedlickas. *The War in Chechnya.* 1999.

Meštrović, Stjepan G., ed. *The Conceit of Innocence: Losing the Conscience of the West in the War against Bosnia.* 1997.

Polokhalo, Volodymyr, ed. *The Political Analysis of Postcommunism: Understanding Postcommunist Ukraine.* 1997.

Quinn, Frederick. *Democracy at Dawn: Notes from Poland and Points East.* 1997.

Teglas, Csaba. *Budapest Exit: A Memoir of Fascism, Communism, and Freedom.* 1998.